Information Security and Technology

Information Security and Technology

by

B.M. Ponnappa
Former Scientist
Defence Research and Development Organisation

Manas Publications
New Delhi - 110002

MANAS PUBLICATIONS
(Publishers, Distributors, Importers & Exporters)
4858, Prahlad Street,
24, Ansari Road, Darya Ganj,
New Delhi - 110002 (INDIA)
Ph.: 23260783, 23265523
Fax: 011- 23272766
E-mail: manaspublications@vsnl.com

First Published 2004

ISBN 81-7049-178-9

Rs. 795

Typeset at
Manas Publications

Printed in India at
RK Offsets
and Published by Mrs Suman Lata for
Manas Publications, 4858, Prahlad Street,
24, Ansari Road, Darya Ganj,
New Delhi - 110 002 (INDIA)

Dedication

This book is dedicated to the unsung heroes of the country—members of the Intelligence community and the security forces. They do their utmost for the nation, in the most adverse, hazardous and dangerous environment, to maintain the internal security of the country and its integrity.

Their success mostly lies buried, unnoticed, under the mandate of secrecy. Whereas, occasional lapses attributed to them are highlighted and blown out of perspective!

I salute them.

May their tribe prosper and get the recognition they justly and richly deserve.

Preface

The word "security" implies a state of "fearlessness", a sense of wellbeing—whether in regard to persons, property, information, an operation or environment. If you look-up in a dictionary for meaning of the word security, it would say- "the state of being or feeling secure", "safety", "that which secures". Achieving such a state is not accidental, but requires taking specific actions—a series of deliberate steps, or following a programme of specific procedures. Such systems have to be planned, designed, implemented, maintained and updated when we consider the security of organizations, businesses or a plant operation etc. The steps may be considered as simple ones, when it is a question of putting up a perimeter wall/ fence, barring and locking up of premises, when not in actual use or occupation. The steps become more complicated, as well as more and more sophisticated, when, one has to look at implementing security of large businesses and important organizations, etc. In such cases, need would arise for installation of intrusion detection and alarm systems, CCTV surveillance, elaborate access control systems etc., along with necessary standard operating procedures or S.O.Ps. Such systems may, even, need to be looked after and supervised by a captive security set-up! As also, increasing resort to use of technology/technical aids, mainly, in conjunction with, but sometimes, even in-lieu of trained security personnel. [Note, that the term "security" *subsumes* "safety". *Thus, ensuring security entails relevant safety activities too.* But, "safety" *does not subsume* "security". Hence, *ensuring safety does not necessarily ensure security*].

No wonder, the present day security managers and security personnel have to possess more than a nodding acquaintance with security technology. In many cases, technology may well be the only possible answer to get security.

Fast paced technological advances have increasingly been adopted to meet varying and multiplying security needs of mushrooming businesses and industries. A host of scientific principles and methodologies available have enabled quick cost-effective solutions to even seemingly "intractable" security scenarios/situations. On the other hand, fallout of technology has also put tools, in the hands of *deliberate intruder/opposition,* to defeat or circumvent such technical security systems. It is hence a *constant, dynamic* "battle" between those who desire security, and those who want to break-in. Thus, security is an area where *"ignorance is certainly not bliss"*. Therefore, a reasonable acquaintance with security technology is de rigueur for anyone who has to do anything with security.

So, how do you go about acquiring this savvy? No doubt there are innumerable books, and several journals too, that address specific or different aspects of security, but few that give in one single place an overall view of "security technology". The objective of this book is precisely to fill this gap. This will help you to appreciate the basic approaches to security, the fundamentals of security technology, the precautions to be taken in their selection, installation, as well as, on training, maintenance of security devices/systems, their limitations, and so on.

The scope of the book has necessarily to be restricted to application of technology, to what is known as "internal security" work. It cannot envisage military/defence areas—that is security applications to meet external threats. Technological applications for latter are usually more capital and manpower intensive and rather different from the simpler, less expensive and cost-effective systems, called for in internal security work. Any attempts to address such areas would defeat the very objective of this endeavour—the result would be too unwieldy and voluminous work. Further, this would also lead to inadequacy of coverage.

Much thought has gone into the formulation of the contents of this book. At the very beginning, I considered a fairly comprehensive approach. This led me to a somewhat unwieldy table of contents, involving over ninety, (yes, nine zero!). Obviously, it would be a parody to call that as an "Introduction" to anything! Straightaway, I could see at least two drawbacks to that approach. Firstly, such an encyclopedic work may find place, mainly, in the bookshelves of libraries and institutions, and only a minority of takers amongst those persons interested in security work/aspects. Secondly, such an elaborate exposition could hardly be accomplished in a handy volume or two, which most persons would desire to have on their personal bookshelf. After considerable deliberation and introspection, arrived at a more logical table of contents for the introductory book. (Ofcourse, my follow-up endeavour would be the fairly comprehensive/encyclopedic *"Security Technology Handbook" or "Handbook on Security Technology"*.

Technology is by nature dynamic, ever growing, and at a faster and faster rate. Hence, no book can expect to remain truly current and upto date for extended periods of time. This effort is therefore aimed, to give a useful and reasonable introduction to the basics. The objective is that you should be able to appreciate the various angles involved in the use of technical aids; their basic principles of operation, the need for clear security objectives; and an understanding of environmental effects necessary for security management. It would also help you whilst making a choice of technology, aspects involved in the design and implementation of systems and so on. You would also appreciate the need for continuous monitoring of the security scenario and the attendant need for upgradation. Further, you would also appreciate, why security personnel have to be carefully chosen, properly trained, have to be highly disciplined, inherently honest, highly motivated and at the same time polite and alert. To quote Samuel Johnson: "*Integrity without knowledge is weak and useless; knowledge without integrity is dangerous and dreadful*"

Suggestions, that could help to improve the content, the treatment of the subject or to make the coverage more effective, are most welcome. Of course, this work cannot include any classified aspects or material. However, this does not affect, per se, the principles and methodologies presented in this book. Classified aspects/situations, merely demand only extensions of normal principles, say an extra twist. Precisely what the situation is and what is done, are not openly talked about, but kept secret on the usual strictly need to know basis.

Contents

Notes

Notes

PART I

Chapter 1

Introduction

"Imagination is more important than knowledge"

—Albert Einstein

What is Security?

If you look into a dictionary you will find many meanings given for the word security, such as "safety", "certainty", " a bond", "feeling secure", and so on. But, when you refer to security technology, and security operations, you are concerned with the meanings: "The state of being or feeling secure", "that which secures", and "safety". In general, the context of such references would be to one or more of the following four specific areas:

1. "Physical Security", that is, security of premises, installations, buildings or such physical assets.
2. "Information Security", that is, security of information in all forms, spoken, written, printed, graphics, documents, recordings, communication channels and so on.
3. "Personal Security", that is, security and safety of individuals, VIPs, groups of individuals, the general public.

(Security personnel consider and talk of only the above three types of security principles/operations, apart from the specialist nomenclatures for individual applications of security principles in businesses, such as retail, hotel, airport, aviation, school, hospital, and so on. *But the actual position is that, there is this all inclusive umbrella requirement of security, which I have termed as operations/process security, as indicated below, as the fourth dimension).*

4. "Operations/Process Security", that is, *security of processes* such as say generation of electricity, water supply, petroleum products refinery, *and operations* such as transportation, aviation, shipping, counter-terrorism, and so on. The two terms may appear to be synonymous, but are distinct, former referring to a continuous series of usually consecutive, interconnected steps; while the latter involves, a series of individual, discrete and generally, overlapping tasks. But, both have hazards associated with them, with adverse impact on the environment/general public.

Before looking into the useful role that technology can play in security work, it would help to have an understanding of what exactly the above tasks stand for, and the security problems that necessitate such activities (involved therein).

Security Problems

Security problems arise basically out of two types of "threats": viz., "Internal threats" and "External threats".

Internal threats: These arise due to problems such as thefts, pilferage, fire hazards, labour unrest, sabotage and so on. These threats usually arise from within the installation or organization, and could be tackled, generally, from within the organization.

External threats: These are threats or problems that arise basically due to external agencies or persons outside the organization. Examples of such threats are subversion, burglary, industrial espionage, sabotage, terrorism and so on. The external agencies concerned may or may not involve employees of the organization, in their such nefarious activities.

The above division of threats is not mutually exclusive. Acts, such as arson and sabotage, could arise due to disgruntled employees within the organization, or due to (instigation from) external agencies. In the former case, the person or persons involved are usually employees, or known and permitted visitors to the organization, and it has reasonable control of the environment; besides ways to tackle the threats. In the latter case, the agent provocateur is generally an outsider and whose environment is usually outside the control of the organization. Thus, the approaches to security, for the two modes of threat situations could/would be generally very different, for the *four types of security tasks, viz. "physical security", "information or document security", personal security" and "process/ operations security"*.

Physical Security

Traditionally, all security operations started with the concept of physical security. It basically deals with protection of the premises against intruders, unauthorized access or attacks on the installations or buildings. This was done by provision of moats, fences, walls and hedges as perimeter protection devices; barriers and drawbridges; gates and doors as access points. When necessary, sentries were posted to examine and control the traffic through the access or entry points. Such, but maybe more sophisticated, age-old physical security measures are still used for premises protection. Locks, safes and vaults are again examples of physical security techniques for safeguarding valuables/spot protection. Technology comes in to aid the security operations, with remote-operated barriers, special fence systems, intruder alarms, automated access control systems, digital/ biometrics/ time-lock systems, surveillance devices and so on. The basic approach is still to erect a physical or "technical" barrier between an unauthorized person or intruder and the premises/location or installation to be protected, and/or have an alarm initiated when unauthorized entry occurs.

Information Security

"Information", as a source for generation of wealth and a means to attain or hold power, or, even, as a threat to the security of individuals or organizations, has gained escalating importance. "Information security" has, hence, grown into a very vital factor in regard to security of individuals, organizations and nations. The problems in regard to safeguarding information within authorized environments have been compounded, in recent times, with the advent of copying systems, pervasiveness of computer systems, and fast and extensive growth of almost instant telecommunications and multimedia facilities; and recently the internet. Thus, whereas leakage of information to unauthorized persons may need no great efforts, to stem such leakage possibilities involve enormous efforts and commitments. Information security measures may start with simple, but effective, control methodologies in regard to generation, flow, storage, and destruction of documents and information. Coding or elaborate encryption techniques may be called for when the information travels over telecommunication links, postal services, or even from one desk to another or into /out of computers. A nation's security may even depend on code-breaking techniques! Hence, *"Cryptology"*, (that is, code making or *"Ciphers "*, as well as code-breaking or *"Cryptanalysis"* techniques), play major roles in securing information.

It is to be noted that, "information security" encompasses "physical security" measures apart from additional special measures called for specifically, to ensure security of the information.

Personal Security

The concept of personal security is not new. Historically, bodyguards have been used by chieftains, important and wealthy persons, kings and so on, to protect themselves from physical attacks on them. Some have even used food tasters to taste their food, to protect themselves from possibility of being poisoned, before taking their meals or imbibing their drinks. The Industrial revolution and the more recent automation, chemical, and other processes, as well as the internet are harbingers of hitherto unknown dangers to the safety and security of personnel. Further, the ever growing and yawning gap between the wealthy, the deprived and the underprivileged have led to the growth of power centres, criminalisation and terrorism. These have radically increased the risks of personal attacks, kidnapping and even assassinations; to the public in general and to *very important persons* (VIPs), in particular. This has led to the growing importance of security techniques to cater to the safety and security of personnel, termed as "personal security".

Please note, that, "personal security" techniques/measures, include in *the first instance "physical security"* and *"information security" measures* apart from procedures very specific *to "personal security"*

Process/Operations Security

This is a recent trend in security requirements. It has arisen, thanks to modern technology; the technology which has given rise to many costly, critical and dangerous processes /operations, which need continuous monitoring and feedback control to prevent unacceptable risks/events that could harm the general public. Examples are atomic power generation, transportation industry, public utilities and so on. These "process/operations" measures are those that are called for specifically to ensure public safety as opposed to the usual safety of only those persons directly concerned with such operations.

Security measures that are required to ensure security of major computer operations, hazardous chemical processes etc. may also be envisaged as "operations/process security" tasks. In view of the possible adverse impact on the community at large, the environment or even the habitat, such situations may require a totally different approach to security, from the hidebound usual "cost-effectiveness" approach (to security). The approach also applies to processes and operations such as municipal water supply, aviation, and utilities etc., which concern the general public or the environment directly, and are not just confined to the institutions or organizations concerned with such tasks.

"Process/Operations Security" envisages as a first requirement, implementation of suitable "physical security", "information security" and "personal security" measures. Concurrently, some special procedures and methodologies are employed, which are specific to "process/operations security". Hence, such operations and activities involve very appreciable organizational efforts and cost, as well as very special attention is required for safety functions and disaster planning. The usual cost-effectiveness criteria, normally considered while implementing security measures, would need to be subservient, in this case, to the all-important consideration of *"public safety and security"*.

Security Management

Security hazards arising out of internal threats and external threats are diverse. Techniques, methodologies and procedures needed for the different situations are many. Host of technical devices and systems are nowadays available, and their numbers are accelerating and spawning.

A security lapse could cost an organization dearly, may result, even in the folding up of the organization. Such factors raise security operations, from the erstwhile subordinate function to the present day "management function".

Security Task

The security task is obviously related to the extent and types of security threats expected. A small business, in a village or small town for example, would have little or no competition; it may have to worry more about recovery of credits to customers and perhaps tackle some minor thefts or pilferage. On the other hand, a large business in a large city, extending over a region or States/country, or even nations would need to worry about strong competitions, and both internal and external threats. In a well run business, the problems in security may well be from its competitors. Thus, there is no single, standard security solution for all types of situations. Hence, the very first task of security management is to set "*security objectives*". This would then form the basis to evolve suitable security plan, appropriate to the situation, and then, organize and implement necessary standard operating procedures, (S.O.Ps), as well as, other relevant security measures.

The security objectives are evolved, naturally, from the *organizational objectives* and the *business environment*. A security survey is hence the next step to identify the security hazards-the "threat assessment" and an "analysis of attendant risks" or "risks analysis". The step that follows would be naturally, to identify suitable solution, and out of the possibilities select the most "optimum/cost-effective" solution. This solution would be, then, implemented.

The above steps may not all be required, in case of simple situations, small businesses etc. However, following the steps would not be harmful in any case. An organization with the primary objective of profit making, for example, would have for its security objective—*"increasing the profitability"*. This would be, usually, achieved by reducing pilferage, theft, fraud, etc. apart from increasing the operational efficiency. On the other hand, an organization providing *"service"*, could well have the security objective *"to improve the reliability and efficiency of the service"*, for getting greater satisfaction of the customers. This may be by reducing breakdowns, diminishing incidence of employee absenteeism, by facilitating communication and improving public relations, etc. Those are, justifiably, management functions too. In this case, security would play a great role in regard to public relations to improve the image of the organization, and ensure employee punctuality etc.

From the above, it is obvious that, all the activities need close "co-ordination", throughout, with the various departments of the organization—Personnel, Plant, Stores, Transport, Finance, Administration etc. That is, from the point of decision for a 'security survey" through "threat assessment" and so on, to the stage of complete implementation of chosen solution(s). And, later on, effect improvements through "reviews" and "upgradations" as found necessary.

Systems Approach to Security

From the above, it may appear that what is needed is a *systems approach to security*. However, this may well be uncalled for, in several cases that you may encounter. In most cases, like small businesses, low investment/non-critical sectors, and so on, provision of adequate locking arrangements and simple physical security measures should be appropriate. Elaborate security-survey, threat assessment, etc., are totally unnecessary. But, as the size, importance, economic worth, and criticality of the organization increases, that is, the cost of security risks mount up, then, the need arises for adopting more and more elaborate, and even *'multi-dimensional"* security measures. Some examples of such measures are—"*intrusion detection and alarms*", "*automated access control system*", "*special security barriers*", "*surveillance,*" and so on. The security operations are no longer in the nature of loss prevention, but are basically "*protection*" against likely "unacceptable risks" to the functioning of the organization.

Does this mean that each and every vulnerable part of the organization needs to be thus protected? The answer is—certainly not. What is needed is to identify the "vital areas", (VAs), "vital points or locations', (VPs), and 'vital operations/processes", (VOPs). These are the areas, locations and operations/processes which are critical to the good health and wellbeing of the organization. Hence, protection of these is the primary requirement of any security arrangements, in the first instance. The vulnerability of these and the attendant risks should be of critical concern to the security. There may well be other areas, locations, and operations/processes, which are vulnerable. But if they are not critical, effects of any security lapse or hazard to such spots on the organization are not catastrophic nor too adverse, and as such they could receive secondary importance /priority as compared to the *VAs*, *VPs* and *VOPs*. This is because of the need for cost-effectiveness of security. No organization has much money or resources to deploy on security functions. Hence, almost always, compromises may well be essential. Hence, the other vulnerable spots may need to be relegated to secondary treatment.

In the case of *VOPs*, in many cases, an exception to the above approach would be needed, as more than cost-effectiveness, safety, and public safety could be the overriding requirement. Hence, whether the vulnerable spots/processes etc. are critical to the organization's functioning or not, if any hazards to these affect safety and security of personnel/public, they must have adequate and appropriate security protection, without fail!

Role of Technology in Security

Technology can play a major and effective role in practically, every aspect of security operations-in laying of security objectives, security survey, risks assessment/analysis, selection of solutions, selection of personnel, protection of plants, personnel, information and other resources, training and in ensuring safety and security of critical operations/processes. With the advent of fast communications, plethora of inexpensive electronic devices of various types, massive and real-time processing capabilities of present day computers, all areas of security operations are pervaded by ever increasing applications of technology.

Technical aids, either help to make security operations more cost-effective or radically improve security performance itself. In most critical operations, technical facilities are indispensable to ensure safety/security. Also, the more the opponent resorts to use of technology, to break into or create security hazards to your organization, the more heavily you will have to depend on what technology can offer. And more familiar you will need to be with technology—be it regarding perimeter security, barrier systems, access control systems, surveillance devices, telecommunications, computer capabilities, encryption, document protection, personnel protection devices, intrusion alarms, explosives, detection and protection. Further, the cost of technical devices and systems are tumbling with time due to technology advancement, and hence, newer and newer applications also arise with time (although the basic principles may remain more or less same). Hence, technological applications in security work can be expected to rapidly increase with time. So, it is very well worth your while to get acquainted with security technology-sooner the better!

What follows in this book would give you a reasonable and adequate introduction to relevant security technology. After going through the first few chapters, you could of course pick and choose to peruse the specific chapters of interest to you, if you are so inclined. And keep the book as a handy reference, as and when the need arise for you to get acquainted with topics which you have skipped earlier.

In the context of safety and security operations, what are technical aids? *An answer to this question should be of concern to anyone interested in security/safety.*

Technical Aids to Safety/Security

Technical aids used in safety and security operations may be divided into two main groups viz. the *"stand alone type"* and the *"dependent type"*. The former is totally self contained and is usually operated manually; examples are fire extinguishers, safes and security mirrors. The latter have several components or units and are connected together to function as a system. The devices may be designed to function automatically, without any manual operation (but usually with a manual override, for extra safety), or may be configured to be manually actuated. Some examples are intrusion alarms, fire alarms, and access control systems.

In general, technical aids used in safety operations have to be, perforce, the *dependent types.* This is because, safety protection-recovery operations are always dependant on continuous sensing of the process environment against unusual or beyond laid down limit excursions of operating conditions, so that the protective/recovery conditions could be immediately imposed, and in a safe manner. The technical device senses for undesirable deviations of the process and sets in motion required corrective actions in real-time.

The *dependent type of device* incorporates two or more functions of sensing, communication, processing, indication or display, control and actuation. Also, quite often, some type of interpretation of the device output, may be required by the security personnel, (the user).

The *stand-alone device* on the other hand is self-contained in functioning. It does not sense, communicate, process or control any information or another device. But, it is used to directly achieve some security function—put out a fire, protect some valuables, minimize effect of an explosion, and so on. Generally, no interpretation is required either, by the persons taking recourse to the device.

Evidently, a *technical aid,* has to provide some sort of assistance in security or safety operations, whether it concerns "physical security," "information security", "personal security", or 'operations/process security". A single device may play multiple roles. For example, a safe may protect a valuable like money or jewels, thus providing physical security. On the other hand, a highly classified document may be kept in it for safe-custody, thus helping to provide information security. Communication facility provides a means for fast transfer of vital messages/ information; and this could alert security to implement in time required security measures, say, an alert against a possible kidnap attempt on a VIP, a personal security task. And, of course, communication, computer processing and actuation devices provide the means for all automated systems and feedback control systems, apart from Intelligence and counter Intelligence operations; and, thus, be vital components of process/operations security.

The chapters that follow will detail various aspects of safety and security management, mention the different types of technical aids as well as techniques that can assist security and safety task. You will also take a brief look at the principles of different sensing methods, characteristics of the systems, as well as various countermeasures to combat threats to security.

Stand Alone Devices

Characteristics:

- # They *perform an independent security or safety function*, without dependence on any other device, link or operation.
- # *Single location* for a device.
- # Generally, minimum or *negligible maintenance efforts* required.
- # Usually, *manual operation* when needed.
- # Examples:

  Safes and vaults
  Security mirror
  Shredding machine
  Fire proof cabinet
  Fire extinguisher
  Bomb blankets

Dependent Devices

Characteristics

They perform required security or safety functions in combination with two or more elements/devices and links, forming the security system and depend on some perceptible change in the environment, in which they exist.
Location could be single, with all elements at one place, or multiple (usually), with the components located at different places, and linked together by wired or wireless communication links to form the complete system or device.
Regular and appreciable maintenance efforts are usually required.
Periodic updating is necessary.
May be designed to operate in an automatic, semi-automatic, or totally manual, fashion, (by designated and trained persons).

Examples

Intrusion alarm systems.

Fire alarm/fire extinguishing systems.

SIGINT systems.

Surveillance systems.

Remote sensing systems.

Automated protection barrier.

Hazardous/explosive materials detection and handling.

Automated access control systems.

Automated turnstiles, entry/exit control.

Chapter 2

Basics of Security Operations

"Eternal vigilance is the cornerstone of Security"

A structured approach to security

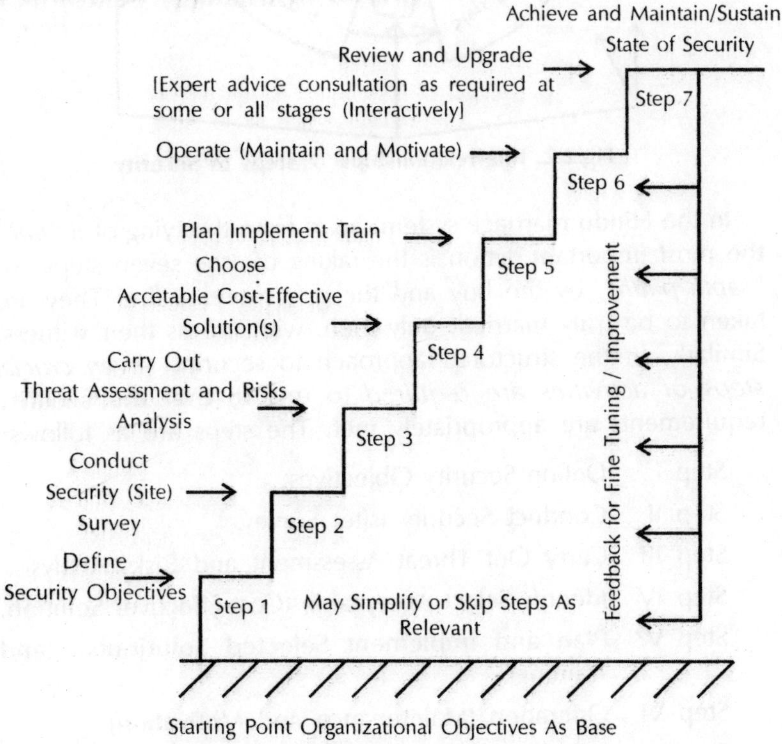

The 7 steps to security, as above, lead (should lead) to a security cocoon around the organization.

Fig.2.1. The Structured Approach to Security ('Sapta-Padhi')

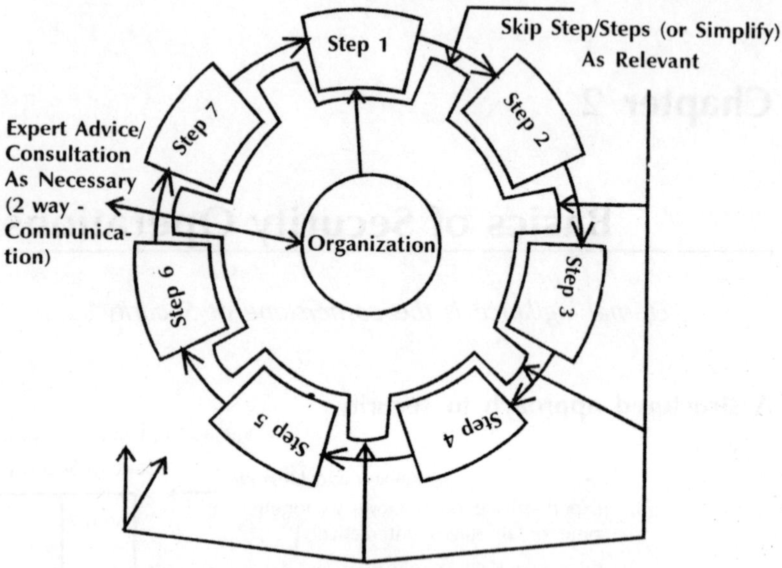

Fig.2.2. Interrelationships- 7 Steps to Security

In the Hindu marriage system, apart from the tying of a "*tali*", the most important action is the taking of "the seven steps" or "*sapta padhi*", by the boy and the girl, round a fire. They are taken to be truly married, only then, with fire as their witness. Similarly, in the structured approach to security, *seven crucial steps of activities are required* to ensure that the security requirements are appropriately met. The steps are as follows:

Step I Define Security Objectives.

Step II Conduct Security (site) Survey.

Step III Carry Out Threat Assessment and Risks Analysis.

Step IV Identify/Select Acceptable (Cost-Effective) Solution.

Step V Plan and Implement Selected Solution(s), (and Training).

Step VI Operation (Maintenance and Motivation).

Step VII Review and Upgrade the Security System (Periodically).

In each of the above steps, it could be of advantage to associate experts in the line, or go in for expert advice/consultation. This would probably save time and lead to a more cost-effective security system. Fig.2.1 gives a pictorial representation.

The above seven steps of structured approach to security are valid whether the situation you face is that of mere physical security, includes problems of information security, has concerns for personal security, or involves all elements, as in an operational/process security problem/situation. This basic approach should be tailored to suit the particular situation faced—keeping it simple, for simple situations in any case; but could be quite elaborate for complex situations, and major organizations. Fig.2.2 indicates the inter-relationships, in the above approach. The various aspects, and activities involved, in the above seven steps of structured approach, are detailed in paragraphs that follow.

Step I: Define Security Objective(s)

The starting point for this step, is obviously, the organizational objective(s). The basic security needs arise out of this. Whether the organizational objective is profit making, service oriented, involves public safety aspects, etc., decide what the basic security objective(s) need to be. Each type of business, or service (hotel, retail, manufacturing, insurance, utilities, transportation, etc.), have their own unique needs of security because of the environment in which they have to function, the competition, the laws and regulations that apply and so on.

The next input of defining security objective is the result from a *swot* analysis of the organization, that is, an analysis of the *strengths, weaknesses, opportunities and threats* of/to the organization. Results of such an analysis are indicative of what could help security and what could hinder security efforts, from the point of view of the structure and personnel within the organization, the competition, the environment, etc. Obviously, security arrangements are easier, and well accepted (with fewer problems), when the personnel are disciplined and well behaved in the organization. The more technical oriented the organization is, the more technology in security that can be introduced, as far as overt activities are concerned such as sophisticated access control.

The other aspect that has to be considered as an input to the security objective is the regulatory aspect—the local / State and national and international laws that apply to the business operations. For example, you cannot issue firearms, or cellular phones, and so on to the security, where, the regulations do not permit the same. Nor, can you frisk an employee, or subject him to a lie detector test, even with his consent, when it is declared as unlawful in that state. You cannot detain or question an employee if the law does not permit it. Such restrictions on security must be taken into account when laying down the security objectives.

For example, you are setting up a factory to produce explosives in a backward rural area. The strength of the endeavour could be that the employees are likely to be simple, honest type, with no inclination for intrigue, or union or disruptive activities. Further, problems of pilferage may be minimal. On the other hand, the weakness would be that they need more training to do their jobs. If, there are plenty of quarrying activities in the neighbourhood, they would create major opportunities. However, if competitive factories come up there, or the region becomes dacoit infested, these would turn out to be major threats. In a rural area, the utilities available may be poor and, hence, internal arrangements for power generation and water supply etc. may be needed- these would be additional vital points to be protected. In such circumstances, "maximization of profits", alone, would not be an appropriate security objective. If security does not provide adequate cover against dacoits etc., the enterprise itself may fail. Then, "maximize profits, consistent with worker safety and security of installation" would be a more appropriate "objective".

Step II: Conduct Security (site) Survey

This step involves detailed study of several aspects—starting with the local, social or neighbourhood environment, the business environment, natural hazards, climatic conditions and so on. These are listed below:

1. Geographical factors: Neighbourhood, business linkages, local safety and health regulations.
2. Physical environment: Meteorological, climatic- sunshine, heat; cold, dust, precipitation, humidity, barometric pressure, altitude, etc.
3. Natural environment: Topographical features/ structures
4. Electromagnetic environment: Radio-frequency interference (RFI), high-voltage lines, high RFI generating industries like welding, RFI sensitive operations in the neighbourhood, like medical units/aviation etc)
5. Biological environment: Insects, birds, animals, fungus, vermin etc.
6. Extent of local services available, and their reliability.
7. Organizational aspects.
8. Identification of *VAs, VPs,* and *VOPs.*

Obviously, many of the above considerations may be beyond you, when the business set-up already exists; and is located, may be, in an undesirable location which cannot be changed. You will then have to do with the situation and provide for the limitations, and if possible, convert the limitations into opportunities. The important thing is to note down and list all points in regard to the above that could have a bearing on security. Please note that, an ideal environment never exists. One has to always make compromises.

GEOGRAPHICAL FACTORS

When there is choice, no doubt a congenial neighbourhood would be selected for setting up the business or industry. A dacoit infested region or highly crime prone areas would be avoided at all costs. You would tend to select a state where the laws and regulations are helpful to your business and reduce security problems. As also, you would tend to avoid countries or locations with over severe health and safety regulations, which have their fall-outs on security aspects too. But, whatever the case may be, the need is to detail all those points of relevance, to evaluate, later, their effects in regard to security.

Obviously, where the neighbourhood is crime-prone, politically active, communally sensitive, has aggressive business opposition stringent safety and health regulations, security hazards and attendant risks to the organization are very high; the security apparatus would then need to be much more elabórate, tighter, more efficient, and highly reliable; even high strung and forceful. Security failures could prove to be extremely costly to the organization, apart from the already high cost of the security system that has to be implemented.

Physical Environment

It goes without saying that the physical environment affects security aspects in a big way. They affect the performance of personnel, performance of equipment systems, create maintenance problems for security equipments, facilities, and so on. The choice of procedures and security methodologies are dependent on these environmental effects. It must be noted that, practically all electronic/ computer systems are sensitive to heat, dust, cold, humidity, chemical contaminants, fungus growth and so on. It is, hence, necessary to have a detailed site survey in regard to the above respects to have relevant data when the question of choice of equipment/facilities and their location/ installation arises. Obviously, rain, snow, fog, dust-storms etc. would play havoc with observation and surveillance system, when the systems are not protected/matched to the physical environment. An unaided guard in a pillbox, normal CCTV system, fluorescent lighting and simple alarm systems would hardly be effective under such conditions. You may, therefore, have to go in for thermal imaging systems, microwave detection systems infrared searchlights and so on. Hence records of the daily variations in humidity, temperatures, extent of rainfall and precipitation, wind, incidence of fog, maximum and minimum temperatures encountered, intensity, types and pattern of vehicular traffic in the neighbourhood and so on are required.

It is also essential to have records and estimates of seismic activities, landslides, cyclones, chemical and nuclear hazards, remote though the occurrences maybe—as they call for strong contingency measures and rigorous disaster planning.

Natural Environment

A detailed site survey is also required in regard to topographic features; elevated structures in the vicinity, etc. which could affect security arrangements. For example, if there is drain going through the location, it could be an easy access route for an intruder. If the soil is soft around the perimeter, an intruder could easily burrow through under normal fences. When there is a tree next to the perimeter, it is an access route for undesirable elements. A lake or a stream straddling or near the perimeter could easily hide the approach of criminals. A hill or a tall structure overlooking the site to be secured could offer ease of surveillance by the opposition and would be a suitable location, for say, rocket attacks by terrorists, and so on. Soft or marshy soil at the perimeter would entail considerable expense on perimeter protection/ patrol paths around the perimeter.

Hence, the inevitable need for detailed record of all relevant topographic features and structures in the neighbourhood. Such a record would essentially help in identification of the techniques that are appropriate for perimeter security.

Electromagnetic Environment

Electronic, computer, technical security systems, communication facilities and so on, are quite sensitive to radio frequency interference. Of course, it is possible to have systems designed to withstand such interference but, at a cost, as in the case of military systems. But, it is also possible to make some local installation modifications, such as shielding, grounding etc. to minimize the adverse effects of such *RFI*; (Radio Frequency Interference), nowadays termed as *EMI, (Electromagnetic Interference)*. Location of the business in an industrial area with welding machines, induction furnaces, etc. In the neighbourhood, could create terrible EMI problems, for *Radio Frequency*

Interference, (or RFI, the old term for EMI*),* sensitive operations and industries.

It is also to be noted that, some *medicare systems* are very highly sensitive to *EMI* and it can be a matter of life and death to patients, on such life support systems. Further, telecommunication links, electronic systems, etc. generate electromagnetic emanations which can be picked up, external to the organization, by interested parties, leading to information leakage-security hazard. This would be particularly so, when the local *EMI is very, very quiet level.* Radiation hazards could trigger explosive materials, and you may need to go in for what are known as intrinsically safe equipment.

It is, therefore, necessary to have a record of the local EMI conditions, incidence of lightning/ electric storms, etc., that is, radio spectrum levels record, to be precise.

Biological Environment

Locations infested by vermin, rats, cockroaches, insects, small animals like rabbits, etc., create their own problems to security. Rats are famous for chewing up cables, hosepipes, equipment wiring, etc. Cockroaches and insects, apart from being a health hazard, can get inside the equipment and affect its performance. Movements of small animals, like rabbits, as well as birds, in and around the location, can create false alarms in security systems. In such cases, apart from insect proofing, rat proofing, as well as availability of suitable storage systems, periodic pest-control measures would be called for. It is, hence, essential to have a record of their incidence and behaviour at the location, and its neighbourhood, to enable implementation of appropriate countermeasures successfully (later on).

Local Services

No business environment can be totally self-sufficient. They have to take recourse to *local services,* such as the utilities, police, water supply, telecommunication facilities, postal services, and so on. Failure of any, or some of these, may affect the business, to a greater or lesser extent, depending on the type of business and internal or alternative arrangements that have been implemented. Therefore, it is important to carry out survey on the reliability and extent of such local services available, to provide for appropriate alternatives.

Organizational Aspects

No security arrangement exists by itself. They are a part of the organization. There has to be interaction between the various departments of the organization. Further, the buildings, installations, spaces in between, special structures if any, all are relevant to how the security must be organized and function. It is thus inevitable, that, the organizational setup, distribution of work and facilities, flow of personnel and materials, vehicular traffic expected, interdepartmental interactions/communications etc., have to be examined and detailed in the survey. The exercise should include details of recruitment policies, procurement methodologies, storage/issue/write-off of materials and documents, communication systems, control, etc. Personnel policies, union activities, incentives and grievance redressal methodologies are of equal relevance. When they are proper, security risks, (particularly, due to internal factors), are considerably reduced.

VAs, VPs, and VOPs Identification

This is the last, but crucial part of the security survey. You list first all the vulnerable areas, vulnerable points and vulnerable operations/ processes. You then examine and determine, in consultation with the management, which of these are vital or crucial to the business or operation. The basis could be that, any failure there would lead to inestimable loss or affect the business very adversely. *(A vulnerable location does not necessarily mean that it needs close security cover.* For example, a waste dump may well be vulnerable to attack/ intrusion, and hence a vulnerable location; but it could have little relevance to achieving organizational objective, and hence not a *VA* for security unless it happens to be important, such as a nuclear waste storage pond.). These are then noted as the *VAs, VPs,* and *VOPs,* to be given particular attention in regard to security arrangements/protection.

Step III: Threat Assessment and Risks Analysis

The effectiveness of security management would be decided, to a great extent, by the depth and extent of activities carried out at this stage. The actions basically flow out of the results of the security survey. The approach is to ask three questions for each of the recorded item of the survey result: ·

Q.1. Can this be a security problem/ security hazard?
If so: Q.2. How may I breach security?
Q.3. What is the attendant risk/cost to the organization?

(Answers to the Q.3 may be sought later on after the *data* in regard to Q.1 and Q.2 have been compiled at the risks analysis stage of the *survey*. It must, however, be a part of the threat profile).

The answers to the questions indicate if a security hazard is present and if so, the extent of the hazard. Each hazard has some vulnerability and risk attached with a security lapse. Also, costs for the resulting risks and for securing against such hazards. Answers to the Q.1 and Q.2 indicate the threat scenario (or threat profile), where as the product of vulnerability and probability of occurrence indicates the risks, costs attached to such failures are indicative of the extent of security beefing up required therein.

This should cover each and every aspect noted in the security survey. You separate critical and non-critical areas, and list them in the order of importance and priority. For example, is sabotage more likely than burglary? If so, is the threat more likely to be external than internal? Is such a threat more dangerous for the assembly line rather than power sub-station? What are the possible routes for the intruder or stay behind to reach the location? What are the weak points or hazards involved along the routes? Is a deterrence system adequate? Would a detection system be necessary? Should it be round the clock, outside office-hours, on all days, including holidays, etc.? Should the detection system alert the local police, or an internal security unit is needed? What is the extent of false alarms that could be accepted? And so on.

This is the most difficult of all steps. Particularly, the problem is to quantify vulnerabilities, probabilities and costs. For example, how would one quantify the relative vulnerability of a nuclear waste storage pond? How can one estimate, quantitatively, the probability of an intrusion at such a location? And what would be the cost attached to such an activity? Ofcourse, it can be done with some effort, where specific need arises. In most cases, at least, what is required is a qualitative measure. However, you should note, that, threat assessment is just *a* tedious process and does not involve too much complexity to execute. In most cases, going through the very process itself may be sufficient to provide acceptable qualitative indication of the vulnerabilities, risks, (and approximations of costs, etc.).

At this stage, you also identify possible threats from internal sources, (disgruntled employees, strikes, pilferage, accidents, etc.), and from external sources, (industrial espionage, failure of utilities etc.).

Step IV: Identification and Choice of Acceptable Solution(s)

Just as in normal problem solving process in management, in this case also, you jot down all possible solutions, even if they appear outlandish. You match the solutions against the requirements of the problem and identify those that appear to be suitable, in the first instance. Then, you tie up with each of these selective solutions, their attendant costs and other implications. You have to now bear in mind, that, the less acceptable the solution is to the personnel concerned in the various departments of the organization, more difficult and perhaps costly, it would be to implement the same. Your choice would, hence, naturally fall upon the solution(s) that is/are optimum in terms of cost, resources required and acceptability.

At this stage, it is also the time to consider the basic security strategies that are possible, whilst selecting the solution(s).

Basic Security Strategies

The basic methodology is the defence in depth strategy that employs a two-fold combination, as follows:

External or outer defences.

(Like Choice of location; access road layout; road barriers; radar/ CCTV surveillance; Perimeter security; and so on.) And;

Internal, local or inner defences

(Defence of VAs, VPs, and VOPs)

Each of the above defense strategy is based on one, or a combination of the five types of possible techniques indicated below:

1. *Prevention* (or denying access, by proper selection of personnel, location and layout selection; S.O.Ps or Standard Operating Procedures need to know principle, access control and so on)
2. *Deterrence* (or delaying access by non-disclosure agreement/secrecy oath/ certification, fencing and access control, patrols, local alarms, etc.)
3. *Detection* (Intelligence, intrusion alarms, surveillance, patrols, access control)
4. *Protection* (prevent penetration of defences, stall or drive away intruders, secured doors/windows, safes/ vaults, access control screening and monitoring, fortification, encryption, and so on), and
5. *Neutralization* (apprehend and deliver intruders to authority, cancellation of access privileges, counter-measures like tagging, automatic lock-in system etc.)

Your choice of solution(s) would include some, or all of the techniques outlined above. It is at this stage that you will decide, whether, mere deterrence or suitable *S.O.Ps* are enough, or you would need to add some detection system(s); or even go in for protection and/or neutralization system(s). Maybe, you may also find need for some structural changes in the organization set-up/ layouts.

The next step is, ofcourse, the planned implementation of the selected solution(s).

Step V: Planned Implementation (and Training)

Once, the appropriate solutions have been arrived at, you could then, proceed with the implementation of these, but on a planned basis, and with appropriate priorities, as relevant. For example, in the first instance, you may need to implement suitable *S.O.Ps* and physical security measures, on top priority, and only then, embark on suitable detection systems, say the actual implementation of the plan has to be systematic. The actions involve several aspects, such as necessary organizational and structural changes to be carried out; selection and induction of necessary security personnel; their training; selection and association of suitable security agency, where needed, to assist in the security operations or even take over the same. (Quite often, where, local police or security force is in a position to provide prompt and quick service. Resort to such already, readily available facility may well be a good solution). You need to ensure proper implementation of the *S.O.Ps,* that have been evolved; design, selection, procurement, installation, integration and checkout of technical systems chosen as part of security solutions, including training of personnel, on the use and maintenance of the security system, and so on.

It has to be emphasized, that, side by side with the implementation of the security plan, it is essential to embark on the selection and training of relevant personnel for the security duties, operation of relevant security equipment/system and their maintenance. This would ensure that, the security operations could start the moment the system is in place, or even ahead, if needed.

Step VI: Operation (Maintenance and Motivation)

On implementation of the security plan, including training of the relevant personnel, you are now all set to carry out the security management function of the organization. You would have evolved your own *S.O.Ps* for the security operations, and easy to follow instruction/ guidelines to the security and associated staff. Where maintenance of security equipment has not been contracted out, you will need also to ensure timely and proper maintenance and repair of the same, as called for. However, the most difficult task would be to keep the motivation of your personnel always keyed up, to sustain high efficiency of the security operations at all times. Further, continuous reinforcement of security and safety awareness, in the organization as a whole; periodic training, and simulated exercises for the security and fire-fighting personnel, are a must.

But, this is not all. You cannot sit back on your *"laurels"*, since security situations are always dynamic, ever changing, with time, environmental changes, organizational changes, change in technology, change in business environment, and so on. Thus, the threat scenario is not static; it is constantly changing. Hence, the necessity for the last or seventh step in the cycle of security operations.

Step VII: Periodic Review and Upgradation of Security System

It is when the selected security system(s) is fully operational that you have to start thinking about when to carry reviews of the system, for identifying any chinks in the system. For, believe it or not, there will always be chinks in any security system, big or small, sophisticated or not. *Perfect security is* not impossible, but is impractical—*as it would be far too costly and would hold true only for a time; not long enough for the efforts needed to achieve the ideal.* Therefore, *periodic review* of security systems and tasks should be built-in, as should disaster plans, in the *S.O.Ps* of the organization. The standing objective of security should be constant improvement. A review is automatically called for, whenever, a change in environment, (unexpected or anticipated), occurs. Particularly, in regard to the *VAs/VPs/ or VOPs*; an organizational or structural change is due, or occurs, subsequent to the security survey, etc. or, after the implementation of the security plan; a change in the business environment/ laws and regulations; and so on. You must take note that, "what is not progressing, is either stagnating or even retrogressing".

ASSOCIATION OF EXPERTS/ CONSULTANTS

Security is a very complex task involving multitude of disciplines, innumerable imponderables, which an organization or business, particularly new one, is hardly likely to be familiar with. In such circumstances, or even otherwise, it pays to bring in consultants, well versed in the field, to assist in the task. This should be done right from the beginning; or at least, for the steps where the organization has the faintest doubt about its capabilities to do an effective job. Such assistance may be sought, either on a piecewise, project-wise basis; or on regular retention.

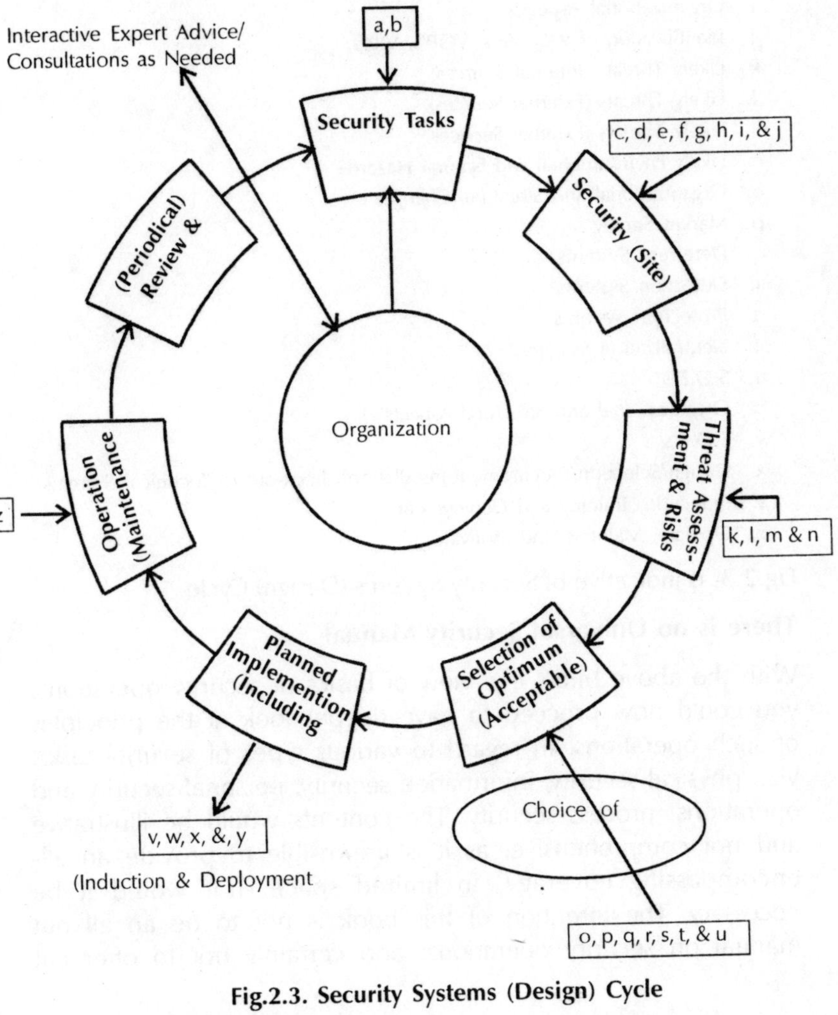

Fig.2.3. Security Systems (Design) Cycle

Legend (Fig.2.3. refers)

a. Swot
b. Local/State/National Laws and Regulations
c. Neighbourhood/Business Enviroment and Safety/Health Regulations
d. Physical Environment (Climatic/MET./Dust/Sunshine)
e. Natural Environment (Topographic Features/Structures)
f. Electromagnetic Enviroment (EME)
g. Biological Enviroment (insects, Birds, Animals, Fungi, Vermin Etc.)
h. Extent and Reliability of Local Services
i. Organizational Aspects
j. Identification of VA's, VP's, VOP's, VIP's
k. Likely Threats (Internal Sources)
l. Likely Threats (External Sources)
m. Likely Threats (External Services)
n. Likely Environmental and Natural Hazards
o. Organizational and Structural Changes
p. Market Survey
q. Deterrent Systems
r. Detection Systems
s. Protection Systems
t. Neutralization Systems
u. S.O.P's
v. Organizational and Structural Aspects
w. S.O.P's
x. Design/Selection/Procurement/Installation/Check-out of Technical Systems
y. Induction, Training and Deployment
z. Operate, Maintain and Motivate

Fig.2.3. is indicative of Security Systems (Design) Cycle

There is no Universal Security Manual

With the above bird's eye view of basics of security operations, you could now proceed to have deeper look at the principles of such operations, in regard to various types of security tasks, viz., physical security, information security, personal security and operations/ process security. The contents would be illustrative and not comprehensive, as it is impossible to provide an all-encompassing coverage, in limited space, nor would it be necessary. The intention of this book is not to be an all out manual on security operations; and certainly not to offer cut and tried solutions to specific security situations. But, to give an introduction to the principles of security operations and technology applicable. Each organization or business must prepare its own *S.O.Ps* and security manual, as appropriate and applicable to their specific security requirements. There can be no single, universal security manual for use, by one and all, and *for all situations.* The only common mantra, that, I can recommend is the *"sapta-padhi", or the seven steps to security operations* given in fig. 2.1.

Before proceeding to the next chapter, there is still one aspect to be looked at the use of technology in security. Technology has, no doubt, become quite pervasive in security operations. But before technology-options are gone into, there are five crucial questions *that need to be answered*—analogous to a quatrain given below, (attributed to Rudyard Kipling):

"I keep six honest serving men
They taught me all I knew
Their names are what and why and when
And how and where and who".

Technology Use in Security: (The five Qs.)

The five questions to be answered for technology use in security are:

Q.1. The Why of technology?
Q.2. The Where of technology?
Q.3. The When of technology?
Q.4. The What of technology?, and
Q.5. The How of technology.?

Q 1. The Why of technology

The steps relevant to this activity are the "security objectives" and "site survey" stages. The reasons may be many, such as:

 # To reduce manpower.
 # To reduce cost.
 # To improve security.

 # To meet security needs.
 # To be competitive.
 # To delay intrusions.
 # To reduce loss/ damage.
 # To warn against impending disasters, and so on.

The above could be *summarized as "to more cost-effectively meet the security objectives (of the organization).*

Q 2. The Where of technology

The steps relevant to this activity are the *stages of site survey and threat assessment and risks analysis.* Some answers to this question may be as follows:

 # To help in perimeter security.
 # To provide security cover to VAs, VPs, and VOPs.
 # To help in access control at entry/ exit points.
 # To improve computer security.
 # To help secure communication facilities, and so on.

These can be *summarized as "where it would be a better alternative and / or more cost-effective".*

Q 3 The When of technology

The stages relevant to this are, *"security survey", and "threat assessment and risks analysis"*. Some relevant answers to the question could be, say:

 # When employees and others are around.
 # When none is around.
 # When security personnel are not in position.
 # When losses are beyond control.
 # When organization/ structural changes take place.
 # At times of crisis/ emergency, and so on.

Technology employed should be tailored, naturally, *to the demands of the security situation.* However, *when deployed, its use should not be intermittent.*

Q 4. The What of technology, (choice of)

The stage, at which, the considerations regarding the type of technology to be used arise, is the step when the possible, acceptable solutions are considered and *selection of the optimum solution(s)* takes place. The types of systems and facilities to be looked at may be:

- # *Local alarm system.*
- # *Remote alarm system.*
- # *Centralized alarm system.*
- # *Reliability (and minimum false alarms type).*
- # *Ease of installation, operation and maintenance.*
- # *Monitoring, recording and analysis facilities.*
- # *Report generation.*
- # *Integration with other systems,* (say access control systems, fire alarm/ protection systems).
- # *Employee acceptability.*
- # *Upgradability.*
- # *Of current technology and in current production.*
- # *Warrantees.*
- # *Cost.*
- # *Dual or multiple technology, and so on..*

Usually, there would be no unique answer, some *compromises may be required. It is always a question of an educated choice- the best compromise solution, at that time.* This *needs proper market survey, and expert selections. Remember that, Murphy's law states, that, "All warrantee/ guarantee clauses become void on payment of the final invoice".*

Q 5. The How of technology, (its use).

The exact manner the chosen technology is deployed and used, are the considerations that arise, at the stage of planning and implementation. Aspects that need considerations are such as:

- # *Sensor locations.*
- # *Communication modes/ facilities.*
- # *Alarm locations.*
- # *Annunciator requirements/ locations.*
- # *Processing and control requirements.*
- # *Integration with other systems.*
- # *Environmental ambience.*
- # *Installation methods (overt/covert?).*
- # *Locations for monitoring/ recording/ report generation and analysis.*
- # *Special power supplies.*
- # *Training of operation and maintenance personnel.*
- # *Who will carry out the installation check out: Where, when and how, and so on.*

No wonder, security technology is a roaring business, with a host of specialist consultants to help out at each and every stage for its induction. So, get yourself expert advice; but, after perusing *the chapters that follow, to help you select the best adviser and that he gives you the right advice.*

Chapter 3

General Principles of Security Management

"Ask to find out. Seek to learn. But, to succeed—communicate and control"

Having gone through the approaches and strategies to effectively tackle security operations, it is time to get acquainted with some basic principles of managing security. You are, by now, quite familiar with the seven steps to achieve security goals. Having systematically implemented the required security plan, how do you ensure security is maintained? This, then, is the task of security management. There are many aspects to security management, and many qualities called for in a security manager. You could readily recall these, if you remember the *"mantra"*: *"Pick of security management"*, standing for the following aspects, (not in order of priority):

- # P: Plan for all contingencies, (and carry out simulated exercises).
- # I: Integrity is vital in security personnel, without this there is no security.
- # C: Communicate effectively to all levels.
- # K: Knack for asking right questions is a common trait in good security managers.
- # O: Organize to optimize security operations, (for efficiency and cost-effectiveness).
- # F: Forge ahead by deliberate leadership, (listen and lead).
- # Se: Systematize every security activity; (S.O.Ps).

- # Cu: Coordinate, for full understanding by all departments' personnel.
- # Ri: Review and improve constantly the security systems.
- # T: Train, train and train, personnel to effectively handle security and contingencies.
- # Y: Yearly plan for improvement in security systems, a must.
- # Man: Manage all security tasks, necessarily by objectives.
- # A: Analyze every problem, from all relevant aspects.
- # G: Guide, build and integrate a cohesive security team.
- # E: Ensure integrity of all security personnel.
- # Me: Motivate everyone, for an active and positive approach to security.
- # Nt: Necessary technology use, is inevitable.

Some elaboration of the above points would elucidate their importance in security management.

Contingency planning and planning for disasters, natural or manmade, is an essential part of security management. Regular simulated practice exercises ensure that such contingencies are effectively handled, if and when they occur, and to minimize any fallout adverse effects, due to such occurrences. Normally, it is hoped that such events will not occur. Even when the probability of such occurrences may be very, very small, the possibility of the event happening sometime (remote though it may be), has to be catered for. Your contingency planning and exercising would then, hopefully, see you through with minimal damage. For example, nuclear reactor buildings are designed to withstand the unlikely, but possible event, of a jumbo-jet aircraft crashing on to it! Fire hazard is a more common danger against which one has to be constantly prepared. It is, therefore, only prudent to evolve and implement plans, and to put it to simulated practice, periodically, right from the beginning; and not wait for any contingency/ disaster to actually occur, before you work out necessary and appropriate action plans!

Integrity of the security manager has to be unquestioned. Security would be seriously flawed, when there is any doubt in regard to the honesty of the officer. No amount of checks and balances in the organization can protect it from security hazards and other dangers, when its security manager is dishonest. It is therefore, imperative, that the organization be highly selective in its choice of the director/ manager/ and or supervisor, to lead its security operations. Choose, without fail, one whose integrity credentials are totally above board; and then, give him every assistance to pick right persons to form the security team/ unit.

Communication, is an essential skill that a good security manager must develop. He has to be able to communicate effectively, not only with his peers and subordinates under him as well as in other departments, but also establish good relations with the top management, right up the ladder, to the presiding "deity" of the organization. He cannot afford to be lax either, in maintaining excellent relations with the local agencies, like the police, utility services, emergency services and so on. It may be advisable to see that he undergoes suitable training in this regard, in any case, by sending him to appropriate courses conducted by reputed organizations in the business.

Knack of asking the right questions is a rare trait. Few persons have this innate, inborn ability. Fewer still, make a conscious effort to develop the same. But this is something that a good security manager will have. In every security situation, it is this trait that leads to a quick identification of the actual/ real problem; and helps to arrive sooner, at the right solution. Such skills help in better management of any situation, (not necessarily concerned with security).

Organizing properly helps to optimize a smooth flow of any activity, whether management or security related. It helps to improve efficiency and cost-effectiveness. When you do not properly organize your security system, you will encounter opposition, sloppiness, security lapses and unpleasant management scrutiny; perhaps, even interference in the day to day running of your unit and operations. A security system will be quite ineffective, when there is friction all over in its functioning. Such daily irritations would consume all your energy and fully occupy your time, to the exclusion of your main task of security.

Forge leadership, an essential element for effective security management. You cannot afford gut-reactions to situations. You need timely, and appropriate responses, well thought out and considering all the relevant factors. This calls for the ability to listen well, with close attention, to what is being conveyed to you about an event or situation, with security connotation. Follow the nuances; ask right questions to elicit relevant details that may well have gone unmentioned. Then, and only then, look at the sum total, to initiate correct response(s) to the situation. Rushing headlong into situations; throwing off the cuff remarks or directions to the staff, is not leadership; and should never be countenanced. *"Listen, comprehend, and then lead."* (Note that, S.O.Ps and contingency plans would have already laid down actions to be taken by all concerned, for most occurrences. So the security manager is not to rush in blindly in any case).

Systematize every security activity. By having well established and well disseminated standard operating procedures (S.O.Ps), you ensure effective and efficient performance. The procedures must be scrupulously observed by all concerned. To remain effective, all lapses or lacunae must be fully investigated and corrective moves initiated. Normally, there should be no gap between discarding of an old established procedure and implementation of a new one. Not a single procedure should be implemented without advance intimation and enlightenment of all concerned. Most often, *S.O.Ps* are the mainstay of security. They basically systematize all activities concerning security, for effectiveness and ease of observation by all concerned. Hence, *the S.O.Ps need to be practical too and not idealistic, even when it may not offer the best security.*

Co-ordination and understanding, is by and large the only way, to get acceptability of activities that leads to effective security. Naturally, all departments of the organization must be fully involved in the evolution of the *S.O.Ps* and accept them, as willingly as feasible. Otherwise, there is likelihood of the procedures being given the go-by or flouted by some employees/ departments, leading to security failures, immediately or ultimately. All departments' personnel must be able to appreciate and understand the security concerns, so that they readily observe the concomitant, inevitable restraints imposed on them, by the *S.O.Ps.* Hence, *no co-ordination means poor security.*

Review and improve security systems on a continuous basis, though you may have a good security system or excellent S.O.Ps. Then, comes along an organizational change, some new buildings or modifications to existing ones, a new environmental or technological threat, and so on. These changes could bring in new security hazards, which have to be catered for. Even otherwise, when any security lapse has occurred, or some lacuna is noted, need arises for updation of security. No security system can remain current and efficient, for any length of time, without needing improvements. Therefore, timely/ continuous improvements to security systems is a necessity, you cannot rest on your laurels!

Training, initial or periodic, intensive or extensive as needed cannot be over emphasized. Apart from the security, operational and maintenance personnel, some training and practice exercises are called for with others too. Say, to handle contingency situations, in regard to security awareness and so on. Training to update capabilities, apart from merely maintaining efficiency of the personnel, is also a necessity. Periodic lectures, seminars and practice exercises are some of the training methods. Training may also be required on how to recognize security and safety hazards, how to behave/what each one has to do during emergencies/ disaster conditions and so on. As long as the normal functioning of the organization is not adversely affected, due to time-out on such training activities, you must fit in as much training as possible for all types and levels of personnel in the organization. (As far as possible, such time out for training should be built into the organizations functioning, as the military do).

Yearly plan, for security upgradation, within affordable cost, is a must. This is the only way funds will be found and improvements are made to security. "No plan" may well mean no additional funds for security. On the other hand, there could even be a reduction of funds, and security system would tend to deteriorate with time. The improvements sought may even be incremental in nature only, if resources are very scarce in some years. But, in some cases revolutionary improvements may be called for on "threat reassessment", with changes in the security environment. And, in such circumstances, total security system upgradation may well be a must.

MBO, (Management By Objective), manage all security tasks necessarily by objectives. The objectives may change from time to time, or its different facets may need emphasis, with changes in the organizational structure, functioning or its long-term objectives. Here, it must be noted however, that the cultural ethos and the societal traditions within which the organization has to function must temper the MBO. For an organization to thrive, the value systems of the organization must be in consonance with the country's cultural background in which the employees are steeped in. For example, most of the western nations may give importance to individual excellence, just rewards and recognition as per merit, hire and fire policy and so on. Oriental nations may value loyalty, contributions to society, discipline, patriotism and so on. The traditions in India tend to make the CEO of the organization a father figure, the employee expects not only permanency of his appointment but also expect the organization to consider his family as an extended family of the company! Question of firing an employee is almost impossible, (so, you need to take all extra care during the hiring part). Loyalty to the organization is all-important and seniority a prized criteria-after all you do respect the elders in India! So, bear the above in mind whilst exercising the MBO!

Analysis is the basic requirement of any problem solving approach. When a security situation arises, you need to consider all aspects related to the problem, and explicitly identify and rule out those which are not of any concern. Also analyze the effects and implications of each relevant solution, after identifying all possible solutions. Rule out those that are not practicable or feasible. Then and only then you could reach the optimum solution, for each such situation. The selected solution should be generally acceptable to all concerned; but realize, however, that you cannot satisfy every one, not always.

Guide, build and integrate a cohesive security team. You will need to select and induct proper and suitable individuals who will meet the needs. Then guide and build a team out of them, which will be well trained, knowledgeable and be supportive of each other. Such a team would be effective in carrying out the security functions efficiently, and appropriately. Security tasks need sincerity, dedication, savoir-faire, impartiality and above all integrity; which you will need to inculcate in your team.

Ensure integrity, of all security personnel with you, by proper selection, at the stage of induction. You should have appropriate background checks carried out for this purpose. You must also set up high standards of integrity and enforce them without exception, but humanely without any harshness. Apart from being scrupulously honest, the team members would need to be highly disciplined, smart in turnout and have the necessary presence of mind and ability to handle difficult people and exacting situations. This is also part of your task of team building.

Motivate everyone in the organization to be positive and take an active role in regard to anything that has to do with security. They must look at security as an extension of their own tasks; an essential complementary measure for the organization to function properly, and achieve its objectives. Each one must be made to develop, to the extent feasible an active concern for security, a very difficult task no doubt. Remember that *"to err is human, to persist in error is devilish"*—St. Augustine; *also "the man who never makes a mistake always takes orders from one who does"*—Anonymous!

Necessary technology, has become, nowadays, an inevitable element of any security operation. There is hardly any security activity where technology does not have a say. A security manager can ill afford to be disdainful or ignore useful role that technology can play in his security tasks. It is of course vital for security management to know which is necessary technology and which has only cosmetic appeal, in regard to their security operations. Associate experts in this regard where required.

From the above, it would be clear, that, *almost all important activities, essential for good and effective security management, could be recalled readily, (hopefully), from the* catch-phrase *"pick of security management "*. You must have noticed that most of the management tools, and some, are readily applicable to security management also, maybe with different emphasis. We could now conveniently take a closer look at the four types of security operations, viz., "physical security", "information security", "personal security" and 'operations/ process security".

Chapter 4

Components of Technical Aids to Safety and Security

"A little knowledge is a dangerous thing"

You may recall that there are two generic types of technical aids viz., the "stand alone" type and the "dependent" type. Examples of the stand alone types are shredding machines, fire extinguishers, safes, bulletproof vests, and so on. The device could be as simple as a lock or be very complicated and sophisticated like transport containers for nuclear materials. The device is however usually a self-contained unit.

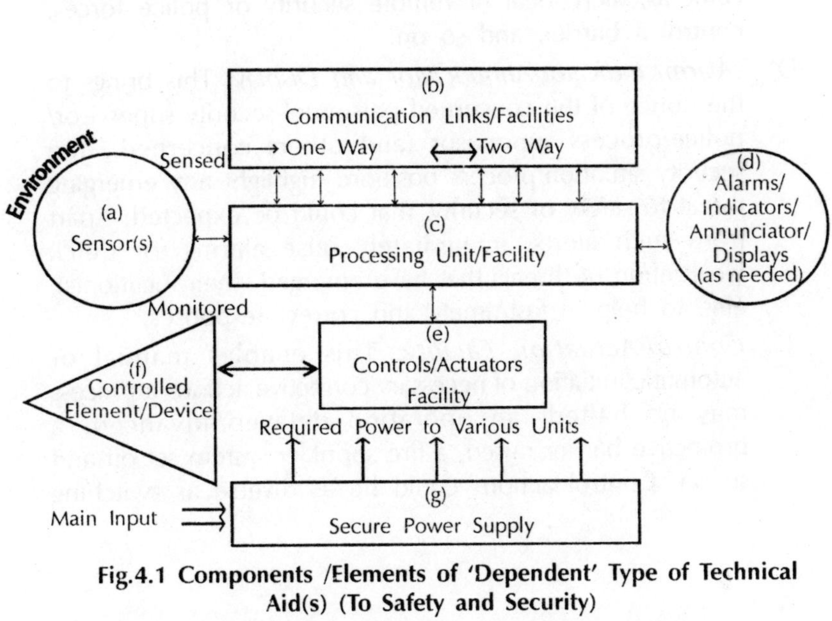

Fig.4.1 Components /Elements of 'Dependent' Type of Technical Aid(s) (To Safety and Security)

The dependent type of device, on the other hand, constitutes more than one component, of several as indicated below, (see fig.4.1):

A) *Sensor(s)*: These sense the surrounding environment for changes and give an output related to some quality or characteristic of the environment that it senses. The output could be an electrical signal that is convenient for transmission to a remote location. Examples are CCTV cameras, card readers, temperature sensors, pressure sensors and so on.

B) *Communication Link or Facility*: This provides a means for carrying the sensed signal to different/remote locations for suitable processing /observation as necessary.

C) *Processing Unit/Facility*: This facility accepts information from the sensor(s) and other sources; analyzes and evaluates the information against preset or predetermined criteria. It then, implements appropriate actions, as well as monitoring the results for further necessary action that may be called for. The actions may be raising an alarm signal, display of suitable messages, activating remote cameras, alert local or remote security or police forces, control a barrier, and so on.

D) (*Alarm) Indicator/Annunciator and Display*: This brings to the notice of the concerned personnel-security supervisor/ police/process supervisor (and others concerned), the security situation/process position; highlight any emerging threat to safety or security, that could be expected. Apart from such alerts, immediately raise alarms for quick localization of threats that have emerged -their location(s), etc., to help in fast/timely and correct responses.

E) *Control/Actuation Facility*: This enables manual or automatic initiation of necessary corrective actions-a process may be halted, an operation delayed/advanced, a protective barrier raised, a fire sprinkler system set off and so on. Control actions could be as diverse as switching "off" of power, stopping an aircraft from taking off (on receipt of a bomb-threat say), stifling a nuclear reaction, shutting of gates, etc.

F) *Controlled Device/Element*: This device is setoff by control signals to perform relevant security or corrective process function to ensure security/safety. Examples are power switch (remotely activated), hydraulically activated vehicle barrier, automatically actuated sliding gates, time-lock-operated vaults, remotely operated fire-extinguishing device, and so on.

G) *Secure Power Supply*: This is an essential facility for any security or safety system. Note that, mains/utility supplies could fail; built in batteries may go dead and standby power refuse to rise to the occasion, sabotage may take place. Total security of power supply, to the security/safety system, even when under active threat, is an indispensable requirement of good security/safety systems.

The simplified block diagram at fig.4.1. is indicative of the above components or elements of the dependent types of security systems.

But it must be noted that the actuation device or "controlled" element may quite often be the human element! You may also be aware that in critical systems, there is often a default condition that is automatically treated as an alarm condition. And protective actions are then automatically initiated like in a nuclear power station, say power to the control element fails due to any reason, then the control element automatically falls into the reactor core to shut down the affected reactor, as a safeguard against a runaway (reactor) condition.

A simple security device may just have sensor(s), and associated alarm indication, and a suitable power supply. More sophisticated system-like elaborate automatic access control systems, may have many sensors (ID card readers), hidden and protected communication links, micro processors, alarm devices, recording and printout units, automatic turnstiles/doors/gates, automatic fire extinguishing systems, time and attendance monitoring and so on.

A) Sensors

Sensor is a device that monitors the environment. It senses any changes in the monitored parameter and produces an output variation, corresponding to the changes. And, in a form that is readily usable, like an electrical voltage/current/phase etc., variation. The functioning of the sensor is based on some physical or chemical etc. principle, that the environmental parameter concerned affects. Usual principles employed are: electro-mechanical, physical, optical, chemical, electro-magnetic, biometrics, thermal, acoustic and so on. Note that sensors can even be the human/ living organization variety. Examples are "sniffer" dogs, "humint", (Human Intelligence), system, and so on.

The *sensor is immersed in the environment, or monitors the environment* (as in the case of CCTV or radar); it senses the relevant changes in the monitored parameter of the environment; and causes changes in the output of the sensor. The output may be made use of as it is, or changed into a suitable form for communication/processing or actuating some device/alarm. The outputs are usually in the form of changes in electric current, voltage, frequency, phase or pulses or combinations of the same.

The choice of sensor(s) and suitable qualification of its output, that is appropriate to the situation, is an important and vital decision. Take for example, an automatic door or turnstile; it may operate by sensing the pressure applied to it by a person desiring a passage through. But then, anyone can pass through such a system; that is, the system provides universal access with no discrimination. When access is to be restricted to authorized persons only, such a system is useless, for the application. You would then need to use some access control system, a biometrics device, and so on, tied up with the door opening system. Such qualification method could be extended to provide all sorts of facilities, like time and attendance recording, access by classification of the types of personnel/ their rank in the organization and so on.

B) Communication Link(s) or Facilities

The signals generated by the sensors, as they monitor the changes in its environment, have to be passed on, usually, to a different location(s), that is, to the locations where the signals can be processed and actuation commands generated for alarms/ annunciators/displays or actuators. Therefore, you require suitable links or facilities to carry out the sensor signals to such locations, and from the processor to the alarm/annunciator/ display etc., locations. Already available telephone, intercom or even power circuits may be used for such purposes. But the preferred method should be to lay separate special wires/cables or wireless links which are secure from prying eyes /unauthorized personnel/ undesirable access. Nowadays, fibre-optic cabling is becoming more and more popular. To protect unauthorized access to such signals, they may be suitably coded or enciphered when passed over the communication channels. Then such signals make sense only to authorized persons/devices which have the proper decode/ decrypt system.

Apart from above, communication links facilities are also required in security operations for conveying information, intelligence, directives, alerts etc., from one person to another, one location to another/many other, between organizations, and so on. *Communication links/ facilities are, thus, vital component(s) of any security system.*

C) Processing Unit/Facility

Signals generated by sensors need to be processed to reduce noise, to highlight or identify alarm conditions, or maybe remove interfering outputs, before it is used to trigger alarm signals, in turn; (on identification of an alarm condition output from the sensor, and so on). Such processing may be local, at the sensor or sensor location itself, or at a remote, convenient location(s), based on sensor signals transmitted over suitable communication link or facility to the remote processing location(s). Such processing may also involve analyzing the signals for threat implications, formatting the outputs for suitable indications or displays at locations (maybe remote) of choice and generation of action commands where necessary. Such facilities are not required, of course, where a simple local alarm type of installation is required; output signal from the sensor(s) directly triggers locally-at the location itself, an alarm-say a siren or /and blinding /flashing lights. However, in most cases, suitable processing facility is a must; and the type of processing provided is indicative of how good and how efficient the system is.

D) (Alarm) Indicator/Annunciator and or Display

When an alarm condition occurs, as determined from the output signals from the sensors, then, it is necessary to alert concerned personnel. Also, the alarm condition would need to be interpreted into terms that could be readily observed, easily noted, and instantly understood, (for what it means/represents), by the persons monitoring the safety/security conditions. Flashing lights and or buzzing sounds are the usual, simple alerting alarm signals. Suitably designed annunciator panels, with a matrix of lamps each with a caption indicating a location, or laid out over a diagram that details the locations, etc., enable a quick identification of the location(s) where the alarm conditions have occurred. Suitable alpha-numeric displays, (alphabets and numerals or AN), or tv type of displays, could provide information on not merely the locations, but also the type of alarm conditions, to be of better aid to the security personnel. Such displays may even indicate the type of corrective action(s) to be initiated by the monitoring personnel.

Alarm indications/annunciators need to have distinctive signals, so that they are easily, and quickly recognized/identified for what they are, by the concerned persons. And this should be so, even, in adverse conditions of ambient noise, bright lights, intense darkness, etc. This will quickly alert the personnel/call their attention to unusual/unsafe, or dangerous conditions, etc. that require immediate response by the personnel/crew, on the spot.

E) Control/Actuation Facility

In most situations manual control is prevalent for interceding in dangerous situations. That is, the actuators/controllers are humans. For example, in the case of a fire alarm, fire fighting personnel attack the fire with help of fire extinguishers, water canons and so on. In a signal Intelligence (SIGINT) setup, the Intelligence supervisor would need to decide whether a special report should be sent out in regard to out of ordinary messages that have been intercepted. Further, he must also decide to whom all such a report should be sent, what other SIGINT actions should be initiated, and so on.

On the other hand, in remote controlled or automated systems, after due evaluation of the signals from the sensors, suitable control/actuation signals may be automatically generated by the system to initiate necessary actions (such as tripping of automatic fire sprinkler system, opening of fire exit doors, shutting down a reactor, closure of a safe or vault operation of a turnstile and so on).

F) Controlled Device/Element

The controlled element or device used determines the basic safety or security function of a technical system. The element may be simple, such as an alarm indicator, or a buzzer. Or it may be more elaborate, like an automatically erected vehicle barrier. It could also be quite sophisticated and extensive such as an electronic countermeasures system that would send out a jamming signal in a specific direction on a specific frequency or frequencies (say on interception of a dangerous radar or communication signal from a hostile location). The device could even be an automatic jammer, which prevents dangerous, electronic, adversary signals from being received in a protected area and, suppress activation of any remote controlled explosive device, and so on and so forth.

However, it is not necessary for a controlled element or device to be always operated by automatic means. They may well be initiated manually; this could be the case most of the times where critical adjustments control, instant responses (human reaction time is too slow), or complicated operations are not involved.

G) Secure Power Supply

This is an important element in any security or safety system. The most sophisticated and expensive safety or security system could become inoperative or even fail (usually at the most critical time), due to inadequacy or failure of its power supply. Hence, reliable system operation needs critical attention to the power supply element as well as its scrupulous maintenance. If, processor or computer is the brain of a system, the power supply is the heart of the system, without which the system is as good as dead. Care has also to be taken to see that the design and installation of the system is such that its power supply cannot be interfered with in any way by ill-wishers.

Depending on the power requirements of the system, the power supply may be by means of suitable batteries, or from utilities/mains supply. Where mains supply is used, it should be supplemented with an in-house standby, petrol or diesel, generator units. Where batteries are used, these may be discardable types or rechargeable types-the choice being decided by the system requirements and the maintenance methodology envisaged.

As mentioned earlier, a specific technical aid or system may, or may not have all the elements shown in the fig.4.1. In many cases, the device may merely have a sensor with an indication, or an alarm, and perhaps a power source for its operation. A hand-held metal detector, for example, has a sensor head which senses the presence of metal close to it, an alarm indication (light and or a buzzer), and an in-built battery power supply, for the operation of the device.

On the other hand, a sophisticated access control system could have multiple sensors, similar to each other or different types, processing or computer units, communication links, local/ remote indicators and display units, printouts and recorders, automatic door opening/closing devices fire alarm system integrated with it, and so on. Such systems would also need elaborate and secure power supply facilities, to power the sensors, the communication facilities, the processors, the indicators/ displays, the controllers, actuators, and so on.

Obviously, the above is just a bare outline of what a technical security system could consist of. Unless you are a technical expert, it is invariably advisable to consult relevant specialists in the business when you have to go in for any technology oriented security/safety system. Ignorance is, certainly, not bliss in such cases. And, a little knowledge could definitely be disastrous! Familiarity with technology and its uses will certainly help to derive the maximum benefit from any consultation projects; enable informed choices in induction of technical systems, their maintenance, installation, operation, training and so on.

Chapter 5

Elements of Physical Security

"Checks and Controls are the essence of Physical Education"

The structured approach to security and the basic security strategies highlighted in Chapter 2 apply equally well to physical security (as well as to other types of security operations). You follow through the "sapta padhi", or the seven steps, elaborately or cursorily depending on the specific security situation that applies. You then apply the principles of defense in depth, the outer defences and the inner defences, having identified the *VAs, VPs and the VOPs.* Your task is then to implement one or more of the five types of suitable techniques of prevention, deterrence, detection protection and neutralization; alone or in combination, as appropriate.

Physical security measures are required to protect property, installations etc., from hazards; both manmade and natural.

Fig. 5.1. is indicative of the principal hazards, manmade and natural hazards, to security and safety.

Principal Hazards

- **Natural**
  - **Normal**
    - **Environmental** (Climatic)
      - Temperature (Heat, Cold, Shock)
      - Moisture, Fog
      - Dust, Sand
      - Pressure, Wind (High, Low, Variation)
      - Sunshine
      - Wind-Chill
      - Rain, Sleet, Snow Frost
    - **Others**
      - Radiation (Cosmic, α, β, γ etc)
      - Polluted Atmosphere
      - Salt Spray etc.
      - Explosive Atmosphere
  - **Abnormal** (Disasters)
    - Floods
    - Earthquakes
    - Cyclones etc.
    - Fires
    - Explosions
    - Tidal Waves
    - Volcanoes
    - Land Slides
    - Meteors
    - Ozone Depletion etc.
- **Man Made**
  - **Usual**
    - **Personnel (Origin)**
      - Pilferage/Theft/Burglary
      - Carelessness
      - Disloyalty
      - Sabotage
      - Arson
      - Espionage
      - Subversion
      - Bombings/Explosions
    - **Others**
      - EMI
      - Radiation
      - Mechanical Stress (Vibration, Shock, Impact)
      - Environmental (Excessive Heat, Cold Pressure Vacuum Moisture etc.)
      - Failures/Loss of Inputs (Power, Water, Air Communication, etc)
      - Pollution etc.
  - **Harmful Intent/Accidental**
    - Fires
    - Explosions
    - EME
    - EMP
    - Radiation (X-ray, Laser, etc.)
    - Aircrash/Train Crash etc.
    - Nuclear Fallout
    - Bombings
    - Kidnappings
    - Assassination
    - Terrorism (Bio, Chemical etc.)
    - Insurgency
    - Space Objects/Debris
    - Poisonings
    - Disruptions

Fig. 5.1. Principal Hazards, Manmade and Natural Hazards, to Security & Safety

Manmade Hazards are:

- Pilferage and theft
- Carelessness leading to accidents
- Disloyalty or disgruntlement leading to above or other problems like fraud, embezzlement etc.
- Sabotage
- Espionage
- Arson
- Fires
- Explosions
- Pollution
- Electromagnetic interference
- Radiation hazard etc.

or More Dangerous Hazards like:

- Air-crash
- Bombings
- Kidnappings or hostage taking
- Assassination
- Terrorism
- Insurgency and war
- Nuclear fallout

Natural Hazards are such as:

Environmental Factors

Mechanical Factors

- Vibration, shock, impact (explosions)

Climatic Factors

- Temperature (heat, cold, temperature shock)
- Precipitation, (rain, hail, snow, ice etc.)
- Fog, moisture
- Dust, sand

- Pressure (high, low, variation), wind
- Sunshine
- Wind-chill

Other Factors

- Natural radiation (cosmic rays, alpha/beta/gamma etc.)
- Salt/polluted atmosphere
- Explosive atmospheres

Natural Disasters

- Floods
- Earthquakes
- Landslides
- Cyclones
- Fires
- Explosions
- Tidal waves.
- Volcanoes

Obviously, the approach to physical security will need to consider the above hazards whilst carrying out the security (site) survey. Then plan out the *defences-prevention, deterrence, detection, protection and neutralization systems* that need to be implemented, taking into account the threat assessment and the risks evaluation.

The security (site) survey highlights the vulnerable locations/ vulnerable aspects of the organization. The threat assessment and risks analysis emphasizes the nature and extent of *security hazards to the VAs, VPs and VOPs,* identified during the survey; and requiring adequate protection. The objectives of physical security measures are to set up appropriate counter-measures around the locations, starting from the outermost boundaries of the premises/organization setup. A basic aspect is to determine as to who and what can be permitted entries and exits to and from the premises/locations; and when, where and how, (including routes to be followed), such entries and exits shall take place.

Suitable barriers, access and exit controls and other appropriate checks are introduced to enforce the above decisions. Hence, *no checks, no controls—means no security* !

There is no such animal as non-invasive security. Security measures do necessarily impinge on movements, actions and behaviour of personnel, to a lesser or greater extent, depending on how good the security arrangements are and how vital tight security is to the organizational objectives to be achieved. There can be no security operation, which will not affect, at least to some extent, the freedom and privacy of individuals who have anything to do with the organization. The effort is to make the security system as unobtrusive, as non-intrusive and as acceptable as feasible, within the security constraints. The decisions *in regard to who, what, where, when and how,* affect *access and traffic controls*; but, the actual type and extent of such control measures to be implemented, depend on the results of the *threat assessment and risks analysis activity.* However, *all security measures are aimed to deny/deter/detect/protect and/or neutralize undesirable intrusions/accesses to assets, (materials or information), and exits.*

Answers to the question *who, decides the authorization of personnel.* The answers to questions *when, where and what, determine the timings and the locations for entry and exit points,* (main gates and doors), and place of work for individuals, location and movements of materials /information. Answers to the question *how, decides the methods of access control, materials control, vehicular traffic* control, the routes to be followed by personnel/ materials/vehicles etc. The standard operating procedures (S.O.Ps) and so on. Thus, the outer and inner defence requirements are arrived at; the first step being to secure the perimeter adequately, to form a security cocoon.

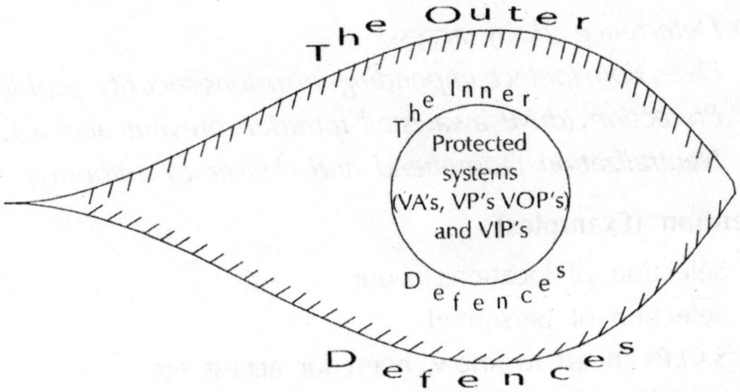

Fig. 5.2 (Is indicative of) The nature of the security cocoon.

"The outer defences" may extend from the perimeter areas to as far out as considered necessary from the threat perception/security requirements, for example government of U.S.A. appear to consider the entire world (outside of U.S.A.), including the outer space as their legtimate region for their 'outer defences', (from their internal security considerations). Israel is not far behind, evidences by their bombing of nuclear facility deep inside another country.

Note: Eye represents an effective long distance outer defence AID for a living creature as it detects likely threats far away. The eyelashes and eye lids form good inner defences for the pupil of an eye (VP), and the whites of the eye (Vital Areas).

Perimeter Security

Activities connected with perimeter security start beyond the actual perimeter of the complex. For example, *"caution"* boards may be erected on the approach road and around the perimeter alerting a person to the fact that he is approaching "private property", a "prohibited area" and that "trespassers will be prosecuted" and so on. Special road humps, or speed breakers may be setup on the approach roads, as it is a good security measure to adequately slow down the traffic. The surrounding areas may be cleared of all obstructions to have a clear view from within the perimeter, for an early warning in regard to likely intrusions or other security problems.

The security measures envisage, naturally:

- *Prevention (deny access)*
- *Deterrence (delay access)*
- *Detection (detect impending-intrusions/security problems)*
- *Protection (drive away/stall intruders/prevent access.)*
- *Neutralization (apprehend and deliver to authority)*

Prevention (Examples)

* Selection of locations/layout
* Selection of personnel
* S.O.Ps (need to know, need for access etc.)
* Vehicle stops and sliding gates
* Access control and so on.

Deterrence Systems (Examples)

* Non-disclosure agreement/secrecy oath/certification
* Barbed tape fencing/perimeter wall/ gates
* Special fence attachments
* Security presence (patrols)/dog patrols etc.
* Local alarms
* Perimeter lighting
* Access control
* Neighbourhood watch system and so on.

Detection Systems (Examples)

* Security patrols
* Observation devices/ systems
* Intrusion detection systems (IDS)
* Access control (alarm) systems and so on.

Protection Systems (Examples)

* Grills and gratings on openings
* Locked/secured doors, windows and other openings
* Secured almirahs, safes and vaults

* Access control screening and monitoring
* Additional inner fence (with IDS and security)
* Electrified fence (where permitted)
* Fortifications and so on, (and in extreme cases, even minefields!).

Neutralization Systems (Examples)

* Local security force (own)
* Local police/security agency force (if they can arrive in-time)
* Automatic lock-in system
* Countermeasures, like automatic dye colouring of currency.

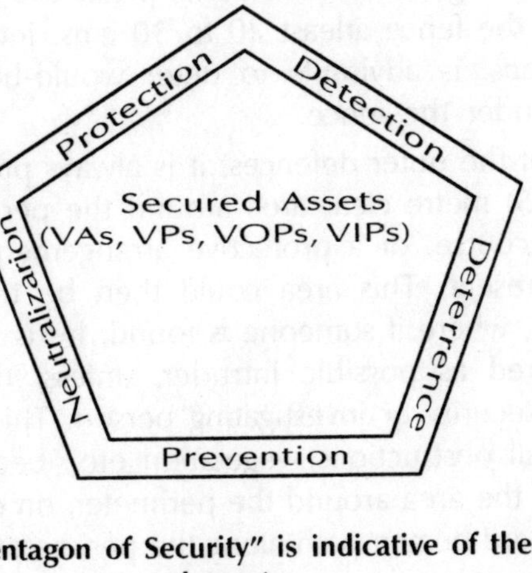

Fig. 5.3 "The Pentagon of Security" is indicative of these security elements.

Note: That there are no explicit boundaries between the security elements/ Techniques and their application, most times, (They are seamless?)

A deterrent activity may help in prevention.

Presence of a detection system could act as a deterrence (when proclaimed/ Advertised without actual details ofcourses.

Prevention techniques may also act as protective element (like a high security wall), and so on. The techniquss need to be optimally matched for specific security scenario, to be effective.

Perimeter Security Guidelines

Perimeter security can vary from simple boundary marking or hedge, through chain-link fencing to very high solid walls with elevated watchtowers, searchlights, elaborate detection and surveillance facilities etc. Nowadays, the erstwhile barbed fencing is more or less passé, except for temporary erections of barbed tape/barbed fence. Chain-link fencing of various heights is quite popular, apart from brick/concrete compound walls, (picket fences are not very popular where security requirements are present). A chain-link fence permits easy visual observation through the fence, unlike in the case of a solid wall where elaborate technical observation or surveillance facilities would be required for the purpose. Where the ground along the fencing is soft, can be easily dug through, some additional protective methods such as embedding the fence atleast 20 to 30 cms. into the ground, in such locations, is advisable to deter would-be intruders from tunneling under the fence.

As part of the outer defences, it is always preferable to have, say, a five (5) metre clear area around the perimeter, wherever possible of course, or a protective arrangement like a moat or stream if present. This area could then be treated as a "no-man's land", where if someone is found, he is suspect and is to be considered as possible intruder, unless, that is, he is an authorized security or investigating person. This area should be cleared of all obstructions, vegetation etc., because it hampers free view of the area around the perimeter, on either side of the fencing. A hard beaten path along the perimeter permits security personnel to move around easily and fast, on their beat or when needed to apprehend any intruders. Such movements of security personnel could be on foot, on bicycles, by motorized vehicles etc. As appropriate to the situation/protected set-up. Suitable elevated observation/watch towers may be needed in case of extended perimeters/obstructed locations, to have a clear gap-less view of the surrounding areas at all times. Security personnel on their rounds will climb up the towers, to look out to spot any suspicious activities in the neighbourhood of the perimeter, for early detection and enable to be suitably countered in time. They may even be continuously manned, where essential, and may be fitted with searchlights/observation devices or surveillance systems, etc.

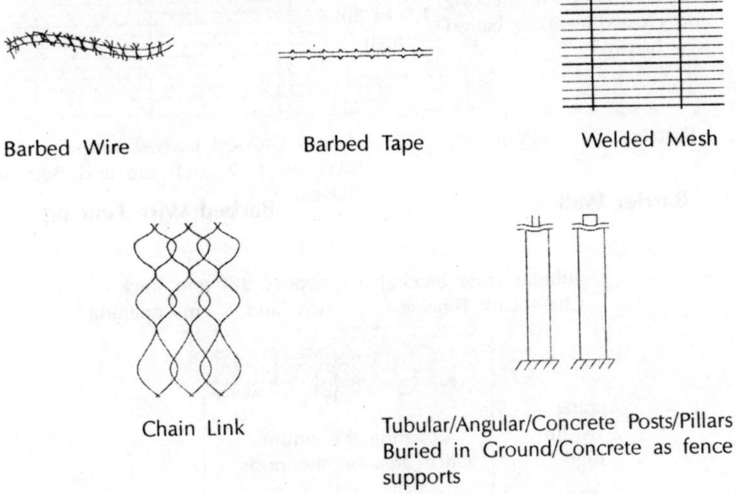

Basic Fence Materials

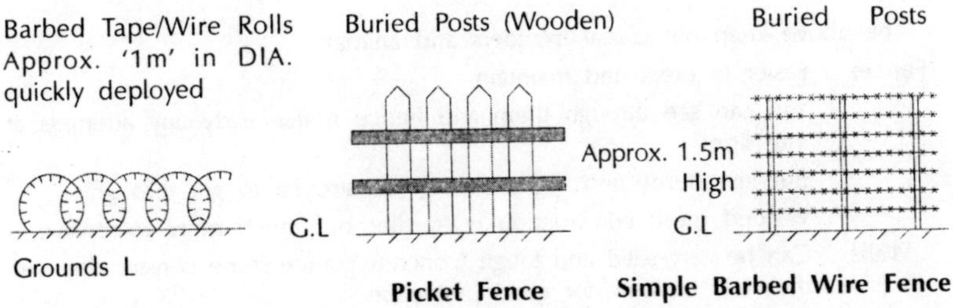

Simple Barriers/Fences

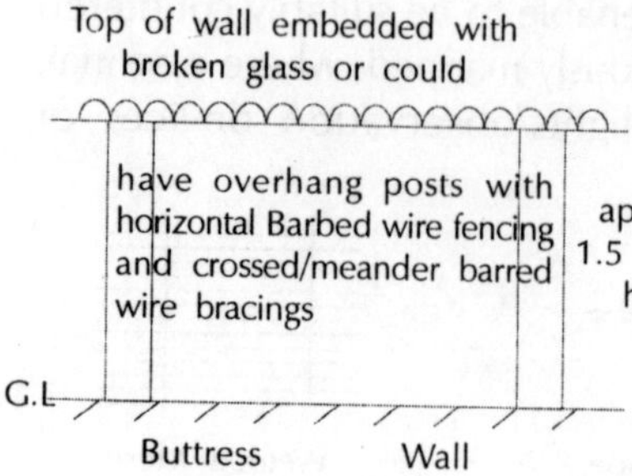

Barrier Wall

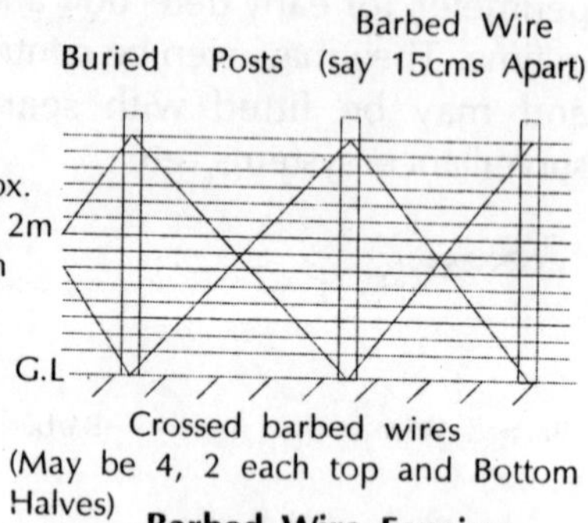

Barbed Wire Fencing

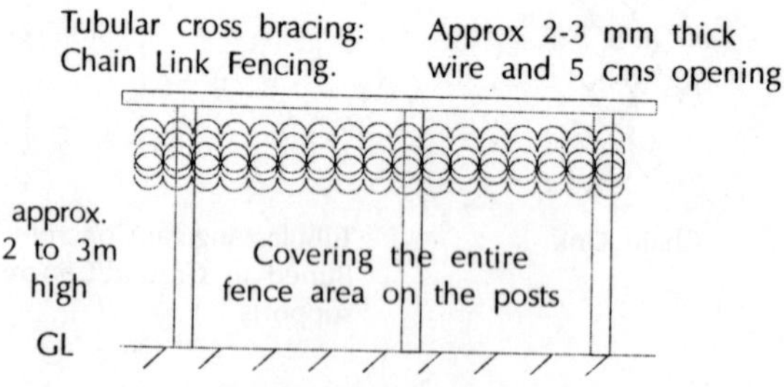

Chain Link Fence

Fig. 5.4 (Is Indicative of) The General Characteristics of Fences and Barriers.

Note:

The above keep out casual intruders and animals

Fences Easier to erect and maintain

You can see through them and hence notice early any attempts at intrusion.

But less sturdy and easily damaged/destroyed to get through

Welded mesh construction is sturdier but much more expensive

Walls Can be very solid and tough (concrete/granite stone construction say) thus can be built for good protection.

Difficult to damage/get through when tough design/construction

Without suitable gadgets no view of proximity (outside) area

Kills curiosity as people outside cannot see inside (activities)

Expensive to build and Maintain (painting, repair etc.)

Overhang fencing may be used atop walls (inward, outward of bothway overhangs) to deter illegal exit/entrance throwing over of objects at the perimeter etc.

The perimeter must have adequate illumination at all times. During dark/overcast days as well as at nights, suitable artificial illumination would be needed. The illumination sources are generally placed about four to five metres from the perimeter (within), at heights of about five metres, or more as needed, and the sources separation and angle are so arranged, as to give gap-less illumination, from within the perimeter, to over the perimeter and beyond.

Perimeter Lighting Guidelines

* Locate lighting poles at least five metres away from fence.
* Space them for proper azimuth overlap and good lighting.
* Position lamp about five metres height.
* Angle lamp to illuminate 'dead zone' within, fence and outside.
* Entry/exit areas to be very well lit (and shadow-less).
* Select appropriate luminaires (true colour rendition is important, where the output of the Cameras/CCTV are used as evidence. Then, when an intruder is caught, the colour photographs/video tapes are better as evidence than mere black and white images, for identification purposes).
* Illumination levels to be far better than twilight condition. (still higher levels of illumination required for colour photography/colour videography).

Table V.1. Details of different lighting conditions, and Table V.2. gives some details of luminaires available.

Table V. 1. Lighting Conditions

Condition	Approximate illumination level (lux)
Direct sunlight	100,000
Full daylight	10,000
Overcast day	1,000
Very dark day	100
Twilight	10
Full moon	0.1
Starlight	0.001

Table V. 2. Luminaires Available (lamps)

Type	Comment
Tungsten lamp	Inadequate
Fluorescent lamp	Satisfactory
Mercury vapour lamp	Good
Sodium vapour lamp (high pressure)	Very good
Xenon/ metal halide lamps	Excellent

High Security Environment

When the area to be secured is very large, and the perimeter is extensive, it is impossible for just a couple of security guards to take care of the security needs. You would then need either a large security force with adequate communication and other technical facilities, or a hi-tech security installation, with a much smaller, but clued-up security force. It is then that the need arises for *intrusion detection (and alarm) system, (IDS).* You will then need to consider whether to go in for *local alarm, remote alarm or centralized alarm system.* We shall however, pend considering this point, till after a closer look at the perimeter security needs of very high security set-ups, like high security prisons.

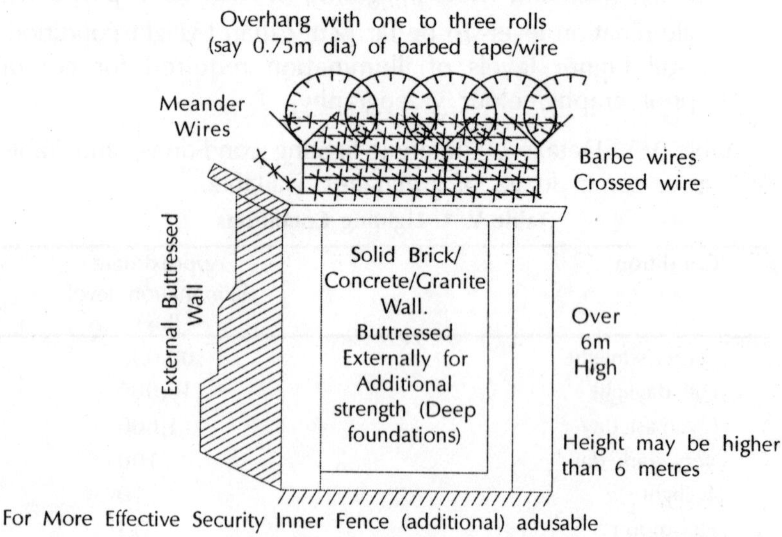

High Security Perimeter Wall

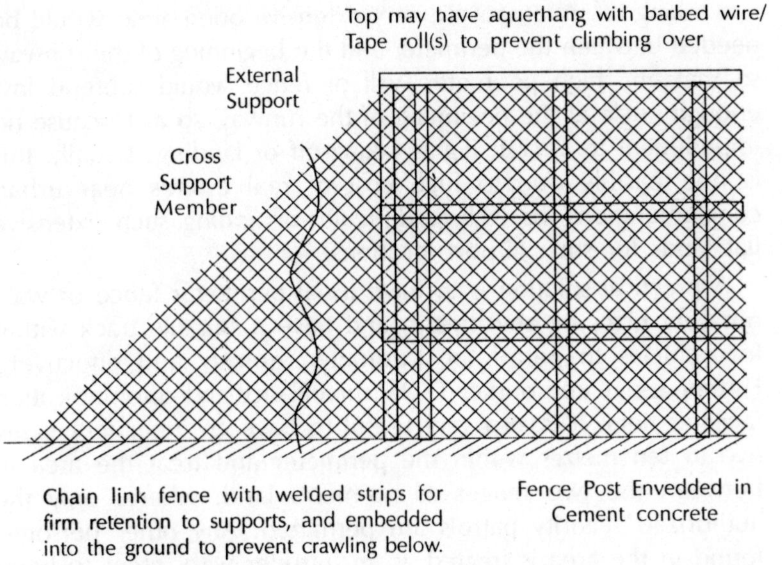

High Security Chain-Link Fence

Fig. 5. 5. Is indicative of high security environment barrier.

Note: 1. Corrider between inner fence/wall and actual perimeter treated as protected/banned area for any traffic except by security personnel

2. Use of suitable detection/surveillance and Alarm systems almost mandatory.
3. Double gates/Doors intandem in a Pound arrangement a must for effective access/exit control.
4. Clear open areas outside the perimeter enables better surveillance/security and minimizes possibility of external intrusions/ assistance to exfiltrators.

Consider an airport perimeter security requirements. An airport extends over vast areas, has expensive installations, and needs strict access control to ensure that only legitimate passengers and authorized persons have access. The perimeter protection has to be excellent to prevent intrusions, damage to installations or hijack situations. However, you cannot afford to have high fences or perimeter walls, as they will cause obstruction to planes landing and taking off. Alternatively, very extensive open areas would be needed between the perimeter and the beginning of the runway, so that any high perimeter wall or fence would subtend low enough angle at the beginning of the runway, so as to cause no impediment to aircraft flights taking-off or landing. Usually, this is not feasible due to high cost of real estates near urban conglomerations, as well as difficulty of finding such extensive flat lands for such airport locations.

A practical solution is to have usual perimeter fence or wall, not very high, by any means, and have a suitable track within for vehicles to patrol the perimeter, quickly and effectively. Further, use of appropriate CCTV surveillance and communication facilities help. It is also very useful to have an inner fence, say five to ten metres within the perimeter and treat the area in between the two fences as no-man's land, where, only the authorized security patrols are permitted. Any other person(s) found in the area is treated as an intruder with intent to harm the installation, and can be quickly apprehended and interrogated etc. Technical security facilities are of immense assistance in such installations to enable a small security force to take care of such extensive facilities. With high mobility of the security patrols, when constant CCTV surveillance/IDS are used, along with an effective radio communication between the security personnel, an inner fence can usually be dispensed with. This is particularly so, when the intruder has to cover a huge area to approach any installation, in order for him to attempt to cause any damage to it.

A set-up, such as a prison, high security on the other hand, is altogether a different kettle of fish. Such set-ups are close to or within urban conglomerations. The installation covers a limited area. It is vital to protect the same from break-ins as well as, breakouts. Hence, usually you need thick strong and very high perimeter walls, which are not easily penetrated, nor tunnelled under. Any attempt, to penetrate or dig under have to be quickly detected and located. Since scaling over the walls is the most popular method, both for break-ins and breakouts, the perimeter walls are made seven to ten metres high, and topped with barbed wire/barbed tape fencing/broken glass etc. It may also be advisable to have on the top, barbed wire/barbed tape rolls, of one to three rolls, for improved security against climbing over.

This is also the type of situation where you need watch towers. The towers must be manned, have technical facilities like searchlights, observation devices, communication facilities and so on; to keep a constant watch over the perimeter and the surrounding and within perimeter areas for unusual activities, threatening movements, intrusions, possible breakouts/break-ins etc. Such watch-towers themselves must be protected from possible assaults and attacks.

This type of security environment definitely calls for the inner fence to delineate a 'dead-zone' or 'no-man's land', between the perimeter and the inner fence or marking. The area in-between is considered as a sterile zone. Persons found entering the zone are to be treated as hostile or intruders, to be apprehended, except for legitimate authorized persons/security patrols. This greatly reduces chances of break-ins/break-outs, by land, (but not from air).

For very high security locations, one may even resort to use of electrified fences, with suitable warning notices displayed prominently and at frequent intervals along the fence, cautioning all personnel approaching the fence of the danger.

Apart from illuminating the perimeter areas adequately, it is usual to install suitable flood-lights and searchlights at appropriate locations, for necessary intense illumination of specific areas of greater security hazard, and for heightening observation/security actions when security breaches occur or are expected. These must have separate back-ups and standby power sources, for failure free operation.

The above are basic deterrents and need to be supplemented by suitable detection and alarm systems, at a minimum. Such a requirement equally applies to the access/exit controls and traffic control. The incoming and outgoing personnel/vehicles and materials must be adequately checked and controlled; also the routes to be followed, locations for loading and unloading as well as parking. Such activities must be monitored and kept under observation at all times. Impeccable record keeping of the activities and their later scrutiny and analysis is a must.

You must not forget that perimeters may have breaches that are natural or manmade due to trenches, ravines, lakes, rivers/streams, forests, hills and storm-water drains, water/sewage pipes and ducts and so on. Perhaps part of the perimeter has shifting soil or sand dunes. In such cases, it may not be feasible to have good perimeter fence or wall, and alternative deterrent/protective arrangements will need to be made. Breaches due to trenches/ducts/pipes/streams, etc. must be protected with suitable gratings at the perimeter penetration points, to prevent ingress and egress of materials and personnel, where permanent perimeter fence or wall cannot be erected due to terrain problems, suitable barbed tape/barbed wire etc. Rolls must be deployed as barriers. Dog patrols would help. Use of intrusion detection/alarm systems should be considered. Strewing such boundary areas with broken glass, nails, rusty empty cans, planting thorny bushes helps in delaying intrusions and give adequate lead time for security patrols to reach the scene in time to tackle any security problem. In extreme cases like protection of strategic locations, one may even have to resort to use of anti-personnel mines strategically buried in such otherwise unsecured areas, *(that is, if legal cover for such actions can be obtained).*

Access Control

All the above preventive, deterrent and protective arrangements at the perimeter are set at naught easily, where there is no proper access and exit control at the entry/exit gates/locations. The reason is that, an intruder can easily get in/get out in such cases, without being challenged by anyone. He could also gain access with subterfuge. Very strict and exacting access/exit control is, therefore, an unavoidable and inescapable feature of good perimeter security system.

Having a strong security presence and heavy gates is not the answer. Good access control involves proper and scrupulous check and control of all entries and exits of personnel, materials and vehicles. This should ensure that only authorized entries and exits take place (and to/at/from the specified locations only). All unauthorized accesses and exits must be denied/noted and acted upon promptly and effectively. It also involves maintaining proper movement control to ensure that even authorized persons/ materials and vehicles follow specific routes and adhere to the locations and times they are authorized for. The methodology must ensure maintenance of suitable records of individuals, materials transactions, vehicles, locations, times and other details, including who authorized the entry/exit/the location and when. This enables later scrutiny and analysis for any breaches of security, their causes etc., and for improving the security further. Hence, a suitable gate-pass system, IDS card system, personnel/ vehicle/baggage search systems, automated access control, attendance time record system, communication between the access points and security/concerned authorities etc., all form a part of good access control systems.

Manual access control systems must be manned, and automated access control systems supervised, by properly selected and trained security personnel. They should be able to sense when trouble is brewing, quick to sniff-out and recognize, intruders as well as unnatural behaviour patterns, indicative of impending security breaches and capable of taking right actions and at the right time. Though security personnel have very responsible position, as may be seen from the above, unfortunately, generally, not enough recognition or respect is attached to such positions. He is the first and vital security barrier against material loss due to unauthorized movements of materials; check against smuggling in of dangerous substances into the premises; positive bulwark against entry of external agents, saboteurs, arsonists etc. Hence, he requires constant training and encouragement, (a place in the sun?).

Access Time

It is obvious, that, authorized personnel must be able to get to their work-spot without losing much time, soon after their arrival at the entry gate. Any delay at the gate should be within a few seconds, at most. Hence, the access control methods used must ensure that, the delay in permitting access to authorized persons is, at most, a few seconds only, (on their reaching the entry point(s)). The access control systems used must be therefore, fast, reliable, effective and also acceptable, to the concerned employees, particularly in regard to any person/vehicle/baggage search procedures.

A whole host of technical security systems are available for intrusion detection and alarm and for access control. Some consideration is given to this aspect towards the end of this chapter.

Area Protection

Having provided adequate perimeter protection, you will come to the second part of the outer defences viz., securing the intervening area between the perimeter and the VAs, VPs and VOPs. Such intervening areas are kept free of obstructions and tall vegetation etc., lest they provide cover to intruders, who have somehow managed to gain entry through the perimeter, and try to sneak through to their target locations (VAs, VPs, VOPs).("*there is a chink in every armour*"). Such areas need to be very well lit, day or night, to enable easy and quick detection of all movements and any intrusions. Also provide limited access routes only, even for authorized personnel, materials and vechicle movements within the areas, to the work-spots, etc., and the entry/exit locations. Persons found loitering /entering the intervening areas, outside of the specified access routes are automatically suspect, and are to be treated in the first instance, as unauthorized persons or intruders. Proper traffic control within the facility is of great importance. Security staff must ensure proper traffic flow, including movement of vehicles to clearly designated parking places. Preferably, there should be separate vehicle parking places for visitors' vehicles where they are permitted within the complex. The vehicle parks and movements must be closely monitored, at all times, for possible security breaches/hazards. Covering the areas with lush grass lawns, flower beds and nice looking plants, small in height (and thus not offering any cover for persons to hide behind), not only beautifies the place but also offers security by keeping persons off limits. Well designed signs, such as 'please keep off the grass', etc. prominently displayed at suitable intervals, will reinforce the message, where needed.

Playgrounds and gymnasiums etc., could also be organized, but not too close to *VAs, VPs, or VOPs.* This helps the employees to relax after their hard day's work and help in improving the *esprit-de-corps,* which indirectly helps in security mindedness, with the sense of belonging that can be so generated.

Protection of VAs, VPs, and VOPs

Perimeter protection is most often linear, along the perimeter; though the fence itself is two-dimensional. Sometimes, two dimensional intrusion detection systems are deployed; maybe a three-dimensional ones in some rare cases. Area protection systems on the other hand are essentially two-dimensional, but will have to be fully three-dimensional or volumetric where attacks from the air/ underground/ underwater are expected. However, for the inner defences, that is, the defences of the *VAs, VPs, and VOPs,* full three-dimensional security coverage has to be planned for, even though the implementation could involve: point coverage; linear coverage and/or volumetric coverage devices and systems. Thus, though it is often referred to as spot security, the security arrangements must form a three dimensional cocoon around the location, with the spot or location in the heart of the arrangements. Thus, it must take into consideration all possible routes to the vital/vulnerable location, from the perimeter/ intervening areas, from a 3-d point of view.

VAs may cover some extended areas, and thus, you apply principles of perimeter and area protection. But *VPs* and *VOPs* are, generally, within a walled enclosure. Their protection systems, hence, start with the walls, windows, doors, ceiling, floors sky-lights roofs, basements, etc., including considerations of ducts, pipes, cable-trenches, under-ground features, trap-doors and so on. For currency, documents, jewellery etc. safes, almirahs and vaults meant for them become *VPs.* On the other hand, in major operations like oil and gas, extensive and expensive structures such as oil-platforms are *VPs*. Similarly, a transport container for nuclear or hazardous chemical is a *VP*. Hence a *VP* can be static or mobile or movable. And, physical security considerations require asking a series of questions relating to each and every aspect of the surrounding areas, the locations, and enclosures/buildings themselves, as well as possible routes, (whether to the locations or the movement parameters for mobile *VPs*). The questions are aimed to elicit what constitutes security hazards (thus threats) and how, as well as the risks that they entail. Only then you can evolve appropriate measures to cost-effectively counter those threats that have serious risks attached to it.

A tree near the building, a trap-door in the roof, air conditioning duct passing over the *VP*, a cable trench or underground drain near safe/vault windows close to the ground etc. are all security hazards. An access door, for example, is definitely a security hazard. Questions that need to be asked are: Is the latch a security problem? Is the lock a security problem? Is the doorjamb a security problem? Can the door be kicked in or a battering ram used to break it open? Can a crowbar be used to pry open the door leaves? Can the safe or vault door be cut open with oxy-acetylene flame, or by a thermic-lance? Or can simple explosives blow it open? And so on. The methods of possible attacks and the risks involved due to the same determine the counters to be employed. How valuable the VP, VOP, how damaging a particular attack can be, the probability of such attacks etc., have to be taken into account for arriving at a cost-effective local protection arrangement.

For example, in the case of safety vaults, the doorjambs are of solid tempered steel and are set in well made concrete walls. The door hinges are well hidden in the jambs and the door bolts securing the door in the jamb are properly located, are of ample size and strength, well matched, as well as, set in deep recesses in the jambs (thus hidden deep inside to deny access for any leverage etc.). The door itself is of tempered steel resistant to attacks by chisels, hammers, battering rams, oxy-acetylene flames etc. It has to be insect-proof, vermin-proof, rodent proof, fireproof, proof against flooding/earthquake, building collapse, etc. The doorjambs themselves must be strongly and effectively anchored to the walls and at a number of strategic locations to offer adequate security. Recessing of the jambs into the wall offer security against exposure of the anchor bolts, etc. There should be adequate recess in the doorjambs for the door to snugly fit in without the risk of intruder trying to insert tools/ jimmy to unlock the mortise/rim locks. Similar considerations apply to the design and construction of windows and shutters.

Similar requirements also hold good for a safe, except that a safe has no concrete wall requirement, apart from need for its mounting on a floor or in a wall. It is constructed of tempered steel. Ofcourse, safes are required to be burglar resistant; contents should be safe from burning, charring, or any damage due to fire, flood/inundation, building collapse, falling down of the safe on to a concrete floor from a height, (due to attack by vandals, earthquake etc.). The protection offered to the contents, from fire, water, heat etc., may be for a few hours. Generally, safes are not designed to withstand attacks with explosives, thermic-lance etc.

Almirahs, on the other hand, may not even withstand attacks with mere crowbars, nor dropping on its corner on a concrete floor. They could be designed, however, to give protection against heat and fire, apart from being insect/vermin proof.

Safes must be installed preferably at ground floor or first floor, unless they are small ones with not much of weight. Some structural strengthening may be required; an architect or structural engineer should be consulted when safes are to be installed at other than ground floor (or basement, if flooding is not a problem). Usually, safes are located at a strong corner of a room, next to a load-bearing structure, and not in the middle of a room where the floor is weakest. When located at ground floor, the safe must be installed at a suitable height to avoid damage due to any flooding. Naturally, location of a safe must be away from other activities, so that the opening and closing of the safe is witnessed only by those directly involved, and others have no opportunity to observe the combinations. No other material should be stored near the location to eliminate fire hazards and unnecessary traffic, possibility of chemical hazards and other similar security risks. Needless to add, that, safes must be procured only from reputed manufacturers; preferably, installation may be by others, (for location to remain unknown to manufacturers personnel).

Vaults should be at ground floor or basement, ensuring that there is no possibility of flooding, fire hazard, corrosion due to chemicals/gases; nor invasions by rodents, termites vermin etc. The locations should not have any underground sewers, water pipes, cable trenches, riverbeds, etc., which could be used for unobserved access to the vault, by criminals, dacoits etc., for their nefarious activities.

If a safe/vault combination is lost, due to any reason, and it cannot be opened, conveniently by a responsible company personnel, it is advisable to call in the manufacturer of the safe/ vault and have it opened under proper supervision.

Locks and Key-Control

In all above cases, where the design of the door, bolt/latches and hinges, their location etc., are proper, the *locks* weakest security link happens to be used to secure the door. The best of locks could be cut through with a hacksaw, levered open with a crowbar or hammered to give way, may be in minutes only. Tumbler locks are vulnerable to picking with a piece of wire or hairpin. Properly designed lever locks are more secure, when it has machine cut levers and keys, tempered recessed hoops, (not hinged), which are not easily amenable for levering, or cutting with hacksaw (hoop must be just large enough to fit the bolt comfortably). Further, the lock should have over seven to eight levers. The body design should be hammer resistant, etc. Night latches must have dead-bolt arrangement. The bolt must mesh in strongly, and to adequate depth into the doorjamb. It should be resistant to sawing (with hacksaw etc.). Any safety-chain arrangement must be strongly anchored, the door-gap when the door is opened with the chain-on must be small enough, and the chain-links strong enough to prevent insertion of any cutting tool and snapping of the chain.

In technology driven societies, use of keyless-locks has grown in a big way, particularly in hotels, condominiums, and so on. The locking arrangements are with or without central computer control. Conventional physical key types of locks are being dispensed with, and digital or keycard (various types) type locks are being extensively utilized. These type of locks are also pickproof, as there are no keyholes or conventional lock-bolt arrangements, which could be attacked.

However, the importance of key-control holds well for all type of locks; whether conventional, magnetic, digital, keyless lock etc. The keys have to be kept safe; whether physical keys, combinations, card keys and so on. Keys can be duplicated, lost and mis-used before the lock is changed. Unsecured combinations may be stolen, or made note of, to unauthorizedly open doors /safes etc. A combination lock should preferably be a four-disc, or better type. Digital locks must have at least a six-digit combination, or even larger, for good security (but not so large that one cannot easily remember the combination, as, this leads to possibility of the combinations being written down, as *aide-memoire*, which defeats the essential security requirement of confidentiality).

Some common aspects of good key control are to be noted. Issue keys to authorized persons only-and directly, [not through others]. Record all the transactions. Educate all concerned in regard to the importance of key security as well as, in the need for immediate change of locks, when any compromise occurs in regard to either the key or a lock. Do not keep the lock floating around either; it must be kept in locked condition, in its proper location. Keep monitoring against any tampering. Duplicate keys must be stored securely with a responsible officer, preferably one who is also likely to be available on location, in case of an emergency. Any loss/compromise of key/combination must be promptly reported to concerned officer/security. The concerned lock/combination should be changed forthwith, with minimum possible delay. The loss of key/lock, as well as changes effected, should also be recorded with details of occurrence, persons involved, the circumstances, etc., for necessary corrective system to be implemented as a consequence. In all cases, signatures of the persons concerned, along with name/designation etc., should also be affixed to the records, for authenticity and any later checks/audits.

Access control systems utilizing revolving doors, turnstiles must ensure that '*tail-gating*' is prevented. After each access, they should remain locked in the shut position. The ratchet arrangements enabling the door/turnstile to rotate in a single direction must be strong and hidden from attacks. Preferably, the design of the facility must enable easy future modifications for full automation, and use of automatic access control systems.

Then you have the air-lock type of entrances, where two doors are used in tandem, only one of which remains open at a time. In such cases, it is imperative to provide either a separate emergency exit for quick evacuation of personnel working there (in case of fire, bomb-threat etc.), or it should be feasible to keep both the doors open simultaneously, in case of an emergency.

Excepting for doors, all openings in the building such as ducts, exhausts, trenches, drains, water/sewage pipes etc. (even underground ones), must have strong wire meshing or gratings to act as physical barriers against entrance or exit of persons/ materials. The meshing used must be close enough, in case of high security environments; to prevent passing through of classified materials, currency, expensive items like diamonds, gold etc., as relevant to the location. Safety arrangements such as fire escapes, emergency exits, effluent controls etc., must be designed taking into account the physical security requirements and vice-versa. For example, gratings used for windows and other openings at the higher floors of tall buildings must not be fully/permanently fixed. On the other hand, such protective gratings must have quick release latch arrangements, and from the inside. Such an arrangement enables occupants to make a quick and safe exit through such openings in case of a fire; or for fire-fighting personnel to easily rescue persons trapped by fire in such floors, through the openings. Otherwise life-threatening delays could occur, as one will have to cut through permanently fixed gratings. Burglars cannot enter the rooms as the grating is firmly fixed, and can only be released from the inside.

Visitors

Sound security principle demands that visitors are at all times properly identified and escorted. Letting visitors wander around the premises, unaccompanied, is the surest way of inviting security problems, and unnecessarily creates hazards to all organizational assets. It invites thefts, sabotage, subversion, arson and so on.

The Stay-Behind

Good security requires, that after duty hours, only those that are specifically so authorized will remain behind and all others leave the premises as per schedule. Also, those that are permitted to stay behind, to work after hours, remain at the specified locations only. The work should also be supervised adequately. A single individual should never be allowed to stay behind all by himself/herself. It is far easier for a stay-behind to do damage to the organization or introduce security problems, where they never existed! Suitable records should be maintained regarding details of such late working.

Technology and Physical Security

At this stage it will be useful to have a quick round-up of some of the types and varieties of technical aids that are available to enhance physical security measures; that is, apart from fences, lighting and so on.

Perimeter Security and Intrusion Detection Systems (IDS)

Outside the perimeter, the region is normally beyond your jurisdiction—it may be public land, private land, and a natural geographic feature such as a creak, a river, a lake, mountain or a combination. This should not deter you from attempting some security measures in the region-like road humps/blocks to control vehicular traffic to your perimeter; make your perimeter difficult to approach/access from the outside, by whatever means that are feasible, with the assistance of concerned authorities. Perhaps green the area, create an artificial lake, and set up a golf course or what you have in mind. You could also install suitable technical devices such as the CCTV, radars, proximity detectors, microwave beams, or seek assistance of trained animals like dogs, geese and so on. Strewing the region with garbage, broken glass, nails or even dangerous devices like fire-crackers or explosives /mines etc. are immoral and quite often illegal. However, with permission of concerned authorities, you could install suitable lighting, mobile or static quick reaction vehicle barriers such as 'tyre-bursters', hydraulically actuated bollards/vehicle stops etc., to deny access to the entry points to suspect vehicles, vehicle-bombs and so on.

Functions of aids

* To detect an impending or actual intrusion.
* To process detected signals to minimize false alarms.
* To alert security (police, security guards/agency).
* Indicate location(s) of intrusions.
* Shorten intervention time for security to reach the spots.
* Ensure suitable segmentation of perimeter to achieve above.
* To detect movements in the 'dead' or 'sterile' zone.

Additionally, the system may cater for provision of suitable records, integrate with fire alarm/fire-fighting system, access control system and so on.

The IDS etc., cannot differentiate, as yet, between security/ authorized personnel, and an intruder/hostile individual. Maybe, time is not far when this would also be feasible!

Segmentation of the perimeter into suitable number of alarm sectors (say segment lengths of 50 to 150 meters), is essential to reduce intervention time, that is, the time needed for the security to rush to the alarmed sector and arrive there to scare away or apprehend intruders. If the intervention time is not small enough, the intruders may be able to initiate or carry out their nefarious schemes and vanish before the security can catch them. Alternatively, you would need a large security force, suitably located around the perimeter, on stand-by. You should also note, that, vehicle movements require longer and maybe different alarm sectors, and much shorter intervention times!

Detection methods used in as IDS may be based on sensing of changes in a single or multiple, (dual or multiple technology), physical, chemical or other phenomena. Some examples of phenomena sensed are given below:

- *Change In:*
  - Mass, pressure, force, strain
  - Temperature, vibration, resistance
  - Acoustic level (infrasound, sonic, ultrasound)
- *Beam Interruption:*
  - Visible light, active infra red (air), laser
  - Microwave
  - Ultrasonic
- *Motion Detection:*
  - Doppler (ultrasonic, microwave, sonic)
  - Ambient light variation
  - Passive Infra-Red (PIR)
- *Proximity:*
  - Capacitance
  - Inductance
  - Electromagnetic
- *Imaging:*
  - Optical
  - Infrared
  - Thermal
  - Remote-Sensing.

Not all the methods of sensing indicated above are suitable for IDS for perimeter security;, as perimeter systems usually have to be linear or two-dimensional types, (perimeter itself being linear). However, where a watch is to be maintained over the region beyond the perimeter, three-dimensional systems like radar and observation devices are needed. Also, *since spurious alarms cannot be totally eliminated in IDS, by using only single sensor type of detection. Therefore, dual-technology or multiple sensors type detection systems are frequently resorted to.*

There are, basically, three types of detectors, viz., linear type, 2-d or area (sensing) type and 3-d or volumetric (sensing) type.

Examples of Linear Type of Detectors:

- *Electro-Mechanical*
    - Taut-Wire
    - Break-Wire
    - Vibration
    - Geophone
- *Optical*
    - Photoelectric
    - AIR, (Active Infra-Red)
    - Laser
- *Electret Cable*

Examples of Area Sensing Detectors:

* Seismic
* Buried Microphone Cable /Electret
* Buried Magnetic Loop
* Buried Hydrostatic (Compression) Hose.

Examples of Volumetric Sensing Detectors

* Proximity
* Radar
* Microwave Beam
* Buried leaky RF cable
* CCTV

Please *note that trained dogs and geese etc, are also volumetric type of detectors,* though animated ones.

There are three types of IDS:

* Observation systems
* Passive alarm systems and
* Active alarm systems

Observation systems

* Enable visual/closer observation of perimeter and surrounding areas for suspicious movements, and from convenient locations.

  Examples:

  - Binoculars (and focus free type), telescopes, binocular telescopes, night vision devices, CCTV, tethered balloon system, RPV platforms.

* When light level is low or inadequate, either air or low light level TV (LLL TV) or thermal imager can be used.
* Observation devices help in distinguishing between false alarms and real Intrusions.
* Note that trained dogs/geese, etc., give advance warning, but usually need active follow-up observations, with CCTV, security personnel, etc.

Passive Alarm Systems

* These sense a change in the local environment and generate a distinguishable output signal, which is treated as alarm condition.
* Processing helps to discriminate against background noise and spurious signals.

  Examples

  - Microphones
  - Vibration detectors
  - Geophones/Seismic detectors
  - PIR Detectors
  - Piezo-Electric Detectors

Characteristics

* Easy to install
* Good value for money
* Noisy (poor signal to noise ratio)
* Rugged
* Proper installation and processing required to reduce false alarms, particularly in noisy environments.

Active Alarm Systems

* One device (called transmitter) *sends out a signal*; another device (called receiver) gathers part of the signal energy and *gives an output.*
* A processor in the receiver makes a decision to deliver alarm signal based on the level or type of received signal (frequency, time, phase, direction, code, etc.)
* Result is high signal to noise ratio.
* Hence, better discrimination (less false alarms).
* Flexibility in distance coverage, (with tandem operation).

Examples

- Switches (various types).
- Laser fence.
- Air beam system.
- Microwave beam system.
- Leaky RF cable system.
- Proximity effects system.

Other Characteristics

* Good detection sensitivity.
* Ease of signal processing.
* Generally easy to maintain.
* More complex.
* More expensive.

Technology and Spot or Local Security (Inner Defences)

You have greater freedom in the choice of technique to be used, as the environment is usually controlled, and hence does not have the problems of the outdoor-such as wageries of weather, movement of animals, movement of vehicles and personnel, relevant to the organization/public and so on. Also, within the building the environment is confined. This means need far less energy is required and smaller distances to be covered etc. Volumetric devices like ultrasonic or microwave doppler systems, CCTV, PIR, (*passive infra-red*), etc., have a great role to play, apart from linear systems like AIR, (*active infra-red*), beam type devices, various types of switches etc.

Alarm system types

Alarm systems can be organized into one of three types or a combination of the same:

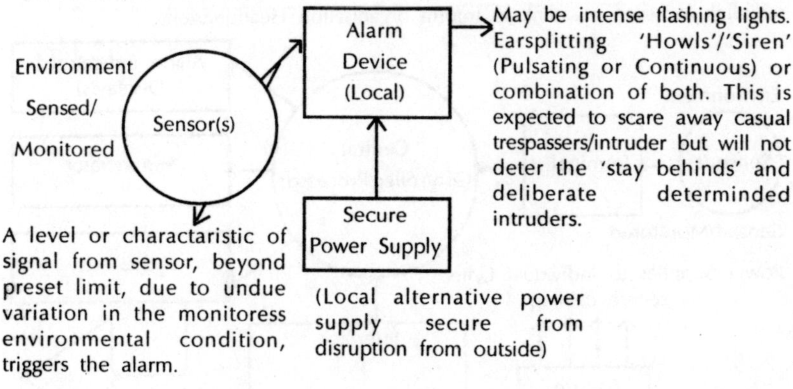

Note: No communication link as such may be needed as sensor, power supply and the alarm may all be in a single unit/enclosure!

Fig 5.6 Block diagram of a Local Alarm System

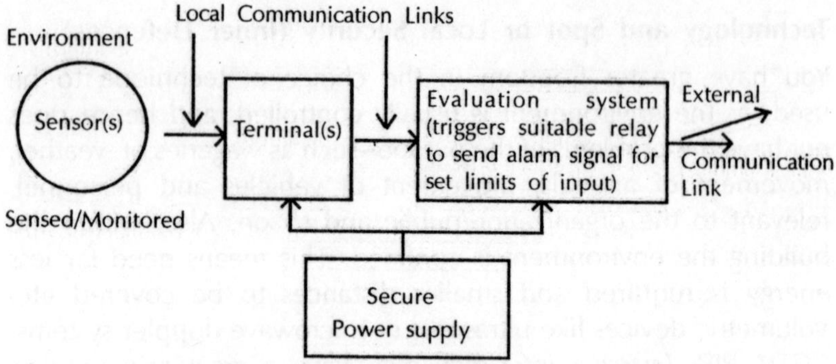

Fig 5.7 Block Diagram of A Remote Alarm System

Note: Terminal(s) collects signals from the sensors and routes them in a suitable (modified) form to the evaluation system (some preprocessing of signals may be done).

Evaluation is to reduce/remove false alarms (as financial implications/penalty involved if false alarms - like due to unnecessary response by local police/security agency etc.)

Communication link(s) for signalling alarm condition signal to remote location_(like local police/security agency)- may be the PSTN/ a leased line/ radiolink (or even a satlink to inform organisation Headquarters)

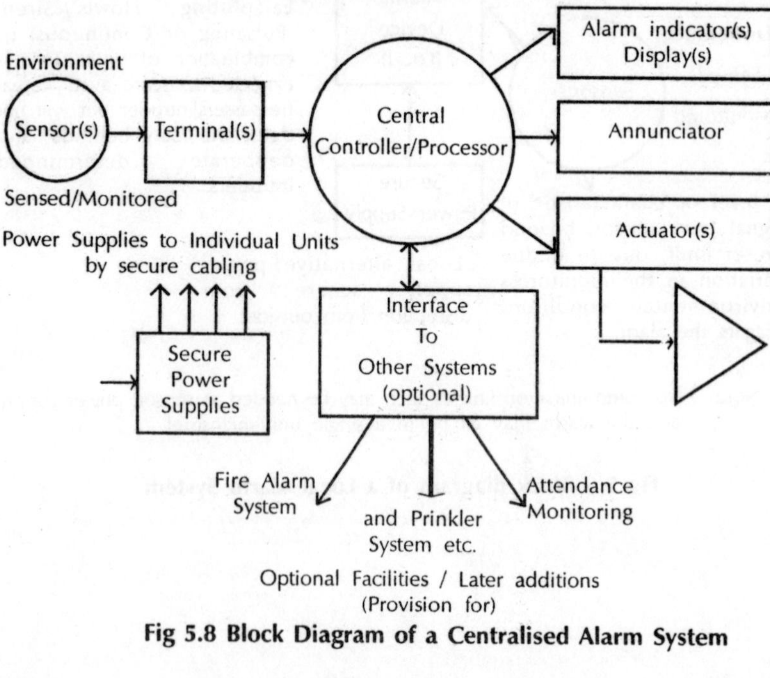

Fig 5.8 Block Diagram of a Centralised Alarm System

Note: Arrows denote communication links

A local security force must be available in-situ to assess alarm situations and handle emergencies directly; and or seek external help (police, fire services) as may ne needed.

Brief description of the types is also given along with the figures.

Care in the use of IDS

Great care is needed in the deployment of technical security systems, such as the *IDS*. Some of the aspects involved are:

* *Everyone to know that some IDS has been installed (*acts as deterrence*).*
* *Only those directly concerned to know what is installed-where and how (*to prevent sabotaging or interference with the system*).*
* *Ensure that the system detects the stay-behind. (*easily forgotten aspect*).*
* *It is imperative that, the wiring and installation are, as far as possible, concealed/camouflaged, (*and the details are treated as classified-on the need to know basis only, to minimize possibility of interference with the system*).*
* *All documentation, wiring diagrams etc. to be kept classified and secure. Details not to be included in open building plans.*
* *Periodic checks by unscheduled attempts at intrusion and analyze results, (*to confirm continued effective functioning of the system*).*
* *Every case of false alarms to be thoroughly investigated (*to bring out drawbacks/lacunae in the system, in order to effect necessary improvements*).*
* *Use of technology without proper training can be disastrous.*
* *Good maintenance cannot be overemphasized.*

Access Control System (ACS)

ACS is the most widely used and vital method of ensuring denial of access to unauthorized persons and control of traffic, (of personnel, materials and vehicles). Objectives of an ACS can be specified as:

* permit easy access to authorized persons-
  - to specified locations only, and
  - at/for specified times
* deny/ prevent access to all others-
  - to unauthorized locations/ facilities
  - at all times.

There can be some bonus facilities available as options, such as:

* provide an alarm at unauthorized attempts at access.
* provide monitoring and recording facilities.
* provide personnel attendance record-locations/times of accesses and exits.
* enable integration of safety (fire and other) systems.
* permit automation of entries and exits.
* provide additional facilities of administrative/ security interest (say, report generation).

Essential Features of ACS are:

1. The challenge: persons attempting access have to give a *password,* show/or use a token (an *ID-card,* a *ticket,* a *key,* an *artifact* and so on), or carries out a specific (series of) operation, such as a key-board operation.
2. The evaluation: compares the *input data/ token/operation* with the authorized version in the system, for a proper match, and
3. The response: *access* is permitted or denied depending on whether there is a *match* or *mismatch.*

Optional features that could be made available are:

* Record of previous attempts at access/exit-persons (ID), locations, times, result of such attempts.
* Suitable alarm on a failed attempt.
* Automation and integration facilities with other systems.

Errors in ACS:

Two types of errors are possible as indicated below:

* *Type I error:* denial or rejection of attempts to gain access by authorized *persons* and
* *Type II error:* permitting access to unauthorized *attempts.*

You must note that, there is catch-22 type of situation. *Attempts to reduce* Type I error, by say broadening acceptance criteria, will have adverse fallout, of *increasing* Type II errors! Also, *trying to reduce* Type II error, say, by making more stringent the ID-parameters, will as a consequence, *increase* Type I errors! Therefore, you have to be very careful in choosing your parameters. *Optimum choice would be, the best compromise meeting your specific security scenario.* No wonder, in access control, baggage inspection systems, etc. a thorough manual check on a random basis of about 3 percent of the throughput is recommended practice.

Access control systems may employ one of three modes, or a combination, for controlling access, they are: authorization, identification and verification.

1. *Authorization* is based on what you know or carry; it is non-personalized, that is, it is non-discriminatory. *Anyone can use and get entry, if they can get hold of it.*

examples*:* password, badge, token, key, uniform, escort, etc.

2. *Identification* is based on a personalized item that you carry-thus, it is discriminatory. *Only the authorized person can gain entry, as he is identified.*

examples*:* photo-ID-card, personalized data coded token.

3. *Verification* is based on what you are therefore, *highly* discriminatory.

Examples: manual ID check-up with photo-ID card; automated access-control with biometric type id-systems, and so on.

The actual provision of access could be done in one of three ways. Manual (here, the security (person), checks the ID and lets person in) semi-automatic (in this case, say the ID is automatically checked by, perhaps, a card-reader; but release of the door for entry, is done manually, (remotely by security), Or, fully automated (say swiping the ID-card, or biometrics check, automatically checks the id of the person, and releases the door /turnstile for entry of the person).

ACS Applications can be for:

* Entrance/exit doors control.
* Half-height turnstile control.
* Full-height turnstile control.
* Vehicle barrier/gate control.

ACS Configurations could be:

* Single-point/stand-alone system.
* Multi-point on-line system, or
* Integrated or distributed system (multipoint, multisite, networked).

There are several types of ID-card technologies in use, viz.:

* Bar-code.
* Magnetic stripe.
* Barium-ferrite.
* Wiegand-effect.
* Proximity-passive type and
* Proximity-active type.

A recent entry, making considerable inroads, is the laser-card technology.

Biometric access control systems differ from card technologies, in that, the former verifies not a carried token, but a *unique characteristic*-physiological or behavioural-such as, fingerprint, (FP), hand geometry, retinal pattern, voiceprint or signature, or a combination. Usage of such systems is fast increasing, particularly in high-security systems. They are also becoming more and more competitive and reliable. Next generation systems could be inexpensive enough for wide commercial (even domestic) mass market. Already, there are applications of hand-geometry systems in the USA in air-travel, colleges, athletic clubs and even for apartment complexes.

What are the criteria for selection of automated ACS? Major criteria to be kept in mind are:

* Population of employees/ visitors/ tradesmen etc., to be catered for.
* Acceptable throughput-rate at the main-gate (s).
* Extent of automation desired.
* Security requirements such as:
    - Levels, locations, time zones, zoning.
    - Exit control, materials/ vehicle traffic control.
    - Tail-gating/ hold-up aspects.
    - Documentation.
* Report generation.
* Emergency/ contingency handling.
* Integration of other systems.
* Environmental factors.
* Possible vandalism.
* Stand-by/ back-up systems.
* Error performance.
* Life-time reliability and maintainability.
* Upgradability.
* Life -time cost-effectiveness, (card-readers, cards, terminals, computers, door-controllers, ancillaries, software cabling, installation, maintenance and so on).

Availability of Technical Systems

Perimeter IDS is available operating on a large variety of techniques such as: acoustic, seismic, geophone, vibration, proximity, electret,

RF leakage, hydrostatic and so on. Break-wire, air, laser, microwave fences etc. are also used. Observation devices such as binoculars, telescopes, night vision systems, thermal imager, CCTV, even radars are employed. Trained dog patrols and geese are also popular for intrusion detection/alarms. Simple convex mirrors located at strategic places and suitably angled helps surveillance by the security, to see around corners etc., and acts also as deterrent, say against shop lifting.

IDS for area security applications do not have as much variety in regard to technical facilities employed. Basically, 2-d or 3-d type of system is deployed, predominantly. Observation devices, search lights, CCTV, time lapse video, thermal imager, night vision devices (NVDS), hydrostatic hoses, RF leakage devices are some of the systems used. Raised wire netting may be used to prevent rodents and rabbits from gaining entry into the buildings. Matrix of geophones/pressure switches or crisscrossing IR or laser beams or acoustic detector arrays may also be deployed.

Spot or local security: physical security measures for vulnerable locations include employing proper access control and use of suitable IDS. The detection devices maybe PIR, AIR, glass-break detector, electro-mechanical devices [such as mat-switches, reed-switches, photo-electric devices, vibration devices, proximity devices, microwave and ultrasonic doppler devices or beam interruption types, acoustic sensors and so on. In addition you may have to go in for smoke and fire sensors, fire sprinkler systems, time-lapse photography/video-recording, plexi-glass/ bullet-proof barriers, time-locks, safes and vaults, anti-lift devices, and so on. Not a day passes without a new device being touted; but they are all based on the fundamental techniques of sensing and suitable processing of sensed signal for alarm conditions.

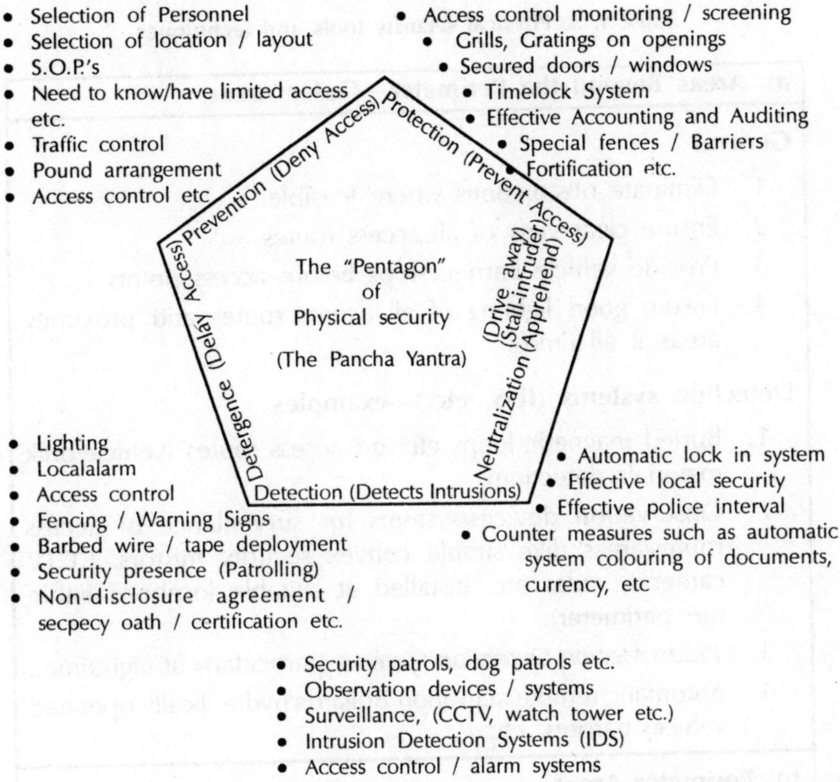

Fig. 5. 9. Is indicative of the "basic principles of physical security, (the Pancha Yantra?)".

Choice of right type of sensors and systems, and their proper installation and check-out/maintenance, cannot be overemphasized.

Table V. 3. Is indicative of the tools and techniques used in physical security.

Table V. 3. Physical security tools and techniques.

a). Areas Beyond the Perimeter—Outer Areas
General 1. Eliminate obstructions where feasible. 2. Ensure clear view of all access routes. 3. Provide vehicle barriers/stops before access points. 4. Ensure good lighting of all access routes and proximity areas-at all times. **Detection systems (IDS, etc.)—examples** 1. Buried magnetic loops etc. on access routes (vehicle/bulk materials detection). 2. Observation devices/systems for surveillance of access routes/areas (like simple convex security mirrors, CCTV cameras, radar etc. installed at suitable locations-within the perimeter). 3. *Video Motion Detection Systems (*particularly at nighttime). 4. Automatic/remote activation Bollards/hydraulically operated vehicle barriers, etc.
b). Perimeter Areas
General 1) Install a good perimeter fence, (see through type). 2) Suitably segment the perimeter (50 to 150 metre segment lengths depending on the location, the nature of the terrain, likely risks involved etc.), for effective intrusion detection/location of intrusions and for timely intervention by the security force. 3) *Ensure effective access/exit controls (*at all access and exit points). 4) Provide sterile zone/(no-man's land) where needed/possible.

5) Ensure effective lighting at all times, the perimeter areas (including the fencing and beyond), the sterile zones, as well as the access/exit points and the areas/routes.
6) Where necessary have suitable pill-boxes/security towers with searchlights, observation devices, communication facilities etc.
7) Ensure that the security Headquarter is located suitably for quick response by the security personnel, reaction force to be able to reach expeditiously the affected, segmented perimeter locations. Should also be suitable for efficient monitoring of security activities (ensure quick access routes from the security headquarters. to affected perimeter and other areas).
8) Clear all obstructions/structures around perimeter areas, which are hazardous to security as far as possible; and strengthen security wherever such obstruction has to remain.
9) Layout suitable patrols as needed/ (patrol paths, foot patrols, vehicle patrols, dog patrols, geese alarms etc.).
10) Provide suitable vehicle barriers/speed breakers, etc. where necessary, (maybe a low solid wall too as an inner fence). A good system is the pound arrangement, opening only one of the two gates/barriers at a time for entry/exit of vehicles/personnel, till proper security clearance of those impounded between the two gates/barriers). This also eliminates the problem of tailgating. Particularly useful for high security environments.
11) Insist on proper traffic control of personnel, vehicles and materials.
12) Provide suitable, secured vehicle parking, unloading/loading areas.

c). Detection Systems (examples)
1) Access control systems (ACS). 2) Traffic control systems. 3) Security time check systems. 4) Communication systems. 5) Surveillance observation systems. 6) Guard Protection Devices (nightstick, stun-gun, torch, silent alarm, sprays, screamer, walkie-talkie, etc.) 7) Intrusion Detection Systems, (IDS): • *Break-wire, taut-wire, trip-wire, etc., devices (*closed-loop current*).* • *Electret Cable System.* • *Proximity sensing device.* • *Vibration detector.* • *Buried geophone/pressure sensing devices.* • *Microphone strings.* • *Leaky RF Cable System.* • *Buried Pneumatic Hose System.* • *Cameras, CCTV, night vision devices.* • *Photoelectric, laser, infra-red (Active IR or AIR) devices.* • *Microwave Beam Systems.* • *Buried Magnetic Cable System, etc.*
d). Intervening areas (within the perimeter)
General 1) Ensure effective traffic control (including: parking, holding areas, loading/unloading ramps, materials, personnel etc.) 2) Keep the areas clear of obstructions/shrubs/rubbish/disposal stores and so on. 3) Ensure absence of possible hiding spots for would be intruders/get-aways/stay-behinds. 4) Have routine patrolling carried out at irregular intervals.

Detection Systems, etc.

1) Microwave doppler radar
2) CCTV surveillance
3) Video motion detection
4) Radar
5) Buried geophones etc.

e). Local or Spot Security

General

1) Ensure effective access/exit control (perhaps air lock doors too)
2) Windows and all openings to have adequate protective grills/gratings/explosion projectile proof glazing (plexiglas) etc. as required.
3) Protect/block any access/exit routes arising out of close by structures/natural features/plant growth etc. (and guard others).
4) Properly secure door structures, bolts/locking arrangements at entrance and exit points.
5) Ensure secure locks and keys control.
6) Use secure almirahs, safes and vaults for valuables, important documents etc.
7) Implement good accounting and auditing systems/practices.
8) Put into effect sound traffic control.
9) Have effective fire prevention/detection/protection/alarm/ fire-fighting procedures and systems in place.

Detection Systems etc. (examples)

1) Access Control Systems, (ACS)
2) Traffic Control Systems/procedures
3) Fire Safety Systems
4) Effective Attendance Control and Reporting System
5) Intrusion Detection Alarm Systems, (IDS)

- Wired Systems-break-wire, taut-wire, trip-wire etc.
- Ultrasonic Doppler Device.
- Acoustic Devices.
- Passive and Active Infra-Red Devices, (PIR/AIR).
- Vibration Devices.
- Pressure Sensing Devices.
- Video Motion Detection.
- Glass Break Detection.
- Proximity Sensing Devices.
- CCTV/Imaging Systems.
- Body Odour etc. detection devices, etc.

f). Locks

1) Locks can be with or without keyholes.
2) *They can be mechanical type, electronic type (*card-key, combination, time-lock etc.*).*
3) Then you have the biometrics combination type.

Note: Mechanical locks are usually inexpensive delaying devices and are hence the poor-man's security.

Keyed type of locks

1) Tumbler locks-disc tumbler type used in the old models of cars. Pin tumbler type with irregular shaped keys (ground on both sides), which provides better delay and a master key is possible.
2) Lever locks use a number of levers. The levers are positioned or designed for a set of specific mechanical displacement or movement which permit the latch or hoop of the lock to move laterally into suitable holes/grooves, (in the shackle or hasp) of the lock, to lock/unlock the lock (the keys have serrated cuts or grooves to match the corresponding lever displacement). A good lever lock should have seven or more non-repeating computer generated combination and machine cut levers/keys. Naturally, these are bulkier and more expensive.

3) Magnetic/electromagnetic locks do not have keyholes and make use of magnetic fields/electric current to unlock. Electromagnetic locks are very widely used in security applications.
4) *Card keys are used with locks that may or may not have keyholes or grooves. Such cards use a number of different techniques such as* the bar code, magnetic stripe, wiegend effect, proximity effect, smart card (with encapsulated computer chip) etc. The lock is basically electromagnetic type with an electronic combination code using one of the above mentioned techniques for release of the locking arrangement. Depending on the technique used, the card is swiped in a grove, or inserted into a slot, held close by or just carried in the pocket, and the proximity, as one approaches, does the required card reading. A card reader reads the code from the card and the release control is local or from a central computer, when the correct preset the card reader senses the encoded combination in the card. Master keying is possible. Alarm conditions can be generated for wrong combinations etc. predominantly used in access control systems; extensively in hotels, large organizations, ATM's etc. Cost varies with the type of system used.
5) Keyless locks are basically combination locks. The lock may be a mechanical type with set of numbers or disc combination settings, or electronic type. No physical key is required to be carried. They operate on codes/ combinations/time settings preset on the locks. The key is the combination digits/number/time (delay or) setting which only will release the lock. The security of the combination lock depends on the size of the mutually exclusive distinct combinations that are possible, apart from keeping the combination (key) secret (extensively used in attaché cases, suitcases, safes, vaults, high security areas and so on). The electronic combination locks could be interfaced with biometrics sensing systems for use in high security environments.

Damage Control and Reviews

"Accidents can happen in the best regulated environment". Therefore, it should not surprise you, that, security breaches can take place, even with the best physical security system implemented. Hence proper contingency plan is a must to maintain effective physical security, under all conditions. When a security breach comes to notice, the first action initiated should be to ensure prompt damage control. When a key to a lock is found missing, you do not get a duplicate key fabricated, but change the lock itself, and replace with a suitable new lock. You could start looking around for the missing key, investigate the circumstances of loss etc., later on/ simultaneously a record has to be made about the change, the circumstances relevant, the person(s) involved, the when, where and why of the changes and the authority for the change. Analogous appropriate actions are called for in regard to any security breach/lapse.

Simultaneously, an investigation is a must to ascertain the reasons for the lapse, identify any lacunae in the security system or procedures, and to fix responsibility on person(s) concerned, where relevant. Such an investigation should also result in concrete recommendations in regard to any changes that may be necessary in the physical security system and updating of the *S.O.Ps* Sometimes, even an updating of the contingency plans may become essential.

It is evident that availability of proper contingency plan, and frequent simulated exercises as a training measure (to enable effective handling of emergencies/security breaches when they do occur), *go hand-in-hand with good security operations.* They help implementation of correct damage control and recovery procedures. For example, in case of a computer system crash, or failure, ready availability of suitable backups and implementation of quick recovery procedures, could well save an organization from irreparable loss or even from positive ruin!

You are now in a better position to look at information security, as effective physical security is a pre-requisite for good information security.

Chapter 6

Basics of Information Security

"Hedges have eyes, and walls have cars"

—An old proverb

Before you can essay on securing information, you need to identify, or answer the question: What is the information that you need to secure? The answer to the question may be debatable. There can be opposing views. The general view is that the information itself, say that you possess some specific classified (secret) equipment, for example, should be treated as classified, and graded accordingly-secret, as top secret when the device itself is graded secret, top secret, and so on. There is the opposing view that, 'the mere knowledge of your possession of a classified equipment should not, repeat not, be treated as a secret; but information on the deployment and use of the equipment must be classified'! So, there you are, the choice is yours and yours only, depending on the situation and environment that you and your organization exist in, as there is merit in both these views! In this connection it is interesting to note that, in cipher system operations you are required to presume that the opposition possesses cipher equipment identical to the one you desire to use. It is only the "key", used by you to "encipher" and "decipher" your messages that should remain secret. Also, with the enormous amount of code-breaking activities going on in the world, not much can be expected to remain secret, for long (except secure systems using "one time pads").

Any statement would logically fall into one of three categories: True, false or may be (Fuzzy logic could push maybe into one of the two categories viz. True/false?). It is imprudent to consider two states only (binary logic, as in computers). Few years ago, an eminent person in a neighbouring country announced that they have the nuclear bomb and the means to deliver the same. Is the statement news? Misinformation? Disinformation? Plain-truth? Influencing? Or, what? The statement could be true, false or may-be (that is, they are very close to having/getting hold of the capability). And now we have North Korea openly announcing their "nuclear capability"-the statements could be facts or mere posturing to get leverage, political, economical or some other "goals", etc. An Intelligence analyst has his work cutout to arrive at the "correct" conclusion. He will need to take into account other relevant inputs he gathers from various sources, in regard to their nuclear activities, posturing, internal compulsions of the country, need for recognition of their 'eminence' in science and technology by other countries, and so on. (In, such cases, it is "Hard Intelligence", and "Proper Intelligence Assessments" that help to unravel the "truth" behind such assertions/situations).

Before you can think of ways and means of ensuring security of information, you will have to, first of all, grade/classify the information into levels. The levels should correspond to the importance/criticality of the information, the extent of damage that can result, if it falls into the hands of the opposition and the extent of efforts that maybe required to protect from/extract by the opposition. You then apply some basic methodologies for guarding the information from the unauthorized, at the same time *enable its legitimate flow*-inside and outside the organization.

Classification of Information

The system of actual classification of information obviously depends on the business of the organization, the information it needs to deal with, as well as the flow of information that is essential to the proper functioning of the organization. In most cases, as in small businesses or personal communications, the classification could be into two groups only: 'Personal', and 'open' or 'public'; in other words 'classified', and 'unrestricted' or 'open'. You may put any name on the two groups, but the generic categories into which the information will fall will be one of the two, as above. Most people may use the term 'confidential' instead of 'personal'. Proprietor of a small business will personally handle his 'confidential' information and let it flow only into the hands of few selected confidants such as, say, his income-tax adviser. His business strategies, his income data, etc. would fall in to this classified category (to be made available only to the limited and specified few). Whereas, all mundane matters, day to day dealings, supply of materials, bills etc. he would group under 'open' information and would be willing to make available to anyone, if required. Such 'open' information could flow through the hands of all his employees, without any restriction whatsoever. But, *not so as regards the "confidential"* information.

Large business houses on the other hand may have many categories of information, which need to be handled by different groups of people, on more or less exclusive basis. That is to say, one group should not have information relevant to another group/different category of information, which, they need not have anything to do with. For example, the Accounting Department need not have anything to do with the strategic planning, nor the stores group be concerned with personnel planning, and so on. That is, the *concept of availability of information to individuals/groups/departments etc. purely on "the need to know basis"* arises. This, in essence, is the core principle for ensuring information security, viz.: *the flow of information, its handling, its storage etc. should be strictly on "the need to know basis only"*. Hence, classification of information in a large business house maybe into three categories only, say, 'personal or private', 'company confidential', and 'unrestricted or open'. Unrestricted documents or information, normally do not carry any classification, as the information can be had by anyone, without affecting information security, and hence, has no need for the classification tag to be mentioned along with it.

Classification is to be prominently displayed on a document for ease of recognition and identification of the class it belongs to. The usual method is to mention the grading, in highlighted capital letters, on the 'top' or both 'top and bottom' of each page. This action is also repeated on the cover page of the file and file cover itself. The cases marked 'personal' or 'private' may deal with material of strategic importance to the organization, usually dealt with only by the owner/Chairman and perhaps members of the board. Information and data, etc. proprietary in nature to the company, which would need wider, but still limited, circulation to others including customers, and still retain confidentiality would be marked as 'company confidential'. Normally, this is the highest classified information of a company that outsiders could come to know/have access to. All other material that the organization/business does not have to bother to secure will come under the 'unrestricted' or 'open' tag or classification. Such information could be mostly of passing interest and their availability of all and sundry would not materially affect interest, business or the future of the organization/business.

Governments may classify as 'unclassified' or 'unrestricted' routine information and specific information that the general public can or should have, say, its plans and programmes for the people, its taxation policies, rules and regulations that the public should know, and so on. Obviously, no mention of the classification is necessary on such documents. There would be considerable amount of information that various departments and organizations of the government should or can have, but the general public may not; that is the flow of such information has to be regulated or restricted. Obviously, such information maybe classified as 'restricted'. Most of the classified information in a government or allied setup would be covered under this classification.

However, there would be appreciable amount of material affecting state interests that would need restriction of its flow, strictly, to a very limited circle. This would need to be classified as 'secret' or some such categorization. There would be other sensitive information, though not state secrets, or which maybe personal in nature, flow of which has to be curtailed to a limited few. Such information could be classified as 'confidential'. Flow of all such information should be highly regulated on the strictly *"need to know basis"*. Classified information of the above two types need great care in handling and strict accounting.

There could always be some material/information of very great importance, say, material that could affect the security of the State, if it was to fall into hands other than specifically designated one or ones. This would obviously need the highest classification. Such a classification is "top secret" or "for your eyes only". Necessarily, such material need to be few and far between, and calls for greatest extent of care in its origination, flow, modification, storage and disposal/destruction. *It therefore calls for personal accounting by the originator and the recipients.*

The above types of classification or grading of information is by no means exhaustive. They are only indicative with the advent of electronic data interchange (EDI), electronic funds transfer, (EFT), facsimile, voicemail, e-mail, and other extensive means of communication, you may need to classify information in other ways. Extensive use of: Computers, multimedia, the internet, telecommunication networks, or the so-called information technology, (IT), have further complicated the issue of information security. The modern society is immersed in its applications. With its easy accessibility and very fast flow of information, that is now possible/happening, it has become essential to compartmentalize information into few more/ alternative classifications.

The following nomenclature may be representative:

- *General=unclassified=unrestricted=public domain*: Such a classification could cover information that can be made available to anyone and everyone without any restriction whatsoever, and there are no limitations on the use of such information.
- *For internal use only*: This classification may be used for information that could be circulated freely, within the organization, but not to be made available to outsiders. Examples are: The company's annual report, company policies and procedures of operation, etc.
- *Restricted*: In an organization some information may need to be restricted to specified management levels, say, supervisory levels. Such information could be classified as restricted.

- *Confidential*: Information, thus, classified could be those limited or restricted to personnel who need to have security clearance, say, those involved in the implementation of the organizational objectives. Usually, it would be the management levels and above. Lower levels should not normally have access to such information, apart from outsiders and the general public.
- *Sensitive*=secret: Sensitive information that need to be made known only to specific units in the organization should be classified in this category, say, information regarding the foreign exchange operations in a bank. Similarly, the financial operations of a business are to be confined to its Financial Department, apart from the board, etc.
- *For your eyes only*=top secret: This, the highest classification for sensitive information dealt with in the organization, *should be restricted to information that needs to be routed to specific individuals only, say, the Chairman and the members of the Board of Directors.* Availability of such information to others could result in unconscionable damage to the security, well being and operations of the organizations. Future strategies and plans of the organization, information on any confidential deals (financial, merger, etc.), are examples of information coming under such a classification.

With the extensive usage of the internet, ever increasing circle of e-business, and the great push on e-commerce activities information security is daily gaining tremendous importance. So, the science (and art) of ciphers, code making and code-breaking, "Cryptology" in short, is no longer the domain of the elite few; nor is its use confined to governments, big businesses, security organizations, etc. (A note on Cryptology may be seen at Appendix "C".)

Organizing for Information Security

As mentioned before, the above way of classification is indicative/representative only. Each company/organization should examine, compartmentalize the information it has to deal with, and (could) use its own terminology, if it so desires. But, it must ensure that all concerned are aware of the exact import of the terminology used. Advantage of using the terminology as indicated above, is that the words are somewhat indicative of the meaning attached to it, in regard to the grade of classification of the information. In any case, with the ever expanding involvement of information technology, or it, in various aspects of business activities, in future, the usual categorization of information into just three or four grades of classification, from security considerations may no longer be adequate.

You may use any type of classification you like for handling information in your organization. But, it is incumbent on you to ensure that, everyone in the organization stick to the same type of classification in regard to all information in the organization, in whatever form it is held. This has to be strictly enforced; whether the information is held in files, in computer disks, in microfilms, in tapes, in print-outs, in reports, inside computers, or in any other form. All must use the same method of grading. This is essential to ensure that a bit of information is graded uniformly in the same category, and prevent wandering of one grade of bit of information held in one form, say a computer disk, coming under another classification when held in some other form, say a file. Otherwise, you could have a calamity in your hands. Imagine, for instance, what could happen when a piece of vital, highly sensitive information, say, in a document, gets fed into a computer as restricted type only! It may then, even get printed out as unclassified type and fall into the hands of general public. So, do ensure that a bit of information has the same, identical classification, throughout the organization, whatever be the form the information is handled in (verbal, written, typewritten, electronic, flowing through telecommunication systems/networks, storage media such as microfilm, magnetic/optical disks and so on).

Yet, another aspect to be constantly borne in mind is that, the value of a bit of information is not static, but is dynamic! Its importance can change with time as well as with other changes to environment, such as restructuring of the organization, change of ownership and so on. Hence, *no piece of information can be considered as permanently belonging to one security grading only*. For example, it is a moot point as to whether there is any piece of information relevant to World War II that still remains in the classified domain! Therefore, along with a system of/ procedure for classification of information you have to *also implement a system or procedure for* periodic review of such information in order to reclassify or declassify them as currently relevant.

Have you considered how long a document or a piece of information has to be kept 'alive', or kept in cold storage in the form of some 'record', or in a 'mortuary'? Does this matter at all? Definitely, yes, it is the third aspect of information security. You have to lay down a policy regarding the life of a document or piece of information when it is created or acquired. May be in your organization a specific grading implies a specific and different life span for the document/information. The periodic review/reclassification would also affect the further span of life of the document/information.

That is not all. You have a fourth aspect to consider too-what to do with a record once its assigned life is over? This is the aspect of destruction/disposal of a document/information. Proper procedure or methodology and the regularity of document destruction/disposal as per such a laid down system, are equally important cornerstones for securing information.

The four cornerstones mentioned above, (the system of "classification", "reviews", "life/duration" and "disposal/destruction" of documents/ information), encompass the field of information to protect, and secure the same from unauthorized access. They are like the perimeter-wall that provides physical protection, basically from outsiders, to an installation within. Adequate physical security also require suitable layout of the installation, proper access control to the various facilities distributed in the complex, within the perimeter, use of locks and other protective measures. And you need appropriate *standard operating procedures*, (S.O.Ps). So is the case with information security too.

Once you have the above four cornerstones in place, you look into the gamut of activities involved in the handling of information. This has to be right from the initial stage of creation/ acquisition of the piece of information. Handling of information also involve its *movement*/flow (verbal, visual, physical, electronic, etc.), within the organization, any modification or transformation, its transmission outside the organization (personal, written, through telecommunication channels, etc.), its extraction or recording, and so on, through its re-classification, to its final destruction and disposal. You need to have accurate and scrupulous accounting, so to speak, *at all stages*. Therefore, you require adequate and appropriate standard operating procedures, (*S.O.Ps*), to be evolved and implemented. These *S.O.Ps* would also require periodic review and updating!

Physical security, a pre-requisite for information security

Any source of information, be it a document, a tape, a computer disk, a microfilm, etc., unless you have proper control of physical access to it you cannot ensure security of the information contained therein. The *S.O.Ps* should *clearly and comprehensively delineate* the physical security measures that have to be followed, specific to the information security operations. These also need to be adequate and suitable for each stage or step of activity involved in: the creation, acquisition, handling, modification, transformation, transmission, recording, storage, destruction and disposal of information. At no stage should the information be left unprotected. Moreover, the system adopted whilst providing ease of access as well as facility to carry out *any required operation on the information* (read, write, copy, transfer, transform, etc.), *as specifically permitted to the authorized*, should totally deny any access to the information *to all unauthorized attempts*. This is an added dimension to the physical security measures called for in information security tasks.

As far as security of tangible storage media is concerned, the relevant physical security measures may be obvious; such as use of lockers, cupboards, safes, vaults in which the documents, audio/video tapes, computer disks and so on can be physically kept and locked up for safe-custody. The locks used could be physical types with keys, or keyless ones, including electronic and time locks. The actual method of handling and storage used for such material media may vary, depending on the type of media-paper, magnetic tape, film and so on. Note that all these have a physical form, though the size and shapes may be different, and the extent of information that, can be stored in each type, do vary enormously. Hence, they are all amenable to physical security measures. The basic techniques of physical security such as physical protection, denial of access to unauthorized persons during handling, movement, and storage apply equally to such physical forms of information and records. Access control methods required could also be analogous to those used for high cost physical items/stores say, jewellery.

Naturally, there would be some differences too in the handling, accounting and storage techniques between the different types of media. Magnetic type of media will need protection from strong magnetic fields, large temperature and humidity variations, as well as protection from shocks and impacts-problems that paper based storage do not face. Also, in view of the voluminous data they can hold as well as the ease and speed, with which the data can be copied, modified, transmitted or even destroyed, far more rigorous and close monitoring of access, handling, movement and accounting systems for such media are called for. Thus, the physical security measures needed in information security operations are not just techniques to merely protect against break-ins, physical thefts or damages to written or recorded information. But, they also call for additional specific techniques to be devised to protect the data/information during the use, handling, movement, storage and accounting of these physical information storage media. Hence, *information security tasks inevitably start with implementation of adequate and appropriate physical security measures.* But, it certainly does not end there!

Information Security Measures

You would have noticed that, the physical security measures to be used are not very obvious when you deal with information in the non-physical *avatars,* such as in telecommunication networks/computers (electronic form), speech, visual images and so on. What physical security measures would you employ to safeguard information held in the memory of a person? An employee talks out of turn to his family members or friends about some confidential matter. He speaks to his boss, who is out of station, over the phone in regard to a classified case. He receives an outside visitor when some confidential papers are on his table, or faxes a confidential document to the company's associates. Such actions can all result in leakage of information (maybe vital and damaging), mostly, unwittingly. Mere physical security measures cannot plug such loopholes. You require additional security measures which, may be classified as information security measures. With the recent explosive growth of it reach, many of the information security measures have to be, perforce, hi-tech add-ons. But some basic security techniques apply to most information security problems of any organization. What is needed is to closely examine the information environment, locate and analyze the possible weak spots, and then identify suitable techniques to minimize possible security breaches. There would be ofcourse, no one hundred per cent guarantee that no information leaks would occur. Accidents do happen, and to err is human! You should, therefore, have suitable checks, control and constant monitoring of the information environment, to quickly locate and plug any leaks. You must also have in position, appropriate contingency plans to counter effects of such unwanted leaks.

Consider the fact that information can be leaked, modified or altered, forged or counterfeited, or even destroyed fairly easily. The need for information security measures is to protect the information from all such 'unauthorized' and 'illegal' operations. Note also that, such illegal activities and unauthorized disclosures maybe 'accidental' or 'intentional'. The security measures must take care of both these possibilities.

Security breaches can occur due to very simple events, or actions. Consider some examples in this regard. An employee casually mentions to a friend, or even an outsider, that he has been promoted and put in charge of an important/sensitive section. "A" sends an important fax message to "B" over the public switched telephone network or PSTN, and due to a *'wrong number'* or crossed connection (if not an inadvertent, or wrong telephone tap), the message reaches a totally different person "C"! Such happenings are not rare 'accidents' at all. You may take any number of precautions to prevent such unauthorized disclosures of vital information. But the basic and common starting point is the 'sensitization of the sender' (and the receiver!), to the possibilities of such accidental disclosures, how the 'accidents' happen, the precautions to be taken and *the need for constant vigil whilst handling/conveying sensitive information.* They have to bear in mind, always, that in all modes of communication the possibility of the information falling into wrong hands exist and guarding against such possibilities must become a second nature to them, at all times. It must be impressed on them not to convey sensitive information over the phone/fax/e-mail or any such system, unless suitable approved encryption or coding is employed. Do not keep classified papers lying around on your table, and particularly so when you are not around. When leaving the room, lock up all such papers. Never carry around sensitive data with you, except on official work, and always in properly locked carriers. Avoid talking about your work when away from work. Even then, on required basis only. Literally believe in the adage that 'walls have ears' and perhaps 'eyes too'. Further, classified information should be passed on *'strict need to know basis only'*. These are some of the elementary and common sense methods that need to be used to ensure security of information.

Thus, the basic techniques of prevention of accidental disclosure of any classified information are 'education' and 'training' of personnel who deal with such information. Constant reiteration of the principles is also essential to keep the individuals alive to the dangers-at all times and at all places. These are the fundamental, basic tenets of information security. *Only thereafter comes application of hi-tech systems and add-ons.*

The above methodology, do not, however, provide protection against 'intentional acts' of leakage/modification etc., of information. The underlying human predilections for anger, greed, jealousy, lust, pride and so on, may drive the possessor of classified information to part with some or most of it, deliberately, unmindful of the damage it can cause to others, or to the organization as a whole. The enemy/opposition could easily subvert such an individual to steal, and pass on to them some vital secrets of the organization or its employees. Or, motivate such person[s] to modify, or destroy some important documents/ piece of information, maybe, even to plant damaging false information. Such subverted individuals may be directed to cause 'influencing', spread 'disaffection', or undertake dangerous and nefarious tasks on their behalf, such as 'sabotage', 'arson,' even acts of 'terrorism'!

A person may commit acts of such treachery due to one or more of the following :

- '*Lack* of bread'—He is unable to make ends meet with what he gets. So he seeks other avenues to supplement his 'income'-that of *'selling secrets'*.
- '*Lust* for broad'—The person is enticed by the 'honey trap', and then has to pay the price, viz., obtain and pass sensitive information demanded of him/her.
- '*Open* to blackmail'—Any unsavory aspect, or trait of the individual, which the organization may not be aware of, is dug out by the opposition. Alternatively, the opposition first entices the person with some goodies like money, maid, special facilities, presents, and so on. And thereafter, with the proof of his misdeeds in their hands, blackmails the individual to comply with their demands for sensitive information or something worse, such as sabotage, with the *'sword of damocles' of 'or else'* held over his head.
- '*Habit* of bragging/bravado'—The person is habitually boastful by nature and desires to impress others about his 'important role' in the organization. He, therefore, boasts of what he does, what he comes to know directly in context of his work, or indirectly from others in the organization, without regard to the sensitiveness of the information, or the nature of people to whom he is *'expounding'*.

- '*Grab* the boodle'—The individual has acquired a taste for high living, a living style he cannot afford on the salary he earns. Hence, he grabs all opportunities (he cares two hoots whether they are ethical or unethical), for luxurious living-expensive holidays, pricey things and so on, that he is offered in exchange for classified information, and other acts of villainy.
- '*Craze* for booze'—The person is addicted to expensive liquor, drugs, narcotics, or such substances, that he cannot afford. The opposition quickly tracks such 'game', and keep him happy with supplies of the person's choice, be it imported whiskey, hard drugs, or psychotropic substances, etc. All they ask for in exchange is classified information, to say the least.
- '*Envy, jealousy, pride, anger etc.*, leading to disgruntlement'—The person is consumed with imagined, or actual grievance of not getting his 'dues'. He is jealous of what his peers have, that he believes he has been "denied", whatever be the reasons. He is envious of his contemporaries and superiors who have gone up in life/ career, and are doing far better. He is angry at the organization for not recognizing his *(presumed?)*'merit', 'achievements'. In brief, he is a totally disgruntled individual with a grouse against the employer/others in the organization. He *becomes a willing tool in the hands of the opposition*, 'to get back at the organization in any way he can'. Then, vengeful acts against the organization, or its people, come very easily, to such a person.

Apart from the above *"seven deadly sins"*, there is also the not so rare problem of '*a cause*' or '*an ideology*'. This includes the more deadly form of 'fundamentalism', particularly the 'religious type' or the 'sectarian type'. A 'disease' that has driven people to commit far more heinous crimes such as, 'assassination', 'terrorist acts of violence' (like exploding bombings, shooting innocent civilians), etc. *Such a person may be prepared even to give up his life in the attempt.*

No amount of 'education' or 'training' will help in such cases. The only solution is 'prevention'. Prevent such persons from entering the organization, particularly as employees. Consequently, the first priority is to prevent access to sensitive material, to such individuals who are, unfortunately, already an employee and you are unable to remove him. However, visitors can be screened to keep out undesirables, with a bit of alertness and tact.

Secondly, and perhaps a more important long term practical answer, ensure that the organization *inducts* only the 'right type of person', both from point of view of growth of the organization as well as effective screening/monitoring processes for 'integrity' and 'absence of all undesirable characteristics' mentioned above. Otherwise, all your efforts at ensuring 'information security' may well be doomed to failure.

The third aspect is to keep 'temptation' away from as many persons as possible by the simple means of not letting people have access to material that 'they do not need'. As far as practicable, keep them also away from modes of 'communication' like telephones, fax machines, email facility, copying machines, even official letterheads and so on. Similar dictum should hold in regard to 'information storage' processes and facilities.

Fourthly, keep in place rigorous system of 'control' for all types of information duplication facilities/processes. Do not permit people to carry into sensitive locations/places having sensitive materials/information items such as cameras, recorders, portable copying machines, memo-corders, and any listening devices. Any *essential* duplication of information should take place only on proper authorization, whatever the duplication process used. It is equally essential to have 'proper monitoring,' and 'accurate accounting' of all duplication attempts that take place (even 'on such duly authorized basis').

Further, you need to ensure that, all extra and surplus copies should be preferably destroyed immediately, instead of taking on account, and stored/filed as numbered copies. The system of destruction applies equally to typewriter ribbons, carbon sheets (used once only), all noting, drafts, etc. Similarly, information and documentation no longer needed and weeded out should be destroyed instead of unnecessarily being maintained in the record room. Such destruction should be carried out under secure, controlled, and properly supervised condition. Also, the weeded out information should be properly 'accounted', with suitable entries in the records.

It is needless to emphasize the inescapable necessity of ongoing, periodic, unobtrusive but efficient monitoring of the behaviour/life style, as well as security vetting of individuals entrusted with sensitive responsibilities/ handling sensitive materials and equipment, or holding critical positions in the organization.

Last, but not the least important requirements envisage the inescapable need for periodic 'audit' of the *accountability*, and 'thorough investigation' of all detected/suspected lapses in regard to the *information security* aspects. You also need to implement promptly, and fully, consequential, required remedial, modified or additional, security measures. You should also remember that there are plenty of conmen, frauds and forgers in the world, and more of them come up as time goes on. It is no longer true to say that 'you cannot fool a really honest man', as he is above greed and is not out to make quick buck. He can easily, and unwittingly enter into an apparently honest deal, and find to his dismay, later, that the transaction was based on bogus or forged documents! Always, you will need to be fully alert, and ever vigilant against such information security lapses. *Do utilize the techniques available for detection of frauds, forgeries and so on. (Experts in the government in this area are called government examiner of questioned documents or GEQD).*

As mentioned earlier, when sensitive messages have to go over public communication networks, suitable 'cipher system' may need to be implemented. You may also need to ensure appropriate 'acknowledgement' and 'authentication' of receipt of the message by the correct 'addressee' only, and not by some unknown/unauthorized person. Where internal communication networks and leased lines are used, when sensitive messages have to be passed over them apart from suitable access control, acknowledgement and authentication processes, you need to ensure that the communication system is 'clean'. That is, others, viz., unauthorized persons, do not have access to the network system or 'tap' into the system. Due to quirks of the telecommunication networks, wrong connection can occur, or messages get delivered to wrong parties. One method of avoiding such situations and ensure that the messages reach only the wanted parties or not at all, is to carry out the following drill, called as call-back technique, is briefly detailed in the next paragraph.

Say, person "A" has a message to be passed on to person "B", (over a communication channel). "A" uses his instrument (whether a telephone, teleprinter, fax unit, a mobile phone or cell phone, an email or computer communication system) to link up to the corresponding receiving terminal of "B". If due to an error in the network "A" reaches some other person than "B", or there is no response/unacceptable response, "A" will break the connection and retry. If, however, a link has been correctly established between "A" and "B" only, then, "A" passes on *a* message to "B" that he has some information to pass on to him, and that "B" should call him back. "A" gets the acknowledgement, for this message, from "B", and disconnects. Now, *"B" calls up "A" and identifies himself, (to "A").* And then, only then, "A" passes on to "B" the sensitive message. "B" then, properly acknowledges the message with authentication, (that it is *"B" that has received the message and none other),* like a personally signed receipt where, *the signature is* unique *and cannot be duplicated by others.*

The rapid expansion and growth in the use of 'office equipment', 'computers', 'telecommunication networks', and connected hi-tech aids in the fields of-document copying, filing, recording, presentation, modifying and transferring of information, have affected all those who are responsible for information security. Not the least of which is need for persons like an information security supervisor, to be quite familiar with *security techniques* of-access control, surveillance and countermeasures, safety and security systems and so on.

"Modernization" being, an important and impressive 'buzzword' you probably tend to go in for the most sophisticated, and up-to-date communication terminals (and system), in your organization. But then, are you aware of the attendant risks involved? Here, 'ignorance' is certainly not 'bliss', but a serious peril that can result in compromising 'information security'! The transmission and reception of messages by telex, and teleprinter, ('TP'), machines involve making and breaking of electrical contacts that result in current pulses in accordance with the 'on' and 'off' telex/TP codes. The electrical sparking that results at the contacts and the pulsed electrical current in the circuits lead to emanations of radio frequency signals in the neighbourhood. This, unintended radio signals, (RF leakage), can be picked up in the neighbourhood with a sensitive receiver, by the opposition. Thus, the machine unwittingly 'leaks the message' to third parties. A similar situation obtains in the case of electronic typewriters and computer systems too. Only, in this case, instead of sparking contacts you have the switching transients as the culprits.

You may be using some 'cipher' system to safeguard security of your messages over the communication links. You may then erroneously believe that your system is safe from the above RF leakage problems. Far from it, you cannot afford to be complacent. On the other hand, you need to be extra careful. Since the message merit coding, they are obviously very sensitive in nature. Cipher system per se, do not remove the RF leakage problem; unless the coding/decoding is done manually and not by some automatic technique involving electric/electronic devices. That is to say, the message is first coded manually and then transmitted over the communication link; so also, the received message is first downloaded and then manually decoded. (Coded messages are typed in/fed into the communication system and at the receiving end, also the coded messages are printed out, and then manually decoded to get at the plain or decoded version). This may be laborious, as against the very convenient method of inputting your plain/in clear message into some automatic machine which, encrypts the message and puts this 'cipher text' out into the telecommunication system; also, deciphers the received message and prints out the decoded version, the 'plain text'. Here lies the peril, whilst inputting the plain message into the system and printing out the plain text, RF *leakage of the clear version of the message occurs.* (Ofcourse, RF leakage of the encoded message also takes place, but would be of no consequence with a 'cipher system' that is designed well). Note that electronic typewriters are also culprits as regards *RF leakage.* So, the usage of encryption/decryption along with it, itself militates against information security, since you then tend to freely pass on classified information, which you would otherwise have hesitated to pass on the communication channel. (The system is now suspect, as the RF leakage from the machine could perhaps be correlated with the coded signal, that is the "cipher text", and the original plain message, or the "plain text"/ "clear text", derived).

Special techniques are called for in such situations. You go in for specially designed and constructed enclosures/facilities, which, adequately prevent the RF leakage generated by the equipment from piercing through to the outside of the enclosure. (This technique is called RF shielding, and the enclosure is known as 'shielded enclosure'). Alternatively, you use only specially designed equipment, which, do not give out any level of RF leakage that can be picked up outside the installation. Such equipment are said to be built to TEMPEST specifications. U*se of equipment to 'TEMPEST' specification, (which are very, very expensive), in shielded enclosures is not recommended.*

Responsibility of a Security Manager

Security manager concerned with 'information security' has his job cutout for him. He has not only to worry about the concrete aspects of physical security but also, has to worry much more about the intangible, even abstract aspects of information security. He has to keep close watch on the types of envelopes and sealing arrangements employed; types of office and communication equipment acquired and the environment in which they are used; also remember that a fax machine can also take out copies of a document, apart from fax transmissions.

He may even have to consider what methods of protection have to be employed when the *opposition is expected to try out even lip reading with telescope or binoculars from across the street, through a window or open door*! He has to equally worry about the integrity of the personnel, their behaviour; whether they have since become security risk and need to be isolated from sensitive areas/locations of work' or, even, need to be removed or dismissed from service. Like that, there are a whole host of things he has to keep an eye on and take care of. He must maintain a constant vigil on material, on equipment, on personnel, over communication systems, on cipher systems, on accounting and accountability, and even over rubbish! So, what principles of information security he has as guidelines? It may be a 'reiteration'. But, reiteration is the essence of 'reinforcement'; so, do observe the principles of information security that are detailed, in the paragraphs that follow.

Principles of Information Security

Many of the principles of information security are just common sense practices. However, these need to be observed with both care and an awareness of the possible methods and procedures that may be used by the opposition interested in you, your job, in your organization and so on. Correspondence and communications, [verbal or otherwise], are the ready sources for garnering information. Hence, they call for special attention. Letters and documents must be sealed in sturdy, non-transparent envelopes that do not tear in transit or otherwise get damaged. Sealing arrangements used must defy/deter duplication, unauthorized or clandestine opening/resealing. Certain chemicals, and sprays, when sprayed over normal paper envelope render the envelope temporarily transparent, thus permitting unauthorized viewing of the contents. No stain is left behind, nor any apparent sign of such actions. (Note, that this method helps in detection of letter bombs too!).

There are other, not so apparent, areas of correspondence and documentation that are vulnerable to information security failures and hence require strict 'vigilance'. Typewriter ribbons, used carbon and stencil sheets, extra copies taken but not destroyed, incorrect document destruction methods used, uncontrolled use of office equipment like plain paper copiers (PPC), poor accounting methods used and so on. Shredding machines are useful for quick and convenient destruction of documents, in the physical forms of paper, films, flimsies, files and so on. No doubt, physical destruction of magnetic tape, floppy disks etc. is feasible. But, as they are reusable items, the equivalent for destruction of information held on them is the bulk (magnetic) eraser. This is, ofcourse, not a solution when you consider the destruction of information held in an 'optical disk' or the CD-ROM, *(compact disk-read only memory).* Use of a high power laser to burn out the information content or actual physical destruction would then be the answer! For destruction of information held on paper, flimsies, film etc., choose the proper type of shredding machine, with great care; depending on the sensitiveness of the information held, the extent of material and speed of destruction required, as well as the further mode of disposal of the shredded material. Machines are available for quick bulk shredding of computer printouts. Such machines convert the paper into strips, say 2 to 6 millimetres, in width. There are other types which shred the paper literally into dust, (actually into tiny pieces of paper, having areas of a few square millimeters); these are low speed devices with not too large a destruction capacity. There are yet other, heavy duty machines that can convert entire, thick files at a time, instead of the usual few sheets of paper at a go, into thin strips, tiny pieces or even sludge of shredded material for direct disposal along with rubbish or garbage! Total security calls for the disposal of the shredded, or otherwise, documents by burning under proper supervision. Use of special types of flimsy paper for extremely sensitive documents, requiring immediate destruction after perusal, are reported; these are supposed to quickly dissolve in water or go up in a puff of smoke when lit (with fire).

Accounting methods used must provide for a check on strict, disciplined use of copying systems and should leave a clear audit trail! When sensitive documents float around in an office with office equipment like PPCS located close by, [no doubt, both on a required basis], apart from proper accounting and close monitoring, special precautions are called for in the use of such copying machines. The record of usage of the copying machine must spell out in its record of use, the date and time of the usage, the name and designation of person, the identity of the document and the number of copies the person has taken on the machine at that time, at a minimum. If the PPC could also leave, directly on the copies taken on it, an imprint of the serial number of the machine as well as a time and date stamp, [may be even the copy number?], the desirable result would be a quick, convenient and effective audit trail. Such a machine would be a boon to organizations handling predominantly sensitive information. Remember that the modern true color PPC could be a counterfeiter's delight. It could give faithful rendition of any document, which does not have excellent intaglio, embossing, watermarks or threads etc.!

Is it feasible to defeat copying of documents in a copying machine? There are reports of special inks, use of which render such documents difficult to copy. Some special techniques could make the documents eye-legible but resist copying actions of a PPC, etc.

Cameras, video and similar devices should be taboo within the sensitive premises of an organization. Use of cameras etc. should be permitted only in other locations within the organization, if at all. There ought to be a time and place for such actions, and under properly monitored, controlled conditions. Sometimes you do need to use cameras and video devices even in sensitive areas, say for some documentation or publicity purpose. Such use must be under strict control and under the personal supervision of a suitable designated person, well versed in information security drills. The person should also monitor the follow up actions of development, printing, pre-production, production and post-production activities and so on.

Extensive modern day use of computers and telecommunication facilities, information technology adjuncts, raises a whole host of information security problems. These need very specialized techniques, devices and procedures to adequately protect the organization from information thefts, illegal modification or erasure of information and so on. Problems also abound due to the nature of the computer-telecommunications symbiosis, environmental problems of electronic noise, interference, cross-modulation, *frightening computer problems such as "viruses", "worms", "trojan horses", "hacking",* and so on. These can lead to data errors, data loss, miscarriage or information sent to wrong parties and so on. *To guard against such happenings in your system, you require special procedures and devices* to ensure the implicit requirements of data integrity, data availability and data confidentiality.

However, in view of its importance to information security *some introduction to* "cryptology" (the science and art (?) of secret writing, or "cipher", and "cryptanalysis", or "code-breaking"), *may be seen at* Appendix "C".

But what do you do regarding the possibility of a 'dissident', a 'spy', a 'plant' or a 'mole' in the organization. He may use some very special methods to smuggle vital information to his 'compatriots' or 'contacts' outside the organization. Such techniques could be difficult to detect with run of the mill methods. Such techniques are termed 'secret writing' or 'clandestine communication'. Here, the secret information being smuggled out is disguised to look like normal, harmless communication such as an 'apparent letter to a friend or an associate'. This may be use of some sort of pre-arranged code between them; use of some common biological fluid or special chemicals for the secret part of the message interspersed in the normal writing, but invisible to the naked eye. For example, the communication may read as, 'in the meeting with Goel today, there was talk about some family problems and movements'. It may actually convey 'in the board meeting today, there was talk about financial difficulties and layoffs'. The receiver of the clandestine message, then, uses some suitable sort of technique to read the hidden message, (like use of 'oblique incidence' light, UV radiation, IR illumination, dabbing with suitable chemical, and so on or, the apparently normal, communication). Or more sophisticated methods may be used like the 'microdot', documents/images compressed into a dot size of photographic film. The emulsion of this bit of film is then transferred and pasted on to, say, a punctuation mark, a period in a typed or printed material of 'normal import', stuck on the envelope, or a stamp, and so on. A more modern version of this could be use of 'laser' writing on a bit of material stuck on any suitable item. Detection of such sophisticated 'secret writing' by the security manager is not too easy a process. However, methods do exist to detect any kind of clandestine communication. But these are limited by the knowledge of such techniques; importance attached to the detection and the extent to which necessary facilities can be created. But, do remember that a brand new technique may be used tomorrow!

Perhaps, the widest known but least understood aspect is the problem of 'electronic surveillance', use of the ubiquitous 'bug' –the 'listening device' for audio/video surveillance, apparently, familiar to the reader/watcher of 'thrillers'! Abroad, hosts of devices and techniques for 'eavesdropping' are advertised and marketed, almost freely. It is, therefore, not easy to stop invasions of privacy of individuals and businesses, as smuggling of such devices is not difficult at all. Nor has the law enough teeth and drive to put a stop to such activities.

Countermeasures are no doubt available, but at a cost and a 'probability' attached to them. The countermeasure techniques vary from the simple to the very sophisticated, depending on the surveillance techniques anticipated to be deployed to suit the particular situation applicable. You term a place has been *'sanitized'* when an operation has been carried forth to check for 'bugs', and remove any found at the place; and necessary efforts are also put in to ensure, that, no new 'bugs' are introduced. Because the action is like sweeping the dirt out of the premises, the operation of sanitizing a room as regards electronic surveillance, is popularly known as 'sweeping', that is you have the place 'swept'! One of the commercial, special equipment used for such a purpose is appropriately called the 'broom'!

The countermeasure task is to be handled only by real experts. Even so, there is no 'total guarantee' that all possible loopholes have been taken care of! Anyhow, remember the saying—'beware of the greek bearing a gift', it could be 'the trojan horse'. 'So do look a gift horse in the mouth'. Watch out for the sophisticated cell-phone presented to you or your household member, or left overtly or covertly/(hidden) in your house, particularly the 'global coverage cell phone'. With its modern facilities of 'silent ringing' and 'hands off operation', it can be a deadly eavesdropping device, remotely switched to listen into your conversations in the room. It also gives very long distance coverage-that of the cell phone, 'global' in the case of the 'global cell phone'!

You may be quite confident that you have designed and implemented systems and procedures that guarantee, one hundred percent, security of information in your organization. Even so, you must provide, in the system, for an immediate, prompt and proper 'alert', 'if' and 'when' any mutilation, leakage, loss or theft occurs, [in regard to sensitive information]; the security aspects of availability, integrity and confidentiality. Only then, you can implement, promptly, suitable damage control contingency plans to ensure continued healthy functioning of the organization. There will always be confidence tricksters, forgers and frauds out to defraud people with false documents, forged deeds and impersonations. There are ample techniques available to protect you, provided you are ever vigilant and not willing to be a fall guy.

For example, suppose 'cipher pad' used for enciphering secret information is compromised or is missing. Unless an immediate alert takes place on the occurrence of this unfortunate event, leakage of considerable amount of sensitive information may be the result. Whereas, when, a suitable alert system is instituted, you can promptly implement damage control activities. You inform all users of that 'cipher pad' about it being compromised and that, they should, hence, immediately stop using it (and also destroy the compromised pad, properly and immediately). Then, suitable, pre-determined, alternative pad should be brought into force, or necessary instructions issued, through secure channels, about further course of action. Simultaneously, immediate and intensive 'investigation and analysis' activity is called for to find the reasons for the security lapse(s), as well as ascertaining the 'implications' of the security lapse. (Any consequential damage due to the availability of the sensitive information that has already been enciphered and sent out, which could have been compromised, and become available to the opposition). You could, thus, implement suitable countermeasures without delay, and limit the possible damaging effects (due to the security lapse). Remedial measures may demand suitable upgrading of the information security system, changes to the *S.O.Ps*, including any changes required in the contingency plans. Such measures need to be arrived at, with great care, and implemented to prevent such security lapses in the future.

Therefore, periodic security checks, audit, good contingency plans and simulated exercises to check the effectiveness of the information security system, play a dominant role in ensuring prompt recovery, quick damage control and denial of much advantage to the opposition in case of any untoward information leaks.

The recent (September 11, 2001) horrendous terrorist attacks on the World Trade Center (WTC) towers show that the most secure means of information transmission is by word of mouth through trusted messengers, particularly when HUMINT is non-available! The terrorists did not use the conventional communication facilities of mobile phones, PSTN, e-mail etc., but couriers were employed during the entire period of years of planning and implementation of their unbelievingly terrible attacks!

(Maybe they followed the principle enunciated in the statement of Benjamin Franklin: *"Three people may be trusted to keep a secret so long as two of them are dead!").*

Chapter 7

A Primer on Personal and VIP Security

"Obscurity often brings safety"

—Aesop

Background

There appears to be no end to the growth of threats to *'Personal Security'*, be it coercion, extortion, kidnapping or even assassination. Whether the causes are social tensions, ever growing economic disparities, communalism, religious fundamentalism business rivalry, territorial greed, political ambitions, terrorism of mere criminal intents there has been a faster and faster growth of such threats in recent times. Though, by and large, such threats are aimed at the affluent and the influential; the simple, innocent common man has not been spared either and most often it is he, who is the greatest sufferer of such heinous activities. We are not talking here of "Personnel Security/Safety" at the workplace, that is security/safety of employees and visitors to an organization, which is covered by 'Industrial Safety' regulations etc., nor are we talking of 'Hostage' situations.

It is no longer infrequent to read about a rich businessman, a shopkeeper, a politician or even a social worker or their children being kidnapped for ransom or other demands-say, release of some arrested villains on an exchange basis. Nor is it rare for an influential person to be threatened, a business magnate being murdered or a politician to be assassinated. Special measures taken to protect such individuals and their families from such threats constitute the security measures covered by the 'umbrella' term—'Personal Security' or 'VIP Security'.

What Constitutes Personal Security?

Whilst considering 'information security' in the previous chapter, you observed how 'physical security' becomes a part and parcel of, and a pre-requisite for, 'information security'. Ofcourse, certain additional security measures, features, and methodologies are also involved and have to be implemented to ensure information security. Such measures are suitably enshrined in the form of 'standard operating procedures' or *S.O.Ps*, 'administrative manual or instructions' and 'security manual or instructions' of the organization. Likewise, in the case of 'personal security' both 'physical security' and 'information security' tasks are closely involved, apart from certain additional procedures and methods required, to arrive at suitable state of 'personal security'. In broad terms, 'personal security' does include the security of the individual in his 'work environment', his 'home environment' as well as when away from them both- that is at 'public places', when 'in transit' between places and so on. Thus, his well-being and security have to be taken care of at all times, and at all places, (he would be at). A very tough task indeed!

There is yet another dimension to 'Personal Security' tasks, viz. the willingness of the individual to both accept and observe the limitations that would need to be imposed on the individual's movements, lifestyle etc. Such a need arises due to the personal security measures that are germane to the individual's safety and security, and hence have to be enforced. You would have noticed that such concurrence of all persons in an organization is preferred and is advisable in regard to imposition of 'Physical and Information Security' measures; but the concurrence was not 'Mandatory'. However, in the case of 'Personal Security', the measures, to be effective, demands willing compliance by the concerned individuals to the limitations that will be called for by the personal security requirements. That is to say, the limitations in regard to the privacy and freedom of the individual, become 'Mandatory' in the case of 'Personal Security'.

Note that, ultimately, your personal security is your own responsibility.

Are you aware of all the personal security measures being implemented on your behalf? By and large you should be, (unlike the case of employees in an organization, who may not care to know the personnel security arrangements made by the employer, for their safety and security). Neither would he bother about the why's and wherefore's of security arrangements. The usual principles of security installations, that, everyone must be aware that security systems have been installed but they should be totally ignorant of what is fitted, where and how it works, (except for the concerned security personnel, that is), does not apply here, altogether. For example, when 'intrusion detection systems', (IDS), are installed, the employees should be made aware that some effective IDS has been commissioned, but only the security personnel must know what is fitted, where and how the system works. Similarly, the employees should not know how exactly an installed access control system works, what are its limitations etc. But, in the case of 'personal security' systems, it is advisable that the person being protected is not only aware of the methods employed but also about its capabilities as well as any drawbacks of the system. He should appreciate the possible 'gaps' and 'chinks' that could occur in the security arrangements, under what circumstances, and what he can do personally to improve the situation. Thus, without the active co-operation of the person being protected, the personal security efforts are bound to be less effective and could, ultimately, end in a disastrous situation, beyond the control of the security.

Personal Security Measures

The extent of variation in 'personal security' measures that are possible is enormous, from very simple 'common sense procedures', to extremely elaborate, highly sophisticated, technology intensive security environment that incorporate the latest in 'physical security', 'information security' and 'personal security' arrangements. The latter would be, ofcourse, highly capital intensive, perhaps need extensive manpower too and need 'money power' to afford such arrangements. Usually, the 'personal security' arrangements are 'unique'- matched to the 'specific threat perception' and the possible outlay that can be afforded, that is, the ability of the person or the organization concerned to foot 'the bill'!

Having an expensive, well thought out, sophisticated 'personal security arrangements in place is 'no guarantee' of 'one hundred percent security'! Against a determined 'suicide bomber' type of attack, who will be 'safe' at 'all times and at all places'? You can only minimize chances of a security lapse leading to a calamity, by using sensible precautions, strict personal security measures and suitable 'contingency plans' of escape from perilous situations, and availability of prompt and competent medical attention on the spot in case of traumatic attacks, that could not be prevented. Such measures should also be in place at 'all times' and at 'all locations'; and 'without exceptions'.

Personal security threats/security measures

Threats to the security of an individual could arise from his immediate environment, from what he does or does not (do), the types of persons he associates with and from persons having access to his proximity. The threats multiply, and take on new dimensions when he is on the move, or in transit between his home and his workplace(s); when he visits friends/acquaintances, when he goes to public places/public or private functions and so on. You need to constantly have a 'security cocoon' around him, [the target]. This should deny the possible 'attacker'—the 'time', the 'place' and the 'opportunity' to launch a *'successful attack'*. You cannot prevent or eliminate, always, 'unsuccessful attacks', when the opposition is so minded. But you can, and should, certainly minimize the possibilities and protect the target from any harmful effects, if and when an attack does take place.

Before you delve into the requirements of 'Personal Security' of high profile persons, (the VIPs), a look at what the run of the mill people can do to safeguard themselves and their families is worth the effort. They cannot afford high cost, sophisticated systems and procedures for ensuring their safety and security. So, what CAN they DO? First and foremost, they should apply the commonsense principles of 'Physical Security' to ensure security of their premises (and belongings). Where feasible, learn the art of self-defense to get out of tough situations, with none or minimum injury. In case of any hold-ups, do not argue but readily/voluntarily give up the purse or other belongings as they are of little consequence as compared to personal injury or loss of life itself. Carry on your person some of the handy modern gadgets that are available for personal protection. Whiff of a spray from an aerosol /pepper spray, sprayed on to the attackers face will temporarily immobilize him, enabling you to make a quick and safe getaway from the scene. Another gadget, when held towards the face of the attacker and pressed produces an almighty, unearthly shriek, which disorients the person for a moment, permitting you to slip away. Yet another, electric torch-like device, called "Taser", when operated (by pressing a button) shoots out a pair of prongs, connected to the device by wires, strikes the attacker and gives him a jolt of high voltage pulse-like a stun-gun. It will temporarily disable and keep him wreathing, (the greatest danger to the assailant, due to the "Taser", would be if/when he falls on the ground-*due to the fall itself*). In the meanwhile, you escape to safety. There can be a host of such devices available, but, when faced with an armed attacker, particularly armed with a gun, do not hesitate and give up your money or other personal belongings. Discretion is the better part of valour, in this case. There is no sense in trying to display your, perhaps inadequate, knowledge of the art of self-defense. Don't you try to dig out your aerosol can, etc. when it is inopportune!. It is totally inadvisable to incite the attacker in such circumstances. Safety of limb and life are definitely more precious than a few thousands of rupees, or even much more!

It makes great sense to keep good neighbourly relations but with the right type of neighbours. With others it is more prudent to keep a polite distance and totally avoid familiarity. You cannot always choose your neighbourhood or neighbours: Some of them couid be unhelpful or even unsavoury types. But, you can certainly be selective and choose to associate with the right types only.

Be unpredictable in your movements to keep the likely assailants guessing. Maybe you will thus also deflect their attention to some other more 'co-operative target'!

Be unostentatious. Do not flaunt your (newly acquired) wealth. A simple lifestyle is an effective camouflage that deflects undesirable attention. Drive home, to your family members, (and the staff), the basic security principles. Inculcate in them the good habit of NOT leaving around, carelessly, money, valuables, jewellery etc. They should be either on their person or safely tucked away under lock and key. Doors opening to the outside should be normally kept closed, bolted, and perhaps even locked when circumstances demand. Safety chain should be kept on, when attending to the door to callers; and use the peephole/video (if available) to identify the calling person(s).

Ensure that the antecedents of the staff/servants have been got verified by the police. The household people must be guided away from mixing/associating with strangers and persons of dubious character. They should associate only with known, reliable and upright persons. It is inadvisable to stay in independent houses if adequate and appropriate security is not available at all times. Particularly, in cities/urban areas, which are usually crime ridden, it is preferable to stay in apartment-complexes, which have proper security arrangements. Avoid crime prone neighbourhood, as far as feasible.

VIP Security

Now let us revert back to the question, How to protect 'High Profile Persons'? Are there any special protective measures to provide security to such 'Targets'? What special actions are called for? First and foremost, study and carry out a survey of all his day-to-day activities. Probably, bulk of his time would be spent either at his *'workplace'/ 'office;'* or at home. Study, in detail, these places and their surrounding areas to put in place appropriate physical security measures. Such measures implemented should be active at 'ALL TIMES'. Some structural additions/modifications may be required, at the locations, to put in place security measures that are effective and adequately secure the specific locations. Obtain necessary approval/funds and carry out the changes needed; whether the changes required are in regard to the perimeter fence/wall, entrances /exits, installation of traffic or other barriers, erection of special security systems and so on. In rare cases you may have to insist on physical change of location itself, to suit the required physical security needs, with alternate routes of ingress/egress, or for quick escape; if such a need were to arise. Such an occasion may arise when a fierce attack on the location takes place, which it is not feasible to withstand, with the physical and other security measures in place.

You would, therefore require suitable installation of devices to give advance warning of any impending attack on the location, apart from adequate security patrols and so on. These may include 'Surveillance Devices', 'Intrusion Detection Systems', 'Access Control Systems' and so on. The *'Security Surveys', 'Threat Assessments' and 'Risk Analysis' etc.*, actions that precede, would indicate what systems are needed to be put in place. In most cases, such technical installations implemented would also need to be cost-effective, no doubt even if meant for 'Personal Security'. However, in case of certain VIPs with a very high threat profile, such cost limitations may not apply. As long as the protective measures are necessary and feasible, cost considerations may not apply in such cases, when there are no available alternative, practical solutions. Even so, there are some limitations too. For example, to neutralize or initiate in advance any 'Remotely Controlled Improvised Explosive Device', (RCIED), or bomb that might have been planted near the locations, (or enroute of the V.V.I.P's planned movements between places), you cannot deploy, say, an 'EMP GENERATOR', (if/when such a device becomes available). The reason is, that such an action could result in temporary or permanent damage to domestic, public and other electronic installations, (TVs, Radios, Pacemakers, Music Systems and so on), in the neighbourhood. Probably, the usual businessman may find it more cost-effective to cough up any extortion/ransom demands, or come to a 'negotiated settlement', in the event of his being kidnapped etc., rather than make a huge outlay on guards and equipment. For him with his profit motive, this would be more affordable than any 'Personal Security' measures!

The next step is to consider what measures would be necessary when the 'target' is on the move. Planned and controlled decisions would be required in regard to all aspects of target's (and his escort's) movements. What alternate route to follow, when exactly to start out, what variations would need to apply in case of emergencies, which of alternate vehicles should be taken and in what order the vehicles should move out/ and their relative positions at various portions of the journey, and so on. Such aspects must be decided in advance of the move. But, *not so much in advance as for the information to become available to the opposition*, maybe by illegal means. So, all information in regard to the movements must be kept secret. It is extremely essential that no information regarding the movements become available to those not concerned with it; and certainly not in advance, in any case. No doubt a moving target is difficult to hit, and faster the target moves the more difficult it is to hit it. On the other hand, the faster a vehicle moves, the more the danger of an accident and greater the chances of it being a fatal one. Hence, the need is to be as fast as possible when on the move, but consistent with safety! How do you prevent smoke bombs, nerve gas bombs being thrown into the vehicle to immobilize it and follow up, perhaps, with a kidnap attempt? Or a grenade being lobbed into the vehicle? You may hence have to go in for a bulletproof vehicle with plexiglas or polycarbonate etc., windows, windscreens etc. You must always remember that use of communication devices, such as telephones, mobile phones, cell-phones, pagers, fax machines, e-mail etc. All entail security risk of information being intercepted, unknown to you. Hence, use of suitable counter-measures, including encryption of messages, may become essential during such communications. Where necessary and affordable use of armed escorts, decoy vehicles, bulletproof transportation, emergency medical retinue etc. are called for. Anonymity of all such facilities should be the hallmark, like use vehicle type and colour that are most common on the road in the region concerned. And so should the occupants merge with the regional background, (in dress, getup etc.), and look innocuous/unnoticeable. Beware of the modern cell phone with its special facilities of 'hands off' operation and 'silent ringing'. Such a device can be planted suitably in the vehicle, entourage etc. to effectively track movements/location of the 'target'. *Recall the cruise missile attack by the Americans on the locations where the cell phone (of Osama Bin Laden), was used!*

The third aspect of 'Personal Security' task if concerned with the measures required to be taken when 'The Target' is at locations other than his home or his business environment, which have already been secured by implementing the steps 1 and 2. What do you do when the target has to appear at public or private places such as 'Hotels', 'Parks', 'Exhibitions', 'Public Functions', 'Places of Worship', 'Stadiums', 'Residences of Friends and Relatives' and similar locations? Such locations may be enclosed or open to the sky; public where the general public have the right of entry/be present, or private where the right of entry could be restricted, the area may be congested, or bleak and sparsely inhabited and so on; the variations possible are many. So, there can be no single solution to the problem. The situations have to be looked at on a case by case basis to assess possible threats, practicable security measures that could be implemented and so on. An 'Reconnaissance', (RECCE), of the area in advance, *(Security Survey),* is a must, even when an earlier security survey record of the location is available. A fresh visit is needed to the place, as some new constructions, additions or changes could have taken place in the meantime, some camouflaged threats may have been put in place recently, some adversary may have hidden himself in the area, and so on. Carry out a fresh threat assessment, analyze the security risks that are entailed and make afresh judgement on the security measures that are now called for. There will be instances where the requirements necessitate the 'Target' to abstain from going to the location, (not attending the function etc.). That is, when adequate security measures cannot be put in place, (and IN TIME), as being impractical or unfeasible.

Do not forget that there is the possibility of the use of 'Decoys', whether by you or by the opposition. 'Duplicates', even, multiple persons of similar looks and appearance have been used in many cases, as 'Decoys' in very many instances. The Iraqi President is a unique case of having multiple persons, (reported to be as many as NINE!), deployed as 'Decoys' for his 'Personal Security'.

Security personnel and security equipment- complement each other.

The objectives of all the above steps are to ensure the basic tenets of 'personal security', viz., 'denial of access to the unauthorized and the undesirable persons' to the proximity of the 'target', and to eliminate all opportunities for any 'attack' on the 'target', even from a distance. Such attacks may be 'close encounters', or distant attacks with 'sniper rifles', 'rockets', 'land mines' planted, beforehand, or even ' RCIEDs'. Therefore, *the very first principle of 'personal security' has to be the assurance of 'total loyalty, reliability and unimpeachable integrity' of employees and household members, who have access to the 'target'*. You also have to constantly watch out for the possibilities of 'blackmail'/'subversions' etc. Before employment, the personnel must hence be chosen with extreme care in regard to the above traits, apart from their abilities to effectively carry out their respective assignments. After employment they must be treated with proper consideration, kept happy and given the *'golden handshake' on termination* of their employment/their retirement. Constant and adequate attention must be paid to their duty environments, their off-duty behaviour, associates etc. Protect them from possibilities of falling prey to the dangers of greed, blackmail, alcoholism, narcotic addiction, womanizing and so on. Periodic screening and rotation of personnel may be a necessity. It is very desirable for the security - personnel to have 'alertness' of the mind and the body as well as 'initiative' and the 'ability to take on the spot independent decisions' that entail the 'minimum risk' to the 'target', when unforseen situations arise.

Having taken care of the dependability of the household and staff, you now turn your attention to the *genuineness of the VISITORS*, and others who desire to approach the 'Target' or get into the neighbourhood. Proper screening of such persons is mandatory, not only for likelihood of carrying any weapons, but also regarding *their 'Real Intent' towards the target.* All the security arrangements and precautions become totally useless, when security personnel themselves permit, knowingly or unwittingly, persons with harmful intent against their employer whom they are to protect. The identity, the authenticity and even the antecedents of the visitors may need to be properly established, and any possible security risk fully ruled out, before they are permitted to approach the target, or his proximity. Such actions may not always be possible in regard to persons found loitering in the neighbourhood of the target's house or location. In such cases you would need to seek the assistance of local police to tackle such suspicious loiterers or vagrants. Obviously, resort to use of suitable technical aids to assist in the screening process becomes a priority. Thus, 'surveillance devices' like the 'CCTV', 'Intrusion Detection Devices', 'Access Control Systems', 'Explosives Detectors', 'Distress Alarms' etc. all are of immense help in 'Personal Security' work.

In case of *VVIP locations*, it therefore becomes *incumbent on the security personnel to ensure regular and adequate screening of the locations and the incoming materials* for listening devices, letter bombs, parcel bombs, explosives, noxious chemicals, bio-hazardous substances, RCIEDS etc. In special situations it may be necessary to also use suitable jamming systems to neutralize possible eavesdropping devices, or radio activated RCIEDS that might be present, and escaped detection during the screening process. Similarly, proper screening has to be carried out on all food articles and beverages that the VVIP is likely to consume against *presence of poisons, drugs, narcotics, radio-nuclide and other such dangerous substances.* Development of compact handheld high power laser devices raises the *danger of blinding* of the VVIP from a remote location by *use of such laser-guns.* This necessitates use of suitable laser protection goggles/sunglasses when possibility of such hazards exists. Cases are not rare of treated telephones that explode when attended to (lifting of the handset), parcel containing poisonous snake, or fruits injected with cyanide. There have also been cases of postage stamps, having poison in the glue, which would kill a person licking the stamp to affix it on an envelope, or new furniture ordered fitted clandestinely with explosives that could be remotely triggered, and so on. The security personnel concerned with the 'personal security' of the 'target' must be, therefore, well aware of all such and similar possibilities and protect the target from such dangers. The security manager concerned with 'personal security' of a VIP can hopefully evolve the necessary and adequate measures to counter all anticipated threats to the VIP. But, only when he is truly conversant with modes of possible attacks, offensive and defensive measures that are possible and techniques that are available to counter all such attempts. Please note however, that, *it may not be cost-effective to plan and implement all measures to protect the VIP* against all types of threats, whether relevant or specific to the particular VIP at that time and place or not.

Target Locations and Movements

The commonsense approach of ensuring that the 'Target's' movements are unpredictable, both in regard to the routes and the time of movements, could go a long way in frustrating the opposition plans for attacks. Predictable patterns in the target's movements make the gathering of information and planning of an attack by the opposition, a very easy task. The villains can then be quick to plan ahead and launch an attack, at his convenience, and to maximum destructive effect.

If feasible, the choice and layout of the premises of the target's residence or work location must conform to general security requirements. For example, no vehicle should be able to drive straight into the premises, unforeseen, from a public, or even, a private road. Approach of any vehicle should be observable from a long way off, (so also, its departure). No doubt, the perimeter fence/wall and the access point barriers/gates must be strong enough to withstand ramming by vehicles driven at high speeds. It should be possible to erect suitable vehicle barriers, (such as rumble strips, road humps, 'bollards', 'tyre-bursters', and so on), at suitable location(s) on the road to prevent a high-speed approach by any vehicle, or even to stop effectively any unauthorized or suspicious vehicle far away from the premises. A vehicle bomb could have deadly damage area, extending to over one hundred meters.

Security staff must keep a constant vigil and lookout for persons loitering in the neighbourhood, even with apparently valid pre-occupations. You never know when they are hired informers or agents of the opposition. Instant and reliable communication facility between the security, at the access points/gates and on patrol around the perimeter/secured area etc. and the security supervisor, as well as the Control Center is a must. Whether the need is to convey information, seek clarifications, pass on instructions/observations, report security-status, to ask for help/ SOS and so on. A record of such communication traffic and its later analysis give pointers in regard to improvements that may be required in the security arrangements.

The security will need to maintain very cordial relations with the local police, emergency services, medical support staff etc. Effective communications facilities are also required with those personnel to summon prompt assistance in case of an emergency that cannot be effectively handled by the security itself.

Actual working areas and living portions of the premises must be isolated from the front office, reception area etc. by the security. As these areas need to be more easily accessible. It may be advisable to have a competent doctor either in the premises itself, or close by for prompt and effective medical attention in case of an emergency. This is essential to minimize adverse effects of untoward happenings that could affect the target's health and well being.

Where a siege type of situation is expected to develop it would be necessary also to stock up provisions, first-aid items and so on. But in any case adequate contingency plans must be available with sufficient simulated drills, so that such unlikely events are promptly and appropriately taken care of.

Internal and External Communication Requirements

You would do well *not to entirely depend on the Public Switched Telephone Network, the PSTN, to maintain communication with the outside*. The PSTN may fail due to weather conditions, equipment faults, line faults, sabotage, accidental or intentional disruption at the exchange, strikes by the PSTN employees and so on. Who can rule out events such as cyclones, storms, lightning strikes, cloud-bursts, falling trees, floods and other such happenings that could result in breakdown of the PSTN services? Hence, some alternative means of reliable communication may be essential, like say special leased lines, captive radio links, (jam-resistant and secure type), etc.

Need for Outside Assistance/Backup

You may well need some protective elements within the premises for immediate ward off of any attacks, till suitable help can be summoned and arrive on the scene. Such outside help could be the local police, special-force from security agencies contracted for such purposes etc.

Screening of Mail/Movement of Items/Vehicles

All incoming letters and packages would need to be screened for letter bombs, explosives and dangerous substances. (It goes without saying that the premises and vehicles have also to be periodically checked, and particularly so after every maintenance/ repair work).

Vehicles are no doubt good means of transportation and even effective means for quick escape from dangerous situations. However, unless they are constantly attended to for timely and proper maintenance/repair, and secured at all times, they could be means for deadly accidents or death traps-accidental or ill-intentioned. It takes no great effort to plant explosives or other devices on vehicles left unattended, for moments only. Access to the vehicles should not be possible for the unauthorized, unreliable persons or those who could be easily subverted. System of watch and checks on the vehicles should enable prompt detection of any attempts at unauthorized access or tampering with its functioning. Only essential modifications should be authorized; and carried out under competent and continuous supervision. And such modifications, say bulletproofing, should be entrusted to only competent, reliable, reputed and trustworthy persons/workshops. The supervision must extend to checks on the use of correct materials, work to specifications, proper workmanship and so on. The vehicles selected for use must be appropriate for the purpose. It should be sturdy, stable and maneuverable, even at high speeds on bad roads, have good pickup as well as safe tyres that do not blow up, if punctured or shot at, (but carry on safely for a couple of hundred kilometers thereafter).

You should note that bullet proofed vehicle may protect the occupants from bullets shot from outside the vehicle but not protect them from explosions within the vehicle or close by, or even from serious accidents. If an explosion of sufficient power blows up the vehicle on the road, even when there is no serious damage to the vehicle, the high 'g' shock would surely leave the occupants with serious injuries/trauma, if not permanently incapacitate, or even kill them.

'Defensive Driving' is a very useful technique that the vehicle driver ought to learn. Such an ability could surely help one to get out of dangerous situations, to escape from pursuits and attacks on the vehicle when on the road, most of the time, if not always; either totally or with minimal damage. It may also enable to immobilize the opposition whilst you escape to safety.

Technical aids in personal security work (explosives detection/ neutralization)

Metal detectors, (MD), whether static or transportable types or hand held types, (HHMD), have almost become synonymous with screening of people for weapons or stolen material, because of their widespread use, in recent times, in screening of the public. All normal weapons and arms are expected to contain some metal content, which the MD detects. That is the reason that MD's will also give an alarm if the person being screened carries enough metal on him in the form of key bunch, coins, penknives, metal belt-buckle or even metal rods/plates inside his body, (used to set some fracture he might have had)! However, you must note that some special alloys may not give a response in the MD. So also, some arms like the Glock Pistol that are made of special plastic material, and hence do not produce any response in the MD. Therefore whilst using MD's to screen people for weapons be sure you have selected the right type of MD, the sensitivities have been correctly adjusted and maintained, (checked frequently for the purpose), and the above limitations of MD's are taken into account and catered for suitably in the procedures employed. Physical frisking, (random sample), of about 1 to 3 percent of the population screened is also usually carried out. Ofcourse, proper training of the operators of such equipment is inescapable. You must also ensure that persons with pacemakers implanted, or similar devices, are not subjected to screening by the MD's unless the MD's used are guaranteed to be safe for screening of such persons.

There are a *variety of 'Explosive Detectors' marketed* that claim to detect explosives. There are even some MDs with built-in 'Explosive Detector' marketed. Their effectiveness must be checked before such devices are purchased/employed. (Some attempts have also been made to incorporate specially designed 'Flash X-ray' walk through doorway detectors, to screen people for arms/explosives. But the likely harm to humans, repeatedly subjected to such screening, has made it a doubtful technique for general use). There are also several 'Portable Explosive Detectors', popularly called 'Sniffers', as they draw in samples of air at the locations being checked, (and check for explosive vapours). The air sample, hopefully, contain vapours or particles of explosives when present, or kept there till recently. And the device responds to such vapours/particles of explosives. The problem here is that, such devices may also respond to other substances in the atmosphere at the location, like cigarette smoke, some perfumes, certain chemicals etc. and, thus, false alarms can result. Therefore, before you consider purchase of any 'Sniffers', do conduct a rigorous test with those devices on samples of all types of explosives you expect it to detect. Equally important is that you conduct tests, as well, on normal substances you expect at the locations of interest such as, cigarette smoke, perfumes, common day-to-day use chemicals etc. Positive and reliable responses must be present to the explosive samples and there should be no spurious responses to the other substances, that is, to materials other than the explosives.

Purely *Gas-Chromatographic* devices are fairly reliable in this regard. But they are not really portable, nor do they give instant or even quick response. They need appreciable time to sample and respond with a strip chart type of display from which the presence or absence of the explosive material is deduced. In most cases this should not really be a problem, as such screening for explosives usually needs to be carried out quite in advance. For better portability, there are also devices with detachable air sampler probes that can reach even nooks and corners. The probe samples the air at the location of interest and is then attached to the transportable main unit, to check the air sample in the probe for particles of the materials of interest you are looking for- explosives, narcotics etc. The probe is then purged of the contaminated air before any fresh sample is taken. (You can also use a number of probes, so those samples can be taken from multiple locations, simultaneously, for quick response).

When you have a package to be scanned to identify what its contents are likely to be, without opening the package, the well known and perhaps the best method available to you is to pass the package through an X-ray machine. Portable X-ray machines are available, which can be easily taken anywhere to screen small packages or parcels. The parcel is placed between the machine and *an imaging fluoroscopic* screen, or *Image Storage Plate, (ISP).* When the X-ray beam from the machine passes through the parcel an image of the contents is formed on the plate (instant and transient display in the case of the fluoroscopic imager, a stored more permanent image which can be seen at leisure/convenience, in the case of the ISP). Such machines, however, expose the operator to unacceptable X-ray radiation, on a cumulative basis, when screening of very many parcels has to be carried out at a time. Therefore, *a more acceptable and convenient portable X-ray device is a Flash X-ray unit*. In this device, only a short burst of X-ray energy is passed through a parcel, (or a letter/envelope), and the image captured on a photographic film, preferably the instant Polaroid type. The operator is, thus, exposed to negligible X-ray radiation, ensuring his safety. Large size packages and baggage need the large, may be transportable, X-ray Baggage Inspection Machines, (*BIM*), similar to those used at airports. Some firms offer BIM along with built in Explosive Vapour Detectors. In recent times more reliable baggage inspection machines are being touted, using highly sophisticated techniques such as Nuclear Magnetic Resonance to positively detect presence of explosives.

When you have to worry about buried explosives, explosives placed at inaccessible locations/ corners etc., you go in for use of probes, spike microphones, microwave or ultrasonic Doppler radar devices, and so on to detect possible use of clock mechanisms. You need to employ mine detectors and metal detectors with suitable probes to search over locations for possibility of buried devices. Special probe attachments permit checking for devices placed underwater. Sophisticated non-metallic buried explosive devices are not easy to detect; they need special procedures or use of special portable radar devices with very narrow pulse-widths and broadband antenna search heads.

It must be mentioned here that, perhaps the most reliable method of detection of explosives, (or to track/detect humans, narcotics, fruits/agricultural products etc. for that matter), is use of the popularly known 'Sniffer Dogs'. Particular breeds of dogs are trained to detect particular types of substances, explosives in this case. Experiments have also shown possibilities in use of animals with long snouts like pigs, for such purposes.

RCIED, triggered remotely by radio, use radio receivers to receive the remote actuation signal. Radiation from the radio receiver of the *RCIED* is picked up, with special sensitive receiving equipment, to detect such RCIEDs. The danger of explosion of such devices could be removed for any specific time, at the suspected location, by use of suitable Jamming device, (JD), which prevents the triggering signal from being received in the RCIED as long as the JD is transmitting its signal near the RCIED. Thus, the *RCIED* can be neutralized. Thus, detection of radio controlled *RCIED* require considerable efforts and use of conventional devices like the probe, the metal detector, a mine detector and perhaps a highly sensitive receiver. Whereas, neutralization requires far less effort but use of more expensive devices- a good jamming device. The former requires search action to be carried out in advance, whilst the latter needs the equipment to be kept 'on' during the period the location is required to be maintained safe. You will observe that neutralization of an *RCIED*, remotely activated by wire or other means, (and not by radio), cannot be achieved by the above method. You will then have to cut the means of communication to the RCIED, that is the wire leading to it etc. to neutralize the device.

In rare cases, you may like to actually blowup any RCIED that might have been planted on the scene of interest, that is INITIATE the device. You have to remember that you must have an idea of the type and quantum, (or the strength), of the explosives present in the *RCIED* that you expect to be present at the location, as also its disposition and any add-ons, (such as steel balls or bundle of nails), etc. only then you can estimate the likely damage area due to its explosion. But initiation of an RCIED is not an easy task, unless you have already located it or actually have the exact remote control for the device. It is possible to devise an electronic device to simulate the signal similar to that of the remote control it you know the characteristics of the system. Alternately, the simulation device will need to produce all possible permutation and combination of expected frequencies of use, types and characteristics of likely modulations and so on; a very complicated task indeed, as hard Intelligence on the triggering mechanism is unlikely to be available, and in time. But, it is not impossible to achieve. Before undertaking initiation of such explosions you must ensure that the resulting explosion of the device is totally harmless to personnel, movables and structures around the location. Therefore, Detection and Neutralization are almost always the preferred methods to tackle such contingencies, rather than Initiation. You may, ofcourse, locate and defuse the device *in-situ*, when feasible, or recover and transport to a safe location where it can be, then, blown up under controlled conditions, without any worries of damaging property or injuring people.

If an occasion arises for transporting suspected explosive devices to some safe location for further investigation, it is best to use special containers for transporting *the device.* Such containers are kept cool, down to liquid nitrogen temperature so that the device remains inactive and do not explode during the transportation. At the safe location, then, the device could be defused or blown up safely, as may be required.

You wear protective armor, that is 'Bullet-Proof' vests, when you need protective measures against possible attacks on your person with arms or guns. 'Bomb Blankets' come in useful to throw over suspected explosive devices to confine and contain the explosion, if it occurs till a qualified 'Bomb Squad' can attend to the suspected object. This would minimize possible damage when the device explodes by smothering the explosion energy and confining any splinters and nails etc. to within the 'Bomb Blanket'; which should be written off thereafter.

When a suspected bomb is found the *'Bomb Squad'* may use a remotely controlled 'Explosive Ordinance Disposal' device, or 'E.O.D', to examine the object or 'Initiate' it from a safe distance. It is a sturdy platform mounted on wheels or tracks and containing battery operated and remote controlled prime mover. Suitable robot arms, also remotely controlled, are mounted on the platform with CCTV camera and high-pressure water jet or some other disrupter facility to neutralize or cause the object to explode, remotely from a safe location. The platform also contains suitable communication facility to the remote location, either wired or wireless or both.

The above is a brief indication of the types of 'Technical Aids' that play a major role in 'Personal Security' of high profile people. Technical devices used in security work are dealt with in some detail in later sections of the book. Hopefully, the above has enabled the reader to have a better appreciation of the large variety of aspects and solutions involved in 'Personal Security' problems; and, perhaps, to reach a sensible and cost-effective selection, to take care of the requirements of his specific problem. You have to bear in mind that in all cases of (security), it is ultimately the man behind the system who is the most important factor. He can be the strongest or, perhaps the weakest link in the security system; particularly where 'Personal Security' is concerned!

Personal Security and Manager's Tasks

A manager of personal security has practically unending problems to contend with, particularly where he has to take care of VIPs. New types of threats arise, as much due to technological advances as due to social, economic or political upheavals. *Dangers can arise in all the four dimensions*—'SPACE' (from air, on the surface and from underground or subsurface/underwater) and 'TIME'.

There have been reports of explosive devices planted, clandestinely, in bridges, culverts and other structures during their construction in the Mid East. The intention being to blow them up at will, remotely, even years later, when concerned VIP targets are expected to traverse the structures! There appear to be well founded reports of MOSSAD, the Israeli Intelligence Agency possessing master keys to almost all well known hotels around the world. The intention being to enable its agents to clandestinely enter the rooms in the hotels to carry out Intelligence operations, (passive or active); against targets who occupy the room. This should not come as a surprise. A clever thief arrested in Bangalore, had a similar modus operandi. He used to stay in different hotels for short periods and prepare duplicate keys to the rooms he, thus, occupied. After days or months he would check into such a hotel, obviously take a different room. When the occupant of the specific room for which he had the duplicate key goes out, he would clandestinely enter, rifle the possessions of the hotel guest and get away with anything valuable! Even otherwise, it is not too difficult to gain entry into hotel rooms, posing as hotel staff, visitor or any other acceptable pretext. Reports have been cited of 'Agents' penetrating even well guarded premises of their 'Target(s)', and planting explosives or other devices in telephones, furniture etc. The purpose was to later on activate them, remotely from a safe distance and safe from capture. It is not easy to apprehend such perpetrators, even when the concerned security organizations are on the job. By the time the organization is able to unravel the threads, gather adequate intelligence to be in a position to trap/apprehend the culprits, they would be long gone, perhaps even to a safe foreign country!

Notwithstanding the above, attacks on VIPs, (on others as well), do take place; more often than not, when they are on the move, or are attending public functions. 'Targets' are most vulnerable in such situations, though perpetrators of such attacks could well be less secure and more likely to be found out and apprehended in those conditions; because of likely high 'bandobast' arrangements. The well known cases of the dastardly and fatal attacks on Lord Mountbatten when on a boat-ride, John F. Kennedy travelling in an open limousine, on Rajiv Gandhi at a public meeting readily come to mind in this connection. They highlight the importance of Intelligence; information security and the necessity for strictly abiding by the physical security requirements that are called for on each specific occasion. They also emphasize the great hazards of public functions, as far as VIPs are concerned.

In this connection, it is worth noting the use of 'Duplicates', 'Clones' or 'Lookalikes' in attempts to mislead and misdirect dangerous attacks on VIPs. You must also take into account that *dangers to VIPs* could occur not merely from snipers, RCIEDs, buried mines or bombs, shaped charges directed towards target locations, vehicle bombs and suicide bombers etc. But could also occur *from missiles, poison gas/chemicals, attacks from the air (light aircraft, helicopter, RPV or UAV, balloons, hang-gliders, par-dropper, dirigibles etc.), or from underwater from frogmen, torpedoes, light submersibles etc.* All such possibilities have to be examined in detail and ruled out or adequately protected against!

Neither is the VIP without danger, when airborne. His aircraft or helicopter may be tampered with, when on the ground. The airborne vehicle may be attacked from the ground with Stinger or similar missiles. So also, there could be danger from other airborne platforms being used as launch pads for attacks. The magic of electronics, computers, micro-miniaturization and IT enable the opposition to choose the optimal time and location for such attacks. They could preposition the required devices/ explosives much before the event and remotely initiate them from suitable, unknown and (perhaps) distant location(s); and usually with total safety to themselves! Therefore, no lapse in 'Personal Security' arrangements would be permissible.

Thus, advance screening of locations and routes of travel, (to and fro), scrupulously securing the 'environment', and close scrutiny and supervision of all maintenance activities are a must. Securing the alternative travel routes along-with a '3 D-Cover', where appropriate could be inevitable in the 'Personal Security' tasks.

At all times, the security manager has to be aware, exactly, the persons to be protected, (the VIP and his family members/ retinue) are, and will be at any given time. So also that the relevant security arrangements at those times and for those locations, are in position and are effective. Provision must also be made that in the unlikely event of a person wandering away from such secured location(s)/kidnap situation etc. for *the* use of devices such as the 'Distress Alarm', by the target under duress. This would enable tracking and putting a trace on the subject, and rush suitable security and emergency medical aid to the target location.

What do you do when a potential threat scenario or a specific threat arises against the personage to be protected? You might have received definite information about a planned attack on the person. The 'information' may even be of doubtful nature. But, you have to analyze immediately and assess the 'expected' threat situation and the attendant risks to put in place, in time, the appropriate countermeasures. These may be reinforcing the proximity security, aborting a planned trip, cancelling attendance at a public/private function, choosing a totally different (alternate) route for a proposed journey or simply advancing or delaying a schedule and so on. In very special circumstances, the action may involve whisking away the person, anonymously, to a pre-determined safe location, where he can be protected with far greater assurance. You have to always bear in mind, that, it is extremely difficult to protect anyone from a determined suicide attack. And hence, *there should be absolutely no latitude permitted in 'Personal Security' arrangements, in spite of any insistence by the VIP to the contrary, when threat assessment indicate possibility of such an attack.*

Since, it may not always be possible to completely avoid an attack; you should also ensure suitable damage control measures to minimize effects of an attack, if it does occur inspite of best efforts of protection. Suitable contingency plans in position should include system of prompt first aid to injured persons and arrangements for their immediate dispatch to appropriate nearby hospital/trauma center, (which is equipped to provide necessary medical attention without delay). Simultaneously, security measures must be tightened around VIP and his family members from fallout of such an attack, and any reprisal/repeat attacks. As soon as possible, any attack must be followed by a detailed analysis of the events leading to the attack, the reasons for any security lapse/failure, and a total review of the security arrangements, to take adequately provide for such contingencies in the future. Necessary updating of all security arrangements should promptly follow.

Do remember that the security measures implemented do not themselves pose any danger, in times of an emergency. Take for example the protective measures used on windows, to prevent entry of burglars, protect from dangerous missiles etc. launched from the outside. When they do not have suitable arrangements for quick removal, or opening from the inside of the room to exit through, (the window), during an emergency, say, a dangerous fire that may occur in the room, the protective element itself, (window bars/grating), could very well become a veritable death-trap! This is particularly applicable in the case of high rise buildings, in the case of upper floors. In such cases, you should ensure metal grills on the windows, which can be quickly released and pushed out, (from the inside of the room, but cannot be tampered with from the outside). Or, do away with grills altogether, but provide suitable glazing along with any necessary intrusion detection/burglar alarm system. Similarly, all security installations/measures must be checked for personal safety, during normal operation, as well as during emergency conditions. To reiterate, all security proposals or implemented security measures must be examined afresh if they pose any safety hazards during an emergency, such as fires/floods/cyclones/thunderstorms/earthquakes/power failure/evacuation and so on. When such an examination evidences possibility of a safety hazard, the security measures/plans must be suitably modified until all such safety hazards are effectively removed. So, 'Security-With-Safety' must be the motto.

To recall the Russian Proverb: *"The Wise Man has Long Ears, Big Eyes and a Short Tongue"!* Further, he must have what Jonathan Swift seems to have enunciated: *"Vision is the Art of Seeing Things Invisible".*

Chapter 8

Principles of Operations/Process Security

"The superior man does not embark upon any affair until he has carefully planned the start"

—I. Ching

You have had a fairly close look at 'physical security, 'information security' and 'personal security' and may feel that there is nothing more left to security tasks, to worry about. That would be a mistaken belief. Because, the sum total of all security techniques come into play when you consider 'operations/process security' tasks. Such tasks encompass *'physical security', 'information security'* and *'personal security'* measures, *but also some additional special measures* specific to 'operation/process security'. The reason is simple-such tasks, apart from the need to maintain the integrity of the operation/process, has also to ensure the 'safety and security of the public', who may or may not be involved in the operations themselves, either directly or indirectly. Protection from 'manmade' and 'natural' 'hazards' may well pose major problems in such situations. Transportation of hazardous materials, nuclear industry hazards, toxic chemical operations and civil aviation are some obvious examples. Hence, a comprehensive look at the operations/process security scenario would reveal the home ground for a close interplay of various security techniques that could be possibly applied. This is quite apparent when you look at the security scenarios of airlines security (anti-hijack measures), nuclear installation security (security measures employed against malfunctions, possible meltdown, natural hazards, protection against terrorist attacks etc.), situations that could lead onto Bhopal gas type tragedies, and so on. Thus, operations/process security demands the ultimate honing of security skills and technology that one could possibly attain. One should be personally familiar with the total system. As John Le Carre states: *"A desk is a dangerous place from which to view the world"*.

Unique to the Operations/Process Security tasks is the essential feature of vigilant and constant monitoring of the 'Operations/Process' that is built into the system, to alert or give an alarm if and when the system approaches an unsafe condition or limit. Such monitoring is a *Real Time effort and not an event based or 'management by exception' type,* that could be prevalent in the 'Physical Security', 'Information Security' and 'Personal Security' scenarios. Another, equally important, aspect is the building in to the system 'Failsafe Features' which would automatically, (in most cases), bring the Operations/Process safely to a stop, when conditions/thresholds are reached which portend danger or unsafe situations; and suitable 'damage control' are initiated where needed. Normally, restart of the Operations/Process would be manually initiated after ascertaining the causes/reasons for the alarm or shutdown; and after making sure that the conditions are now safe for restarting of the operations/process. Further, 'Contingency Plans' are inevitable concomitants to Operations/Process Security Systems. And when dangerous conditions occur, such plans are to be automatically called into force, without need for any go ahead signals.

One may well question the need to provide 'Physical, Information and 'Personal' security measures when suitable safety systems are built into the 'Operations/Process' systems, along with damage control/contingency measures to protect the system from entering unsafe operating modes. Such a question is superfluous, and 'de-trop'. In fact, *'Physical'/ 'Information' and 'Personal' security measures* precede implementation of the 'Additional Measures' that are called for in the 'Operations/Process' security tasks, (in which all security measures are closely interwoven). Let us consider some dangerous possibilities. A workman may tamper with the limit switches of a vital machine to render it dangerous. A saboteur could set in motion dangerous situations by unplugging or making ineffective safety devices. A disgruntled or subverted employee may disarm an alarm or automatic recovery system. An arsonist may cause a dangerous fire resulting in damage to property and injuries to personnel. A terrorist may simply blowup the works. Or a 'Hacker' inserts a deadly virus into vital computer operations and so on! Such unsafe or insecure situations would be result of absence of suitable 'Physical'/ 'Information' and/or 'Personal' security measures in the system. The 'additional' security measures of 'Operations/Process security, by themselves, would not be able to stop the above dangers. Thus, the need for suitable 'Physical'/ 'Information'/ 'Personal' security measures as prelude/concomitant to 'Operations/Process' security tasks. Most often, it is the human element that is the cause of failures in systems, even in spite of built in safety features. The reasons could be either due to sheer negligence/ignorance, or due to deliberate tampering/interference with the security systems (ignore alarm conditions, delay damage control actions, change contingency plans and so on). Take the case of a coalmine inundation, which caused scores of miners to lose their life; because the guard on duty at the surface, at the lift, casually left his place of duty. So, when the alarm of (inundation) was sounded, the contingency plans/ damage control actions could not be initiated in time, the man on duty, who was to initiate the actions, being absent from his station-a case of sheer negligence!

Episode of Nanda-Devi loss of nuclear power pack (mountain peak).

Decades ago, there was a lot of hullabaloo about the case of a lost nuclear power pack, in the Himalayan mountains-the Nanda Devi peak, to be exact. A Plutonium based power pack had been lost many years earlier during an expedition to the Nanda Devi. The pack could not be retrieved, as it was lost in an avalanche, and sank into the snow. Such power packs are usually well protected. But, there could always be an unlikely event of the integrity of the unit getting breached. That would be pretty dangerous. Hazardous Plutonium could then leach and leak into the water sources originating around the region of the Himalayas; and become a deadly hazard to fish, fowl and humans living downstream and dependent on the water. The mighty and holy river Ganges originates in that area and flows through heavily populated regions of India. A high power expert committee of scientists deliberated on the problem and arrived at the conclusion that the only answer was to continuously monitor the water source, at the source, for any contamination by the noxious Plutonium. If and when any trace of Plutonium were to be found, an instant alarm should be raised to stop the people living (downstream) from ingesting the water, (or the aquatic creatures, like fish, originating from the river) for the duration the contamination is present and is not removed/stops. Such a task has to be carried on year after year after year in view of the very high half-life of plutonium-thousands of years! Or until the lost power pack could be retrieved somehow!! This is a great operations security problem. The task is thankless, boring and hopefully uneventful. The persons entrusted with the task could thus become negligent, careless, casual or complacent and not do his job properly. The maintenance of the equipment facilities utilized for the purpose may suffer and give wrong indications. The alarm system may fail to operate when needed because of disuse and lack of necessary checks. Even the people may not give required attention and importance to an alarm if raised. Contingency plans for supply of potable water, when such an eventuality occurs may have got buried in records and cannot be recollected by anyone, and so on. Hence, by the time the failure is noticed after such a contamination occurs, it may well become a national catastrophe due to extensive health problems in the people of the region (as well as dying animals and so on). This example is illustrative of what mammoth problems "Operations Security" could encompass.

In general, people are conscious, at least to some extent, about process security, because of safety regulations imposed upon them when they visit any factory, chemical plant, food processing unit and so on. Visitors are made to wear caps, helmets, overall; remove shoe, lighters/matches, tuck in loose clothes; avoid going near machinery; abstain from smoking and so on. But, they are far less aware of operations security.

We could look at an operation as a series of inter-linked and interwoven steps of activities that lead to achievement of desired goal, or state of affairs. An operation may thus culminate with the achievement of a single goal, securing of an objective, such as launching of the IRS satellite or surrender of the militants in the operation 'BLACK THUNDER'. Or the desired activities may continue, as in the case of airlines operation, railways operation and so on. Notice that a process too is a series of interconnected steps/activities leading to a desired result viz. a product(s), say cracking of crude oil to get petrol, kerosene, etc., obtaining a pharmaceutical preparation, a chemical and so on. Processes are usually repetitive or continuous in nature. For security considerations both the words may be used interchangeably. The security elements, however, in actual practice could well be different. Processes involve more of automation and technical control, whereas, operations usually involve considerable human interfacing. However, both may well entail hazards to personnel and the general public. Hence, the great emphasis on public health and safety which go beyond the general tenets of 'Physical Security', 'Information Security' and 'Personal Security'; but encompasses them also! A few examples will make clear the necessity for the addition of *'Operations/Process Security'* as a distinct classification in security operations, with its special requirements and security activities (as essential concomitant to safety and security of the operations).

Nuclear power generation—an example of operations/process security

Take the case of nuclear power generation. The safety regulations that have to be implemented go far beyond the normal requirements of factories act and public health safety regulations, that, most industries are concerned with. Every aspect of the processes involved, every nook and corner of the location and the environs/environment, each and every person at the location (even as a passerby) and the materials that pass through have to be closely and systematically organized and monitored. This is to ensure that neither harmful radioactivity arises, nor imbibed or passed on. Total containment and punctillous accounting and auditing of nuclear/radioactive materials must be ensured at all times, and at all places, to ensure that no misplacement, or loss of such materials occurs at any time. (Further, any such occurrence is spotted immediately, and appropriate corrective measures instituted forthwith). The system must provide an immediate "red alert", when any untoward possibility/event is in the making. Suitable contingency plan has to be in place to quickly locate any missing material and to immediately launch effective damage control methods. For example prompt detection of loss of radioactive needles used on a cancer patient in a hospital at Bangalore, and helped in the quick recovery of the items, as well as in the identification, and suitable treatment of all persons unwittingly exposed the radioactivity from the needles. Immediately the loss was detected, a specialist team from the Bhabha Atomic Research Center, (BARC), rushed to Bangalore with suitable detector equipment. The team investigated the loss, scoured possible locations at Bangalore, to promptly locate and secure the missing needles. This was essential to prevent/minimize the general public getting exposed to the radiation from the needles by being present, (unwittingly), in the neighbourhood of their location. They would be unaware of the consequences to themselves too, and are likely to contract radiation sickness, by being subjected to dangerous levels of radiation, which would result in radiation sickness-difficult and time consuming to detect/treat.

In view of the likely horrific danger to the public and the environment, very special and stringent precautions/security regulations have to be observed in the preparation, storage, transportation, use and disposal of nuclear material as well in the design, construction, utilization, maintenance and dismantling of nuclear installations. These include but extend far beyond the conventional physical, information and personal security measures and techniques. For one thing, effective shielding, remote handling, remote detection and control are de rigueur.

Design of most buildings in other industries, usually have to follow only the normal building codes applicable for the region. (With the use of modern technology and materials, the factor of safety, or factor of ignorance as some may call it, coming down for such constructions from the earlier more than 5 (five) to maybe less than even 2 (two). In the nuclear industry the position is different. The factor of safety has to be increased to take into account unlikely events, such as a fully loaded jumbo-jet aircraft crashing into the building. Even then, there should be no damage to the radiation shielding, and no spilling of radioactivity as a result of such an accident. It is mandatory to monitor the daily and cumulative radiation dosage the workers are exposed to in the environment. Strict accounting of all nuclear materials is essential at all stages of handling/processing/storage/transportation/ use and disposal, as already mentioned earlier. Transportation containers gets specially designed with adequate shielding integrity, even if the vehicle carrying the containers get involved in a serious accident. They also prominently display the logo indicating radiation danger. Special security arrangements are also needed when a mass of nuclear material is moved around, to protect against dangers of loss, hijacking by terrorists etc. Apart from effective containment of radiation, information about the move, the route to be followed, the time schedules etc. are kept secret, to avoid possibilities of hostile attacks, whilst on the move. The material is also physically secured against all but determined assault on the container. The location of the material whilst on move is monitored by reliable means, at all times until the package is delivered at the destination, safely and intact. *Periodic and stringent audit is carried out to ensure that the accounting is proper and is a true reflection of the position on the ground.*

Resort to advance Technology and Technical Security devices

Extensive resort to Advance Technology and use of technical security devices is hence a necessity to achieve the above needs. Extensive use of Intrusion Alarms, Access Control Systems, Telecommunication Systems, Special Packaging Techniques (including use of Electronic/Time Locks, Coded Communications, Proximity Alarms, Failsafe Shielding, Vehicle Locating Systems etc.), is not uncommon. The design of the transport container ensures that the integrity of the package is maintained even if the train or motor vehicle carrying it crashes, even at high speed. The system ensures that only the authorized person can unpack the material from the package/container. This is to make sure that the material remains properly shielded, and protect the environment from its radioactivity even when unauthorized persons make attempts to break into the package unwittingly or intentionally.

All steps of the processes involved are designed to be in the failsafe mode. For example, if the power supply to the reactor were to fail, the control rods automatically drop down to instantly stop the nuclear reactions. This prevents any runaway condition that may lead to the nuclear core meltdown or the "China syndrome". All stages of operation are designed so that there is no spillage of radioactivity at any location, at any time and under any condition of operation/non-operation-however unlikely it be! Further, in the unlikely event a spillage does occur, suitable contingency plans are invoked and implemented automatically to control the spillage and to contain and limit possible danger and damage to the environment and personnel. If such an unlikely event were to pose danger to beyond the confines of the reactor areas, the system has to ensure an immediate alert and alarm to the general public of the possible danger. The general public, in the region, has to be constantly briefed of what they have to do when such an alert/alarm is raised. They may even have to be evacuated to safe places when such an event portends a major hazard or a nuclear disaster. Suitable arrangements must also be ensured to take adequate care of such displaced persons, until they can safely return to their homes. Appropriate disaster warning and control systems have to be part and parcel of such process security tasks. Above also calls for facilities for a quick and thorough screening of the public for identification of those with high level of absorbed radiation. The facilities must include suitable recording and analysis of the data and methodology for effective treatment of affected persons, *in situ* if feasible, but definitely in time. Thus, safety, integrity and security of plant/equipment/ plant personnel and the general public as well as the environment involved are the prime features of Operations/Process Security tasks. Biotechnology and some Chemical processes may also need equivalent or perhaps even more elaborate security arrangements.

Airlines operations, is yet another example of operations/ process security

Consider another typical example of Operations/Process Security-Airlines Operation. The operation involves co-ordinated activities connected with airports, aircraft, air lanes, ground support systems, ground-staff, airlines personnel, passengers, cargo, communications, ticketing/reservation systems and so on. Apart from such an extensive list of interconnected of tasks, it is also concerned with suitable surface feeder transportation, hotel accommodation for aircrew and stranded passengers etc. To add to the above normal activities, you have to worry about connected aspects of possible air crashes, flight cancellations, maintenance operations, etc. To top this all, there is the frightening possibilities of bomb threats, sabotage and hijacks. Thus, airlines operations involve all aspects of security viz., Physical Security, Information Security, Personal Security and its unique needs of Operations/Process Security.

The first area of concern in regard to security objectives of an airline operation is, naturally, the safeguarding of its own assets-physical/material, vital data/information/tangible and intangible facilities and personnel. These include airports, airstrips, aircraft, hangers, maintenance facilities, operational installations (radar, communication facilities, reservation and ticketing, baggage handling and so on), training establishments, personnel, etc. Usual Physical, Information and Personal Security appropriate to the situation for such establishments will meet the objective. But, the flip side of the coin—*safe guarding the operation and the passengers and the public pose unique additional* requirements of safety and security that make airline operations a typical Operations/Process Security Scenario.

Thus, the airport, aircraft, hangers etc. may be secured with physical security measures such as perimeter security, area security and spot/local security (Outer and Inner Defenses). The running operations maybe protected with information security measures such as proper document control, encryption, auditing and so on. Appropriate personal security measures may be deployed in regard to crew, maintenance operations etc. But, these measures are insufficient and inadequate to cover bomb threats, hijack attempts, or extreme type of situation-terrorists attacks on airborne aircraft (say shooting down with ground-to-air missiles). Possibility of such threats to security of passengers and the public necessitate additional security measures which may also include more elaborate physical, information and personal security tasks.

Hence, arise the need for screening of passengers and their baggage for weapons and explosives. This brings in the concept of cooling down period for cargo, before their loading into an aircraft. (It must be mentioned, however, that with the availability of electronic timers, clocks etc., a cooling period of erstwhile just over a day is no longer adequate as a safe period of time. Because, the time for any hidden explosive to go off can now be set for days, weeks or even months, or even set off remotely! This is not to say that, such cooling period of over a day or two would be now redundant. Remember, that a watch or a clock is still the most easily available and, perhaps the most inexpensive timing device one can get and use). So also, extensive use of technical measures such as CCTV and baggage screening systems, effective Access Control Systems, personal frisking measures, use of explosive detectors and dog squads, elaborate communication facilities, continuous surveillance of vital areas and spots and so on. No wonder any package left unattended in an airport is promptly whisked away and subjected to close scrutiny/cold storage.

The method of ensuring that every passenger whose baggage has been loaded into an aircraft does board the aircraft, before the aircraft is permitted to take off, is no doubt a good security precaution. But this in itself is not good enough, since it does not eliminate the possibility of say a passenger, heavily insured, blows up the aircraft when airborne, so that the insurance beneficiary is well taken care of. Or, a terrorist suicide bomber gets aboard with a bomb in his baggage; or he somehow convinces a passenger to carry a package for him in that passenger's baggage/ clandestinely introduces the bomb into that passenger's baggage, which then gets loaded onto the aircraft. The aircraft can then be blown up conveniently. Only means to avoid such possibilities, is to properly screen every baggage that gets loaded onto an aircraft that will be taking off, or has passengers on board.

Constant monitoring and effective contingency plans are mandatory

Ofcourse, the parallel action of having appropriate and effective contingency plans for all possible dangerous eventualities is of vital importance. The emergencies may arise, whether expected or unexpected, due to technical troubles, human failures, natural catastrophes, man-made crisis or calamities such as hijack or hostage situations and so on. It must be observed that it is not adequate to have wonderful contingency plans unless all concerned in the operations, the passengers included are fully educated/trained as to what each one has to do, how and when and under what conditions. Such emergency situations are normally rare and are unlikely to occur, hence need constant reminder and reinforcement of actions to be taken, if an emergency does occur. It is always advisable to test and improve on the effectiveness of the plans, by well devised, and conducted simulated exercises, wherever feasible.

Obviously, a system of constant monitoring of the environment go a long way for timely and effective implementation of such well thought out contingency plans. This is necessary, not only to deny opportunities for occurrence of such emergencies, but also to give an early warning of incipient emergence of such situations. Therefore, this constant monitoring of process/ operations is the inevitable and concomitant requirement for operations/process security.

Call for Special Requirements

Operations/processes involving high voltage installations, hazardous chemicals, high power explosives, nuclear materials, hazardous biotechnology products, and other such substances require special, elaborate arrangements; considering not only the day-to-day, but second to second, or even nanosecond state of affairs. No wonder everything could be special about it-special environment, special buildings, special containers, special handling, special transportation techniques, special storage arrangements, special inspection and maintenance facilities and, of course, specialist personnel, (specially trained for the purpose). Disaster warning and population evacuation procedures may also have to be catered for to handle contingencies. Use of easily recognizable danger signs, logos are used to caution, and keep the unwary away from the neighbourhood of such hazardous operations/ processes, materials etc. Populated areas and environmentally unsound regions must be avoided in the storage, transportation, preparation and handling of such materials/processes. Several examples of such areas can be sited. Regions, that are earthquake prone, or seismically active. Locations where the underground-water tables could get polluted. Areas where strong wind movements could carry the potentially dangerous, accidentally spilt, or leaked material to the surroundings. Places where heavy precipitation occurs that could carry the hazards to far off areas, and so on. Hence, Operations/Process Security tasks require involvement of variety of specialists and experts in diverse fields to ensure the safety and security of the tasks.

Offshore-oilfield operations, yet another example of Operations security

Another typical Operations/Process Security Scenario reveals yet other dimensions of such tasks—Offshore Oilfields Operations. The security requirements become nationally and internationally important commitments. All equipment, facilities, interconnections, components etc. used therein must be certified and maintained "Intrinsically Safe", that is, in using them, there is no possibility of any arcing, sparking, generation of corona etc., which could set afire inflammable fluids. This is an inescapable safety requirement. The platforms themselves are likely to be located in isolation, perhaps, in international waters, and maybe near international/national shipping routes and perhaps an international air-flight corridor is overhead. Hence, movements of ships and aircrafts in the neighbourhood cannot be totally debarred. Nor can movement of subsurface crafts, (submersibles etc.), near about the rigs be prohibited. Unless, that is, they are likely to endanger the safety of the rig/ environment. It is also impractical, normally, to bedeck the rig with expensive deterrent/protective gear against intrusions. Nor can it be converted into a fortress with all manners of defensive gear or weapon systems to protect it from likely threat of attacks from the air, sea or the subsurface. But nothing prevents one, (on the other hand it could be essential), from mounting on the rigs effective communication gear, comparatively inexpensive intrusion detection and alarm/alert system and suitable contingency plans. These are essential to have an advance notice of possible hostile attacks on the rig and enable timely and safe shutdown of the rig and evacuation of the oil-rig personnel to safety, when such an occasion arises. You need to guard also against the unheralded possibility of occurrence of natural hazards such as tidal waves, hurricanes etc. Sufficient facilities must exist to provide adequate notice to allow timely evacuation of personnel and safe shutting down of the rig. From the overall economic and security points of view, it makes sense to have a multiplicity of platforms spread apart and lay multiple underwater pipelines, (which follow different routes and perhaps terminate at different locations (terminals on land)). It is almost impossible to protect and guarantee the safety and security of a few rigs and a single pipeline, however sophisticated and complex the protective system you employ. Ofcourse you need a system for quick shutdown of the operations, in case of an emergency, to prevent a blowup or runaway type of operations, or deliberate sabotage by villains. *The basic tenet is* "not to put all eggs in one basket", and to protect the "eggs" from damage or cracking up, due to accidents etc., by suitable effective packaging.

Small is Beautiful and Distribution of Assets

The above basic concept of redundancy for superior security is extendable to other operational security scenarios such as Transportation, Power Generation, Energy Sector, Healthcare Operations and so on. In so far as security scenarios are concerned it would appear that "small is beautiful", and "distribution of assets" *is advisable, whether it is wealth or costly installations* !

Summary of Suggested Security Practices

NOTE that, Operations/Process Security envisages the complete range of security principles, the well-known aspects of Physical Security, Information Security and Personal Security, as well as, additional security aspects that are peculiar only to Operations/Process Security scenarios. (These are the particular concerns regarding safety and security of the public, the environment etc., apart from that of the operations/process themselves).

Physical Security Measures

You do need the perimeter fencing with limited access/entry points installed, maybe, with access control turnstile gates, guarded by security personnel to check the identification of those (and vehicles/materials movement etc.) seeking access to the controlled area, (maybe even exit control). In special cases, Automated Access Control Systems maybe used, backed up with security guards; and these may function with ID Cards (Magnetic Stripe, Proximity principle, Smart Card, Wiegand, Barcode etc.) or even use some biometrics sensors for access/exit control.

In case of extended perimeters, you may need pillboxes or watch towers for the guards to obtain an unobstructed view of the perimeter and the surrounding areas. Perimeter lighting, as appropriate, is usually de rigueur. Suitable tracks will be required along the perimeter for the patrolling. When guards are few in number, or in special circumstances, you may need to provide them with trained dogs to accompany them during the patrols. In major installations, time clocks may be required to keep track of the guards to ensure effective patrolling. There may also be a need to provide the guards with suitable communication facilities such as hand held radios, so that they can keep in touch with each other and the central control, as well as seek for prompt assistance when needed. As per requirements of the security scenario the guards may carry suitable protection devices-from the simple baton/nightstick, to more sophisticated stun-gun, bullet proof vests, etc., apart from the regulation flashlight, to help in the subjugation of an intruder when called for.

It is not always necessary to have the security/guards as employees of the business/organization, but can be contracted with a suitable security agency. But, when guards are your employees there are a few worthwhile benefits. Their loyalty to the organization, better incentive to do their duties properly, greater familiarity with the facility as well as better knowledge about the company personnel. This may well lead to better liaison with all concerned and more effective control on security aspects, and perhaps less absenteeism, far less turnover of security personnel.

On the other hand, contracting out of security have the advantage of absence of unionism, less expense, flexibility to increase and decrease the number to suit time to time/emergency requirements and perhaps greater objectivity on the part of the guards. Further, the contractor may provide the guards with suitable special stores to help them in their tasks. However, there is the flip side to this too. High turnover of the personnel, usually due to not too attractive career opportunities, less or no attachment to the organization, less awareness of the facility and its personnel and so on. Further, there is the big question of the exact liability of the guards and the contractor in case of a security lapse leading to consequential losses/ damages/calamities, even when the negligence of the security personnel is established. Therefore, for Operations/Process Security scenarios it could be inadvisable to go in for contracted security.

Between the perimeter and the actual buildings/installations/ facilities, to be secured, lie areas, which, you need to ensure, are free of obstructions to avoid any blind zones, as far as security aspects are concerned. It is best ensured at the design and layout stage of the project with proper layout of the buildings and installations, and other allied structures that may be required. The layout design must take into account the needs of suitable landscaping, layout of lawns, beautification of the areas, etc., as well as requirements of perimeter lighting, lighting of the installations as well as the areas in between.

The buildings themselves must have minimum required access and exit points and other openings, consistent with safety requirements, to minimize security problems. Provision of windows at low levels-close to the ground and structures providing ease of access, are positive invitations to likely intruders. It is essential to remember, that, any large opening—windows, skylights, trenches, trapdoors, gutters, large water or effluent/drainage pipes, air-conditioning inlet/outlet/ducts—are all possible access/exit points for intruders as well as for the stay-behind perpetrators. All such openings have to be properly protected with suitable grills, gratings, alarm systems and so on.

The door layouts, the design of door jambs, doors themselves, the hinges, latches etc. must be appropriate and of adequate strength for the enclosures and contents to be protected. The system should be resistant to battering, levering, sawing, hammering and so on. Where high security needs are present, the design may have to envisage deterrence against use of drills, gas cutting, the thermic-lance, explosives and so on. It would be very foolish to have sound door design and layout, without effective locking arrangements, key control etc.

The design and layout of the buildings and facilities should provide appropriate compartmentalization from security and safety requirements. Such compartmentalization also enables additional security access controls to be introduced to control the movements of personnel, materials, goods, transportation units and vehicles, to and from critical locations, strictly on need basis, (as well as enhanced fire safety measures). In high security areas, suitable biometrics access control systems may be installed. Such biometric systems use fingerprint, palm-print, voiceprint, retinal pattern, signatures, etc. or a combination of them. Further, use of digital locks, time locks, intrusion alarm systems, and so on, may be considered. Computerized records of entries and exits of materials, goods, vehicles, and personnel may be resorted to, for further checks, analysis of patterns, audit, investigation of security lapses if and when they occur and so on.

In many cases, resort to suitably designed CCTV system may be a great advantage. You may or may not require both day and night coverage. Where night coverage is essential you may have to go in for suitable low light level TV or LLLTV cameras for surveillance of areas with inadequate light or normal ambient light only. Such cameras can easily provide good enough images, day or night, without need for extra illumination. Thus, with properly positioned cameras with their characteristics—such as field of view, focal length, sensitivity and resolution etc., should be selected to match the surveillance requirements, and effective coverage of the total facility. (Perimeter and surrounding areas, exits and access points, vehicle parking areas, loading/unloading areas, buildings and installations, vacant areas and structures in between, as well as inside the buildings and other complexes). It is the usual practice to go in for cameras with fixed orientation and fixed focal length systems only, except for special circumstances where one may be required to have zoom, pan and tilt arrangements. Appropriate recording and playback facilities help in audit and analysis of security situations, particularly in case of critical area coverage such as banks, lockers, high security locations etc. This is great when you need to recreate the situation just before, during and after an incidence of intrusion or security lapse. You can examine the situations through the recording by scanning it at various speeds, forwards and backwards, with freeze frame where required to spot the problems, gather evidence and so on. Such operations should be failure free and must have suitable backup power supplies. Obviously, necessary expertise is a must too.

Vehicular traffic has to be strictly regulated. Parking must be in designated parking places and well monitored. No vehicular traffic must be permitted in hazardous locations, except on strict need basis and use of vehicles specially designed for such applications. Proper record of all vehicular movements (and materials/goods/persons) must be maintained for later checks as needed.

Information Security Measures

Screening of personnel will be to appropriate degree of "tightness" as relevant to the Operation/Process. But, all employees must be screened periodically, for their loyalty, integrity, behaviour etc. against possible subversion, alienation, ideological influencing and so on.

Strict enforcement of laid down security procedures in regard to use of locks, safes, almirahs, vaults and so on is inescapable. So also, in regard to the introduction and use of office equipment, computer facilities, communication systems, presentation systems and so on should be in consonance with appropriate security policies and procedures. Such facilities need to be constantly monitored and checked for presence/introduction of privacy intrusion techniques like listening devices, telephone taps and so on.

Handling of information, (particularly sensitive information), its creation, modification, storage, transmission and destruction should be strictly in accordance with appropriately laid down security policies, procedures and techniques, including requisite auditing. Suitable cipher systems would need to be used in communication, computer and information processing systems to ensure required security.

All sensitive information, in any form (oral, written, typed, mimeographed, printed, maps and graphs, magnetic and optical media and so on), sensitive and critical materials must have strict, and suitable procedures for generation, recording, inspection, storage, transfers, disposal, destruction, accounting and auditing; and the procedures must be properly enforced.

Note that "Information Security", and thus "Operations/ Process Security" too are facing major, fresh problems due to the Internet. In earlier days of Computer Viruses, they used to propagate through the medium of spurious/pirated software and floppy disks. But now, the use of the Internet is getting more and more widespread, with its readily accessible Servers, (of the Internet Service Providers, or ISPs), and use of even on-line connections to millions of computers all over the world. Thus, computer "Viruses", "Worms", "Trojan Horse" and "HACKERS" can have easy access to infect, corrupt, and affect computer operations all over the world, and almost instantly through the Internet network. The problems that are/will be faced are innumerable. To mention a few watch out for *masquerading or impersonation, misinformation, misrepresentation, programme manipulation, fraud for gain, cyber forgery, unauthorized access, interception, unlawful and heinous activities of peddling pornography/enticement of children and the unwary etc. Ofcourse you also have activities for fun or personal gain-such as hacking/spoofing/network overloading/planting of viruses/ worms/Trojan Horses/junk mail, and all manner of scams. But there are still more heinous affairs as highlighted recently in newspapers,* "Internet turning child sex industry into global scourge"!

Cyber crimes can be broadly grouped under the following:

- Hacking for fun, gain, spite, etc.
- Committing fraud by Unauthorized Access, Interception, Programme Manipulation, Computer Forgery, Tampering with ATMs, Manipulating Bank Transactions/EFS, E-Commerce Irregularities, etc.
- Telephone "Phreaking", Internet Time Theft, etc.
- Sabotage and Vandalism like creating Computer System Breakdowns by introduction of Virus, Logic Bombs, Worms, Trojan Horses, or Sabotage/Vandalism of Computer Hardware/Software/Auxiliary Equipment/Installations, targeting planning and execution of terrorist activities, etc.
- Interception/Theft of Trade Secrets or other Classified Material in Computer system, etc. and
- Use of the Internet to with intent to commit Criminal/ Terrorist Offences of Pornography, Gambling, Spoofing, Masquerading, Extortion, Kidnapping, Luring the Innocents, Hate Mail, etc.

The danger is not of mere vandalism as such but even "CYBER-TERRORISM", an all-together different ball game, where even well established and up-todate National Security Agencies may well flounder! You should also be aware that the economy all over the world is becoming more and more Internet-driven; so the damage can create widespread havoc-all over the world! *You can safely expect the twenty-first century to be the epoch for Cyber-spying, Cyber-crimes, Cyber-terrorism, Cyber-wars, Cyber-Intelligence, Cyber-detectives and so on!*

Note that the worst virus attacks on computer systems have been through the Internet e-mails, particularly ones with attachment, be it Code Red, Nimda, etc. Here are some (simple) methods to minimize the dangers.

- Use difficult passwords, that include both letters and numerals.
- Use the computer off-line, except when you actually do need to go on-line.
- If the system has a number of ports, keep only those ports open as are essential to function at that time.
- Use proper virus protection software, (and keep updating the same without delay; they can be usually downloaded free!).
- Invariably make regular backups, at least of vital/critical data and software.
- Use firewalls between your computer and the Internet/on-line connection.
- Do Not, repeat DO NOT, open attachments unless you are certain of the origin and the relevance of the mail (and its content). Preferably, confirm from known sender that he has actually sent the mail AND the attachment, (attachment could be sent without knowledge of sender by infected computer to all e-mail addressees, automatically!).

Then, you can also expect an exponential increase in credit card frauds/scams. Unauthorized use of someone else's credit card-lost card/stolen card/cards intercepted from mail, etc. the villain gets hold of genuine card numbers by various means, including hacking into the Internet/interception of mail/telephone/ e-commerce orders, or conspiracy with someone who legitimately gets access to the numbers like a hotel/establishment cashier, and then misuses the number to order stuff/facilities/tickets etc. through the Internet/telephone, etc. A common method used by unscrupulous traders is use of multiple copies of sales receipts/ invoices and later submit false receipts to claim amounts from the unwary card holders account. Even duplicate/multiple "copies" of genuine cards and spurious cards that appear to be genuine are fabricated to simultaneously use at many places to get maximum gain in a short time and then discard those particular cards, prepare new ones to carry on the scams. Then of course you have to watch out for getting less than what you are entitled to, like an ATM closing the operation by dishing out less amount than what you processed for and you get no redressal from the Bank either!

You should also observe that, there is continuing interest and exploitation of mobile/wireless connection to the Internet, (as is being increasingly catered for at airports and other places, abroad). Busy people are likely to quickly open their laptops to use such readily available connections to carry out their urgent messaging/business through the Internet. In such situations, unless the lap-top/palm-top/mobile user conscientiously uses encryption, others in the vicinity could easily pick up vital information/data. (In view of the open wireless connection freely broadcasting the transmission).

So, all you security guys-wake up*, and do, quickly, emerge from the "Old and Traditional Security Outlook."* Take your rightful place in the *"New Security Tribe". Stand up and be counted amongst* the Technology-CYBER-savvy, *and* forward looking "Security-Wallahs!" Luckily for us, India has world leaders in IT, both in the academic field and in the industry. (Then we have teenage geniuses too like Ankit Fadia, whose book "The Unofficial Guide To Ethical Hacking" was released by Macmillan India Ltd., is understood to be creating waves of admiration abroad, supposedly, even in FBI circles!).

Contingency plans, disaster management/disaster warning and evacuation

Operations/Processes must have appropriate CONTINGENCY PLANS in place, apart from necessary Standard Operating Procedures (S.O.Ps), relevant to them. They are essential to enable effective tackling of any untoward incidents, accidents, emergencies, hazards or disasters (manmade or natural, and to protect from health, occupational and environmental hazards). Each and every stage of the operation/process/facility must have incorporated in the system suitable mechanisms to protect against all possible and probable causes for failures, accidents and creation of hazards; and these must be FAILSAFE. Threats from organized crimes, labour unrest, arson, intrusions, kidnappings and abductions (needs EXECUTIVE PROTECTION programmes too), bombings, terrorism and so on should be properly guarded against.

(First of all what exactly constitutes a disaster must be exactly spelt out in the procedures to enable prompt and appropriate actions/procedures to be called up and quickly implemented to manage that particular disaster, when it occurs. Obviously, this is necessary to obviate the likely questions of who should do what, and when; since the persons involved and the activities relevant could be quite different for different types of disasters. It is essential to have a forum to spread awareness amongst all concerned, including the general public; and to lay down sensible and practical guidelines/codes for construction, hygiene, municipal facilities etc. to be covered in the areas likely to be affected by specific types of disasters. No doubt, effective communication and public alerting/warning systems, that function even under all adverse environmental conditions/disasters are indispensable. Detection systems such as thunderstorm/cyclone warning radar, properly located are of tremendous help in providing early warning of impending disasters. Protective facilities, such as bunkers and underground/shelters setups to safely house/feed etc. the affected public during disaster periods, (and the aftermath), have to be built and run properly. Suitably trained emergency services to promptly/correctly and effectively respond to disaster occurrences is a major task in itself. Without all the, above effective disaster management will remain a dream and a talking point only).

No patchwork methods can help much to protect against natural disasters. It requires advance planning and putting in place suitable systems and porcedures. Floods, thunderstorms, cyclones, earthquakes, tidal waves, land slides, lightning-strikes etc. give little or no advance warning of their occurrence. Most of the man-made hazards on the other hand could well be disasters waiting to occur, when not properly monitored and controlled. Building collapses, aircraft crashes, dangerous leakage of hazardous materials/radiation etc. are preventable when safety requirements are NOT flouted; and suitable protective machinery exists against tampering. Implement suitable DISASTER WARNING system, along-with relevant, and a well-planned evacuation procedure. Effectiveness of the same should be tested, periodically, with simulated exercises.

Ofcourse, a Disaster Warning system without suitable Emergency Services and Procedures would be like having a cat without teeth or claws to save us from the menace of mice!

Check on Employees and Visitors

It is a must to screen all visitors, suppliers, manufacturer's representatives, external service/maintenance personnel etc. Their movements within the facility must also be controlled to need basis only, as well as, suitably monitored, till their safe exit.

Periodic sensitization of the employees for security awareness and security requirements is always advisable, and cannot be over-emphasized.

Sound monitoring procedures and good maintenance practices for all stages and aspects of operations/processes cannot be over-emphasized.

It must be noted that detection of electronic listening devices and techniques is an extremely difficult process and is best left to the experts in the line. It is weli nigh dangerous for any amateurish efforts. Do not be taken in by persons offering quick fix solutions and facilities in this regard.

Carelessness of employees can be a troublesome problem—a phenomena best addressed by sound security procedures, periodic training, constant monitoring, strict vigil as well as effective and uniform enforcement at all times.

Relaxation of Security Measures

Occasional relaxation of security procedures may be called for in exceptional circumstances like disaster situations, need for unexpected evacuation. It is essential to have suitable well thought out simplified alternatives for implementation during such occasions, and which are properly supervised in accordance with relevant contingency plans. Even then, movements of personnel, processing and movements of sensitive information/ material, their disposal and destruction must be capable of being audited.

Technology Use

Encourage use of reliable technological aids to safety and security, wherever effective/ helpful. They should be constantly monitored and properly maintained for proper functioning. Should review periodically use of such gadgets to upgrade suitably, as required. Such a need may arise due to technological developments, environmental changes, mere passage of time making the system outmoded/unreliable, system changes, organizational changes and so on.

Salient features specific to Operations/Process Security scenarios may be summarized as follows:

1. Operations/Process Security Tasks envisage emphasis on *Public Safety and Security* considerations, apart from embracing and encompassing the usual Physical, Information and Personal Security aspects. Cost-effectiveness, profit and Efficiency of Service become subservient to the above all important needs.
2. Consequently, Intelligence inputs to safeguard against internally, as well as, externally generated threats become highly relevant.

3. Protection against the, so called, Acts of God, natural and manmade hazards, etc., need serious consideration, and mandatory Contingency Plans against such disasters in the making.
4. Most often, such Operations/Processes are spread over wide areas and or/several locations. Some examples are- nuclear power generation, shipping, airlines operations, transportation industry, oil production and distribution, and so on.
5. Appropriate Contingency Plans are invariably needed.
6. Hazards/Disaster WARNING arrangements to alert in time the population in the neighbourhood, even to far-off areas/ regions under possible danger, in case of failures or occurrence of a dangerous situation, are a must. Obviously, this would call for continuous, perhaps extensive monitoring of the system and its constituent parts for an early warning of any impending failure situation, (and for a prompt institution of necessary corrective/remedial measures.). Suitable evacuation procedures may also be essential, in regard to certain kinds of operations.
7. Fail-safe safety controls/facilities to prevent damage/minimize hazards/contain dangers in case of any unexpected failures/ hazards are essential for each and every stage of Operations/Processes that could pose danger.
8. Periodic specified inspections, preferably by an independent body, are mandatory.
9. To ensure timely, correct and accountable actions, responsibility and the necessary authority are specified and delegated together to each level/control person/point.
10. Must have secure, fast, relevant and reliable, internal and external communication facilities for the system.
11. The smallest of failures may entail extensive and critical investigation and follow up analysis. So also for any recurrent or major failures, ofcourse. This could be by an independent /statutory body. Usually, the recommendations of the body are to be implemented,

mandatorily and with minimum possible delay. More often than not, the restart/continuation of the Operation/Process would be contingent on such compliance (implementation of the recommended remedial measures).

12. Failures are usually attributable to design inadequacy or poor maintenance (and occasionally to the human factor of negligence; despite adequate and mandatory training of the concerned personnel before they are involved in the Operations/Processes).
13. Rigourous maintenance and upgradation of the system is the norm.
14. The system should have, in-built into it, suitable manual override features, for a quick and safe shutdown of the Operation/Process, (or parts thereof), when need arises. This is essential to prevent a 'runaway' type of situation, and to minimize hazards/damages if an unexpected failure/ dangerous situation occurs, and the built-in automatic "fail-safe" system performs inadequately or totally "fails" to function.
15. To take care of new threats that may arise for any reason, continuous vigilance and lookout are called for, as also suitable counters to be instituted in time against such possible new threats.
16. It is always advisable to maintain a watch on fall-outs and fruits of technological advances that could be incorporated/ integrated into the system to upgrade its safety, effectiveness, efficiency, possible cost-savings and so on.
17. Computer facilities involved in the system performance are to be fault-tolerant type or of redundant configuration. The system may require suitable electronic countermeasures (EMC, TEMPEST techniques and so on), to protect it against electronic surveillance. Special features of safety and security have to be in place such as stringent Access Control, specific Authorizations, effective Identification/Authentication, appropriate Cipher techniques, Rigourous Audit, quick and reliable Recovery

Procedures/Facilities, ensuring reliability of Personnel, multi location multiple Back-up Memories and so on.

18. The locations and design of the facilities should fully take care of the environmental hazards of all types, and not merely those related to the climate and geography, (heat, cold, humidity, dust, salty atmosphere, precipitation, seismic occurrences and so on). The system must be protected from both, manmade as well as natural hazards.

It should be noted that after the *September 11, 2001* terrorist suicide attacks on the WTC Towers, with the resultant horrifying tragedies, the whole complexion of Operations Security and Disaster Management concepts calls for some radical thinking. What is also sickening to observe is that, an investment an estimated a mere few hundred thousand US Dollars (with long term secret planning and making the plan work) had resulted in an estimated over ONE HUNDRED BILLION US DOLLARS of DAMAGE to the US ECONOMY alone! This is apart *from the fallout on economy of other (comity) of nations*! It does not, of course, change the principles enunciated above. What might have saved the Americans from far greater tragedies, perhaps, was their clear thinking and prompt actions that led to the immediate grounding of all flights, diversion of flights already in the air, stopping of the (underground) train movements, prompt harnessing of Emergency Services/Disaster Management Procedures, etc. It is clear that such problems of terrorism; extortion, kidnappings etc. cannot be tackled effectively, by conventional approaches of "Law and Order". They require National (many times even International) efforts. The imperative for immediately establishing a unified *National Level Organization cannot be overemphasized (*call it by any name-be it *HomeLand Defence System*, like in the USA*)*. And it must have Local, Regional and National units, with well-coordinated efforts for effective functioning. Also, *effective Disaster Management Systems/ Procedures* as well as availability of good *Emergency Services can no longer be ignored.* (The Interpol would not be able to handle the anti-terrorism tasks at the International level. Perhaps, a suitable, separate permanent International setup may be needed under the auspices of the UN). It is heartening to note that the Government of India is actively on the job to set up a suitable Disaster Management Authority.

Supplementary Security Techniques

There are security tasks, which can be considered as supplementary to the four types of security operations, viz. *'Physical Security', 'Information Security', 'Personal or VIP Security' and 'Operations/Process Security'.* Some examples of such techniques are 'Forgery and Fraud Investigation', 'Patents and Copyrights Protection Techniques', 'Protection Techniques Against Counterfeiting', 'Forensic Science/Technology', 'Detection of Spurious Drugs' and so on. The techniques/tasks may be self-contained, like use of UV illumination to detect counterfeit currency, and tackle local crime. Or, they may involve physical security, information security etc. operations to counter serious crimes such as counterfeiting, which impinge on National Security.

Many such techniques find normal usage in Crime Investigations. Some examples are: Comparison Microscopes, Handwriting Analysis, Typewriter Characteristics Recognition, Fake Currency Detection, DNA 'Fingerprinting' Applications, Footprint and Tyreprint Identification Techniques, Interrogation Techniques, use of Analytical Instruments such as Chromatographs, Spectra-Photometers, Polarographs, Spectral Comparators and so on.

Ever extending reach of bio-hazards, continuing and ever spawning environment pollution, spread of biotechnology and its newer and the infotech revolution etc. Go on adding newer and perhaps more deadly threats to national security. Thus, as time progresses, instead of few people, a very small percentage of the population, being involved with security work, much larger groups of people will be involved in such tasks. For example, in future, terrorist threats to the general public from NBC agents could arise that are even targeted against just individuals, maybe at random say through the postal system. Such threats are extremely difficult to counter by the organized agencies and it is the people themselves who would have to safeguard themselves, by and large! As it is, with the growing threats of personal assaults, burglary, extortion, abduction/kidnapping etc. Private security and body-guarding agencies are mushrooming every day. With the widespread enlightenment on the security weaknesses of credit card operations and info-tech products, larger and larger percentage of the population, particularly those using computers or credit cards are becoming more and more security conscious and tech-savvy. Thus, 'security technology' will no longer be the play-field of security-wallahs only, but may well become a talking point for the general public too!

With the incidences of "Bio-terrorism", (*introduction of Anthrax into the postal system* in the USA, in the post WTC attack period), the world has been stood on its head. "Operations Security" has a totally new dimension to actually take into account and handle, what used to be a hypothetical threat. These attacks have put great economic stress on the operations of the transportation industry, entertainment industry, power generation systems, municipal systems of water supply etc., post and courier operations, travel and tourism industry, and so on. That is practically any system where there is an interface with the public. This has in turn brought in uncalled for, unexpected and extensive economic burdens on the nations, and the population in general. The perpetrators being shadowy figures it requires Herculean and quite expensive Intelligence and covert operations to home in on them. Neither does it seem possible to deliver them, their agents/protectors/persons providing safe havens to them to quick justice with the existing laws and legal procedures. To add to the confusion there are human rights activists "to protect the rights of these terrible modern day predators" at the cost of the poor innocent victims, whose rights are freely trampled on by the terrorists and quite ignored by some activists. The normal democratic Law and Order approach that a hundred guilty ones may go scot-free in order that not a single innocent person gets punished, will not work in the context of terrorism, and in regard to those who assist and provide shelter to terrorists. Justice has also to be swift, sure and maybe even ruthless. The fact is that when a "terrorist" is let go in order to save a few innocents, the result may well be that the released terrorist wreaks havoc on hundreds or thousands of innocents, later on. History of terrorism is witness to this fact! The moral of the story is that, you cannot reason or bargain with the *"Devil"-the 'terrorist'*; he is a breed apart with no morals to speak of (there can be no justification for killing/maiming of the innocents!). So, do not shed tears for a slain terrorist, or his henchmen; shed them for their innocent victims! Fortunately, recently, the Central Government has passed the POTA or the Prevention of Terrorism Act. Though some States do not agree to implement it, some of them have own state laws perhaps as stringent or more stringent than the POTA!

Now for the question, is there a total and permanent solution to terrorism? Can terrorism be completely wiped out and eradicated from the surface of the earth? The simple answer is a categorical NO! There will always be the fringe elements, the lunatics with twisted sense of morality or greed for making a quick killing by targeting the unwary innocents. With the increasing divide between the rich and the poor the world over, the growing sense of frustration and alienation amongst isolated groups in societies there will always be some inescapable acts of terrorism here and there, which, unfortunately, it is impossible to prevent (like any crime for that matter!). So, in absolute terms, terrorism per se cannot be prevented. But, widespread terrorist acts can be prevented and contained, as also fallout of such isolated acts minimized. At a price of course of dedicated sustained efforts by all concerned, the general public included.

Consider the threat of Bio-terrorism. You can contain the threat and limit possible damages by instituting certain positive regulations and actions. First of all, there has to be strong deterrence against committing of a terrorist act by anyone. This calls for a swift, sure and exemplary punishment, to not only the terrorist but *also to those who aid and abet in the programme*. Justice has to be swift, for it to have any deterrent value. Cases dragging for years in a court can by no means be a deterrent. On the other hand, it could lead to other terrorist acts to force the release of the seized perpetrator of the terrorist act, at worst.

At best it enables the terrorist to plan further acts of terrorism whilst happily cooling his heels in prison/encourage human rights activists to get him released on bail, to further perpetrate his acts of terror! Cases are not rare where prisoners, (criminals and terrorists), hatching their nefarious plots from the safety of the prison. There have also been any number of cases of detainees/ under trials escaping from the clutches of the law, whilst being taken from place to place, or by prison breakouts, whilst the normal legal processes are progressing at their painfully slow pace.

Justice has to be certain, so that persons planning any terrorist act will understand that they will be caught and will be subjected to quick punishment. And the punishment has to be exemplary, for it to have real deterrent effect. A mere *wrap on the knuckle* could only be an encouragement to the perpetrator to carry on, with perhaps a redoubling of his efforts to commit further acts of terrorism! In brief, to deter terrorist acts there has to be special regulations and fast track justice system for proceeding against apprehended (suspected) terrorists, as well as persons who aid and abet them. (Keep the normal laws and procedures for the run of the mill criminals only, who do not affect the security of the society they operate in, nor impose a heavy financial and other burdens on the society/state). No wonder many of the western nations which face/have faced terrorist problems have already enacted new laws to specially tackle the problems of terrorism, (that include inter alia summary detention, speedier law processes and harsher punishments, etc.). Also recently, India has promulgated an ordinance in regard to terrorism, and will have hopefully some sort of a special law to adequately tackle the bane of terrorism.

The above is only a part of the story. There has to be an effective Intelligence system to render an early warning of possible and specific terrorist occurrences. You also need a pervasive, efficient public health system which is highly responsive and fast acting to effectively handle emergencies (such as could be caused by Bio-terrorism (or calamities such as epidemics, earthquakes, fires, floods, etc.). Obviously, they need to be provided with the wherewithal to not only handle the victims/casualties but also to quickly analyze and arrive at the causes of health concerns. That is an early detection system. This in itself is also not sufficient. You need to have in place a system for surveillance of events/ occurrences of public-health import for an early warning of possible dangers, and to institute a quick alert to all concerned; to effectively tackle possible emergencies that could affect the public health.

You now need to have in place a system and resources to quickly, (in time), supply on the spot the required health care facilities of appropriate drugs, vaccines and so on. Fortunately, we in India have an excellent pharmaceutical industry which can be primed by the government suitably to be an adequate resource to meet contingencies prognosticated by Intelligence alerts and early warning by the public health system.

The general public also has their bit to play. They need to be constantly aware of the dangers and take adequate precautions, like being suspicious of questionable parcels/mails received by them (and packages etc. left unattended at public places). It is better not to even touch them but report the event to the nearest police station (or others concerned). If suspected contents have spilled by accident, make sure that you keep people and pets away from the area until all necessary safety actions have been taken. As a (personal) safety measure, the best thing that can be suggested is to immediately scoop it all back and seal it in a Polythene bag; to be handed over to the police or the designated agency. Wash the hands and face with soap and water, (preferably have a good bath) and inform the agencies concerned. Do not try to treat yourself with self-help but quickly go to the nearest hospital. *It is best to strictly follow the guidelines laid out by the competent authority,* in all respects (precautions, prevention, detection, first aid, treatment, reporting, etc.).

There is no gainsaying the fact that curbing terrorism requires international co-operation. This is particularly so when you consider the multiple *avatars* of terrorism—*Narco Terrorism, Nuclear Terrorism, Bio Terrorism, Chemical Terrorism, Space Terrorism, Cyber terrorism and so on*! The close nexus between terrorism, and money laundering, illegal trafficking (in arms, narcotics, etc.) and organized crimes is unquestioned. It is, therefore, heartening to note the recent developments of international cooperation between nations to tackle terrorism *after the Sept.11, 2001 attacks on the* World Trade Center, (the knocking down of the twin towers of the WTC). It is also a point to rejoice that the recent Moscow Declaration (Sept. 6, 2001, by Prime Minister Vajpayee and President Putin of Russia) reportedly *includes the vital sentence,* "Whatever be the motive of their perpetration-political, ideological, philosophical, racial, ethnic, religious or any other-terrorist acts are unjustifiable". *For terrorism in any form, whatever be the raison d'etre-is horrific, deplorable, to be condemned by all; and put down firmly, without any hesitation.*

In view of the recent spreading scare "anthrax scare", a few words in regard to major known agents for Bio-Terrorism that one speaks of, may not be out of place. These are Anthrax, Small Pox, Plague, Typhoid, Botulism, VHF or Viral Haemorrhagic Fevers, Mustard Gas, SARIN, VX (there are, ofcourse, other possible agents like TULAREMIA, HCN, and so on). Ofcourse ,with the fast developing bio-technology-the gene manipulation techniques-could well lead to more dangerous, far more deadly viruses with far more widespread and horrendous consequences, to the state and the public, of Bio-terrorism in the future!

- Anthrax (*Bacillus Anthraxis*): It is a hardy bacterium whose spores are highly resistant to heat and can live on for years and years. They can get into the body through cuts and breaks in the skin, by ingestion or by inhalation. Once they get in, they rapidly multiply and produce toxin, which cannot be countered. So, *treatment with antibiotics like Ciprafloxacin/penicillin can help* only at the initial stages, before the discharge of the toxin by the invading bacterium. The symptoms of the anthrax infection vary with the method of entry into the body by the bacteria. Infection through the skin leads to appearance of rashes after a couple of days, and they turn black with fluid filled vesicles. When the entry is through the mouth by eating/drinking infected substances, nausea, retching, stomach pain and fever occur. The deadly meningitis may follow this!

Maximum fatalities occur in cases where the spores are inhaled. In this case the symptoms are those of the common "flu"-cold, fever etc., plus nausea.

- Small Pox (*Variola Virus*): It is a hardy, deadly and contagious virus. Infection could lead to death unless protected by a vaccine. Since the disease is expected to have been eradicated from the surface of the earth, permission of WHO is needed to produce and stock the vaccine, which it is unlikely to do as widespread vaccination may create more of a problem. High fever and rash are the main symptoms. The rash later turns into permanent distinctive "pockmarks" in the survivors of the attack.
- Plague (*Yersinia Festis*): A highly contagious and deadly disease spread by infected rat fleas. If not treated promptly it is almost always fatal. Prompt treatment with Antibiotics is the answer. If the bacteria invade the body, within three to four days of their reaching the lungs, fever and delirium appear.
- Typhoid (*Salmonella Typhii*): Unhygienic food and drinks are the main route for the spread of this disease, which is long drawn out and debilitating. Antibiotics like Ciprafloxacin (and suitable diet restrictions of course) are the quite effective treatment for the attack. One has to guard against a relapse too. Symptoms are high/recurrent fever, loss of appetite, etc.
- Botulism (*Clostridium Botulinum*): The entry methods for this deadly nerve toxin is through broken skin, the lungs or the intestines. It has paralyzing effect before fatality occurs. An antitoxin is likely to arrest the fatality, sometimes. The symptoms are nausea, slurred speech, diarrhoea, and dizziness.
- VHF refers to family of viruses like the deadly Ebola and Marburg viruses. There are no known treatments for illnesses caused by attacks from such viruses. Preventive vaccines are available reportedly only for two of the viruses viz. yellow fever and argentine haemorrhagic fever.
- Mustard Gas, known as a blister agent, was widely used during World War II. Dispensed in vapor/liquid forms it

gets absorbed through the eyes, skin and the mucous membranes, and causes injury to the eyes/skin and the respiratory tract etc., while there is no known antidote (reported). However, damage (to body tissues) limitation possible by immediate de-contamination of all potentially exposed body areas within minutes of such exposure.

- SARIN is a highly toxic chemical that can cause death within minutes of exposure to it. (Remember the terrorist SARIN attack in the Japanese underground train?). Entry into the body can be through the skin, by ingestion or through inhalation. Effective and immediate decontamination is the antidote! Running nose, watering of the eyes, excessive sweating, laboured breathing, nausea, affected vision are some of the symptoms. Death is by exhausted muscles and glands that ultimately stops one from breathing!
- VX, like SARIN, is a highly toxic compound both in the gas form and in the liquid form. Its entry; into the body, effects on the body and antidote are also similar to those for SARIN.

One last point before we close the chapter. What should be done about hoax calls? Hoax calls have to be handled as if it were genuine, as you cannot know in advance that it is a hoax call. You just cannot afford to ignore them. Until all the relevant security actions have been taken, the required security procedures have been gone through, and proper investigations have been carried out, no one is in a position to identify a hoax call, for what it is. The result is a great deal of wasted efforts, uncalled for high mental stress, in the general public apart from the people directly connected with the related security activities, as well as totally unnecessary economic loss to the nation. Hoax calls also have the unfortunate effect of likely subsequent degradation in the security system and loss of public faith in the system and their morale. Therefore, no one should shed a tear when the perpetrators of hoax call are severely dealt with, even to the extent of meting out to them punishment that one may otherwise feel is quite harsh.

PART II

Chapter 9

Safety and Hazards Management

"Hindsight Explains the injury that, foresight would have prevented"

—Henry Cabot Lodge

The words, safety and security, appear to be practically synonymous, two sides of the same coin. But, there is a distinct difference. The word "security" subsumes safety, but not the other way around. It is interesting to see the meanings for the two words as detailed in a dictionary:

Safe: Uninjured; free or secure from danger or evil; unharmed; sound; affording security; not risky; cautious; trusty; sure; certain; no longer dangerous.

Safety: State of being safe; freedom from injury, danger or risk; safekeeping or custody.

Secure: Free from danger or apprehension; safe from attack; reliable; in safekeeping; to make safe or secure; to make safe against loss etc.

Security: The state of being or feeling secure; safety; certainty; that which secures; a pledge or a guarantee etc.

The word security conjures in one's mind protective actions against basically, some type of active "internal" action against external possible threats (from a burglar, an intruder, failure of an external service like telephone breakdown, adverse acts by an external agent-such as sabotage, etc.). These are basically open-ended and can extend to any type of perceivable external threat.

The word safety does not connote any such 'deadly' visions; it confines itself to protective actions against possible 'accidents' and 'hazards' during normal activities and living conditions. The hazards could be natural or man-made ones.

Safety and Hazards Management extends from the home environment through safety at work, to safety at public places. The activities cover a very wide range of disciplines encompassed by diverse activities such as: Construction safety, fire safety; electrical safety; health safety; safety from hazardous chemicals and poisons; environmental safety; safety from disasters, and so on.

Basic Approach to Safety

The basic approach to safety is to take all actions to minimize the hazards, to contain its effects, assess the risks and institute suitable prevention and protective measures for the future. Have suitable first aid and safety net in place.

As the old saying goes, "accidents (do) happen in the best regulated families", and health hazards do abound in every aspect of living; more modern and hi-tech the living, the more the health hazards and possibility of accidents happening. Every accident has an economic penalty attached to it. The Bhopal Gas tragedy of December 3,1984 claimed over 10,000 lives. 15,310 death claims are reported to have been adjudicated and over 3,00,000 claimants are understood to have been awarded an average compensation of more than Rs.25,000/= each for personal injuries suffered due to the disaster because of accidental release of methyl-isocyanate into the atmosphere.

Any number of things may cause accidents. It could be due to simple occurrences such as-falling objects, slipping on steps or flooring, falling into trenches or pits, stumbling over obstructions, mis-stepping or slipping while climbing. Or, it could be due to deliberate malicious actions such as tampering with protective systems like limit-switches. What is worse is that accidents could be direct results of negligence and poor management of resources and facilities. Some examples of this are-faulty storage / unauthorized access or poor handling/transportation of dangerous substances like-poisons, hazardous chemicals, radio-active materials, P.O.L. (petrol, oil and lubricants); radiation or fire hazards; poor industrial waste handling/storage; poor safety training/management, and so on.

Apart from accidents resulting in dangers to health, physical injuries even fatalities, they can have serious economic connotations. Accidents could damage plant and equipment, they could destroy work done, result in loss of man-hours, lead to disruption of productive activities due to time lost on accident investigations, loss of confidence, reputation and so on; in extreme cases, even closure of the factory.

Compared to above, any extra expenditure involved in improving safety measures has to be looked at with a receptive approach. Such a balancing approach is necessary, as most of the accidents are preventable with good safety management, who is dedicated, and has a committed approach to the implementation of safety and health regulations/procedures.

By and large accidents are results of human error. Hence, what is most important is to change the human behaviour to reduce possibility of human error. Further, in factories, and organizations health and safety measures should involve training of workers towards occupational safety. (Note that, although imposition of suitable punishment to those whose carelessness or negligence results in an accident may be unavoidable, relying on such measures as means for preventing accidents is likely to be unreliable, and not very useful. The basic approach to health and safety should involve the following:

- Risk assessment
- Prevention
- Protection/containment and contingency plans
- First aid/accident investigation
- Safety net
- Safety audit and
- A safety officer/adviser to oversee the above activities.

In the first instance, the safety procedures should lead to make the workspot safe, as well as the personnel in the location also remaining safe. This means, that the premises, plant, equipment, materials, processes, access, transport, storage, disposal, supervision and competence/capability of the personnel and systems must be adequate and safe. Also, personal behaviour, personal hygiene, discipline and personal health when at work all needs to be proper. Protective personal gear must be used, and used properly, wherever necessary. Thus, the very task for ensuring safety at work needs a comprehensive risk assessment exercise for evolving the essential safety procedures and put in place requisite safe work environment. This includes the appropriate induction and training of personnel too.

Simultaneously, suitable contingency plans must be evolved, put in place, and relevant personnel trained to correctly implement such plans, when any contingency arises. The plans should envisage containment of adverse effects of accidents, if they do occur, such as protection of people and the environment, in case of such a contingency. Further, suitable first-aid facilities should be catered for.

Risk Assessment

It involves a close look at all the activities, the locations, the environment, workers' competence, installations such as plant and machinery at the workspot, and so on. Taking all these into account you need to evaluate the hazards to the health and safety of the workers and other personnel who could be at the location/workspot. You must check on the preventive methods that are practicable, to assure improved protection, and incorporate them suitably into the activities of the organization. You also need to ensure that only workers with adequate competence and training have access to areas and plant/machinery which have dangers/risks attached in their operation.

Regarding quantification of risks, risks analysis etc., you may glance through the relevant paragraphs in Chapter I. Somewhat similar considerations apply here too.

Prevention

Apart from the above, you need to create the standard operating procedure, (S.O.P.), for the health and safety management in the organization. This will require the participation by all personnel: management, workers, supervisors, clients, contractors, security/ administrators and so on. (Factories act/ regulations covering health, safety and welfare of employees, spell-out the minimum requirements in regard to health and safety at work, including the role, the duties and responsibilities of employers, the employees and other personnel on the spot). All relevant safety and health data and information should be disseminated to everyone, to make them, not only aware of the same, but also, to consciously utilize the knowledge in their day-to-day (respective) work, (to the extent relevant and necessary). Emphasis must be on the anticipation and avoidance of hazards as well as creation of proper environment and behaviour towards health and safety at work.

For a proper appreciation and implementation of such *S.O.Ps*, it may be essential to nominate or appoint a person to be exclusively in charge of safety management, to bring about the necessary co-operation, co-ordination, commitment and training in the personnel of the organization and others involved (like visitors, contractors etc). He also needs to ensure that all actions/activities leave an auditable trace to enable proper investigation to home-on to the real causes of accidents and when they do occur, so that proper remedial actions/procedures could be instituted, apart from fixing of responsibilities that would be required.

What should be obvious is, unfortunately not very apparent, that, health and safety is the responsibility of everyone at the workspot. So, effective training is a must to improve safety management, and to bring about necessary changes in human behaviour, so that the tendencies for accidents are minimized. Thus, leading to reduction in injuries and fatalities, as well as avoidance of economic /time loss. The personnel on the spot have to take care of not only their own safety, but also ensure safe behaviour and conduct of the employees, for whom they are responsible. So also, ensure safe behaviour of others, (like visitors) in the location, as may be relevant.

Prevention means, you avoid risks wherever practicable, and not total elimination of risks-which may be impractical, or totally uneconomical. Evaluate the risks that cannot be avoided. You must, then, reduce the effects of these residual risks by matching worker to work, proper training, proper supervision, use of protective measures, incentives and so on. People at work have to be protected from risks to their health and safety due to the work related and other activities at the spot, and in the neighbourhood. Adequate control has to be exercised in the storage, handling and use of dangerous substances like poisons, explosives, hazardous chemicals, flammable substances etc., and prevent people from getting hold of such materials illegally. Note, that you use such hazardous materials only where essential, and unavoidable. Release of dangerous, noxious and offensive substances into the environment/atmosphere must be controlled and prevented as per regulations in force/knowledge of their adverse effect on the environment /habitat; where proper regulations are not yet in force. It is the responsibility of the employer to ensure proper and timely maintenance of the plant and total system to keep them risk-free at all times. And also to ensure safe and risk-free arrangements for the storage, handling, usage, transportation etc., of all material, substances and equipment as well as implement necessary instruction, training, supervision and dissemination of relevant safety and health related information. Also note that, the activities of the organization should not endanger the safety and health of people not in his employment, whether at the workplace or in the surrounding region etc. So, the employer should induct only properly designed, (from safety and health considerations), and environment friendly equipment and systems. Obviously, both, people at work, and the public, (includes children also), should not endanger the safety and health arrangements in any way, by interfering with any health, safety, or welfare measures in places.

Protection Methods, Containment and Contingency Plans

Use of personal protective equipment like gloves, goggles, footwear, helmet, protective clothing, etc., are the very last resort to reduce the risks due to hazards. Recourse to such aids arises after all possible preventive systems and actions have been instituted. Containment and contingency plans are also protective arrangements, which are designed/evolved to protect mainly, not the system so much as the personnel, and the environment from the hazards, when due to any untoward reasons the preventive elements fail to contain the risks.

Take, for example, a nuclear reactor where, due to reasons beyond control, a leak develops, say in the coolant. If not contained, the leaking coolant will carry hazardous nuclear radiation to all over the plant and the environment. It hence, becomes necessary to design and implement suitable containment chambers/methods/procedures to ensure that, if and when such untoward happenings occur, the leaking coolant and radiation are contained within a limited protected volume; until mopped/rendered harmless and released/neutralized etc. as relevant and feasible. Such containment methods are designed into the system, and, what is more important is, that they are put in place before the system is permitted to function. For example, a nuclear reactor dome is designed and fabricated to be able to withstand the contingency of say, a Boeing 747, jet aircraft crashing into it by accident.

Protective systems must also include safe storage of hazardous substances, from accidental and unauthorized access/release into the environment. This applies to materials such as drugs, poisons, hazardous medical waste, nuclear wastes/material, explosive substances, and so on. The protection could include physical protection systems, intrusion alarms, 24 hours security cover, and so on. The storage itself could be in exclusive well-protected rooms/buildings/locations.

The protection and containment systems are implemented before the commencement of the operations.

On the other hand, the contingency plans may or may not be in position before the functioning starts, though it is always advisable to have such plans evolved and provided for at the outset itself. (It may look like locking the stable after the horse has bolted).

In spite of all preventive and protective measures, occasionally, some unexpected events could occur, say an earthquake or flood, which results in breakdown of the preventive/protective measures. It is then, that putting into force appropriate contingency plans becomes all important, and vital-to help in the containment of possible dangers; protect the environment/habitat, etc. It may also be essential for the protection of the personnel on site (and perhaps the general public/and or environment in the neighbourhood, as well), from the adverse effects of the accidents/hazards, resulting from the contingency. Such plans also help in quick restoration of the facility, to enable normal operation to recommence as soon as possible.

Protection, containment and contingency plans are independent, but, interrelated actions. They are clubbed together to indicate that, when preventive actions are not enough, from practical, economic, or other reasons, it is then essential to institute suitable protective, containment and contingency plans.

First Aid/Accident Investigation

When, inspite of all precautions, an accident does take place, it becomes important to ensure that prompt, and requisite first aid is provided. Also, simultaneously, or soon as possible, institute necessary accident-investigation proceedings. Delayed action in this regard may result in some loss of objectivity, non-availability of all relevant information, possible loss of crucial evidence, and so on.

First-aid is required to save the injured from dangerous consequences of the initial injury, like excessive loss of blood, respiratory arrest, choking, and even possible death due to blood loss, etc. Hence, rendering of prompt first aid is a vital activity/drill that the organization must ensure as it could be a matter of life and death for the affected party. The organization is held responsible for any drawbacks or lacunae in this connection.

First aid and accident investigation are clubbed together to indicate that the two actions need to be instituted immediately an accident takes place. Former, to promptly render urgently needed assistance to the accident victims, to save them from further injuries and grave danger because of the injuries already suffered. And the latter, to ascertain the reasons for the accident, how it could have been prevented and future course of action to eliminate or minimize the possibility of such an accident happening again. No doubt, the two sets of actions are disparate and are distinctly different. However, they are clubbed together since both sets of actions need to be taken up without delay, immediately after any accident take place.

Some useful details on first aid may be seen at Annexure "A".

Safety Net

When accidents occur, the result could be heavy financial loss to the individual or the organization. Therefore, you require suitable safety nets to protect from such losses. For example, an organization may retain functionality by having standby operational sites. This is definitely the case for major computer facilities; where they must go in for suitable back-ups, multiple operations in the same location, or, preferably, at different locations. However, in most cases, insurance is the well known, and extensively used safety net—whether *for* individuals, or organizations. Such safety nets are necessary to help to reduce losses due to untoward happenings—accidents and disasters.

Safety Audit

In safety management and loss prevention activities, you must ensure that suitable safety audit facilities/procedures are built-in. Such features lead to timely highlighting of aspects that could lead to accidents in the future. Hence, safety audit features enable suitable corrective methods, systems and procedures to be incorporated. That is to constantly improve safety management, even when there are no changes in the organization/operations/ equipment/plant/personnel, and so on. Safety audit is an excellent means to ensure-timely maintenance of plant and machinery, proper training of personnel, and in time, implementation of/improvement to safety procedures (much before any lacunae in the same could result in accidents).

Whatever are the measures taken, in isolation or in combination, to take care of safety requirements (precautions, warnings/alerts, prevention, protection, containment and /or contingency plans), safety audit has to be incorporated into the safety-system/procedures, and without fail. Without it, safety and disaster management would bè quite inadequate, and only lead to partial success.

Safety Officer/ Safety Adviser

In any large organization, to ensure proper safety and hazards-management, it is advisable to have a suitable person appointed exclusively to look into and supervise all aspects of safety/hazards management systems, procedures and all relevant activities. Loading existing executive with the task as just one of his responsibilities, is fraught with great danger for the organization. Such an organization can be accident prone/have hazardous working environment. Safety management is a full time job, and requires a very competent person to handle effectively the multi-disciplinary, and multifaceted actions required at all times; and throughout the organization, as well. It also includes initiation and review of necessary training of workers, outlook of employees, and behaviour of visitors etc.

Hazards

Hazards are basically of two types viz. natural and man-made. However, origin of some hazards could be natural or man-made. For example, a fire may be due to natural causes, as in the case of a forest-fire or a fire caused by lightning; or it may be man-made, such as due to-arson, electric short circuit, P.O.L. ignition, etc. Similarly, pollution, though mostly man-made, could also arise, and over extensive areas too, due to natural causes (like the super-cyclone over Orissa, the major forest fire in Indonesia spreading smoke over hundreds of miles, blanketing even Malaysia).

Natural Hazards

Natural hazards may result in disaster in a micro-scale affecting a very small area or region; or could be on a macro-scale affecting large, extensive areas. It could even be on a global scale affecting nations. Preventive measures may not always be possible. But protective measures are possible such as early warning, first aid and other disaster mitigating methods. And those should be necessarily implemented. Major natural hazards are listed below, roughly, on the basis of their increasing spatial extent, or area coverage, (note that ESD and gas leakage basically originate because of the present day way of life):

- Electrostatic discharge [ESD]
- Gas leakage [radon, methane, hydrogen sulphide etc.]
- Wind, rain, snow, fog, dust, hail
- Thunderstorm, lightning
- Flash-floods
- Landslides
- Avalanches
- Heat/cold wave
- Earthquakes
- Droughts
- Floods
- Cyclones, typhoons, twisters, hurricanes
- Volcanoes
- Radiation [UV, IR, cosmic ray, ozone depletion etc.]
- Global warming

(A nuclear holocaust could out-beat all the above mentioned natural hazards, in regard to the extent of coverage and damage to the population and the habitat).

ESD and gas leakage aspects will be covered later, as they are also man-made hazards.

Cold, Heat, Rain, Snow, Fog, etc.

Under normal conditions of the above natural environmental conditions, one can arrange for suitable protective measures against the adverse affects due to these natural hazards. But, extreme environmental conditions can be dangerous hazards for humans. For example, working under extreme cold conditions/ biting winds etc., is liable to cause accidents because of dulled mental faculties, weak muscle reactions, possible arthritis or bronchitis. This is particularly so, when proper, protective clothing, warm footwear, or protected/hospitable work environment is missing. Hypothermia (that is, extreme cold), could result in frostbite due to freezing of tissues/lack of blood circulation, and could well end in gangrene of the extremities of limbs, like fingers and toes, when prompt and appropriate attention is lacking. Skin could stick to very cold surfaces, when it comes in direct contact (with them). The elderly persons and children are more easily affected by intense cold (if not properly protected). The problem could well become critical and deadly dangerous when the body temperature goes down to 28 degrees celsius, (normal human body temperature varies from person to person and is about 37 degrees C/98.4 F), because of such cold conditions/situations.

Similarly, high humidity, hot sun, radiant heat, hot air blasts/atmosphere, or high local (ambient) temperature will lead to one or more body reactions such as yawning, sweating, headache, giddiness, fainting fits, cramps, or even lead to sudden unconsciousness. In extreme cases of such heat exhaustion, immediate medical attention would become necessary. Further, it has been observed that, if the body temperature reaches a high value of about 43 degrees celsius, fatality is to be expected, (due to cerebral injury). Adequate drinking water and proper cool environment are the minimum essential pre-requisite for the work to be carried on effectively and safely.

Heavy rain, intense snow, blanketing fog, swirling dust storm, etc. will adversely affect work and worker-safety, as well. For example, tools can slip, heavy loads could slide, persons may fall, machinery stop/seize, vehicles capsize, and so on. So also, unexpected, dangerous overloads may occur, structures collapse, and so on. Hence, work would mostly grind to a halt. Further, it becomes incumbent to provide suitable protection to the (partial) work already carried out, for the machinery, etc. during such occurrences. During such periods, you have the responsibility, too, to ensure suitable arrangements for the safety of the workers, as well as for them to stay safe.

Heavy rain also adversely affects radio communication systems, radar systems and most systems that depend on *electromagnetic wave,* (EM), propagation in space. It degrades performance of equipment and installations used in the open such as CCTV, intrusion detection systems, transportation systems, etc. It also decreases the effectiveness of people when their activities/work are perforce out in the open/under exposed conditions. Impact of heavy downpours (rain) can cause erosion of exposed surfaces (like soil for example), and lead to unexpected stresses on structures, (not catered for in the normal design). Water logging that may occur can result in the degradation of materials/items, (in regard to their strength, surface coatings, corrosion, etc.), or even make them inoperative/destroy, (exposed units such as electronic and electrical equipment/machinery, even some mechanical equipment could get damaged such as automobiles becoming rusted and inoperative).

Snow, Sleet, Hail, Fog, Wind, Floods, etc.

Snow, sleet, hail, etc., are well known for their danger to transportation. They result in slowing down of vehicle traffic, create traffic jams, and even disrupt movements of transport vehicles, movement of personnel, etc. Further, they can also lead to structural damages because of the resulting unexpected over-loading (of structures). They could even stop use of essential machinery, too. Like heavy rain, snow/sleet/hail etc., can also adversely affect equipment/systems whose operation is based on EM propagation. Personnel directly exposed to above hazardous conditions of the environment, unless suitably protected/exercise due care, may well be subjects for injuries, or even fatalities.

Fog and whiteout can be expected to have similar effects as humidity and rain, with the added problem of greatly reduced visibility. Whiteout results in extremely cold climates with heavy fog, (fog droplet size of 1, to more than 50 micrometres). This results in total diffusion of the available light, the consequence being very much reduced visibility, may be right down to zero visibility. Normal fog, on the other hand permits varying visibility, (maybe up to about a kilometre), depending on how light the fog is.

Strong winds can have adverse effects too, on structures, and personnel exposed to it. So do heavy duststorms, and sandstorms, what to talk of landslides, earthquakes, floods etc. As you cannot prevent the occurrences of the above hazards, you take whatever protective actions you can implement. On a long-term basis, suitable modification to the habitat, (say, raising a wall of suitable trees, suitable strengthening of structures, erection of bunds, quakeproof shelters, and so on), may possibly influence the occurrences/their effects, to some extent. But it is more immediate, and more practical to reduce the impact of such hazards, by suitable protective, or mitigation techniques. Protective systems include proper design of the habitat, use of appropriate clothing, and so on. Mitigation techniques, on the other hand, include long-range/disaster planning, deployment of early warning systems, system for rescue operations, disaster communication system, relief and rehabilitation programmes, and long-term measures like erection of bunds to prevent flooding, quake-proof shelters, evacuation measures/protective shelters against cyclones, etc.

It should be noted that, it is not always feasible to have adequate early warning about an occurrence, for all types of hazards. For example, an earthquake may occur within a few seconds of any detection system that is currently in use. Global warming is something that people are being warned about, for years. And, it is not something that would be a sudden calamitous event, (it will insidiously creep on the people, if suitable counteractions are not instituted, and carried out continuously, by the global community). A *few minutes* is all the time that may be available for saving oneself from a "flashflood"; whereas *at least several hours* of *advance warning* could be available regarding "thunderstorms", "hailstorms", etc. With availability of modern meteorological techniques of atmospheric sounding/ satellite imagery/radar observation etc. and analysis, fortunately, it is now feasible to have a *few days advance warning* as regards- "cyclones", "floods", "heat/cold waves", "landslides", and "avalanches".

More information in regard to the above natural hazards is given in Annexure "B".

Chapter 10

Manmade Hazards

"When you live next to a cemetery, you cannot weep for everyone"

—Russian Proverb

Manmade hazards are the result of the way individuals, groups of persons, the society and nations live. The effects may be purely local, regional, or even global depending on the type of hazard involved. Most of the types are usually localized in effect, such as:

- ESD
- Construction hazards
- Industrial/occupational hazards
- Radiation hazards
- Electrical hazards
- Pollution (noise, etc)]

On the other hand, there are some other manmade hazards, which can result in, either purely local damage, or result in extensive areas or even regions being affected, depending on the containment measures/procedures adopted. Examples of these are:

- Chemical hazards
- Nuclear hazards
- Fire hazards
- Pollution (chemical, nuclear etc.)
- Biological hazards.

It is worth considering the above in some detail, as these hazards may be encountered in the day to day activities of individuals, at home, at work or at leisure (public places), etc.

ESD

A report says that, a dentist, attending to his patient, touches the patient, and the hair on his (patient's) arm singes! The reason this happens is because of *Electro-Static-Discharge, or* ESD. Such static electricity is generated in the working environment, when one moves around on floors carpeted with nylon or acrylic floor coverings/ the person is wearing synthetic clothing, and the air around is dry. The static charge is generated due to friction with the carpet fibres/air molecules. This electric charge is stored on the person, (as humidity is lacking for the charge to dissipate into the atmosphere-humid air conducts electricity due to the water content). And, the charge so accumulated is quickly conducted/transferred, when he touches, or comes in direct contact, with anything or anyone, (who can conduct the charge to earth, thus neutralizing it). Wearing insulating stuff such as-nylon socks, rubber-soled footwear etc. act as barriers to the charge conduction, and thus add to the problem. Effect of ESD can easily be observed, when one removes synthetic clothing he has been wearing, in the dark. Sparks can be seen to jump between the body and the clothing being removed, (may be accompanied by some cracking noise), making the hair stand on end, (that is raising goose bumps). Humidity in the air prevents build-up of electrostatic charge as the humid air acts as conducting medium. It is best to avoid synthetic floor-covering/synthetic fibre clothing, eschew use of synthetic furniture such as plastic chairs. Also, avoid a dry air environment. Touch some semi-conducting item like a wall, before you come in contact with a person, or any conducting material like metal. Such an action, will reduce/eliminate ESD problems; since the charge then, leaks away through the wall to earth, instead of sudden transfer, all in one go-which can result in shock/sparking, etc.

In manufacturing processes, etc. contact and separation of two dissimilar surfaces generates static electricity, when, one, or both the surfaces are poor conductors of electricity. When the two bodies are in contact, the potential difference between them is of the order of 1 volt. On separation, movement of the charges, (due to the potential difference), is impeded by the high resistance of the surfaces. Hence, the excess charges are retained on the surfaces. This leads to a large increase in the potential difference, order of kilo-volts, which could accumulate with repeated contact, and separation of the surfaces. Thus, assembly, disassembly, transportation, intermixing, etc., of dissimilar materials often leads to ESD generation. So also, when liquids having high resistivity flow in pipelines, or high resistivity powders produced in grinders moving on conveyor belts fall into metal containers, they have potential to generate ESD. This can lead to potentials of as high as 10 to 40 kilo-volts.

ESD is a high-voltage, but low-current phenomenon. The high voltage aspect leads to formation of sparks, under suitable conditions. Individuals can acquire as high as 10 kilo-volts or more, walking over synthetic carpeting. But, because of the low current aspect, they will get only mild electric shock (and not fatal ones), when this discharges on contact with metal etc. Hence, ESD is, usually, non-incendiary in nature. However, even this low current will be catastrophic in certain activities like assembly, maintenance/repair of sensitive electronic systems; particularly, those using devices such as FETs (Field Effect Transistor). For this reason, in such businesses, the personnel use suitable conducting wristbands to earth ESD to the ground whilst working on the electronic devices/systems.

However, ESD could be very dangerous when it occurs in explosive atmospheres/atmospheres with inflammable gases present. Resultant sparks could set-off explosives or ignite the inflammable substances. Energy value required for ignition is between 0.001 to 1 milli-joule (mJ). Chemical dust clouds may require over 5 mJ. (mJ = 1/1000 of joule; note that, joule is the unit of energy which is equivalent to unit of power working for a duration of one second, that is, Watt.Second).

How to effectively manage ESD hazards? You could try the following safety precautions:

- Prevent/Minimize/Reduce potential for *ESD* generation, with suitable design/operating procedures.
- Use appropriate methodology, to prevent charge accumulation in the processes and personnel.
- Ensure proper design and layout of system, to prevent occurrence of sparks.
- Prevent formation of explosives/flammable atmospheres.
- Make sure that the System has good/ proper:

Earthing and bonding.
Humidity.
Conductivity, (maybe with ionization/electrically conductive additives, where needed).

You could avoid use of synthetic clothing, furniture, carpeting etc.

Gas Leakage

In the natural environment, rotting carcasses/plants and vegetables evolve noxious gases, such as *Methane, Ammonia* and *Hydrogen Sulphide*. (Pollution generated by mankind adds many other gases such as *Carbon Monoxide, Carbon Dioxide, Sulphur Dioxide, Nitrous Oxide, Chlorine* and so on. This is apart from extremely dangerous pollutant like-*Lead, Cadmium, DDT, Mercury, Benzene, Dioxin*, and so on). Accumulation of such gases can take place in-hollows, cavities, trenches, wells, tanks and sewers. This can have dangerous consequences for the unwary, who get down into such places, without adopting necessary precautions (of testing for the presence of such gases; and taking relevant protective measures). Dangerous explosions can take place, also, when such gas accumulations occur; due to accidental ignition-because of some sparking, lighting of a *beedi*/cigarette, etc., in the neighbourhood.

Radon

There is a *naturally occurring dangerous gas*—RADON, which occur in rocky soil due to disintegration of radioisotopes that are present in them. The gas is, thus, slowly released to the atmosphere above. Reports suggest that Radon accounts for about 50% of the natural background radioactivity exposure of humans, and is particularly becoming a major concern in the West. Focussing of their efforts to build very energy efficient houses, with little or no ventilation to the outside means that the gas accumulates, in such ill-ventilated homes. This results in continued exposure of the residents to the, (consequent increased levels of), gas. Some recent studies (by the National Geophysical Research Institute, NGRI), indicate that, in some parts of India too, the problem of RADON gas has to be taken note of. For example, their studies indicate that in Hyderabad, many houses are built on the rocks, which have been found to have relatively very high content of radioactive elements such as Uranium, with consequent release of high levels of Radon gas as the radioactive element decays. Hence, the Radon gas can build up to dangerous levels in such houses, if proper ventilation is not ensured. Having closed basements and garages built into such houses greatly increases the danger further, because of the gas build up in such enclosed places finding its way into the living areas, through access openings like doors, pipes, air-conditioning ducts, and so on.

The hazards that can be expected are dangerous to the blood forming organs, the testis, eyes, skin, and increased lifetime risk for all types of cancer. For example, when Radon gas is breathed in along with air into the lungs, the Alpha particles, that the gas releases, directly damages lung cells and leads to cancer. Radon-decays to form radioactive isotopes, (solids), with short half-lives. These isotopes transform into radioactive aerosols that emit alpha particles. The small aerosol particles when inhaled, get deposited in the respiratory tract, irradiate the region with alpha particles, which creates havoc. (You may look up the section on ionizing radiation hazards and the chapter on nuclear hazards, covered later on, in this connection). The solution to this particular hazard is really simple-reduce radon accumulation in the home/office environment, (by proper location and good design of buildings, ensuring good ventilation to eliminate the possibility of the gas accumulation), the locations, where you spend most of your time.

Construction Hazards

When you think of safety at work, you immediately consider industrial/occupational hazards as the main aspects you must deal with. Obviously, these would apply to running facilities/ continuous occupations (and not sporadic/occasional pieces of tasks). On the other hand, construction activities are, usually, on-and-off types and at different locations. There are considerable hazards associated with such activities too—different kettle of fish. Safety management of construction hazards, hence, needs to be dealt with, separately.

Construction hazards include physical, chemical and biological hazards. Physical, because of use of implements, tools and machinery in the construction activities of digging of trenches, formation of earthworks, transportation of materials, erection/ use of scaffoldings, use of light and heavy tools themselves, and so on. Chemical hazards arise due to use of chemicals/gases, explosives, any site contamination and so on. And biological hazards turn up as a direct result of the health hazards arising out of the chemicals used, fabrication work and so on.

Thus, construction sites are full of physical hazards because of excavations, scaffoldings, structural frameworks, roof-works, tunneling, pits, cranes, iron-working, use of concrete-mixing and other machinery, road-works, demolition work, materials and waste accumulation, movement of personnel and materials, use of transport and other vehicles itself, and so on. Further, working out in open is the invitation for the environmental and other hazards of extreme cold, heat, hail, deluge, snowfall, falling objects, and so on.

Repeated and continued use of high frequency vibration devices, like pneumatic drills, is capable of causing injuries to hands due to the vibration. The danger starts with slight tingling or numbness of fingers, then leads to whitening of fingertips, and painful onrush of blood, and so on. The remedy is to use suitable vibration isolators, proper gloves, and ensure good circulation of blood into the hands.

Persistent exposure to high levels of noise, such as those arising from use of pneumatic tools, heavy machinery etc. itself, can be dangerous enough to cause irreversible loss of hearing, partial or complete deafness. Such extremes of noise pollution are also great irritants to others in the neighbourhood. Muffling of noise production and noise reductions by suitable re-engineering, as well as use of appropriate protective ear-cover, etc., are some remedial measures.

Health hazards also occur when harmful chemicals such as asbestos dust, silica dust, noxious gases, welding fumes and so on are inhaled or ingested. So are extensive uses of materials such as: solvents, adhesives, paints, lubricants etc. Inhalation of the vapours can lead to headaches, dizziness, vomiting, or even unconsciousness followed by death. This is particularly true where such operations are carried out in confined spaces, particularly without proper ventilation. In such instances, it is essential to have proper protective devices (breathing masks, protective clothing), apart from good ventilation.

Chemical hazards, biological hazards, radiation hazards, electrical hazards etc., are dealt with in some detail, later on.

Occupational Hazards

Some or many of the above-mentioned manmade hazards, may be present as Occupational Hazards, to a lesser or greater extent, depending on the industry and the occupation. Hence, safety and hazards management is a vital task in most industries. Ergonomic aspects are also important, not only from point of view of improving efficiency of operations, but also as they impinge on the operator's health and safety. The hazards and safety management aspects are specific to the industry and the occupations involved. It is not necessary, therefore, to enumerate the different industries, which are a legion and ever growing, and the specific hazards/safety engineering relevant to the same; but dwell at some length on the various types of hazards, already listed in the above paragraphs.

Special symbols are used for safety—CAUTION/WARNING—against possible hazards in the work environment, at home, out in the open, and in public places (like the cautionary road signs and fire hazard indications). Wherever a particular symbol is seen, it indicates the presence of that particular hazard, at that location; and denotes that relevant safety precautions should be taken while one is working or, even, merely present at the location.

Radiation Hazards

Radiation is, basically, nothing but transfer of energy by electromagnetic (EM) waves like, X-rays, radio (RF) waves, laser output and so on. Or, it may be particles such as neutrons, alpha and beta particles, electrons and so on. Main radiation hazards are from IONIZING RADIATIONS, such as from X-ray machines, from radioactive sources, or due to thermal effects of electromagnetic radiation, LASER, (Light Amplification by Stimulated Emission of Radiation), etc. The effects may be, thermal heating up of tissues/body parts or the whole body; or genetic type-involving mutation of cells, or genetic material, etc. Ionizing radiation is that electromagnetic radiation or particle radiation that causes breakup of gases into ions and electrons/positrons. RF waves are basically non-ionizing radiation, as the absorption of the energy usually results in heating up, or thermal effect, and not in a breakup of atoms/molecules into ions.

Common sources of ionizing radiation are the various types of widely prevalent sealed radioactive sources used in: smoke detectors, medical diagnostic/treatment devices, industrial non-destructive testing devices, (used to check integrity of pipelines, joints, castings etc.), radiograph systems, some types of explosives vapour detectors, and so on. Effect of exposure to the radiation could be nausea, skin-burns, dermatitis, loss of hair, or even cancer. Obviously, the severity of radiation injury depends on the dosage received, apart from the type of radiation, the duration, and extent of exposure (whether part or the whole body has been exposed), to the radiation. Effect of acute radiation can be notices in a few hours, or weeks. But, evidence of effects due to chronic radiation exposure is difficult to detect, as they are usually delayed, and may become evident, perhaps, after years. In such cases, particularly, it can be difficult to distinguish the effects, from similar effects that could have arisen due to other causes. These hazards will be dealt with at greater length when considering nuclear and biological hazards.

LASERS

When laser devices are around, *lookout for eye damage, skin burns etc., unless proper protective actions are taken.* Depending on the type, and intensity of the laser beam, the particular laser device could be safe, that is, it will not cause biological damage. Basic safety precautions to be used are, to be cautious at locations using lasers, use adequate and suitable goggles while working with lasers. Totally avoid aiming a laser with the naked eye, nor should you look at the laser source, (or even reflected laser radiation), to prevent retinal burns. So warn all personnel and visitors, at the location, of the potential danger.

Sometimes, Cryogenic (liquid nitrogen/ liquid helium) cooling is used in laser system, and laser radiation detection devices. This can be hazardous, unless extra care is taken, to avoid contact with the coolant, (to prevent skin-"burn"). It is advisable too, to wear asbestos gloves and a facemask whenever you handle such coolants. Do ensure adequate ventilation, since these coolants, if/when vented into air tend to condense oxygen from the air, (as oxygen liquefies at the lowered temperature of the air, due to the evaporation cooling by the vented liquid nitrogen/liquid helium). This also necessitates that you have to ensure that any hydrocarbons lying around are not cooled to such an extent that liquid oxygen will condense on it. This is to avoid resultant formation of highly explosive mixtures that are very sensitive to shock; and hence result in unexpected/dangerous explosions.

Do note that *high-powered lasers cause other dangers too.* Such a high power laser beam, when it impinges on materials like glass, can cause sudden shattering of the material due to the very rapid heating caused by the laser beam. Dangerous flying shards of the glass can well be the result. Hence, suitable protective enclosures are a must around such high power beams (the optical path, lenses, diffraction elements, etc.), and the brittle targets.

Great care is also called for whilst irradiating any biological specimens. This is essential to prevent any scattering of the specimen cells to the atmosphere, that could result in the release of dangerous pathogens into the environment (due to mutations or otherwise of poisonous, cancerous, or infectious specimen/ material).

Ultraviolet Radiation

Exposure to *ultraviolet, (UV), radiation can result in injury to the cornea (of eyes).* Therefore, it is dangerous to use sunglasses that do not have UV absorbing capability. Actually, it is more dangerous than not using any sunglasses at all. This is because such sunglasses reduce the visible light entering the eye, thus causing pupil to open further to see better. This, in turn enables more UV energy to enter the eyes, and hence cause more damaging effects than when no sunglasses are used. UV radiation is relatively easy to shield. Most plastics, glasses and other materials, which absorb visible light, are also opaque to ultraviolet radiation. So, if you do use sunglasses, use only those with certified UV absorbing capability.

Did you know that UV radiation could also ionize air and produce toxic levels of ozone, in the atmosphere? Ozone is a highly reactive agent. It could hence be harmful to men and materials. It is a strong oxidizing agent and reacts with materials like rubber. A concentration of ozone in air of as little as one part per million, (1ppm) is sufficient to cause noticeable effects on health of people exposed to it. A concentration of about 10 ppm is expected to cause severe illness.

UV radiation also results when electric conduction takes place in gases (apart from the normal occurrence in sunlight, due to ionization of air).

Radio Frequency (RF) Radiation

You are familiar with the mains AC power frequency of 50 cycles (Hz) (and 60 Hz in the USA, JAPAN, etc). Even higher frequencies like 400 Hz are sometimes used in special power generators, as in the case of aircraft supplies. At these frequencies, the wavelengths are huge. At 50 Hz, for example, the wavelength is six thousand kilometres (6,000 kms.)! Hence, to radiate energy at such low frequencies, the antenna required will need to be of the same order of length; so you do not expect radiation at such frequencies. The definition of RF band, however, covers a very wide range of frequencies-from 300 Hz to 300 GHz (i.e. 300,000,000,000. Hz)! This includes the well-known HF, VHF, UHF/microwave and radar frequencies.

The human body absorbs RF radiation to varying degree, depending on the radiation frequency, the body structure-skin, blood, muscle, bone etc. Water being the main constituent in the human body, the primary result of such absorption of the RF energy is-heating, i.e. thermal effect. The extent and the distribution of the energy cannot be easily quantified, because of the difficulties of direct measurements as well as the large number of parameters involved (in RF radiation), such as-frequency, power level, type and extent of modulation, antenna characteristics, distance involved, exposure duration and so on. Therefore, though there is a large body of literature in regard to RF radiation hazards to human beings, (RADHAZ), there is no universally accepted standard quantifying the hazards. (Note that RF radiation hazard to Electro-Explosive Devices, or EEDs, is known as HERF). However, an International Committee on Non-Ionizing Radiation Protection was established in 1991, for investigation on all forms of non-ionizing radiation.

There are standards laid down by different countries in regard to undesirable RF radiation from devices/equipment/systems, so as to control unwitting occupational and in public exposure of personnel to such radiation. That is, to reduce and minimize RF radiation hazards to users of equipment/personnel in the vicinity, RF leakage standards set limits to such RF leakage from consumer items and commercial/professional equipment systems.

There are also standards to minimize mutual Electromagnetic Interference (EMI) between equipment systems, i.e., to ensure

Electromagnetic Compatibility (EMC). Special standards are laid down too to minimize/ prevent possible ignition of flammable substances/explosives, or EEDs.

However, due to lack of agreement between nations as to what exactly are the hazards to humans because of RF radiation, some of the countries have evolved their own standards regarding permissible RF leakage from consumer and other equipment. Some of the examples are: consumer devices such as, TVs, Microwave Ovens, Hairdryers, Electric Shavers and professional and commercial systems like, Transmitters, Medical Equipment and Electronic Systems. They have also evolved limits for radiation intensity and duration to which individuals maybe exposed. There are also different standards laid down in different countries for mutual interference free operation of equipment systems, that is, Electro-Magnetic-Compatibility or EMC. For Military systems, there are very elaborate EMC standards, and TEMPEST specifications lay down limits to prevent any information pickup, by the opposition, from RF leakage from electronic systems.

Very special methodology, design and procedures are needed to protect electronic systems from damage or deterioration in performance, due to what is called as the Electro-Magnetic Pulse or (EMP). Luckily, EMP has no direct effect on human beings, though it can "kill" normal equipment systems based on electronics—for example, an automobile using electronic ignition system could come to a halt, and refuse to run! You will come to know more of EMP when dealing with nuclear effects.

Whether an individual is exposed to whole body radiation or partial body radiation mainly depends on the frequency of the radiation, (and to some extent on proximity). At lower RF, the wavelength of the radiation is very large compared to the largest dimension of the body, the height. But as the frequency increases, the wavelength decreases till it becomes comparable to the human body dimension. Hence, absorption of RF radiant energy increases with the increase in frequency, till it reaches a peak. This peak is around the frequency at which the body length corresponds to slightly less than half-wavelength; (the body is then said to be resonant with the radiation frequency). Thereafter, the radiant energy absorption becomes more and more partial body type, but the rate of absorption remains about the same-near the peak. For the human body, the resonance occurs at frequencies varying from about 250 MHz, for a child about 0.5 metres tall, down to about 60 MHz for a 2 metres tall person. For the purpose of laying down limit for human exposure to RF radiation, an increase in the rectal temperature by one degree C, due to the RF energy absorption in the human body, is taken as the Specific Absorption Rate, (SAR). A SAR of 0.4 W/kg is used as a basis for occupational safety. SAR is, however, not practical or measurable on a human being. Also, some parts of the body have higher absorption than others like knees, elbows, and head. For estimation purposes modeling is used, or computer simulation. But both have inadequacy due to the heat-regulatory mechanism of the human body. Further, when a person is effectively at earth potential (bare feet directly on the ground for example), the resonance occurs at half the above-mentioned frequencies, and the radiant energy absorbed is twice that a person would absorb, compared to when he is effectively insulated from earth.

Research results indicate that the eyes and the male testis are most prone to heat-effect, as they do not have direct blood supply to carry away the local heat, and thus take away the heating effect. Hence, one has to take due precautions when working with (or in the neighbourhood of) RF systems/devices which have high RF leakage. This is particularly so at microwave frequencies. Do avoid being in strong RF fields, such as those near high power radar/radio/TV antennas.

Conductive items like-metal wire, metal fences, metal scrap, metal grills etc., can themselves act as RF generators, when subjected to strong RF radiation. This can also give rise to sparking, arcing as well as ignition of flammable vapours/materials. Hence, do remove such material from locations where strong RF fields are likely to be present. At lower RF of up to, say, 100 MHz, there is also the danger that contacts with such objects could result in shock and burns, as if the direct source of radiation has been touched. You should be equally aware that before climbing any RF antenna masts, you must ensure that the antennae are not energized (that is, there is no transmission), for the duration of the work. Even then, it is advisable to wear suitable harness to keep you close to and attached to the mast. This will ensure that in case you lose your hold of the mast, it will save you from deadly falls, resulting from any RF shocks you may get whilst you are going about your task, on the mast. You should also wear suitable protective gloves, to save your hands from cuts, abrasions, burns etc.

Considerable confusion exists in regard to "Non-Thermal" effects, such as cancer, due to RF absorption in the human body. RF sources using very high voltage could produce some X-ray radiation, as a by-product. Such X-ray radiation hazard could arise in case of TV sets when the TV tube shielding is damaged/misplaced or badly installed, (during checkup/maintenance); since TV sets use high voltages of the order of 15 to 25 kV, (hence sitting near its proximity is also inadvisable). Radiation hazards also exist with microwave ovens. It is inadvisable to have your face close to the oven, looking into it, whilst the oven is "ON". Also, the look-through glass of the oven maybe cracked, indiscernible to you, the gaskets damaged or become imperfect RF seal thus letting RF leakage through, and so on, thus exposing you to leaked-through high RF energy. Similarly, hazards arise when you use your cellular radio, often and very close to your eyes/head. Note that those who wear medical implants, like pacemaker, could have serious problems with the units going haywire, due to such exposures to RF energy. (It is best to use only properly approved and tested equipment, which are also, properly installed and maintained, and also exercise due care not to expose them to undue RF radiation). Avoid use of high power cellular or other RF devices, and reduce the duration of exposure. So also, exercise extra care when around electronic devices that could have RF leakage, such as microwave ovens, computer systems, TV sets, and so on. Use of cellular radios when you are on the move, driving, could turn out to be deadly dangerous, due to serious accidents that could result as a consequence, because of the resulting inattention (to driving). Many states/countries ban use of cellular/mobile radios in vehicles, when on the move. Cellular radios are now being offered with quantified specifications on their radiation parameters to help consumers to choose one that is likely to least affect them, radiation-wise that is.

Filtering, shielding, bonding, grounding, orientation, timing of operation, and distancing from radiation sources (that is avoidance) are the basic means of reducing RF radiation hazards. It must be noted, that testing for RF leakage or susceptibility to EMI, involve laborious and expensive methodologies, and hence, are not too prevalent, particularly, on large systems.

Table X.1 Radiation Hazards

Types of Radiation	Characteristics	Effects	Precautions
A) **Laser** (Light Amplification by Stimulated Emission of Radiation	* Emit ionizing radiations * Radiations differ in wavelength, continuity, pulse, coherence etc.	* Responsible for causing eye damage which could even be irreversible in severe cases. * Skin rashes, burns and blisters.	* Use of proper shades to shield eyes. * Prominent display of warning/caution notices. * Removal of unnecessary furniture and fixtures from laser prone locations. * Prevention of all undesired reflections and sound operating procedures.

Types of Radiation	Characteristics	Effects	Precautions
Ultra Violet Radiation	* Emit ionizing radiations. * Capable of producing toxic levels of ozone. * Apart from sunlight, they are emitted by furnaces and during welding only.	*. Lead to sunburns, skin cancer and rashes. * Effect cornea of the eye, besides causing Conjunctivitis	* Wear protective UV blocking goggles. * Use proper clothing, sunscreen or devices etc. * Do not get exposed to strong sunlight (direct or reflected).
Radio Frequency Radiation	* Emit non-ionizing radiations. * Passes great range of frequencies, power level, type, modulation etc	* Responsible for thermal effect. * Cause serious biological changes in human body * Damage heat-effect prone organs like eyes, testis etc., and even human tissues. * Responsible for cancerous developments	* Avoid/ reduce exposure to high power cellular or RF devices. * Keep away from strong RF fields. * Cover eyes and body properly when exposed

Electrical Hazards

Practically, everyone, who uses electricity or an electrical apparatus, should be aware of electric shock hazard. Many may also know that contact with a live electric wire could lead to electrocution; but not many can claim to know that *electricity can cause wounds, injuries, or conjunctivitis* (apart from consequential injuries like broken bones as a result of falls sustained due to an electric accident). Neither would you be aware that an electric shock could turn out to be deadly, when it is totally unanticipated and catches you unawares. Further, electricity can become a serious fire hazard. It is not too many years ago, that, a devastating fire, as a result of a minor electrical short-circuit/sparking in the building wiring burnt down the famous Vigyan Bhavan, at New Delhi. Fortunately, timely evacuation of the building took place and there were no casualties. On the other hand, the fire, resulting from an electrical short-circuit, in the Uphaar theatre at Delhi, was an unmitigated human disaster, and caused a large number of deaths. So it would appear, that, adequate knowledge of possible electrical hazards and relevant safety needs are not too well known, despite repeated occurrences of a number of deadly electrical accidents/ fires due to electrical short-circuits. Further, note that, an electrical accident could become an explosion/ detonation hazard, when it occurs in an environment laden with flammable gases/substances. Breakdown or failure of electrical equipment could also lead to consequential hazards, like-in operation theatres, life-supporting systems, fire detection/suppression systems, transportation systems, and so on.

It is doubtful whether many people are aware, that, there can be a toxic hazard also associated with electrical hazard. Overloading of conductors, overheating of wires, terminations, loose contacts, sparking at terminal strips etc. can lead to release of toxic gases due to PVC or other nature of insulation, terminal strips etc. Note also that electrical conductors can pick up sufficient energy that could be dangerous enough, by induction in the presence of strong RF radiation, static radiation from thunderclouds or lightning. This could cause sparking, arcing, and even result in dangerous explosions where flammable substances/gases are present. Ofcourse, there is the ever-present danger of shock and/or electrocution, also, if you are anywhere near such conductors, during ongoing thunderstorm activities.

To ensure electrical safety, the best approach is to scrupulously follow the safety instructions, and prevalent national safety codes during selection of material and equipment, design, installation, operation, and maintenance of electrical installations/systems. It is best to go in for fire-resistant cables and materials; check for effective earthing; ensure that all terminations are firm and sound, (and that there are no loose contacts at all). Provide proper interlock switches, where necessary. You should use appropriate barriers/screened protective enclosures, without fail, where required. It is also essential to protect the electrical installation/system from rodents, cats, birds, vermin and others, whose activities could cause electrical shorts and accidents. Exercise due caution in the use of electrical devices/ apparatus, to ensure not only your personal safety, but also the safety of others. Check the device to see that it is in good condition, that the wiring is not frayed, and for poor contacts of switches and terminations. Do not touch with bare hands any naked conductors, but always use protective gloves, in such situations. Only, "INTRINSICALLY SAFE" equipment should be used in hazardous locations of flammable or explosive atmospheres, such as petrol storage depots and petrol bunks, for example. Do protect your eyes with proper goggles, when in the proximity of in use-welding units, electric arc machines, electric furnaces, or similar devices. Be fully aware of First-Aid requirements for electrical accidents. Only properly qualified and experienced personnel should carry out any maintenance, or repair work on electrical units/circuits/ systems/installations.

Chemical Hazards

The twentieth century saw an explosive growth in the use of chemicals. (From consumer conveniences like detergents and cleaning agents, through agricultural inputs of insecticides, pesticides, and fertilizers, to life saving medicines as well as life threatening drugs and poisons). Ubiquitous chemicals are in widespread use, whether in industry, agriculture, domestic life or public utilities. *Though, the use is for the "benefit" of individuals/society,* the toxic properties of chemicals so used, are often ignored or forgotten. The manner of usage affects the toxicity, to differing extent. One may be toxic when ingested; another when inhaled; yet another one, when it comes in contact with the skin (or through scratches, cuts or wounds; the breaks in the skin may even be invisible). Some chemicals are dangerous in many ways or in combination. Body openings are the most common, dangerous entry points for many of the hazardous chemicals/poisons.

The toxic effect of chemicals can be immediate and acute, or become apparent over long term usage/on chronic exposure. The ill effects may well manifest later, much after the consumption/exposure to the hazardous chemical. The type, the amount of the hazardous chemical exposed to, the method of introduction into the body, the duration of exposure, the nature of the person (body condition), etc. all have their say on the damaging/ill affect on the individual. Chemicals can be corrosive, harmful, damage equipment systems, pollute the atmosphere/the environment, and endanger the habitat.

In most cases, there is a threshold limit for the quantity of the chemical exposure beyond which only harmful effects occur. This is known as the Threshold Limit Value, or TLV. Below the TLV, the material is considered, (hopefully), as harmless. However, this danger limit is not a fixed value, as it varies with the age, growth, constitution, health, etc., of the individual exposed to the danger. Thus, a child, the old, and sick ones are more easily affected. Therefore, the TLV for them is much lower. On the other hand, the young, adult, healthy and well-grown persons would require higher doses of the substance for it to become dangerous; that is, a higher TLV.

Most chemicals are dangerous by themselves, but some are dangerous in combination only. For example, like 'drinking and driving do not go together', drinking and consuming anti-histamine drugs (like Avil) or sleeping tablets is very dangerous and can be fatal. Whereas, separately, within specified amounts, they are considered beneficial. It is essential to know which chemicals are incompatible, the difference between an oxidizing agent and a reducing agent, those which have high affinity to each other, and so on. For example, peroxides are oxygen rich, (oxidizing agent), and should not be juxtaposed with a reducing material like aluminium powder, as an undesirable conflagration may then take place.

Similarly, mixing of some immiscible liquids can be dangerous. Petrol is lighter than water and does not mix with it. It is, therefore, dangerous to try to put out a petrol flameout by throwing water on it; the petrol will float on the water and the fire will spread faster. The fire may even spread into drains and cause explosions too. The Bhopal Gas Tragedy is a case demonstrating the danger of introducing water into a chemical container not fully purged and clear of all traces of a dangerous chemical it contained. There are many chemicals, which react very violently with water, generating heat, corrosive and deadly gases, including possibility of explosions.

On the other hand, there are also some flammable chemicals, which are miscible with water. In such cases, a gentle addition of water to a spillage will mix and dilute the concentration gradually down to safe levels. Thereafter, the spill could be flushed down the drain, safely. This permits very easy and effective handling of such spills, where they are not otherwise harmful to the environment/habitat.

Note also, the difference in movement of gases. The dangerous carbon monoxide and carbon dioxide gases generated in a fire, move upwards with the draught created by the expansion of gases due to the heat of fire and in rushing flow of air. It is, hence, safer to hold a wet cloth to the face and crawl along the floor to a safer lower level, while getting away from the fire. On the other hand, in case of a spill of the deadly chlorine, the gas is heavier than air and tends to settle down seeking and concentrating at lower levels. In this case, it would be most prudent to keep upright and walk away towards a higher level, say upstairs!

Many chemicals are well known by popular names, and usually, not identified by their chemical formula or scientific name. Everyone may have heard of Vitamin C, but not many will recognize ascorbic acid; who has not heard of aspirin, but do you know it is called acety-salicyclic-acid! (There are some exceptions; sulfuric acid is well known, but how many are aware of its common name-vitriol?).

The physical characteristics of chemicals also vary widely. A chemical may be in gaseous, liquid, solid or dust form. Their storage requirements also vary; may need to be kept in a cool, dry place, away from direct sunlight, away from source of heat, not exposed to air, kept in a freezer and so on. Some may need isolation, or total separation from some other specified substance, to which it has great affinity, or incompatibility. A chemical may be basically inert, very active, corrosive, flammable, or even explosive. Hence, handling, storage and transportation, etc. of chemicals, require specialist knowledge, expertise, great care and strict adherence to national and local safety procedures and requirements.

The toxic nature of a chemical is its inherent characteristic. It depends on its composition, (that is its formula). However, the aspect of how and which way it is hazardous, depend on many aspects. The mode of application, the frequency of exposure, the concentration involved characteristics of the person concerned, (age, bulk, health and other such considerations), as well as the duration of exposure or time delay before application of suitable remedial measures, may all play a part. Risks attendant on its usage and the hazards are interrelated. Thus, when used in the specified way a chemical, (medicine, drug, cleaning agent and so on, all coming under the generic name of chemical), is beneficial, whereas, it can be very harmful and dangerous when used improperly. For example, sulfuric acid is a very useful chemical in industry, or even in the domestic environment, (a car battery cannot function without its dilute sulfuric acid), when carefully handled and used on an informed basis. However, it is highly corrosive, deadly, and dangerous acid in its concentrated form. It causes severe burns and rapidly destroys tissues of the human body, on coming in contact with the skin, (recall the acid throwing crimes of some lunatic people!). Thus, with the acquisition of comprehensive knowledge of the chemical, use of appropriate and scrupulous procedures, elaborate accident prevention programmes, and correct handling, the hazards of the highly dangerous and toxic chemical can be controlled and reduced to be practically a risk-free proposition. But, any flouting of the precautions/procedures can result in deadly consequences.

The TLV, (Threshold Limit Value), for a dangerous chemical is often mentioned in terms of parts per million, (ppm). That is to say, so many parts of the hazardous chemical is present in one million part of air, (or in the substance in which the undesirable chemical has got mixed up, leaked into or found). Sometimes, the TLV for the chemical may be below the detection level, by the human senses in any case. Take, for example, a chlorine gas-air mixture. The sense of smell can detect the chlorine when it is present in air, in concentrations of order of few parts per million, (say, 5ppm or more); whereas, such a concentration is deadly for humans, as the TLV for chlorine is a mere 1ppm. The TLV is, naturally, different for different chemicals, and it varies over a very wide range. The TLV for carbon dioxide, (Co_2), is 5,000ppm, whereas, the TLV for carbon monoxide is far lower, a mere 50ppm. Arsine gas, on the other hand, is very deadly, with the TLV of hardly 0.05ppm!

In view of the above, it is very important to know the properties of chemicals you are likely to encounter, to prevent dangerous accidents from happening and to ensure the safety and protection of people, and the environment. Inspite of all care, an accident could occur. It is, therefore, also necessary to have effective, and safe disaster plans to handle such contingencies. Therefore, great care, scrupulous specifications, proper inspection, elaborate recording and audit are required in the design, production, packaging, labelling, transportation, storage, juxtaposition/isolation, use and disposal of chemicals.

Chemical hazards are widespread throughout the world with over an estimated 100,000 chemicals being used in domestic and industrial applications. Considering this, the safety management in chemical applications appears to be pretty good, except for a few unfortunate incidents. On the other hand, nuclear applications have been deliberately controlled, to far more limited extent and locations. This is because of any nuclear accident having likely lasting, very widespread, and horrendous risks to humanity. Therefore, an entire chapter, that follows, is devoted to Nuclear Hazards.

Chapter 11

Nuclear Hazards

"Vision is the art of seeing things invisible"

—Jonathan Swift

Nuclear hazards are the invisible types and, they *can entail Horrendous Consequences.*

"I'm an Optimist, but I'm an Optimist who carries an Umbrella"

—Harold Wilson

An interesting situation arose a few decades ago in the country. This concerned the Nuclear Hazards—the problem of not being able to retrieve a Plutonium Battery lost in the Nanda Devi Mountain, of the Himalayan mountain range. There were hot discussions in the media, reporting about loss of the nuclear (Plutonium based) battery in an avalanche, during an expedition to the mountain in the early sixties. Naturally, there was considerable agitation in the minds of the public too, about the possible dangers of the extremely hazardous nuclear material of the battery leaching into the mighty river Ganges, which would disastrously affect the people, animals, and the fish that depend on the waters of the river. The deliberations of a high power group of scientists arrived at the conclusion, that, the only solution was to have a continuous monitoring of the waters of the Ganges in the higher reaches, near the mountain. Immediately, on finding any trace of the poisonous Plutonium, the population downstream was to be warned against use of the river water, as long as the traces of Plutonium persisted. *This was because it was not possible to retrieve the nuclear battery, which had got buried deep in the snow and it was not possible by any means to locate it.* It is possible to appreciate the problem only when you are aware of the nature of the products of nuclear activities and their effects on living beings and inanimate systems that civilized societies have come to depend upon. This is more so with the proliferation of uses of nuclear technology, what with nuclear power generation, nuclear weapons, nuclear batteries in satellites, nuclear medicine, irradiated food, use of radio isotopes in fire alarm system/ industry/explosive detectors and so on.

Ionizing Radiation

Almost all the products of nuclear reactions have the characteristics of *IONIZING RADIATION.* These are EM radiation such as, X-ray and Gamma ray; or corpuscular radiation like, Alpha and Beta particles, (electrons, positrons), Neutrons, Protons and heavier particles (like Nuclides or Radioisotope-that is a chemically identical radioactive substance having the same positive charge on the atomic nucleus, but has different atomic weight). Such radiation is capable of breaking up atoms, or molecules into ion-electron pairs.

A nuclear explosion results in many products:

- Intense pulse of Electro-Magnetic energy, (the *Electro-Magnetic-Pulse, or EMP*);
- Energy in the form of a ball of fire/heat wave;
- High-pressure blast, and
- Particle radiation, the Transient Radiation Effect or *TRE, (or TREE,* when considering its effects on electronics).

It will be, perhaps, worthwhile to know a bit more about these and their affects on living beings and material systems, without going into the intricacies of nuclear science.

Alpha Particles

These are nuclei of helium atoms with a positive charge (positive ion). Their typical energy level is of the order of 5 MeV. (Note that one electron volt, or eV, is the energy gained by an electron when it moves through a potential difference of one Volt. Hence, 1 eV = 1.6 x 10 raised to the power of (-12) ergs, that is 1.6 x 10 raised to the power (-19) joules. The unit eV is used to refer to the energy levels of particles to indicate how energetic they are). They travel in straight lines and have low penetration, (about 5cms in air), and can be stopped by a thin sheet of paper, or body skin. But, the danger is that, they are intensely ionizing and interact strongly with matter. It penetrates soft tissues and heavily ionizes, creating more ionizing particles to break up more cells. Therefore, when ingested, the alpha particles are deadly as they damage internal organs. Similar damage to tissues under the skin can occur in case of cuts and wounds, when exposed to alpha particles. (Hence, the brouhaha about the lost plutonium battery. Any plutonium leakage into flowing water would result in widespread exposure/ingestion of plutonium atoms, even by mere consumption of fish of the river exposed to the hazard. It would also be extremely difficult to remove traces of the poisonous plutonium).

Beta Particles

These are electrons (negatively charged particles), or positrons (positively charged particles). They have high velocities, approaching the speed of light, being much smaller in size. They have much greater penetration power than the alpha particles, in view of small size and relatively high energies. Consequently, these particles also have high ionization potential. With far lesser energy, (order of say, 0.5 to 3 MeV), they penetrate up to over a metre in air, and penetrates into the sub-cutaneous layers of the skin. These particles can thus affect the superficial body tissues and the lens of the eyes.

Gamma Radiation, **X-Rays, and Bremstrahlung**

These are basically, electromagnetic (EM) radiation. They may be termed as photons. The radiation is highly penetrating. For example, 1 MeV (energy) gamma ray will reduce to half that value, after penetrating as much as 10 cms. of soft tissue or water. Such rays of even a few keV of energy can penetrate about a mm into soft tissues. Therefore, the radiation can be, biologically, very damaging. (Note that Bremstrahlung is the EM radiation emitted when charged particles accelerate, or decelerate). The severity of radiation injury depend on-dose, dose rate, extent of parts of body irradiated, type of radiation, and so on. Acute exposure may show early effects within a few hours to few weeks. Whereas, chronic exposure may show delayed effects, with a latent period of even tens of years. (Note, however, that exposure to some other types of hazards too may show similar effects).

Clinical effects for acute whole body radiation may show only with a radiation dosage of about 50 to 100 rads, (rad stands for Radiation Absorbed Dose-the historical unit for energy absorption, which is about 100 ergs/gm of material-or more). The *current unit* for the *absorbed radiation dose* is the *gray (Gy)-quantity of ionizing radiation that results in the absorption of one joule of energy, per kg of the (absorbing) material.* (Thus, one gray = 100 rads, and one rad = 0.01 Gy). Symptoms of radiation sickness may appear for irradiation levels of *1 to 2 Gy.* With exposure to 3 to 4 Gy of irradiation, fatalities are to be expected in 50% of cases. Higher levels of exposure would lead to early and certain death. (Note that, the rad, the historical unit of irradiation, is the energy deposited/or absorbed in materials as indicated above. It is *approximately* equal to *100 ergs/gm* of the material. For example*, it is 87 ergs/gm of air,* but as much as *97 ergs/gm of water).* When relatively small areas of the body are exposed to acute but local radiation, local, significant symptoms appear, such as loss of hair, erythma, and even radiation burns at very severe exposure levels.

As usual, genetic effects are very difficult to assess, as they take years and years, and perhaps appear only in the progeny. And it does require statistical assessment over a large population too, for validation. This is the crux of the problem.

Maximum permissible dose/dose rate for public, as well as occupational exposures are laid down by relevant national standards, and by the International Committee on Radiological Protection, (ICRP).

Protons

Protons are nuclei of hydrogen atoms. A proton has a positive charge of one unit. As a proton is over 1800 times heavier than electrons, protons are more difficult to deflect.

Neutrons

Neutrons have the same atomic weight as protons, but do not have any charge. Like Gamma rays, they have great penetrating capabilities. Maximum dosage applicable would be as for EM radiation. Normal practice in this regard is to apply the most restrictive limits as per the ICRP. Since there is no charge, they are difficult to stop. But, Hydrogenous matter like water slows them down, (it is hence that, water is used as the moderator in light water reactors). Note also that Gamma ray is emitted when a neutron is captured. Neutrons are classified as per their energy level as, thermal or slow neutrons, (less than 1 keV), intermediate neutron or fast neutrons (greater than 100 keV).

Radionuclide

These are far, far heavier particles or radio-isotopes, which occur as results of nuclear reactions. You may well recognize some of the well-known radio-isotopes viz.: Carbon 14;Cobalt 60; Strontium 90; Iodine 132 and Cesium 137.

Radioactivity

Naturally occurring elements have Atomic Numbers from 1 to 92. Elements with Atomic Numbers higher than 92 are produced artificially, in the laboratory by scientists. Thus, man has *produced elements having higher atomic numbers,* of 93 to 106, artificially. The atomic number of an element is its number in the Periodic Table, where the elements are arranged in the order of their atomic weights, with the lightest one, Hydrogen being in the first place. Elements with an atomic number of 83, or more are known to be *Radioactive.* Such elements undergo nuclear re-arrangements to reach a stable configuration, with the emission of gamma rays and sub-atomic particles. High atomic number nuclides emit negative beta particles (electrons), whereas, proton rich nuclides emit positive beta particles (positrons). *The unit of radioactivity is the Becquerel, indicating the number of disintegration per second.* (Traditionally the unit was Curie, the number of disintegration per gram of Radium, the element discovered by Madame Curie. One Curie equals 3.7 x 10 raised to the power ten Becquerels). The *nuclides decay to form stable atoms.* The time taken for the radioactivity of the nuclide to fall to half its original value is called the 'half life' of the nuclide. Thus, the number of disintegration per second at any time is proportional to the amount of the unstable nuclide present.

The biological effects of radiation on humans, depends not only on the radiation dose, but also on the type of radiation, (its quality factor, or Q), and other modifying factors. *That is,*

REM (or rad-equivalent-man) = (rad x Q x modifying factor).

REM is the traditional unit of *absorbed radiation dose equivalent.* The current unit for the same is the Sievert (Sv). (Note that rad or gray is the unit of deposition of energy, as mentioned earlier) Thus,

One Sv = 100 rems and one rem = 0.01 Sv.

RBE or, Relative Biological Effectiveness, is an alternative unit to the quality factor Q. It is defined as:

$$\text{Thus RBE}=\text{Q}=\frac{\text{Absorbed dose of reference radiation}}{\text{Absorbed dose of given radiation with same effect}}$$

Q varies for the type of irradiation (alpha, beta, gamma radiation or particles/nuclides involved), and whether the radiation is external or internal to the body. For X-ray, gamma and beta radiation, the Q value is unity, or 1; so that for these radiation's, rems and rads are equivalent. For neutrons, Q depends on the energy, (i.e., as per keV); and it varies from 2 to over 10. For alpha radiation Q can be taken as zero for external irradiation, as the unbroken skin can stop the radiation. But it can be as high as 20, for *internal irradiation,* as it very adversely affects internal organs/cells. Thus, obviously, *alpha radiation would be most damaging, followed by fast neutrons.*

Background Radiation

Some background radiation is always present in nature. These arise from *Extra-Terrestrial, Terrestrial and the Local Environmental origin, and are termed as background radiation.* At mid latitudes, the extra-terrestrial radiation level is about 300 micro Sv/ yr. (or 30m.rems/ yr.). Terrestrial background radiation level is of the order of 2 mSv. / Yr., (or 200 mrems / yr.). The environmental background radiation depends on the nature of the soil; whether rocky, granite type, sandstone structure etc. It could vary from 200 micro Sv / yr., (at a height of 1 meter in air). Living in a granite house may expose one to radiation level of about 5 mSv / yr., (or 500 mrems / yr.!).

Much higher levels of background radiation exist in some parts of the world; like Kerala beaches with Monazite sands. The radiation level for monazite sands can be as high as 20 mSv. / yr., (or 2 rems/ yr.).

Radiation-Internal to the Body

Some naturally occurring radionuclides, such as potassium, radium and lead are present in the body and give rise to sources of internal (background) radiation. This is of the order of 200 micro Sv/ yr., (20 mrems / yr.).

Annual radiation dose limits

The ICRP has specified limits for annual radiation dosage that a person could be subjected to. It varies from 5 mSv / yr. for the general public, to 50 mSv /yr. for a classified worker, (that is, an occupational hazard), as whole body irradiation. The dose can increase to as much as 500-mSv/ yr. for parts of the body-like the hands and the feet.

Nuclear Explosion Hazards

The types and extent of hazards that occur due to a nuclear explosion is dependent on the type of nuclear burst. *Nuclear explosions are classified as—Underground Bursts; Underwater Bursts; Surface Bursts; Air Bursts or Low Altitude Bursts; and High Altitude or Ex-Atmospheric Bursts.*

The energy generated in a nuclear explosion is distributed amongst four mechanisms. These are in the form of-1). Electromagnetic energy, (*gamma rays and X-rays, about 5 %* of the total energy), 2). Particle radiation, (*neutrons and radioactive particles,* with *about 10 %* energy), 3). Thermal radiation*, (visible, infrared etc.*, energy of *about 35 %) and 4).* Blast/Shock wave, about 50 %, (the balance of the energy output of *about 50 %,* of the explosion). The actual distribution of energy, amongst the four mechanisms, varies with the design of the bomb and the type of burst. The highest dose rate is the gamma pulse emitted within the first microsecond. The other effects strongly depend on whether the explosion is on the surface, or is ex-atmospheric.

Fig.11.1. Indicate the relative intensities and time relationship, as well as, the duration of the various effects resulting from a nuclear explosion.

Underground Burst

An underground burst has minimal damaging effect on the environment, when the explosion is deep down in the earth, apart from a crater and some little radiation and fallout released into the local atmosphere/soil. This is because the ionizing radiation, neutron flux, nuclear fallout, blast and the thermal effects are all contained within the earth. No doubt, there will be some seismic movement and earth tremours in the surrounding region. At Ground Zero, i.e., the earth surface right above the burst, collapse of structures can be expected, as well as, within a small radius of ground zero. Since there is no ionization of the air above, the ELECTRO-MAGNETIC-PULSE, or EMP, with its horrendous damaging power on electronic equipment and electronic based systems, is missing.

Underwater Explosion

An underwater explosion, on the other hand, would throw up a huge geyser of water up into the atmosphere, which when collapsing causes a tidal wave that rapidly travels outwards from ground zero. This can, obviously damage/ sink ships, vessels and structures enroute, and submerge/devastate low-lying areas and coastal areas in its route. As a result of such an explosion, *the water itself becomes radioactive, it will spread out all around the ground zero, and remain radioactive for a long, long time.*

Surface Burst

A surface burst is one that takes place on the earth's surface or in the atmosphere, close to earth's surface. In this case, the damaging effects on the environment and living beings can be widespread and deadly. Such an explosion will have the typical effects as expected of a nuclear explosion, viz., EM radiation, thermal radiation, blast, and fallout, to a limited or more widespread damaging radius/frequency of EM radiation, depending on the height of burst and the yield of the explosion.

Air Burst

A high air burst or low altitude burst is the one which takes place in the atmosphere at altitudes of order of hundreds of metres to kilometres, up to within 20 kms. Increase in the frequencies of EM radiation and increased radii of damage due to the other nuclear effects can be expected.

High Altitude Burst

A high altitude or ex-atmospheric burst is one, which occurs above the atmosphere, at heights of order of *40 kms or more.* High altitude nuclear explosions can disrupt communications, damage/ degrade performance of electronic and Tele-communications based systems. This is because of the EMP or the Electro-magnetic pulse that results. In this case, *other nuclear effects, such as shock, heat wave and radioactive fallout are not present at the ground.*

EMP

The ionizing radiation from a high altitude burst, (x-rays, gamma ray), breakup the air molecules at the denser layers of the atmosphere at 20 to 40 kms altitude. The electrons so generated are called Compton electrons (because of the Compton effect). The movement of these electrons in the earth's magnetic field generates a very high amplitude electromagnetic pulse, the (direct) EMP. This pulse is directed towards the earth. Since the pulse has very steep rise time, (less than a few nanoseconds) and very narrow width, (fraction of a microsecond), it results in high energy RF radiation components, from very low frequencies to ultra high frequencies. The EMP penetrates the walls and windows of unshielded buildings, induce high currents in interior / buried conductors and directly or indirectly causes system failures or degradation, and over a very wide region of earth, (to a radius of upto thousands of kilometers from ground zero).

Typically, EMP levels of 50 kV/m to100 kV/m are expected at the earth surface, over an area of 3,000 kms slant range, for a high altitude nuclear explosion of 10 Megaton yield and burst height of 400 kms. And 90 % of the energy is expected to lie in the *100 kHz to 10 MHz frequency range*. Remaining 10 % energy would be distributed in the *1 kHz to100 kHz range and 10 MHz to 100 MHz* range. For surface bursts, on the other hand, 90 % of the energy would remain in the 0.1 to 10 kHz frequency range; and the balance below 0.1 kHz and up to 1 MHz. The voltage levels could be less than 1 kV/m, and energy distribution over 10 kHz to 100 MHz, for low altitude bursts (with the energy concentrated in the lower frequencies).

It is very difficult, and expensive to try to protect from EMP systems like the telecommunication and power networks. Systems and devices like computers, cars/vehicles using electronic ignition/ control, the simple electronic clocks/ watches, and so on will instantly fail; unless they have been protected from EMP damage by special design/production techniques called *"EMP Hardening"*. Hence, transportation systems, such as the railways and air traffic would be disrupted. An EMP event knocks out electronic based systems, permanently or temporarily. This is particularly so for semiconductor based ones, as the EMP damages or upsets the front ends/ input stages, affects cable link-ages and internal circuitry. Therefore, complex systems cannot be fully protected, *particularly by any 'fix' approach,* from the damaging effects of the EMP. The best and least expensive method is to accomplish the necessary hardening of the systems right from the planning, designing, through installation and commissioning stages. It must also be emphasized that actual testing for 'EMP proofing' is impractical and too expensive, in most cases. *EMP modeling, simulation and lab testing of sub-systems may, however, be an acceptable solution.*

EMP effects are not very widespread or significant in case of low altitude or surface bursts. For such events the thermal radiation effects, the blast and nuclear fallout effects are far more devastating and significant. However, it must not be forgotten, that, systems such as power grids and telecommunication networks extend over wide regions; and any disruption or damage to the same at one point, say, due to localized EMP effects, could thus extend over a far greater area.

Sudden huge increase in RF noise, ionization etc., are the side effects of a nuclear explosion that cause radio links to fade or blackout; at least for several hours. This is particularly true of short-wave communications and satellite based communications. *Nuclear explosions could create ionized layer above the earth, which could persist for months together, with consequent adverse affects, on some forms of communication (particularly HF communication), for far longer periods.*

System Generated EMP (SGEMP)

Space borne systems like satellites are subjected to gamma and x-ray radiation when a nuclear explosion takes place in the vicinity, within its line-of-sight. The radiation interacts with the system to produce EMP, which is *termed as* SGEMP. SGEMP voltage levels of order of kV/ m are reached. Thus, such systems could become non-functional, unless suitably protected by 'EMP hardening methods'.

Thermal Radiation

The enormous and sudden release of energy in a nuclear explosion, in a surface burst or a low altitude burst results in an instantaneous overheating of the atmosphere to beyond incandescence. (*Thus, looking towards the same would result in immediate blindness*). The overheated gases promptly speed outwards and upwards, forming the well-known mushroom shaped cloud. The intensity of the radiation is measured in calories/ cm.sq. The sudden and violent air movement creates a

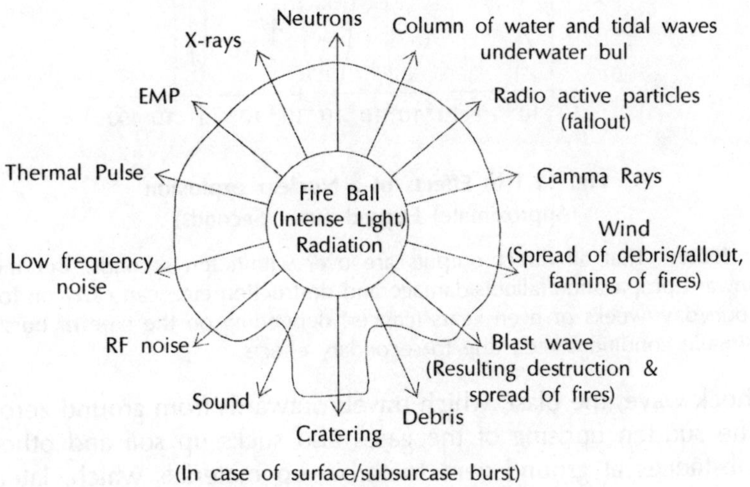

Outputs due to a nuclear explosion

(Ranges, duration, intensities etc depend on type of "Burst", magnitude of the nuclear explosion -KT, megaton, etc.)

Fig. 11.1(a) Output due to a Nuclear Explosion

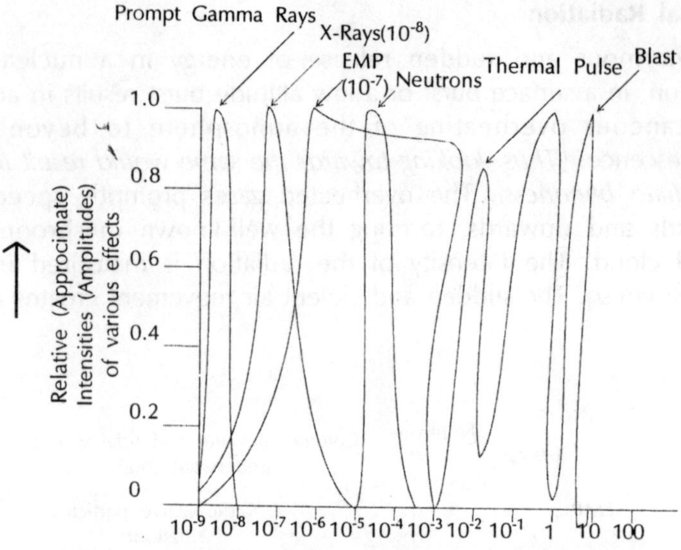

Fig. 11.1(b) Effects of a Nuclear explosion
(Approximate) Elapsed Time (Seconds)

Note:- That all direct outputs are over within ten seconds. But the onward propagation/fallouts/damage and destruction etc., can carry on for hours/days/weeks or even years (cancer) depending on the type of burst, climatic conditions etc., due to secondary effects.

shock wave, the blast, which travels outwards from ground zero. The sudden uprising of the gases also sucks up soil and other substances at ground zero to throw up materials which, later, rain down over a widespread region as radioactive fallout. This fallout follows the atmospheric movements high above, and could thus travel far outwards from ground zero.

The Thermal Radiation is a transient, lasting for a fraction of a second, as may be seen from Fig.11.1. Hence, the best bet for you is to remain or hide behind a wall, or even a tree. This could be protection enough from the direct effects of the Thermal Radiation. But alas, this may not save you from damage due to any consequential raging fires, explosions of flammable material and so on, (in the path of the direct thermal radiation). Table XI.1. is indicative of the thermal radiation damage effects. The danger zone may extend to a far greater radius than in the figure, because of consequential fires/ explosions etc. When out in the open, hiding in a trench, or a deep depression/cavity in the ground may be adequate to protect you from the direct thermal radiation. When indoors, be sure to stay away from windows and other openings, and from flammable and explosive materials, which could catch fire/explode.

Shockwave/ Blast

As mentioned before, the Shockwave/Blast due to a nuclear explosion occurs as a direct result of the rapid movement of the overheated atmosphere. *Like the Thermal Radiation, the Blast is also a transient phenomenon.* The intensity of the blast is measured as the overpressure in pounds per square in, (or PSI), above the normal atmospheric pressure. Table XI.2. is indicative

A 20 Kiloton Atmosphere Burst At 500 Metres Altitude Results In

Thermal Flux (calories/cm^2)	Approximate Distance From Ground Zero (In Metres)	Effect On Humans (When in Open/Exposed)	Effect on Equipment in Open
24	1,000	Dress gets burnt	Effect
12	1,500	Dress is scorched	On Equipment
8	2,000	Exposed skin gets 3rd degree burns (is Fatal)	Nelligible Due
5	2,700	Exposed skin gets 2nd degree burns (is Dangerous)	To the thermal
3	3,000	Exposed skin gets 1st degree burns	Radiation Pulse

Note: Easy to Shield against the Thermal radiation pulse by staying in a shelter. (Even Behind A Wall)

Table XI.1 Damaging effects of thermal radiation from a nuclear explosion

For A 20 Kiloton Burst At 500m Altitude

Blast over pressure (PSI)	36	24	10	3
D or Damage to	Heavy Machinery	Heavy Equipment	Vehicles	Light Equipment
Approximate Distance (From Ground Zero) (kms)	0.4	0.6	1.2	2.5

Note: Blast Efects are negligible on Stores/ Equipment/ personnel when in under ground shelters.

a) **Blast Effects Due to a Representative Nuclear Explosion**

b) **Fallout** from a nuclear explosion can have deadly and long lasting effects on the environment and living beings. But it has negligible effects on most equipment, only routine de-contamination may be needed.

c) **EMP** has negligible effects on living beings. But can prove fatal to electronic systems and electronic based functions/systems.

Damaging effects and extent of EMP depends on the severity and Altitude of the nuclear explosion.

1) In surface bursts about 90% if energy distribution is between 0.1 to 10 KHZ; with remaining enelgy in frequencies down to 10Hz and above upto one megahertz (1 MHZ).

Also the energy density is about 3 order higher than for an exo atmospheric burst.

2) For a high altitude/ Exo atmospheric (nominally at over 40 Kms) burst 90% of energy lies in the frequency range of 100KHz to 10 MHz; remaining energy distributed from 1KHz to 100KHz and 10MHz to 100MHz.

Note:-

(i) EMP is a very sharp/Short pulse with a rise time of a few nanoseconds (n. Sec.) only and duration of about 100 to 200n-s

(ii) A one megaton burst at 400 Kms altitude may result in an enormous area coverage of about 3000 kms radius from grounds zero being affected by EMP.

(As the resulting radio line of sight is huge).

Yeild in Kilotons (High Altitude Burst)	1,000	1,000	100	100	10
Approximate Distance (kms from ground zero)	1,000	100	1,000	100	100
Approximate Electric Field (in KV/Metre)	15	1,000	1.5	100	15

Table XI.2 Blast Fallouts,, EMP Effects of a Nuclear Explosion

of the blast effects. The overpressure rapidly falls away, as the blast pulse moves away from the ground zero. Close to ground zero, the destruction of buildings and structures is usually total, except for concrete bunkers/shelters built deep underground, and has enough earthwork/concrete protection above it. Depending on the range/ intensity of overpressure, the blast can destroy/ damage buildings and structures in its path. Further, note that the consequential damage zone could extend far outwards, due to flying projectiles and debris. The blast overpressure region decreases as the altitude of the explosion increases. And *for altitudes of above about 30 kms, blast damage may not amount to much compared to the other effects.*

Underground shelters/ bunkers not only protect against blast, but also from the thermal radiation and radioactive fall-outs. In this regard you could get sufficient protection by having above you, say, just 50 cms of earthwork! As further benefit, having earth as a buffer above you reduces the gamma radiation/neutron flux that could reach you, by a factor of as much as 100/ 20, respectively. Hence, staying inside an *underground bunker,* with earthwork above you, (concrete would be of still greater assistance, but not inescapable), *is the simplest means for* immediate survival *of both men and electronic equipment.* You would, ofcourse, need further elaborate arrangements for continued availability of clean air, wholesome uncontaminated food and fluids, suitable medical supplies, appropriate waste disposal arrangements, and so on for surviving over a long period, after a nuclear explosion that affects the neighbourhood.

Transient radiation effects (TRE) on electronics (TREE)

Transient Radiation Effects, or (TRE), refers to the effects caused primarily by the gamma radiation, neutrons and X-rays that are released *almost instantly* (within millionths of a second of the explosion). When you consider the effects of these on electronic devices and systems, the terminology becomes TREE (Transient Radiation Effects on Electronics). TREE is of particular concern when considering communication satellites. *The radiation* impinges on the atmosphere and causes the ionization of *the air molecules.* This *ionization leads to a far greater absorption/attenuation of radio waves as they propagate through the atmosphere, till the ion-electron pairs recombine.* This could take hours. As a consequence radio communication could be disrupted for hours. You may recall that such radiation also directly affects solid-state/semi-conductor devices and systems, temporarily or permanently, in the form of upsets/deviation in performance, or even damage/destruction. As far as upsets/deviation in performance of the devices are concerned, the damage zone maybe limited to within a couple of kms only, or could well extend to tens of kms, depending on the yield of the explosion. Neutrons affect the performance of such systems at a much larger range, than gamma radiation. (This could be even hundreds of kms, as against mere tens of kms for gamma radiation). Neutron exposure is measured as neutron flux, that is *the number of neutrons/ cm.sq.* Whilst, gamma radiation is measured as rads, and dose rate as rads/sec. For low altitude bursts, depending on the height of burst and yield, no effects may occur due to TRE radiation beyond few tens of kms. Table XI.3. is indicative of the extent of the effects of TREE. Electronic devices/ equipment and systems that are designed to operate unaffected in the presence of TREE are known as radiation hardened devices/ sequipment/ systems.

Nuclear Waste Disposal

The nuclear industry, whether nuclear power generation, weapons production, production of radio-isotope based devices, (for medical diagnostics/treatment, fire detection systems, instrumentation and so on), produce highly radioactive wastes. The wastes may be in the form of solids, liquids or even, gases. *The half-lives of the waste materials could extend to even thousands of years or more*! Hence, the problems of waste management, (that of collection, storage, disposal, strict accounting etc.), are stupendous. In view of the great danger posed, by any

TREE
A Representative 20 kiloton yield Nuclear Explosion

(Approximate) Height of Explosion (kms)	(Approximate) Distance from ground zero (in kilo metres)					
	Gamma Radiation (in Rads)			Neutron Fluences (Neutrons)/cm^2		
	(D)10^4	(U)$_{10}3$	(T)$_{10}2$	(D)$_{10}13$	(U)$_{10}11$	(T)$_{10}9$
0 (Surface Burst)	0.7	1.1	1.5	0.5	1.2	2
3 (Atmospheric Burst)	0.8	1.3	2	0.7	1.6	2.8
30 (High Altitude Burst)	1.7	3.5	6	1.8	13	48
300 (Exo-Atmospheric Burst)	2.5	8	250	1.9	19	190

Table XI.3 Damaging effects of transient Radiation Effect (TRE) on ELECTRONICS (TREE)

Legend: D Indicates Damage Level
U Indicates Upset Level
T Indicates Threshold Level
For Electronic Circuits/ Functions/ Systems

Note: 1. A dose of 200 Rads is FATAL to Humans.
2. Approximately, $4.4 \times 10^8 n/Cm^2$ Neutron fluence gives a dose of one rad.
3. A Dose RATE of 10^{10} Rads/Sec is DAMAGE Level; whilst a Dose Rate of 10^6 Rads/Sec is Acceptable.
4. Note large increase in 'T' Ranges for high altitude and Exo-Atmospheric Bursts.
5. Nominally A nuclear burst at >40Kms Altitude is terned as Exo-Atmospheric burst.

loss/misplacement of the highly radioactive and long half life radio-nuclides, to the environment and the public, *extreme care has to be taken in their handling, safe-keeping and faultless accounting; and at all times to come!* Because of possible terrorist threats, the wastes have also to be well protected!

There is, as yet, no single proven, universally accepted method for nuclear waste management (*how do you prove in advance, or even after the fact, the reliability and effectiveness of any method, for the coming thousands of years* ?). Concentration, inert packaging, (by fixing in ceramic/ glazing); containment in strong stainless steel drums and their burial in deep rock strata, (whose locations are proven to be unaffected by any likely earthquakes, and possible plate tectonic movements), are some of the methods developed/ being considered. Even, loading the wastes into space rockets and launching it out into deep space, (maybe *into the Sun to be* 'consumed' *by it*), has been proposed by some imaginative people. Naturally, you have to keep in mind that earth based arrangement must be protected and remain safe for hundreds/ thousands of years, even with occurrence of natural/ manmade, hazards, like floods, hurricanes, tidal waves, possible leaching of water/hazardous chemicals to the underground locations, mishaps, etc.

Irradiated Food

The issue of irradiation of edible stuff, to safely clean and better store foodstuff (both cooked and uncooked), is still under intense debate by supporters of the technique on the one hand and opponents on the other. Many contend that, the proven methods of cooling, freezing and smoking are the methods to be used; and *irradiation is only a solution in search of a problem* ! (?)

Irradiation techniques involve bombarding food to be preserved, with gamma ray, x-ray, or accelerated particles. Such bombardment presumably kills bacteria; causes subtle chemical changes in the food, etc., and thus delays its deterioration. Hence, the foodstuff so treated can be safely stored for long periods. Supporters of this system of treatment of foodstuff, claim that irradiation system is safe, and that the food retains intact its taste, and smell etc. Besides this there is no toxicity because of the process. (The food to be treated may be vegetables, potatoes, fruits, poultry, seafood, and so on). However, some consumer organizations, particularly abroad, express reservations about the safety and keeping quality/durability of food, so processed.

International Nuclear Event Scale, (INES)

The INES is a measure designed to help people connected with nuclear industry/ research/ installations/ nuclear related operations, such as nuclear medicine, instrumentation, to put nuclear related events in the proper perspective related to nuclear hazards and to report nuclear events. The events are ordered into eight types, from zero to seven, (safe threshold to major accident), as indicated in the Table XI.4.

Table XI.4. (INES Scale)

Event Classification	INES Scale	Hazard Rating for Event
Accident	7	Major Hazard (entails widespread health and environmental effects).
Accident	6	Serious Accident, (significant Off-site effects).
Accident	5	Accident with Off-site Risk
Accident	4	Accident without Significant Off-site Risk
Incident	3	Serious Incident
Incident	2	Incident
Incident	1	Anomaly
Safety Threshold	0	Below Scale, No Safety Significance

Nuclear, Biological and Chemical, (NBC) Safety

In military doctrines, NBC safety plays a very major role. Basic principles are that of suitable dispersal of personnel and assets, proper shielding and use of protective clothing, and appropriate de-contamination procedures. To protect against the EMP hazards, special techniques, called EMP Hardening, are used for devices and equipment systems, apart from their being suitably shielded and grounded. Use of specially designed concrete underground bunkers, or shelters located deep in rocky-mountains, for both men and materials are de rigueur. Such shelters have to be totally self-contained as regards adequate supply of uncontaminated air, water, and food, and energy requirements; as well as proper and adequate waste disposal arrangements. The shelters are also designed to provide adequate EMP hardening for equipment systems used therein, and remote actuation for antennas to be raised above the ground, when blast and EM Pulse hazards have passed, to re-establish vital radio-communication, etc.

The above require complex and expensive efforts, and maintenance support. It is, thus, impractical to apply the principles adequately for NBC protection of the civilian population. Suitable moderate cost underground shelters are however feasible. Such shelters could offer adequate protection against blast and thermal hazards of a nuclear explosion, and limited protection against nuclear, biological and chemical fall-outs. This is ofcourse, provided appropriate early warning systems are in place, in the first instance, to warn the civilian population well in advance of occurrence of such dangerous events. Even when NBC hazards start out over a limited area, they can soon dangerously extend over very wide areas, because of consequential damages of blast and thermal effects, (like fires, flying debris etc.), and the carriers for the NBC fall-outs-mainly movements of contaminated air, water, effluents, animals and human beings. However, effects of these could be minimized by scrupulous attention to provision of clean air, water, foodstuffs, fluid intakes, and medication, that remain uncontaminated; as well as by suitable shielding, effective de-contamination systems, and isolation from affected carriers. Who can claim that safe living in the modern world is easy?

The concept of the NEUTRON BOMB, to some extent, mitigates the related danger to civilians because of the conviction of the military, that, nuclear deterrence is the mantra for security. The idea is to produce a low yield nuclear bomb that generates, on explosion, copious neutrons but very low thermal, blast, and nuclear fallout effects. When launched on a military target such as a cluster of tanks, such a bomb would not pulverize the tanks or the equipment mounted on/ contained therein, but would instantly kill the personnel in the area, including those inside the tanks. This is tantamount to a neutralization of military concentration, with the added advantage of being able to use the enemy equipment in the subsequent battles, against the enemy (!); and has no extensive hazards to the civilian population in the neighboring areas, to boot. Such a nuclear explosion thus becomes, basically, a tactical weapon rather than a strategic weapon of mass destruction (and therefore does not have the lasting attendant danger to the environment, of the conventional nuclear weapon explosion, that makes the region uninhabitable for long periods to come).

The menace of NBC hazards has assumed terrible connotations, as far as the civilian population is concerned, with the spreading tentacles of terrorism and extortion. How to protect a city from terrorists who have got hold of a "suitcase atomic bomb", (purported to be available with the erstwhile Soviet Union, and its constituent states, and the USA), and then threaten the population with dire consequences if their untenable demands are not met? Unimaginable havoc can be created by such lunatics if they get access to, say, the city water supply and dump in a fistful of deadly Plutonium dust, a bottle full of dioxin, a thermos load of cholera germs, and so on. It would be devastating, to say the least. (Some analysts have surmised that, the terrible Surat plague pestilence was caused by dumping of mutated strains of plague in the city refuse, by motivated, dangerous individuals).

The worst scenario for a nuclear power station is the China Syndrome (apart from the dreaded possibility of a terrorist takeover of a nuclear facility/power station and their blowing up the installation!). The control of the fission reactions in the reactor, if lost, the reactions accelerate without being limited by the control elements. This leads to overheating of the core and causes what is called as the "meltdown" and the reactor could "blow-up," spewing radio-active materials into the environment.

Ever since the caveman discovered how to make fire, mankind has been living with the ever present the dangers of accidental fires. This hazard has been growing in leaps and bounds to become the ever-present risk in modern life, particularly in urban conglomerations. In view of its importance *Fire Hazard merits* a separate chapter to briefly highlight the problems and the dangers of fires, as well as the methods to tackle the hazard.

Chapter 12

Fire Hazards

"Dig the well before you are thirsty"

—Chinese Proverb

So, do have necessary fire precautions in place, without delay, in advance of a possible fire occurrence!

Fire Hazards

Fire Hazard perhaps, *is the most widespread and troublesome of all hazards, in modern times.* The reason is not far to seek. The "bare necessities" no longer satisfies the modern man. He has to clutter up his life and surroundings with trappings of modern living like furnishings, furniture, carpets, cupboards, appliances, cooking ranges, heating devices and so on. And then you have condominiums and residences adjoining each other, shopping complexes, amusement parks and so on. Almost all of them are fire hazards, either by themselves, or by reason of their "neighbours". Further, a fire hazard adds it to the dangers of most other hazards too, as a by-product you may say, a consequential hazard that multiplies the danger manifold by its occurrence when other hazards are running out their course. Therefore, it is important to understand, at least, the basic principles of "Fire Safety". Answers to questions such as-"why and how things burn? What actions can be taken to prevent occurrence of a fire, that is "*Fire Prevention*"? How can fires be detected? How to ensure "*Safety of Life,*" when a fire has occurred? How to "*Suppress fires*" in the making, or incipient fires and "*Fight fires*"?" provide the basis for "Fire Safety Management".

Why and How Things Burn

For a fire to occur three components have to be present and combine, at that location. A fire starts only when *adequate supply* of *all the three elements*, viz. fuel or combustible material, oxygen and heat, (all three) exist, or come together at one place, the location where the fire occurs. There will be NO fire, at all, unless these three components *forming the so-called Fire Triangle* are present, and in adequate quantities/proportion.

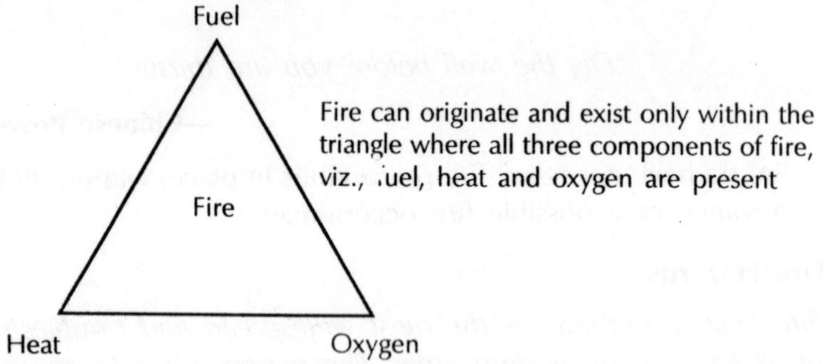

Fig. 12.1 The Fire Triangle

Note:

1. All three components of the fire triange viz., fuel, Heat and Oxygen must be present for a fire to start/sustain.
2. When anyone of the three components is absent i.e. fuel (Obviously), or heat or oxygen, there can be no fire.
3. Hence, fire prevention methods have to ensure that at any location the possibility of all the three components coming together never arises.
4. To reiterate there is no fire, or fire dies in case of any of the following.

a) There is no Fuel/ combustible (even if plenty of heat and Oxygen is present). So if you remove-deplete fuel supply in a fire, the fire dies.

b) Adequate heat is absent a fire cannot occur of sustain. So, if you remove heat from a fire like by dowsing it with water, the fire is quenched.

c) Adequate oxygen supply is not available, even when fuel is aplenty and heat is present no fire is the result. So if fire is started of Oxygen, the fire is extinguished.

The Fuel or the Combustible material is the substance that catches fire. It is the first essential component for a fire to occur. The combustible substance maybe dry paper, dry wood (furniture, logs, shavings, etc.), inflammable gas/liquid or solid materials, (LPG, kerosene, petrol, charcoal/coal, waste materials like-cloth/newspapers/computer printouts and so on). Therefore, without such a combustible material being present, a fire will NOT start/nor SURVIVE, (continue). So, *all fires die out, when the combustible material that was present gets exhausted.* That is, unless additional fuel supplies come up-say due to the fire spreading to nearby locations which have combustible materials readily available, or structures collapse, adding further fuel to the raging fire, etc. Hence, if you take away the fuel, the fire cannot continue any longer and it dies. Therefore, *depriving a fire of* further supply of *fuel* is a very *important means to fight fires.*

Oxygen is the second essential component of a fire. Without it a fire cannot start or continue. A fire or a flame is sustained only when there is a continuous and adequate supply of oxygen. The oxygen may be from the surrounding atmosphere, or, as in some cases, it may be inherently present in the composition of the material, (and that oxygen gets liberated during the fire, to sustain the fire). When you starve a fire of oxygen, the fire is smothered, and it dies out. Therefore, *starving a fire of oxygen* is another *effective means for fighting a fire.*

The third component of a fire is Heat. This is the thermal energy that raises the temperature of the combustible substance till it catches fire, (when oxygen is available). The fire, thus, starts and then liberates enough heat to sustain/spread to nearby areas where stores of combustible materials are present. Without continued supply of adequate heat, the reactions those sustain a fire stop, and the fire dies out, (without your having to do anything). No wonder, the most prevalent, common and popular method of putting out a fire is to quench it with a healthy dose of cold water (thus *removing the heat,* by cooling it). Further, when you throw enough cold water on a fire, it *also starves the fire of oxygen* and smothers it, as the layer of water prevents the oxygen from the atmosphere from reaching the fire. Further, because of the heat the *water turns into steam, the blanket of steam also starves the fire of oxygen,* (note that a lot of heat is also taken away from the fire when the water turns into steam). Thus*, throwing water on fire deprives it of two of the components that are essential to sustain it.* Naturally, this method is to be preferred, as it turns out to be both easy and very effective; and water is normally inexpensive, and is available in plenty. Unfortunately, you *cannot use this efficient system, for fighting fires of inflammable liquids* (fuels) like petrol, as the fuel spreads along with the water thrown on it, thus spreading the fire too.

From the above, it is obvious that when you take away any one, or more, of the three essential components from a fire, (the fire triangle refers), the fire dies/cannot occur. All fire-fighting methods, therefore, involve techniques for depriving the fire locations of one, or more of the three components, viz. fuel, oxygen and heat. The actions maybe-prevent accumulation/ further addition of combustible substances, starve or smother the fire of oxygen, or remove heat, *alone, or in some suitable combination,* (at the location, and its neighbourhood).

Before you consider fire safety, you first need to understand and be able to recognize *what constitutes* a fire. There are various types of fires—Diffusion Flame or Flaming (*Glowing combustion)* Fire, Smouldering, Premixed Flames, Detonations/ Explosions and some special kinds of fire-events, such as Boiling Liquid Expanding Vapor Explosions (BLEVE), Open Flammable Cloud Explosions/Fire (OFCE/OFCF) and Boilover/Slopover Fires. Let us consider these, briefly.

Diffusion Flame

Most fires have diffusion flames. The commonest examples of such flames are the domestic stove (LPG, gas, or kerosene, liquid), or the laboratory Bunsen burner, and the ordinary candle (made of wax). The stove uses gas/liquid fuel, the lamp uses liquid fuel, and the wax candle is a 'solid' fuel device. All of these (fuels) burn with diffusion flames. A study of the candle flame will reveal that at first the solid combustible becomes a liquid, and only thereafter, this liquid fuel turns into a gaseous vapour. And it is the gaseous vapour, that participates (with oxygen and heat) to form the fire/flame.

You will notice that when a candle is lit, the radiant heat from the lit match, or the lighter flame, melts the layer of wax at the top, next to the wick, and heats it up into liquid fuel. The hot liquid rises up the wick, by capillary action (and so does the kerosene in the wick stove, or lamp). The temperature of the liquid rises further, as it rises up the wick, and vapourizes the liquid wax. This hot gaseous fuel breaks up into highly reactive hydrogen, hydrocarbons and carbon atoms. These reactants actively react with the oxygen of the atmosphere and burn to produce more heat, in the process. This process is an exothermic reaction; that is to say the reactions *generate heat.* (Note that in endothermic reactions *heat is absorbed by the reactants,* for the reaction to take place). Note also that the nitrogen atoms in the reaction zone also heat up, during this combustion process but do not take part in the reaction, except as heat carrier. The heat so generated during the reaction, heats up the top layers to melt more wax, also heat the liquid wax, thus, produced to vapourize it and further heat the resultant gaseous fuel. The result is that the vapours participate to sustain the reaction and the combustion process. The candle flame is luminous because of incandescent carbon atoms that are present; so incomplete combustion results in smoke and soot too. Gas flames *burn at a higher temperature* with little or no carbon atoms present. Therefore, (provided that there is adequate supply of oxygen for complete combustion), the gas burns with a bluish flame. (However, note that *some fuels burn with a flame that has NO luminosity at all!)*

In a flame, the rate of reaction is dependent upon the rate of flow of the active reactants, (viz. the combustible substance, oxygen and heat), into the reaction zone. When flow of fuel is more than required for proper combustion to take place, with the available rate of flow of oxygen, inadequate and incomplete combustion results. This leads to release of unburnt carbon particles etc. alongwith the hot gases resulting from the combustion. *Temperatures of the order of 1,000 to 1,400 degrees celsius could be expected in the combustion process.* Note that gas flames are not tied up to the fuel (gas) source. The source could be far away, and the gas piped/leak to the location where the gas is actually burnt/flared. This may be the reason, perhaps, why gas flames have a much lower tendency to generate smoke in the combustion process, (unlike liquid and solid fuels). You can more easily/exactly control the gas flow into the reaction region of the flame to ensure complete combustion and get a clean blue flame, with no sooting.

You will note that before a liquid fuel can burn, it must be vapourized, into its gaseous form. When this action takes place in a wick system, as in a kerosene wick lamp, the flame is usually small, stable and also closed, that is not undulating. But, a liquid fuel will burn without a wick too, and steadily, when in a container/or vessel. And whether the flame is closed or open, depends on the fuel area exposed to the atmosphere. When the area is large, the flame will be wavering/pulsating. When the area is very large, say over 1 metre across the flame would turn turbulent. Also, do note that a running liquid fire could be a catastrophe. This happens when, say, there is a leak in a fuel pipe at a high elevation and the liquid fuel runs down to lower (ultimate) ground level. If now the fuel leak catches fire, (gets ignited), as the combustible fuel is flowing down, a running fire results. Such fires are very difficult to extinguish, (unless, of course, the fuel supply runs out).

You notice that most solid fuels do not melt, (Paraffin/candle-wax are the exceptions, in this regard). On heating the molecules at the surface of the fuel pyrolizes, breaks down into smaller components, (something like O_2 molecules breaking down into O + O). This process generates the volatile gases, which are flammable vapours, of the fuel. Pyrolysis is an endothermic reaction, (the substance absorbs heat for the reaction to occur), that breaks the material into a range of simpler products/ molecules, like hydrogen and carbon monoxide, as also more complex molecules/tars. In this connection, it is seen that wood decomposes at fairly low temperatures of about 200-350 degrees Celsius. But, about 10 percent of it, (the /charcoal), the material that remains after the flame dies out, requires much higher temperatures of the order of about 300-500 degrees. There is considerable heat loss from the burning surface of wood, as the temperature there will be more than 350 degrees. Much of the heat loss is by radiation to the surroundings. Hence, not surprisingly, when such surfaces are closer to each other, as in the case of closely positioned logs of wood/or heaped charcoal; they burn much more efficiently than single log of wood, or widely spaced charcoal lumps/logs of wood.

Smouldering

If you have watched wood burn, you would have noticed that, when the flame dies burning charcoal remains, which still gives some heat. This is because, when wood burns the flame goes out when all the volatile gases from the wood are consumed. Then, it leaves behind the hot, porous, carbon char, or burning charcoal. The charcoal undergoes slow oxidation as it comes in contact with the oxygen of the atmosphere. The process is called Glowing Combustion or Smouldering. The temperature lies between about *500 to 750 degrees C*, during this portion of the reaction. If you carefully watch the glowing charcoal, you may see a pale blue flame, (due to the smouldering reaction). When the charcoal is fully burnt, what is finally left behind is ash, on which fire has no further effect and there is no further reaction, since there is no combustible material left in it. It should be noted that about 1/3 of the total heat energy released in a wood-fire is due to the smouldering reaction of the char/charcoal.

Smouldering is not peculiar to wood, alone. Better exercise due care as even porous heaps of solid materials like sawdust, plastic foam etc., will smoulder when ignited, or a burning source is held next to its surface. The smouldering zone will slowly spread throughout the layer. The combustion process is like that of charcoal. Initially, pyrolysis starts at the surface releasing volatile gases, and then smouldering occurs; and it propagates outwards along the layer, starting from the location where the ignition source initiated the reactions. Heat from the combustion zone is transferred and raises the temperature of the material ahead of it. As soon as the temperature reaches 200-300 degrees C, most organic material present, start decomposing by pyrolysis. Then a char is formed that begins to oxidize/smoulder. Though the gases released may be similar to those produced during a flaming, fire in this particular situation no flame is present as the critical rate of flow needed to sustain a flame is not achieved. But, there is an exception. *If the layer of material is thin smouldering cannot take place.* A thin layer has too high a heat loss to the surroundings for the smouldering process to occur. For example, it has been noted that *sawdust with particle size of about 1mm will not smoulder unless the layer thickness is over about 3 cms* There is thus a minimum thickness for a combustible for smouldering to take place. (So, better avoid storing such combustibles in heaps or closely packed).

Smouldering fire is, perhaps more dangerous than a flaming fire, because it can carry on unnoticed for considerable time-even months for large fuel heaps, (for the fire to progress from the bottom to the top heap, of say, a saw dust heap metre thick. The duration of the fire is proportional to the depth of the heap). *The indications, late to appear, are a dark patch on the surface, then a musty smell, and only thereafter a charring appearance. When there is as increased* oxygen flow, say, due to wind, fan etc., the smouldering fire could well change into a flaming one. You can resort to only one way to stop such a deep seated smouldering fire-break up the heap to bits that have thicknesses less than the minimum thickness for the material, (that will not smoulder). There is a further danger of smouldering fires. When flames occurring on the surface of such a material heap die, you are relieved the fire is over. But this may not be so, smouldering may be continuing deep within the heap!

Smouldering can occur in heaps of a large variety of materials of organic origin, such as paper, sawdust, fibers, hardboard, foam rubber, and so on. So also, some synthetic materials like-polyurethane foam, phenol formaldehyde could smoulder. There is yet another situation where smouldering can occur. When a flammable liquid deposits as a thin layer on, say lagging used for thermal insulation on pipes, (a fibrous material), any local increase in temperature could initiate slow oxidation at the spot. Slowly, over a period of time, (maybe several days), this oxidation will lead to smouldering, due to the liquid fuel. Then, *the great danger is that the smouldering can change into a flaming* combustion—*a terrible hazard,* where there is a flammable environment—such as the terrible fire that occurred recently in a petrochemical terminal at Vishakapatnam.

Premixed Flame/Explosions/Detonations

It was noted earlier that in a diffusion flame, the fuel vapour is totally consumed in the fire, as adequate supply of oxygen is present. Therefore, a blue flame results as no carbon particles are left unconsumed to be luminous. The fuel oxygen mix is said to be "Stoichiometric"; that is the chemical equation of the reaction is exactly balanced. Incidentally, the stoichiometric mix generates the maximum energy output, or heat generation for a given volume, and hence also the maximum temperature for the flame, too. But a fuel/air or oxygen mixture need not be stoichiometric, and can still burn, albeit not so efficiently. The ability of the inflammable mixture to burn depends on the concentration of the fuel in the mix.

Consider the case of a kitchen that is closed up, but has a LPG cylinder that is leaking. The leaking gas fuel mixes up with the air in the kitchen to form a fuel air mixture, and you now have a situation where the fuel is premixed with air. (We presume that there is as yet no ignition source, like a sparking electrical circuit, or a refriegerator close by with its automatic switching "ON" and "OFF" of its compressor that could cause sparks). If now someone opens the kitchen door and switches on a light or lights a match, the premixed fuel/air mixture that has filled up the kitchen ignites and a "premixed flame" quickly propagates outward from the point of ignition. Obviously, the fuel /air mixture is unlikely to be stoichiometric, as the concentration of the gas in the mix varies with size of the leak, time, volume of air in the kitchen, any circulation of air and the burning that takes place. Tnerefore, this flame cannot be a "Diffusion Flame". It is actually called a "Premixed Flame", as it is a result of fire in a premixed fuel/air mixture.

In this connection you have to take note of what is called as the "Limits of Flammability" of the fuel. Just because there is a leak from a LPG cylinder, does not mean that there will be a fire when there is an ignition source. It is necessary for the gas concentration to reach a minimum, and also the concentration should not exceed a maximum, for the particular fuel for it to actually get ignited and a fire to occur. The lowest percentage concentration of the fuel gas in the fuel/air mixture is its "Lower Limit of Flammability ", (or the LLF), below which it will not burn. That is the reason why oil companies advise kitchen windows to be kept open so that the concentration of any LPG gas leak will not reach its LLF. And the maximum percentage concentration of the gas in the mixture beyond which the fuel /air mixture will refuse to burn is its "Upper Limit of Flammability", (or its ULF). The LLF and ULF are specific to each combustible material and the limits may be fairly close together, (as in the case of Butane and Propane constituents of LPG; the values being 1.9 and 8.5 for Butane and 2.2 and 9.5 for Propane, respectively). Or they may be wide apart, (like for Hydrogen, 4 and 75, and Acetylene, 2.6 and 80). Below the LLF, the concentration of the gas is not enough to generate sufficient heat to sustain a flame. Above the ULF, the gas/air mixture is so (fuel) rich that there is not enough oxygen to support combustion. The limits of flammability are not fixed, since temperature, oxygen concentration, and pressure (to some extent) affect them too. When the atmosphere is oxygen rich it can be deadly with pre-mixed fuel fire, because, then the ULF of the fuel increases drastically. For example, Methane has a LLF of 5 % which remains almost unchanged, even in a pure atmosphere of oxygen, (as against about 20 % oxygen normally present in air). But, on the other hand, the ULF for Methane increases to as much as 60 % in such an oxygen rich atmosphere!

A pre-mixed flame travels in the gas/air mixture at a velocity that depends on the fuel and the temperature of the flame. The velocity is large enough for damaging effects in normal buildings, (being of the order of 0.5 m/sec, to an upper limit within 2 m/ sec. but quite small when considering wide-open areas/explosive type of fires. (When the fuel/air mix itself is moving, then that velocity also has to be added).

In certain situations a pre-mixed flame can cause an "Explosion" or "Detonation". Take the case of a LPG cylinder, which is a closed vessel, with flammable gas/liquid inside. If now a pre-mixed flame propagates into the cylinder,two things happen to suddenly increase the pressure of gas within the cylinder. 1) The heat generated by the flame increases the pressure, and 2) the effective volume of the combustion products would be far in excess of the initial volume of the unburnt gas, and this results in a great increase in the pressure inside the cylinder. (If the gas were outside the cylinder then, obviously, there would have been an increase in the volume due to its combustion and not a rise in the pressure). Ofcourse, the walls of the cylinder will cool the gases with time, but for a fraction of a second there will be a pressure burst. The result is an explosion, when there is a structural weakness in the cylinder/the cylinder is not designed to withstand the pressure buildup with suitable factor of safety. (Recently, there was a report about six people sustaining severe burns and four houses getting damaged in a gas cylinder blast at the Bangalore Development Authority Quarters, due to gas leakage because of carelessness of house inmates. They did.not properly switch OFF the cylinder, (regulator) knob at night. Consequently, gas leaked from the cylinder throughout the night. The inmates were, ofcourse, fast asleep and did not smell the gas leaking. When a light was switched ON in the morning, there was a massive explosion; the house roof collapsed and three adjoining houses were also damaged, with the common walls connecting the building collapsing, etc.).

Obviously, there is always the danger of an explosion, when a flammable gas is stored/processed, (in a building or installation), at a temperature above its flash point. It can happen with flammable liquid fuels like petrol too. Ofcourse, in the case of a flammable liquid the occurrence of a pre-mixed flame itself depends on its volatility and how low the flash point is (apart from its limits of flammability). (Flash Point of a flammable material is the temperature at which the pre-mixed flammable mixture ignites to form a flame, as the temperature is raised. When the temperature is raised further till a continuous burning of the fuel results, that temperature is known as the Fire Point of the material). Thus, because of its narrow limits of flammability (1.5 to 7.5 %) petrol can be safely transported in tankers. Further, even when petrol spills in a room, because of its high volatility the petrol vapor/air mixture quickly reaches a concentration of beyond the ULF of 7.5 %, and therefore it is safe from ignition. But, when you empty a petrol tank it remains a hazard for quite some time, thereafter, because the petrol vapour present in the tank, (initially 100 %), turns into a pre-mixed fuel/air mixture with the air gradually leaking into the tank. This pre-mixed petrol/air mixture, then, tends to form a violent explosion on ignition. So it is that, the danger of an explosion in a petrol tank(er) arises when you empty it, and the fuel/air mixture reaches down to a concentration of below its ULF. So do keep reasonable amount of petrol/fuel in your vehicle tank to minimize possibility of an explosion. This is also the reason why kerosene can be stored very safely at room temperatures. Its very low vapour pressure, apart from its high flash point of 54 degrees C, makes the fuel/air mixture reach a concentration that is below its LLF. (And the high flash point makes it difficult to ignite too. But let the ambient temperature reach above 54 C, then kerosene turns into as dangerous a flammable fuel as petrol is). No wonder heavy fuel oil have to be pre-heated for it to catch fire (ignite), because of its very low vapour pressure (high viscosity) and high flash point. Note that, actually, a pre-mixed flame is nothing but a sort of explosion, (a sudden, fast travelling conflagration), under normal conditions itself!

On the other hand, a detonation can occur when a pre-mixed flame travels in a pipeline and encounters an obstruction/ or a bend, etc. These cause turbulence, and momentary increases in the flame velocity, (due to resultant sudden pressure and temperature increases, caused by the turbulence). The net result is generation of supersonic Shockwave, with velocities of the order of 1,000 m/sec. to as much as 3,500 m/sec., (compare this with the normal velocity of a premixed flame, of less than

2 m/sec). A Shockwave of such high velocities is termed a detonation.

Pre-mixed flames could occur in (flammable) solids too. Solid fuels, if they burn by releasing volatiles, can form a pre-mixed explosive atmosphere when heated to ignition. For example, when a fire starts in a building the inflammable volatile gases released by the solids combustibles like wooden furniture etc., form a fuel/air mixture pre-mix. If the doors and windows are shut, there may not be enough oxygen for the fire to start raging. If now someone opens an outside door or window to the building, the sudden inrush of air into the building subjects him to the dangerous explosive pre-mix flame that blasts out-the well known "Flash Back" or "Back-Draft", that the fire fighters worry about. (This is something akin to the case of gas fuel in enclosed space-the LPG cylinder). Obviously, heating of any solid fuel in enclosed spaces is dangerous. And a solid fuel dust/ air mixture, is perhaps more hazardous, (as it is similar to a flammable gas/air pre-mixed atmosphere), and have burning velocities that can be very high. Hence, coalmine have to take care to suitably treat coal dust to prevent their dispersion. Otherwise, any minor ignition could lead to a deadly dangerous coal dust explosion that quickly propagates throughout the mine.

Metal dust explosions develop high overpressures. So even small amounts of metal dust fuel can result in heavy damage, when ignited, because of the consequent explosive force of the pre-mixed metal dust/air fire that occurs. Propellants are nothing but pre-mixed solid fuels, which also produce hell of a lot of hot gases, on ignition. High explosives are also pre-mixed solid fuels. But, they detonate (creates shock waves) and produce pre-mixed flames with high velocities, on ignition/detonation. Note that metal dust explosions involving metals like aluminum and magnesium are devastating in their vicinity due to their very high rate of pressure buildup-order of even 1,000 bars /sec.

Bleve/Slopover/Boilover/OFCF/OFCE

These are some special types of combustion events connected with mainly inflammable liquid fires, and generally in industrial environment.

BLEVE stands for Boiling Liquid Expanding Vapour Explosion. Such an occurrence can arise when a flammable liquid is contained in a sealed or partially, (not fully), vented vessel, and it gets heated, say by an unexpected fire nearby. Continued application of heat makes the liquid fuel boils, generating flammable fuel vapour. If the containing vessel has any structural weaknesses like cracks or fractures, the fuel flashes out, the hot gas/vapours turbulently mixes with the atmospheric air to form a pre-mixed expanding flame-a veritable fireball that rapidly expands to form an explosive blast. The fast expanding fireball can burn up everything in its way over a wide region, and the broken structural materials of the vessel, and anything else in the way of the blast, become missiles flying all around to add the devastation directly caused by the BLEVE. Road tankers and rail tankers carrying highly inflammable materials are reported to be responsible for many a BLEVE occurrences, when they got involved with some fire or other. Such BLEVE occurs from within 10 minutes, to a delayed period of as much as an hour later after the tankers become involved with a fire. Actually, the general public is daily exposed to what may be termed as minor-BLEVE because of someone's carelessness-a leaking domestic LPG gas cylinder that explodes on a spark igniting the leaking gas that results in the explosion, soon thereafter. The best way to prevent occurrences of BLEVE is to keep the vessel cool with jets of cold water to ensure that the fuel inside remains cool, and does not heat up to generate flammable vapours creating overpressures. (Ofcourse, this is apart from the normal precautions of seeing that a fire does not occur nearby, and ensuring the structural integrity of the container/and no leaks, etc.).

SLOPOVER/BOILOVER are expressive terms that describe exactly what happens during such fires. A flammable liquid, say crude oil, contained in a tank or vessel slops-over the edge of the tank, *(Slopover),* or it boils-over the sides, *(Boilover),* after the liquid fuel gets ignited due to a fire nearby. The process takes some time and is not instantaneous. And they occur only in flammable liquids that have a wide temperature range of boiling points, like crude oil which fractionates into a number of inflammable distillates that have different narrow temperature ranges of boiling points. They do not occur with flammable fluids that have a narrow range of boiling point temperature, like petrol and diesel.

For both types of fires to occur, you start with a tank of flammable heavy oil with a mixed/wide temperature range of boiling points. If the tank/vessel is now exposed to a fire close by, flammable volatile form on the surface of the oil and ignite to start a fire on the surface. With the surface temperature reaching the boiling point of the surface oil layers, the vapours continue to feed the fire on the surface of the oil. While the top surface layers of the oil boil in this manner the temperature below the surface layer, say a few centimetres below, however remains cool; may be even at the normal ambient level in the case of heavy oils like the crude oil. This is so because the heavy oils being opaque, (not transparent), the radiant heat from the top surface is not easily transferred down to beyond the top surface layers of the oil. Several hydrocarbon fractions, from light petrol to the heavier fractions culminating in fuel oil and tar, constitute the crude oil. Therefore, the fire at the surface makes the lighter fractions with their lower boiling point fractionate towards the top surface, in the first instance. This is followed by the heavier fractions with higher boiling points, and so on. This results in the heavier fractions at the top start to sink towards the bottom of the tank/vessel. These layers of heavy oils are, however, much hotter than the lower layers of the crude oil, and when they move downwards they form a sort of "Heatwave" moving towards the bottom of the vessel. Since, the boiling surface of the oil could reach a temperature of as high as about 350 degrees C, the Heatwave could have a temperature of about 300 degrees C!

Suppose now, when the heatwave is close to the boiling surface of oil the fire fighting guys arrive and direct fire fighting foam on to the surface. The foam instantly flashes into steam because of the intense heat it encounters and the steam by forcing into the Heatwave causes a part of the flammable fuel to flash out in hot foam of oil. And the hot fuel-foam causes the nearby oil mass to "Slopover" the edge of the tank/vessel. A Slopover can help sometimes, because when such a "Slopover" causes a major portion of the oil in the tank to be thrown out of the tank, it enables the oil fire to be put out easily.

The Heatwave can be big trouble, when the tank/vessel was not thoroughly dried of all water traces before the oil was poured into it, (and, a thin layer of water remains at the bottom). As the Heatwave moves towards the bottom of the vessel and reaches it, the layer of water at the bottom instantly converts to steam, because of the high temperature of the Heatwave. This flash of steam, (which is also high in volume), in trying to get out violently blows out the hot oil content of the vessel/tank over a wide area around. And this "Boilover" is in the form of fast expanding, hot, flammable foam of oil (with its temperature already near the flashpoint of the flammable oil). Boilover is dangerous as it spews flammable liquid fuel over very wide areas causing massive destructive fires all around.

You can prevent a Boilover in the first instance by making sure that there is no trace of water left in the tank/vessel before you fill it with the flammable heavy oils, or by promptly putting out the fire at the surface of the burning fuel. By keeping the lower portion of the tank/vessel cool, say, by directing jets of cold water there, you can slow down the movement of the Heatwave towards the bottom of the tank. This will delay the formation of a Boilover. And that gives you enough time to issue suitable warning to all concerned, for the personnel and costly equipment to be moved out to a safe distance, before the Boilover occurs and spreads its deadly blanket of flammable, hot, foaming oil all around the tank.

Since, it is easier to fight an oil fire when a Slopover ejects out major portion of the fuel in a tank/vessel, sometimes it may be an advantage to intentionally create a Slopover of an oil fire. This can be done by directing jets of water on to the boiling surface of the burning fuel. But ofcourse, you have to remember that you do not have the problem of Boilover/Slopover if the oil on fire happens to be petrol or diesel, that is a fuel with a narrow temperature range of boiling point.

OFCF/OFCE stands for Open Flammable Cloud Fire/Open Flammable Cloud Explosion, respectively. OFCF is said to occur when a cloud of flammable fuel vapours gets ignited and burns as a Flash-fire. Such a fire may not do any/much damage. On the other hand, an OFCE could have a devastating effect all around the surrounding areas. An OFCE occurs when you have a large enough volume of pre-mixed fuel vapour/air (cloud) that gets ignited, and the resultant flash-fire detonates the cloud into an explosion. So, watch out for the possibility of such an event when you fill a huge balloon with hydrogen gas!

Note that a flammable liquid fuel can burn in many ways-as a "Pool-Fire", as a "Flash-Fire", as "BLEVE", as "SLOPOVER/ BOILOVER", "OFCF/OFCE", etc. The very same quantity of a flammable liquid fuel burns for different periods of time depending on the type of fire that occurs/can occur. Thus, a given quantity of the fuel may burn as a "Pool-Fire" for several minutes. The same amount of the fuel could burn up within a couple of minutes as a "Flash-Fire". On the other hand, that quantity of the fuel would last hardly a couple of seconds when it goes up as "BLEVE", less than a second when an "OFCE" is involved, and not more than a few milliseconds if it is a "DETONATION"! Consequently, the rate of release of energy of combustion increases proportionately with the type of fire involved, and hence, the extent of damage/destruction potential of the fire.

Hazards of Smoke and Spread of Fire

Smoke is nothing but hot gases from a fire, and that supports and carries with it particulate matter, such as unburnt carbon particles, tiny droplets of liquids that result from Pyrolysis. Some of these products are oxides of carbon, nitrogen, hydrogen, sulphur as well as complex ones of high molecular weight. The hot smoke cools down as it moves away form the fire and deposits as an oily layer on solid surfaces (such as kitchen walls-when gas cooking ranges/stoves are used). Except for diffusion flames and some fuels (like hydrogen, carbon monoxide, white spirit, formaldehyde etc,), almost all (fuels) fires produce smoke.

Also, understandably, fuels with oxygen as a constituent in the molecules produce less smoke than "equivalent" composition materials, but which are without the oxygen as one of the constituents in its molecules. Thus, Alcohol (Ethyl) has oxygen in its molecules, (C_2H_6O or CH_3CH_2OH), and burns with less smoke than Ethane, (C_2H_5 or CH_3CH_2) which has no oxygen "content". This is also the reason why hydrocarbon "plastics/polymers" like Polyethylene, (popularly known as Polythene), and Polystyrene, which has no oxygen in their molecules, generate copious smoke (far more than wood, which has oxygen present in its molecules).

Most often, the smoke from a fire can be more deadly than the fire itself. Far more deaths are reported to have occurred from effects of smoke than as a direct result of fires. Apart from the dangers of oxygen deprivation and toxicity due to smoke inhalation, smoke also causes loss of visibility and disorientation of fire victims, thus, preventing them from moving in the proper direction towards safety. Smoke can also cause a fire to spread to neighbouring areas, remote from the source of fire. Further, to add to the problems, smoke hinders fire-fighting personnel from effective fire-fighting/evacuation/rescue attempts. The toxicity of smoke depends on the materials consumed in/exposed to a fire. Smoke can have dangerous toxic products like—Sulphur Dioxide (SO_2), Carbon Monoxide (CO), Hydrogen Cyanide (HCN), Hydrogen Chloride (HCL), Phosgene, etc.

Smoke moves upwards from the source of fire, unless there is a lateral movement or swirling due to any breeze/wind, that it is subjected to. On reaching the ceiling, smoke spreads out to form a layer by moving horizontally outwards along the ceiling. It moves to higher levels through openings such as-doors, windows, air conditioning ducts, chimneys, ventilation openings, piping, trap-doors and so on, on towards the top of the building, and dissipates into space. Wind movements can accelerate the spread of smoke and to far away from the source of fire. When smoke accumulates below the ceiling it radiates heat back into the room adding to the radiant heat from the fire itself. This quickens the spread of fire by increasing the burning rate, and as a consequence of the heating up of other combustible objects close to/around the fire to ignition and catches fire.

Talking of heat and the temperature in a room with a fire that has occurred there, the temperature of the room varies in four identifiable stages during the growth and death of the fire. These are known as—1) The Pre-flash, or growth period of the fire 2) The Flashover period; 3) The Post Flashover period, or Fully Developed Fire; and 4) the Decay period. Initially, the temperature of the room increases very slowly, the Pre-flash or Growth period of the fire. Then the temperature grows almost exponentially, the Flashover period when other combustible objects in the room generate enough flammable volatiles for the fire to flash over and start producing additional heat energy in the room. The temperature in the room now reaches a peak and starts to fall slowly. This is the Post Flashover period or the stage of the Fully Developed Fire. Now the temperature of the room starts to fall quite rapidly and the fire has reached its Decay period. During the course of the fire, any movement of air increases the oxygen supply and heat transfer and can accelerate the growth and spread of the fire.

When the flammable volatiles generation in the room is adequate to spread out and fill the room, and with a sufficient and continuous flow (from the fuel sources in the room), a transition occurs in the fire that involves the whole room on fire-the Flashover. Ofcourse, a Flashover may not always result in a fire. This is particularly so when the fuel source is all by itself, away from other likely combustible items in the room, so that fire spread is prevented. It may also happen that the rate of fire is small and the fire quickly dies out by itself, because of poor ventilation and lack of adequate oxygen supply. Or the fuel source for the initial fire /oxygen is small, and enough heat is not generated to spread the fire to the nearby objects, and thus ensure fire growth.

When the room is fully ventilated, obviously, there is enough oxygen supply available and so the rate of fire then depends on the availability of flammable volatilize, generated by the available fuel sources in the room. On the other hand, if the flow of air is limited/controlled due to poor ventilation etc., the result is a less intense fire. Sometimes, this could create major problems, the problem of "Flashback" or "Backdraft", etc! The heated combustibles in the room goes on releasing volatiles only part of which gets burntup, as adequate supply of oxygen is not available. The flammable vapours that are not consumed fill the room, and spread out to even remote locations, as hot flammable gas that could get ignited causing major fire spreads or be accumulate to result in a dangerous "Flashback"(when air rushes in due to opening of a door /window etc.). So, it should not surprise you to learn that hot flammable vapours released in a fire, (say at the corner of a big building like a godown), could flow right across the entire length of the godown. It could then exit remotely through a ventilator, or chimney etc., at the other end and catch fire there to create havoc far, far away from the original source of fire!

There is also a unique type of fire—"Flames in an Air Stream" that can occur when a breeze is blowing over a large pool fire on a flammable liquid surface. When the breeze blows over the poolfire, the flames bend closer to the hot burning surface, and heat it up further. This generates more flammable vapours of the combustible liquid, and causes a pre-mixed flame to be carried along with the flow of air (caused by the wind). So, this can result in spread of fire, downstream.

Fire Classification

For fire fighting purposes etc., all countries do not classify fires on identical basis, that is, there is no uniform classification of types of fires. However, the ordinary fire may be classified as:

- Class A fire: These involve *solid combustibles, which smoulder/generate ambers,* (such as wood, paper, and textiles).
- Class B fire: These *involve flammable liquids,* (liquids such as alcohols, petroleum products like petrol, solvents, etc.). Such flammable liquids may be categorized into two types those that are miscible/dissolve in water, and those that are immiscible/do not dissolve in water. Fire extinguishing methods are different for the two types.

- Class C fire: Fires that *involve flammable gases* or (*flammable) liquefied gases.* And then you have the special category,
- Class D fire: *Metal fire*

Electrical fires are not classified in any separate category, as the fuel encountered in the fire, and the fire fighting methods to be used fall into one of the above four types (or classification) of fires.

Usually, different types of fire extinguishers are required and are designed specifically to fight one or more types of fires, (such as CO_2, Halon, Foam, Powder, Water jet, etc.). However, *Halon 1211 may be used, and quite effectively too, on most classes of fires.*

Metal Fires

Metal fires are totally different kettle of fish, a class by themselves that need very special handling. Almost all metals burn, even the inert ones (these burn when in a finely powdered condition). Some metals like calcium, lithium, magnesium, potassium, sodium etc. are easily ignited. They are, therefore, known as combustible metals. Metal fire flame temperatures are high and the surfaces are very reactive too. To add to the problems, unfortunately they also react exothermically, (generate heat during the reaction), with all common extinguishing agents, (like water, carbon dioxide, nitrogen, Halons etc.)!

Particularly, potassium and sodium catch fire as soon as they come in contact with water. So, as a must precaution, you have to store them in some light oil or paraffin. On the other hand, Phosphorus automatically ignites if/when it comes in contact with air. Therefore, you normally store phosphorus under water! (Such containers should be isolated as far as possible and fire brigade personnel should be informed of their locations). So also, you must take care to see that the containers, do not leak, or get misplaced, get knocked over, the water evaporate/oil loss occur, etc. It cannot be overemphasized that all dangerous chemicals used/stored in an organization/location must be, invariably, recorded and listed. You must also make particular note of the safety requirements for such substances, in transportation, storage, handling and use, (as you would for dangerous poisons). Good accounting, auditing of such dangerous chemicals and periodic review for removal and proper disposal of such stores no longer required are essential for safety requirements, apart from any other considerations.

It is easier to control a metal fire when it occurs in a closed space. When metal burns in an enclosed space, it can be easily deprived of oxygen, by replacing the oxygen present in the closed space with a suitable inert gas, say Argon or Helium. The inert gas can be introduced into the space under pressure to drive out the oxygen and replace it. But do make sure the inert gas you are introducing does not react with the metal that is burning!

On the other hand, a metal fire out in the open is very hard to tackle, and is dangerous. The only reliable means appear to be to use inert powders to smother the fire (by forming a coating on the metal surfaces that prevent contact with air, and thus arrest combustion). Specially formulated powders are commercially available, but substances such as salt and soda have been used in view of their ready availability.

Ignition Source (for start of a fire)

A fuel (fuel vapour/volatiles) has to be ignited for it to catch fire and burn. Considering the fire triangle, you would believe that heat is an essential input for a fuel to ignite and flare up into a regular fire. But this is not so. Ignition could take place due to a variety of causes. A spark resulting from, either, mechanical friction or an electric make/break of contacts could be adequate to cause ignition. Even a corona discharge (due to ESD) may do the trick. A hot surface of an electric iron, an oven or a soldering iron could be the culprit. Further, note that *Spontaneous heating, or an exothermal chemical reaction could equally cause ignition.* Note that in a diesel engine the fuel air mixture ignites due to the heat generated by a rapid compression of the mixture, (during the compression stroke in the cylinder), that is Auto-

Ignition takes place. There could be other causes too for ignition, such as *radiation, shock etc.*

Fire Extinction

From the above, it is noted that there are innumerable sources of ignition that could start a fire. But, *as far as extinction of a fire is concerned, the Fire-Triangle is all that one has to remember*—the basic, essential elements for a fire to occur/ sustain, viz. fuel, oxygen and heat. Once, all the fuel present is consumed by a fire the fire dies, unless additional fuel supply occurs, due to the spread of fire or otherwise. This is true, provided, the necessary elements of heat and oxygen continue to be available for the fire to persist. When the available fuel exhausts, a fire dies a natural death, even when plenty of heat and oxygen is still present.

There may be ample fuel available, but if the oxygen supply is choked or cut off, the fire cannot persist. So also is the case, when enough heat is taken away from a fire, say by throwing enough water on it. Then, the fire cannot sustain. (Hence, this is the most popular and effective way of fighting a fire and/or its spread-that is cooling the surface of the fire with water). Blanketing a fire with water, apart from removing heat, also cuts off oxygen input, thus smothering the fire, particularly when copious steam formation occurs. Similarly, in case of small fires, you can put it out by smothering it with sand.

In fire fighting, chemical agents play a great role in view of the small space they occupy, (that is their compactness), which is a very major advantage in storage and transportation of the Extinguishant to the site of a fire. Thus, stored in small cylinders, carbon dioxide, nitrogen and Halon gas are used extensively as fire fighting/fire extinguishing agents. However, they have the flip side too, they are toxic in fairly low concentrations, and are hence a biological hazard. This necessitates immediate evacuation of all personnel to a safe location, before fire-fighting efforts commence with such agents. (Ofcourse, sometimes, you may be able to effectively fight a fire with low enough concentration of such fire-extinguishing chemicals).

It is not surprising that major flaming conflagrations, such as oil well fires, cannot be put out by above means. In such cases it is not only necessary to remove heat of flame from the reaction zone, but it is also essential to shift the reaction zone (so that there will be either too little fuel there, or too much of it to sustain a flame—the LLF/ULF). The popular, and perhaps spectacular, method of doing this is to detonate a high explosive charge to distort the reaction zone, in such a way that heat release is highly reduced so that poor combustion results, and this causes the flames to be "killed". And thus the fire extinguishes.

Use of Water in Fire Fighting

Water is obviously an ideal fire-extinguishing agent in view of the excellent physical properties it possesses for fire fighting purposes. It is indeed unfortunate that water cannot be used to fight certain types of fires. For example, *any attempt to put out petrol fires and electrical fires using water, as the Extinguishant is extremely dangerous.* Petrol and other lighter petroleum products float on water and therefore the combustibles/fire spread around, when you try to douse such fires with water. This causes the fire to spread, instead of killing it. Similarly, use of water on an electrical fire, particularly in high voltage installations, is like asking for great trouble. Since water, specially, saline water, has good conductivity it will reduce insulation (resistance), thus lead to increased current flow, and result in arcing etc. All of which actually worsens the fire rather than help to put it out. Therefore, in such situations, use of water to fight the fire actually increases the hazards of fire rather than reduces it.

Apart from the above-mentioned situations, water is the most frequently used extinguishing agent. Major advantages are that *water is readily and plentifully available, in most places, is inexpensive, and is certainly NOT a bio-hazard!* It's most useful characteristic in fire fighting is its ability to remove tremendous amount of heat, particularly, when it is converted to steam. For water to boil and fully convert to steam, one litre of water needs to absorb about 2,500 kJ of energy! Further, in this process it generates over 1,500 litres of steam, which greatly helps to blanket a fire and smother it, by effectively depriving it of oxygen. Please note, that *in cold climates you have the problem of water turning into ice at about zero degrees C,* (this is of course altitude dependent). Therefore, *at sub-zero temperatures, water is quite difficult to use as a fire-fighting agent.*

Some special chemicals can be added to water to improve its fire-fighting efficiency, in a number of ways. Wetting agents increases the ability of water to adhere to materials such as-thatched roofing, haystacks, and to quench such fires faster, and better. To fight fires even better, fire-retarding chemicals can be added. This is usually done to fight forest fires, more effectively. Anti-freezing agents depress the freezing point of water, (down to as low as 10 degrees C). Water then becomes useable; to fight fires at sub-zero temperature environment. Viscosity of water may be increased so that it can reach farther from the fire fighting hose nozzle. To reduce the friction to the movement of water through the hose and the nozzle at high pressures, substances called as 'thickeners' are added. This enables the water jet to reach farther. You can add to water a "foam concentrate", to convert water into foam by aeration so that it expands into a much larger mass consisting of bubbles. Throwing or projection of such foam, onto, say, a burning liquid fuel, spreads it around and helps to smother such fires. (This property has made *foam* a fire-fighting aid, by itself).

You can control a water jet, directly (manually) only when the water pressure in the jet is within a few kegs. When the pressure is high you lose control of the fire-fighting hose/nozzle, because of the high reaction force, (like the kick back from a rifle as you fire it, or like a bucking horse the hose bucks in your hand in every which way). It will whip around violently, and this can cause damage/injury to you or to those/things around you.

You can estimate the reaction force, or kick back, approximately by the rule of thumb:

$R = 1.6\ PD^2$, where R is the reaction force in *kgs,*

P is the water pressure in *bars,* and

D is the diameter of the nozzle in *cms.*

Thus, when the water pressure is say 3 bars, and the nozzle jet diameter is say 15 mm, the reaction force would be about 11 kgs, and it is small enough for such a jet to be controlled by a person with his bare hands. But, suppose you increase the jet diameter to 25 mm and raise the water pressure also, to say 7 bars, the reaction force increases to about 70 kgs. This is far too high a force for the hose/nozzle to be handled manually. You will then definitely need some sort of mechanical gadget/arrangement for controlling such high-pressure water jets.

Nowadays, it is rare for one to encounter fire-fighting facilities such as the erstwhile primitive system of keeping buckets of sand and water, at strategic areas in a building/installation. These have given way to water points with coiled hoses and nozzles at suitable locations, strategic and easy to access. And, water is fed to such locations from suitably located, raised storage water tanks. The pressure required for the water jet is the gravity feed, in most cases. The water tank is kept at a location raised as high as possible in the building or its neighbourhood. And *this water tank is used exclusively and specifically for fire-fighting purposes only,* kept quite separate from other water tanks, meant for normal purposes of domestic/industrial/other usage.

In many modern constructions, particularly multi-storied ones, sprinkler systems are installed for *automatic water dispensation in case of fires, at those specific locations where an incipient fire is detected.* The sprinklers are brought into action either manually when a fire is noticed/alarm is sounded, or they are automatically triggered, by suitable warning signals from a properly designed and installed fire detection system. (The triggering occurs, usually, after a specified designed delay using heat, smoke, flame or other types of fire detectors). The deliberate delays are introduced to take care of suitable validation procedures that are intended to eliminate/minimize possibilities of false alarms, etc. (In older systems fusible plugs were used to keep the sprinklers normally blocked. They melt and open up to allow flow of water, only when the ambient temperature rises, to say 65 degrees C, because of a fire in the vicinity of the sprinkler head). Even when a sprinkler system is unable to totally put out a fire, it has major advantages of limiting the spread of fire, and keeping the fire under control until the fire fighting teams/equipment arrive on the scene, to take charge of fire fighting operations.

A sprinkler system is, basically, one of two types—either a 'wet' type or a 'dry' type. In the 'wet' type of system water is continuously present in the pipes, ready to flow-out of the sprinkler as soon as the system is triggered. In cold environments, as water may freeze and refuse to flow in such systems, you then resort to the 'dry' system. Here, the pipes/system is filled with air under pressure. This air is replaced with flowing water when a fire actuates the fire alarm system. The fire alarm triggers the system to release water into the system, driving out the air that is present. Sometimes, a hybrid system may be used with advantage. This is a suitable combination of the two types of sprinklers—"wet" as well as "dry", to more effectively meet specific situations, or environment.

When a sprinkler system is in use you must ensure, particularly during installation/maintenance tasks, that the openings/orifices of the sprinkler heads remain clear of obstructions, and do not get painted up. Otherwise, they could get clogged up to totally stop water flow, or the water flow become less effective, when a fire actually occurs and the system is triggered to operate. You also need to take special care to ensure that plenty of water, and of right quality, is available at all times. Further, there must be the required minimum pressure. The system must also be clear of all obstructions to enable free flow of water for fire-fighting operations, as and when called for. Do *make sure that, under cold weather conditions, NO freezing of water can take place in the system.*

Use of Foam as a Fire Extinguishant

When you encounter liquid fuel fires, then, it is an advantage to resort to use of foam, a special solution of water in which bubbles are built up by aeration with air, nitrogen or a halogen, (Halon types). The bubble formation expands the volume of the concentrated solution very many times. The concentrate also provides stability for the foam to sustain itself for some time, and not collapse soon after the bubble formation. Since, this type of foam is formed by mechanical means, it is known as *mechanically generated foam.* It is also feasible to prepare fire-fighting foams using chemical means, as some chemical reactions also generate (fire-fighting) foams. It is but natural for such foams to be known as *chemically generated foams.* An important characteristic of foam is its expansion ratio, (the ratio of the volume of the foam generated, to the volume of the 'concentrated' solution from which the foam is generated). Fortunately, the expansion ratio of a foam can (by suitable design) be made to lie anywhere between about a low 5, to as high as 1,000! This enables matching the foam to the type of fire it is used to fight. (LX, or Low Expansion, foam has an expansion ratio of about 5 to 15; MX, or Medium Expansion, foam has an expansion ratio of around 50 and HX, a high expansion, foam an expansion ratio of up to 1,000).

When foam is projected over a burning surface, usually burning liquid, it spreads over the surface smothering the fire, (and cooling it to some extent too). *HX foam has the advantage of totally filling up a volume, whatever is the shape of objects within the volume.* But, this is a disadvantage in that, persons who might get caught within the foam become completely disoriented, and they have no means of knowing which direction to move, to get out of the place. Also, you need to worry about the time taken for the water to drain out after the foam has been deposited on a fire, (the 'drainage' time). *High delays/ drainage time could adversely affect fire-fighting operation itself, as well as the post fire-fighting operations,* of cleaning up and normalizing the situation.

Foams can be designed, with suitable concentrates, to produce a thin film of the inert bubbles, over a fire, that not only try to smother/ put out the fire, but also prevent flammable vapours from rising. And it can also greatly reduce the radiant heat. The *overall result is an enormous reduction in the tendency for the fire to spread.*

Use of Chemical Powders in Fire Fighting

Special chemical powders are available to fight fires, particularly those of solid/metal fuels. These chemical powders react with the burning surface to prevent it from releasing flammable vapours/ volatiles, and thus stifling the fire. Some cooling may also be expected as a side benefit. It is important to ensure that the size of the powder particles is correct, for their proper dispensation over the fire. The particle size is usually kept around 40 microns. These particles shatter into much smaller particles when they come in contact with the heat of the fire (could be down to even sub-micron levels), and fight the fire much more effectively. Proper storage of the chemical powders is a problem. They could get compacted when stored, thus losing their effectiveness. Such compacting leads to problems in their discharge to fight fires, and also results in unsatisfactory extinguishing action. Therefore, when they are stored for long periods of time, *frequent tests on such Extinguishant are essential, in regard to their continued effectiveness for fire-fighting purposes.*

Use of Inert and Other Gases to Extinguish Fires

You have seen how fluids (like water, foam), and solid chemicals, (in powder form), may be used to extinguish fires. Inert and other gases (such as carbon dioxide, nitrogen or halogens, like Haleness), are also highly effective extinguishant that are widely used to fight fires. One of *their main advantages is, that they can be stored conveniently and can be easily located in tight/crowded places,* (because of their ability to be compressed and stored in very small volumes). By directing at the high pressure such gases, in adequate enough concentration, onto a fire (location) you can smother and kill the fire, particularly small ones. The concentration required of such extinguishant depends upon the gas involved. It is high for carbon dioxide and nitrogen, but it is low and varies for Halon, depending on the type of Halon used. But, note that many Halon types are dangerous to humans in the concentrations required to fight most fires, which is of the order of 5%. When Halon is going to be deployed to put out a fire it is, therefore, advisable to evacuate humans and pets from the neighbourhood, particularly in closed spaces. Concentrations of carbon dioxide gas and nitrogen that would be required to affect humans dangerously are far higher. Unfortunately, higher, (hence dangerous to humans), concentrations of these gases are also needed for fire-fighting to be effective with these Extinguishant.

Use of Halon fire extinguishers has increased rapidly in the country. The reasons are not far to seek. With the ban on CTC, (Carbon Tetra Chloride), as a fire extinguishing agent, and other types not suitable for use in aircrafts, electrical systems and for portable use, (hand held types), such as in vehicles, apartments and so on, Halon fire extinguishers have made a rapid entry in the country. There are several Halon fire fighting agents: *Halon 1011 (CH_2BrCl), Halon 1211 ($CBrClF_2$), Halon 1202 ($CBr2F_2$), Halon 1301 (CF_3Br) and Halon 2402 (C_2Br2F_4).* Though Halon 1202 is perhaps the most potent fire-extinguishing agent*, it is also by far the most toxic.* Halon 1301 was found to be the next best, most stable and least toxic of the lot. It has a low boiling point. Halon 1211 is *NON-TOXIC, NON-STAINING, NON-CONDUCTING and ANTI-STATIC.* Hence, it has found widespread acceptance as a popular fire extinguisher (including for aircraft systems and for portable types). However, in the work environment of normally occupied locations, total flooding with Halon 1211 is unacceptable, as immediate, prior evacuation is required in such situations. Also, because of its low boiling point, (high volatility), you have to keep it away from sources of heat/direct sunlight. Note that, Halon 1301 can be used, even in such situations, provided the concentrations is kept under 10%. Both Halon 1202 and 2402 have high boiling point making it difficult to exploit its potential. *But they find application in systems for explosion suppression.* Most other Halon types are very, very toxic. However, it is to be noted that, the developed countries are now making a move to ban use of Halons, as it is considered to contribute to ozone layer depletion. (With the recent reportedly successful experiments with high power laser to recreate ozone in the atmosphere, would the situation change?).

It is an advantage that carbon dioxide can be liquefied and stored in the fluid form, and in suitable steel cylinders, at normal room temperatures. The pressure levels required are around 50 atmospheres. However, note that *when the room temperature is over about 30 degrees C, the gas can exist only in the gaseous form, and not as a liquid.* Further, surprisingly, at pressures below 5 bars the gas can exist either as a gas or as a solid-and not as a liquid! Also the solid carbon dioxide sublimates directly into its gaseous form, without passing through the liquid phase, (at 76 degrees C). *These characteristics of the gas could create problems, while dispensing the gas to fight fires.* If the nozzle design is improper, the gas could solidify as the pressure drops to 5 bars, and clog the nozzle. As the liquid CO_2 flows through the nozzle, in the process of vapourization the local temperature drop could be below 78 degrees C! The CO_2 immediately freezes. (This frozen solid form of CO_2 is called snow). When the nozzle design is proper the heat from the surrounding atmosphere sublimates the snow into gas form, and thus unblocking the nozzle. And the gas gets dispensed over the fire to extinguish it.

Nitrogen gas, on the other hand, cannot be liquefied until very, very low temperatures are reached. Therefore, for the gas to be used on fires as an extinguishing agent, *you need very large volumes of the gas to be stored, and at very high pressures too, for the quantity of nitrogen to be adequate to fight a fire. Further, unfortunately, nitrogen reacts with burning metals to form nitrides.* (In such cases, your choice is to go in for fully inert gases like helium, argon, neon etc., which are also stored in the compressed gas form).

You can more effectively fight a fire at its incipient stages. So, earlier the fire is detected, more easy/effective the fire fighting is, and so can be the fire-extinction. Hence, reliable and early fire detection assumes great importance in both manual and automatic methods of fire fighting. Obviously, fire detection devices have to depend on some aspect or characteristics of a fire such as heat, light (ultra violet/infra-red), chemical, or physical products released in a fire. People respond quickly to smell and smoke, but to a far lesser extent to heat (and flame). So, when people knowledgeable about fires are around, and are also alert, you can expect them to detect incipient fires faster and raise a fire alarm earlier than, perhaps, most automatic fire detection systems. When such fire alarms are promptly acted upon, it results in quicker and more effective control of a fire. (Note also that most automatic fire fighting systems have some specified delays before the sprinkler etc. comes into action).

Fire Detection

It is all very well to know what an excellent method (an informed) man based fire detection system would be. But who can afford to employ a number of persons, trained in fire detection, and positioned all over the place to raise a fire alarm, when (an incipient) fire starts somewhere in your building? No doubt, it may be great to have trained alert humans to detect/smell out incipient fires. But, usually, they would be otherwise occupied. They also need to sleep, and several may be required to adequately cover a spread out installation, apart from the expense of their upkeep, maintenance, pension etc! So, *it would be sensible and better to go in for some sort of an automatic and reliable fire detection/(and alarm) system*. Fortunately, there are several types of fire detectors commercially available, which have been found to be very useful in fire detection systems. Basically, there are three types of fire detectors: *Heat* (temperature, rate of rise of temperature) *detectors*, *Smoke* (smoke particles, combustion products) *detectors* and *Flame detectors*.

Heat Detectors

Heat detectors take advantage of the fact that heat or a rise in the ambient temperature results in a change in some physical or electrical characteristic of many materials. And, such a change (due to heat) can be easily used, as criteria, for existence/occurrence of a fire, (since heat is invariably present where there is a fire). Heat expands bodies and cold contracts them is a well known principle that is usefully extended to fire detection. Small expansion of metallic sensor elements/volumetric expansion of suitable liquid in a small container can be suitably magnified several folds to provide reliable signals for a fire alarm. Or, a change in the resistance of a thermistor/ resistor element can be the criteria for a fire alarm. A popular method was to use a fusible plug which melts at a specified high ambient temperature which will not be normally reached (say 60 degrees Celsius, since in some places summer could be as hot as 55 degrees). But such a temperature would be definitely exceeded during a fire melting the softening/plug, a clearly discernible change that is used for fire alarm/automatic fire extinguishing activities. Yet another method is to use the expansion of a gas sealed in a thin tube, (same principle as is used in pressure gauges, barometers), or differential expansion of a bimetallic strip due to a rise in the ambient temperature to signal presence of a fire. Even variation of the refractive index of air (due to its expansion) due to the heat of a fire, has been used, with an optical beam detection device, for fire detection. So, *you do have a very wide range of fire detectors to choose from, to meet your (exacting) requirements.*

But, heat detectors are not all that wonderful for fire detection because of certain inherent problems. One main problem is that the time to respond to the heat of a fire is quite high. Usually, this is a disadvantage in fire fighting. Consider a situation where the (ambient) temperature at which the detector signals occurrence of a fire (to trigger a fire alarm) is 60 degrees C, and suppose the rate of rise of the ambient temperature is, say one degree/ minute, (considered usual at the initial stage of a fire). If, now, the normal room temperature happens to be only 30 degrees C, a simple calculation indicates that the detector would need a full thirty minutes (to reach the 60 degrees) before it signals the presence of an incipient fire!

Some detectors, however, have a fast response like the ones that work on the change in refractive index of air. Use of a visible beam of light would be impractical, due to the normal violent fluctuations in the ambient light levels. You would, therefore, need to go in for an infra red (IR) beam of light.

Flicker and fluctuations in the refractive index of the air in the room because of the heat of a fire has far less affect on IR. Note that this type of detector has also got the major advantage of its being able to cover, and adequately, large volumes of space with a single detector unit. Further, IR beam detectors also respond to smoke particles. But then, cigarette smoke and humans/ intruders moving around in the area may also trigger an alarm! Fortunately, ionization type smoke detectors do not respond to cigarette smoke or body-heat, and are therefore very popular and widely deployed.

Smoke Detectors

Smoke detectors detect the presence of smoke arising out of a fire at the location. They use one of the *two principles*—photoelectric (*optical*) or ionization (using a radio-isotope source) type. Smoke is nothing but particles of combustion products released in a fire. The particles may be solid or liquid, with dimensions varying from smaller than about one milli-micron, to a much larger size/larger than 10 microns. (1 micron is equal to one millionth of a metre; and one mill-micron equals a thousand-millionth or one billionth of a metre, in size). When the particle size is *larger than about 0.3 microns they scatter visible light and hence are seen as visible smoke.* Note that, particles at pre-ignition stage are very small, about 0.1milli-micron to 0.5 milli-micron; whereas, smouldering fire releases smoke particles much larger in size, (say 0.1 to 1 micron). A flaming fire may release far larger size particles, of unburnt material. Therefore, *an optical detector will fail to detect pre-ignition combustion products* and the smaller range of smoke particles released during smouldering. *Fortunately, an ionization detector is particularly well suited to detect such smaller size particles.* It is advantageous to combine in one housing both types of detectors, to detect smoke particles, both small and big in size.

However, you must note, that there are situations where smoke detectors will fail to detect a fire. Neither the optical nor the ionization detector will detect alcohol or similar fires that do not release any smoke particles. Therefore, in such hazardous environments, you must take advantage of a suitable combination of fire detectors say, *combine smoke detectors with detectors sensitive to rate of rise of temperature.* One type of detector will not be effective in all types of environments. Evidently, smoke detectors will have problems in a kitchen environment, where with food cooking smoke is bound to be present, most often than not. Thus, the need for going in for a judicious choice of detectors that match the particular environment in which it is to function is of paramount importance.

Ionization detectors work on the basis of a difference in the ionic current in a chamber with ionized air, when in normal ambience and when some smoke particles enter the chamber. The detector uses a dual chamber housing, an inner chamber and an outer chamber, and a radioactive source, usually Americium 241 (quantity of around one micro-curie) to ionize the air in the two chambers. The inner chamber is virtually closed whereas the outer chamber is open to the environment so that smoke particles and invisible gas products of any fire at the location can penetrate into it. Normally, a small current will flow in the circuit, since the difference in the currents arising out of the ionization occurring in the closed and open chambers will be negligible. Smoke particles and invisible gas products of combustion at the location enter into the outer chamber, resulting in an increase in the current flow in that chamber. This results in a distinct difference in the currents in the two chambers. And this differential flow of current, (after due amplification ofcourse as the current by itself is too small in value), is used as the signal, to trigger a fire alarm/ initiate automatic fire extinguishing activities. The detector is an effective early warning device for fire, as they also detect micro-particles of smoke and invisible gases produced during the incipient stages of a fire, (that is the pre-ignition stage). *It is a tough, reliable and sensitive detector, which is also stable in operation under extremes of temperature.* Therefore, it, is no wonder that it is very popular in most business environments. But, do note that due care has to be exercised during any repair/disposal of such detectors. Only the manufacturer should undertake such jobs, due to possible biohazards because of the radio-active source used in the detector. (This is particularly true after a fire when the source would get exposed from its housing).

FLAME DETECTORS

The flame characteristics are used in the Flame detectors to indicate presence of a fire. These detectors have the fastest response time, as mentioned earlier, since the ultraviolet and infrared radiation from the flame, that is used for the purpose of fire detection, travel at the speed of light to reach the detector. Needless to say that you have to eliminate, as far as possible, the UV and IR radiation from direct sunlight from reaching the detector environment in order to get rid of any (unwanted) responses to the sunlight. To also avoid false alarms due to other causes (such as an electric heater, presence of carbon dioxide or water vapour that absorbs IR, etc.), and to discriminate from responses to them, *the flicker frequency of the flames of the fire is used,* with advantage, *in the detectors.* The response is optimized for flicker frequencies lying between about 1 Hz to about 15 Hz. (Note: small pool fires are expected to have a flicker frequency of about 15 Hz, whereas large pool flames have flicker frequency of about 2 Hz). Obviously, Flame detectors do not respond to fires at the pre-ignition or smouldering combustion types of fire, but to flaming or glowing combustion types only. But the detectors do have the additional advantage of ability to cover large volumes of space (say, for general surveillance for fires in the region). If installed in open areas, scintillation/reflections of extraneous light could adversely affect the performance of such detectors. Then, it is essential to use some sort of signal integration to make sure that the responses are for persisting signals only, (say, those that persist at least for a few seconds). This would prevent such transitory inputs from affecting the detector performance. A further advantage with these detectors is that they respond even when obscured to some extent by grime, grease, smoke, fog etc. However, *these detectors* also *do not respond to alcohol, hydrogen etc., fires,* which burn with an '*invisible*' flame !

A discussion on fire detectors will not be complete without some mention of some other types of detectors. There are quite a few types of such detectors, available. Gas sensors indicate presence of flammable gases. Particle detectors detect micro-sized particles such as those released during pre-ignition and smouldering combustion processes. Sampling detectors enable monitoring of large areas, by sequentially sampling at one place, the air samples from different locations. Use of ultrasonic/ microwave sensors is also possible (to detect presence of smoke, heat, combustion products etc. in the air at a location), *for indication of a combustion process in the location, etc.*

You must note that detectors only provide an output signal (*variation*). The variation in the output signal needs to be processed further, to eliminate/minimize false alarms before a fire alarm is sounded, (say, by a central control unit). Usually, it is a central-control unit that generates/signals initiation of fire fighting activities. The activities include alerting the fire brigade, sounding the fire alarms within the area it monitors, initiate automatic fire extinguishing procedures, unlatch emergency exits, identify and signal the zone(s) where fire has been detected, sound remote alarms, and so on.

Fire Alarm System

From the above, it is clear that fire detectors are not the be all and end all as regards fire fighting. Fire detectors are only a part of a fire alarm system. They constitute merely the important sensor portion of a fire alarm system. And, there could be other types of sensors used also, like CCTV surveillance, workers present who are also trained to observe and alert (when an incipient/ initial stages of a fire/fire itself occurs) the management, and so on. Where extensive areas/locations have to be monitored for fire occurrences, a central monitoring system and a centrally controlled fire alarm system become a necessity. The system will then include, apart from sensors, telecommunication links, reliable power supplies, manual fire alarm points, (break-glass devices), etc. The telecommunication links carry the sensor signals to the control unit, as well as the output alarm/activation signals from the control circuit to the output devices of the system, (such as bells and sounders, remote signaling units, automatic fire sprinkler systems and so on). The reliable power supplies are essential to keep the system functioning even when the power supply mains get disrupted due to a fire etc. The fire alarm points enable manual triggering of a fire alarm by alert personnel (employees/visitors etc.), from strategic points within the area so monitored, and so they also constitute a part of the fire alarm system. Note that the central control system has the all important function of processing the incoming signals from the detectors to assess whether the signal is actually indicative of a real/incipient fire at a particular location(s)/zone(s), or whether it is a false alarm. And only after this decision the system initiates relevant audible and visible alarms, and other fire fighting (signals) actions. Fire fighting actions could include remote alarms, automatic fire extinction, (sprinklers, gas/foam release, etc), opening of emergency exit doors, operation of fire dampers, highlighting of escape routes, (special signs, special illuminations), and so on.

The fire alarm system is expected to respond to alarm signals in less than about 200 milliseconds. And it is usual for the alarm signals themselves to have a duration of at least a second or more. The sounders and remote alarm should sound within few seconds of the fire detection/initiating trigger signal. In areas occupied by employees/personnel, alarm bells must definitely sound within few minutes, (to enable the people to promptly implement established fire-fighting procedures/quickly evacuate in an orderly manner, when required). Sounders must be loud enough to be clearly heard all over the area it is expected to cover, and be quite distinct in nature to be quickly identified as a fire alarm. The desirable sound level is 70 dB. at a distance of 3 metres from the sounder. It is usual to choose for the alarm signals *two or more fundamental frequencies within the sensitive audible range* of 300 Hz to 3 kHz. Communications systems employed to convey signals to and from the central control must be reliable, (whether leased line approach, dedicated wiring, automatic telephone dialing or other types/combinations are used). Remote alarms should also sound within 5 minutes of fire detection. Naturally, power supplies employed in/for the system must be reliable, and also have suitable back-ups. Manual, quick and positive initiation of an alarm, (say, the break glass type), must be provided for. They must be located at appropriate points spread throughout the building /installation. All devices and wiring etc., must be proof against any vandalism.

An elaborate and expensive fire alarm (and automatic fire extinguishing) system is totally worthless if it does not work when most needed, that is when a fire breaks out anywhere in the area (that the system keeps under surveillance). Therefore, leaving the maintenance aspects totally to the system supplier could be inadequate, inadvisable and could well turn out disastrous! This is particularly so in large, extensively spread-out, and workforce intensive organizations/installations. In such cases, it is advisable to appoint one person to be totally and exclusively responsible to oversee all fire-safety activities in the organization. His tasks would vary from simple actions such as dissemination of all relevant fire-safety information to everyone, employees and visitors alike, to more elaborate and onerous duties of checking for adequacy, proper control and implementation of anything in the organization that has to do with fire safety. He has to ensure that appropriate fire installations are setup; and that they are frequently and adequately checked and maintained. He has to see that the fire safety and fire fighting operations in the organization are well understood by all concerned. It would be his job to evolve and have instituted appropriate fire safety procedures. Further, it would be he who has to ensure necessary training of all personnel in the organization, in concerned areas of fire protection–fire safety, evacuation, fire fighting procedures, etc. He must also make sure too that adequate number of manual fire points are spread around and located at suitable spots; and that those are kept fully operational at all times.

A good fire alarm system must have suitable in-built self-test facility too. It must be possible to quickly check that the detectors and the alarm system as a whole are in proper operational condition. And it must be also possible to have a quick identification and replacement of defective devices and circuitry in the system. To enable this, purely temporary bypass of sounders may be provided for in the system design. But ofcourse this should not be at the expense of missing a likely real fire situation. Any defects found should be immediately rectified forthwith, without any delay. This could well mean location of suitable spares at the installation itself, or in the neighbourhood. Note that most fire detectors maybe checked for proper operation by holding close by to it a hot air blower (hair dryer for example), the flame of a cigarette lighter, etc. It must be emphasized that systematic and periodic maintenance checks are essential to ensure that the system and all its constituent parts are always fully functional; and that any defects that may arise are promptly noted and immediately rectified.

Perhaps, the toughest tasks for the mankind in the twenty-first century is to ensure an effective control of environmental pollution, and minimize biological hazards. The risks and dangers of natural hazards pale into insignificance compared to the enormous, lurking dangers of unbridled pollution. This is all the more so as the dangerous effects of environmental pollution could be insidious, go unnoticed, played down or just swept under the carpet. The problems are multifaceted and have major economic implications on industries, societies and the nations. Therefore, unless societies, nations and the man in the street work together-towards well defined goals of controlling pollution-in a deliberate, co-ordinated and emphatic manner-the biosphere/the habitat is in for terrible times, maybe even extinction of the living species, in decades to come. *Environmental pollution and bio-hazards are closely connected; so, they are considered together in the next chapter.*

Chapter 13

Pollution and Biological Hazards

"The one sure way to conciliate a tiger is to allow oneself to be devoured"

—Conrad Adenauer

This can very well be *true of Fire, Pollution and Biological Hazards!*

POLLUTION and BIOLOGICAL HAZARDS are the unwanted baggage that the modern society is made to bear. This is mostly because of the increasing, rank consumerism, and perhaps selfish desires of comfort and conveniences, (this is particularly true of the throwaway concept, in lieu of the age-old reusable philosophy), that is also fueled by the greed of quick profits and the rapid technological advances/capabilities and offerings. The castaway products become "enduring rubbish", wastes that refuse to go away and clutter up/pollute the environment, cause undesirable biohazards for decades or even aeons!). The problems are exacerbated by the lack of will in the concerned regulating authorities to effectively control the menace (of *pollution and biohazards*) because of spheres of influence and possible high cost of implementation of the readily available remedial measures. The hazards remain despite the high cost to society and possible adverse affects on the national/world economies/habitat in the long run, that arise due to the non-implementation, in time, of the possible remedial measures.

To a great extent, "Pollution" is usually a by-product of production processes, products of daily consumption/usage of hosts of goods, materials and substances, (that maybe results of newer and newer applications of technology, or creation of new wants in modern life). Some well-known examples of pollution are vehicle exhaust pollution, pollution due to smoking, pollution due to use of chemical processes, etc. Generally, pollution is not due to any incidental contamination during a production process that may occur due to an accident nor primarily due to any spurious product deliberately produced and marketed, illegally/unlawfully. (Though, these could also result in pollution and biohazards, like the polluting industries which thrived in the heart of Delhi until the Supreme Court stepped in to clean up and have them removed from the metropolis.). Health hazards may also arise because of the method of usage. For example, use of virgin material plastic bags for packaging food/edibles may not cause harm to humans (unless they are burnt, as garbage, when they release noxious toxins into the atmosphere, the reason why synthetic furniture and furnishings are deadly as fire hazards). Whereas, use of recycled plastic bags for such purposes may have serious consequences to humans when they consume the edibles so packaged, due to contamination of the plastic material during the recycling process! Animals (cattle, animals in the zoo and so on) may unwittingly consume discarded plastic bags, with dangerous consequences to their lives. Pollution leads to *known* (immediate*) and known/unknown* (long-term) biohazards *to humans, animals, etc.*, that is to the living planet.

Almost everyone is affected by the serious problems of *environmental pollution*. Environmental pollution basically consists of two components viz., atmospheric pollution (*air pollution and noise pollution*), and earth surface pollution (which includes also water sources pollution, that is pollution of *wells, ponds, lakes, underground sources* such as *bore-wells, streams, rivers, and oceans*). No doubt, there is space pollution with the floating debris of innumerable satellites, space probes and other objects, launched and orbiting in space till their ultimate descent into the earth's lower atmosphere and burn up/fall onto the earth surface. However, they are not as yet of major significance as far as any direct effects, on the human habitat, are concerned. Space pollution can therefore be ignored for the present, except by those involved in space launches (*unless lot more space debris of space based nuclear power units start falling back to earth, with their consequential nuclear hazards potential!*).

Atmospheric Pollution

As indicated above, atmospheric pollution include air pollution and noise pollution. Atmospheric Pollution is suspected as leading to possible ozone depletion in the *Ozone Layer*, (about 50 kms above the surface of the Earth, the region called the Stratosphere). Earth surface pollution includes pollution of the earth soil and pollution of sub-surface strata. (The hazards of RF Pollution are not included here, since they have already been covered under Radiation Hazards). Neither does the term pollution cover the deliberate activities of anti-social elements of flooding the society with spurious or adulterated substances of consumption, whether milk, drinks, foodstuff, drugs/medicines or substances used in the preparation of toiletries, edibles, liquid refreshments and so on. Pollution is usually an offshoot or fallout of valid, legal activity, where, during the design, production, use, maintenance and disposal of so called amenities of 'the good life' proper and adequate control is NOT being exercised to maintain a clean environment.

Environmental pollution is, and is going to be the main source of problems in achieving quality of life, *nay-even sustaining life itself*, both for humans and for other living beings; let alone the problems of its adverse affects on materials, structures and buildings! In modern living conditions, environmental pollution control will assume a center stage in society. It will remain a herculean task too, that may well be never ending. Environmental laws need to be stringent, have to be enforced with religious fervour, entail exemplary punishment and require total commitment by everyone in the society-man, woman and child-in order to be effective and ensure a clean environment. Otherwise, having a clean environment all around us, will remain a utopian dream!

Air Pollution

Air Pollution is one of the worst and extensively prevalent hazard that the modern man faces, particularly in the urban conglomerations and built up areas. This is because of the countless factories and electric power generation systems, etc. that have cropped up (and continue to crop up, near urban areas, consequent to the industrial revolution and its fall-outs), and because of the ubiquitous concentration of the automobile population. Air pollutants consist of particulate matter (solid and liquid) and gaseous pollutants. The automobile exhausts spew out into the atmosphere gases and particulate substances that are dangerous, particularly, to humans and animals, and to other living organisms too to some extent. The extensive use of CFC refrigerants in the older technology refrigerators and air-conditioners, as well as in aerosol spray cans also apparently contribute to atmospheric pollution. Other major causes could be the occasional major eruptions of volcanoes, spewing out thousands of tonnes of volcanic ashes into the atmosphere, and the major forest fires-like those that have occurred recently in Indonesia.

As if the above problems are not enough, now and then major disasters take place, mainly because of human failures and the resultant accidents (whether due to design inadequacies, poor maintenance or sheer negligence). Two such disasters come to mind in the recent times—the Bhopal gas leak tragedy and the Chernobyl nuclear disaster, which occurred in 1984 and 1986 respectively, and resulted in thousands of deaths, and many more thousands seriously affected. Further details on these may be seen in the annexures on chemical hazards/nuclear hazards respectively.

Most industrial processes release pollutants into the environment in the form of gases, dust, smoke, effluents etc. (Hence, the safety of health of workers, and of people in the neighbourhood, is a major concern). *Gaseous pollutants* include oxides of sulphur, oxides of nitrogen, carbon monoxide, carbon dioxide, chlorofluorocarbons, (CFCs), hydrocarbons, ozone and other oxidants. Dangerous *Particulate pollutants* in the form of dust, fume, mist, smoke or spray-include compounds of antimony, arsenic, asbestos, benzene and its derivatives, beryllium, hydrocarbons, lead, manganese, mercury, nickel, nitrates, phenols, vinyl halides, (even sand dust) and so on. As a matter of caution, regulations enforce suitable control of hundreds of chemical compounds, including the above mentioned ones, to safeguard clean environment.

Whilst gaseous pollutants affect human health by some sort of chemical reactions with the human organs, particulate pollutants may lead to physical reactions and/or chemical affects leading to hazards to health. For example, exposure to dust in the air we breathe in may lead to copious watering of the eyes, violent bouts of sneezing and coughing, that are *physical reactions.* Whereas, dust inhaled into the lungs can lead to more serious and invidious hazards (long-term affects include damage to alveoli of the lungs, loss of lung capacity, and even cancer etc.). Particularly, dust of chemical compounds, inhaled or ingested, can result in extremely dangerous consequences to the humans, and animals. Industrial and public health standards lay down some minimum levels for the pollutants as *'safe levels'*. But it is a moot point as to whether any (minimum) levels can be considered entirely safe to the biosphere, over a long, long period. Insidious adverse affects of the so-called 'safe' levels of pollution may remain dormant and come out into the open and become evident, much later. For example, effects of the hazardous substances identified as carcinogens may become evident years (even decades) later, with the actual onset of cancer, (which may well be twenty to fifty years later), when irretrievable damage has already occurred. Several dangers of air pollution are listed below:-

a) <u>Dangers of Lead Pollution</u>

One of the biggest problems that society faces today, particularly in the urban environment, is the automobile exhaust, whether that of petrol driven vehicles or diesel operated ones. (In case of diesel vehicles the main danger lies in the sulphur content in the diesel oil, and the copious particulate pollution in the vehicle exhaust). It can have immediate and lasting harmful effects that depend on the extent and continuity of exposure of the victims, particularly children. Leaded petrol, the ordinary kind extensively used, leaves *lead in the exhausts* that seriously affects the health of those exposed to the fumes; children to a far greater extent. Smelting operations, work on/reconditioning of lead acid batteries are also major sources of lead pollution. Lead is also used in daily life objects such as paints, bathroom fittings and so on. The dangers to health that *lead poisoning* leads to are understood to include the following:

- *Coma, convulsions and even death,(at high levels of inhalation/ingestion).*
- *Anaemia, both in adults and children.*
- *Impaired fertility in adults.*
- *Adverse affects on the kidneys of adults.*
- *Children become hyperactive, their growth can be impaired, their I.Q. reduced.*
- *Reduction in attention span of children, impaired reading and learning abilities.*

Lead absorption is through the lungs, by inhalation, and through the digestive system when ingested. Absorption is 50% for inhaled and about 10% for ingested, except in children the absorption can go up to 50% in the digestive system, (ingested). Once absorbed into the bloodstream, only a portion of the lead gets excreted whilst the remainder accumulates in the liver, brain, kidneys and bones. A person needs to supplement his diet with salts by consuming milk, for calcium, and green/leafy vegetables for zinc, iron and magnesium. Fortunately, use of catalytic converters for newer models of petrol vehicles has been made compulsory and, atleast, in urban areas lead free petrol. (However, note that the catalytic converters themselves have hazards associated with their usage, since they are understood to produce *benzene a dangerous carcinogenic* (cancer producing substance)). It is understood that new regulations are under consideration of the Government of India in regard to controls on work on lead acid batteries.

b) Dangers of Inhalation of Particulate Matter

Next time you liberally sprinkle on yourself talcum powder after a bath, think twice. Hold your breath, or better still, exhale. Do remember that the protective abilities of our respiratory system have certain built in limitations. It has wonderful ability to keep out from the lung cells, (the alveoli), particles of matter larger than about 5 micrometers (that is, 5 millionths of one metre, or five thousandths of a millimetre!), in diameter. Hair in the nostril and the mucosa, the mucous lining inside the nose, keep out large size particles, which, you blow out/take out as snot. (Do take care to *blow one nostril at a time, and that too not violently*, lest you burst a blood vessel). The mucous lining/the cilia, (tiny hair), in the bronchi have the ability to propel smaller size particles back towards the throat, by the movements of the tiny hair, (like flagellation?), and thus preventing their entry into the lung cell sacs. And you get rid of the mucous bound particles by either expectoration or by swallowing. (But, *if you take in a violent breath, all bets are off. Your lungs then act like a vacuum cleaner and sucks in the particles along with the breath. The particles may then bypass the protective mechanism, and get directly into the alveoli of the lungs!).*

Particles smaller than 5 micrometres escape this protective action and can reach the alveoli, where they deposit and get embedded. This irritates the lung tissues. In an attempt to remove the irritation, mucous gets deposited on the site leading to lung malfunctions, reduction in lung capacity, pulmonary edema, cancer etc. Note that most particulate pollution vary in size from a mere fraction of a micrometre to about 10 micrometres. *So when you powder a baby, watch out. A baby does not know to hold its breath. Do not dowse the baby's chest, chin etc. liberally, directly from a tin of talc; lest the baby inhale the talc dust directly into its lungs. It is much better to use a powder-puff, to gently powder the baby without generating any cloud of talc.* (Also, if you go in for a facemask to protect you from polluted atmosphere, do make sure that the built-in filter has the ability to stop micro-particles smaller than 5 micrometres in diameter, apart from capabilities to absorb/neutralize polluting harmful gases/chemicals in the air you breathe in).

c) Dangers of Carbon Monoxide (CO)

Carbon monoxide gas is present in the motor vehicle exhaust because of incomplete combustion in the engine. And so, CO does not get converted into Carbon Dioxide, (CO_2), and water. Ofcourse, all internal combustion engine systems, such as engine generators, and electric utility stations using fossil fuels for generation of electricity, also produce some amount of CO. This however, is mainly present close to the source, which is inherently static (not spread all over as in the case of vehicles, due to their mobility). Carbon monoxide gas is a dangerous, deadly air pollutant. Therefore, the permissible exposure level for the gas, for an 8 hour (usual work period) exposure is a concentration of the gas of less than 10 parts per million, ppm. *CO gas when inhaled damages the inherent oxygen carrying capacity of the red blood cells. This can leads to oxygen deficiency that affects the central nervous system, bring about cardiac/pulmonary changes, and leads ultimately to respiratory failure and death.*

d) Dangers of Carbon Dioxide (CO_2)

At low concentrations, CO_2 leads to increased breathing rate to make up for the reduced oxygen intake in the air we breathe in. But, in this case the concentration is measured in terms of % rather than in parts per million. At higher concentrations on the other hand, the rate of respiration is reduced. And that leads to oxygen deprivation, which causes rapid unconsciousness, and even death. *CO_2 in the atmosphere is believed to lead to global warming, and its consequential adverse effects on the habitat. (Hence, it comes under the umbrella term of 'Greenhouse Gases').*

Sulphur Dioxide (SO_2), Nitrous Oxide (NO), Nitrogen Dioxide (NO_2) and Ozone (O_3) Pollutants.

SO_2, NO, NO_2 and Ozone also arise as atmospheric pollutants due to the sulphur content in fuels, as well as the combustion systems in vehicles and industrial processes. High temperature processes result in the production of NO due to the nitrogen present in fossil fuels, and the atmosphere itself. The NO gets converted into NO_2, by further oxidation. Ozone, a highly oxidising agent, is produced in the atmosphere, indirectly, by chemical reactions of hydrocarbons in vehicle exhausts, oil refineries etc. with sunlight as a sort of catalyst. Ozone, being highly reactive, reacts with hydrocarbons in the air ultimately producing organic compounds and acids that further pollute the air around us. Thus, ozone, which is so useful in the stratosphere to practically stop dangerous ULTRAVIOLET rays from reaching the surface of the earth, is a very hazardous pollutant when it is present in the lower atmosphere.

SO_2 adversely affects the activity of cilia, (the protective mechanism that drives the particulate matter that manage to get into the respiratory tract, away from the lungs and towards the throat), constricts the bronchii and cause bronchitis as well as abnormal accumulation of fluid in the lungs, (pulmonary edema).

Nitrous Oxide, (NO), is called the 'laughing gas', since in small quantities it induces laughter. But in higher concentration the gas is used as an anaesthetic. NO_2 can produce pulmonary edema, when present in high concentration in the air we breathe in.

Presence of Ozone in the air leads to dry throat, headache and a change in the respiration. Being a high oxidant it can lead to pulmonary edema etc. even when present in minute concentration levels of a few parts per million.

e) Dangers of Hydrogen Sulphide (H_2S)

H_2S is an extremely toxic gas. At low concentrations, even as low as 0.3 ppm, its presence is detected by its distinct smell of rotten eggs. The gas is generated in sewers, in oil refining-where it is flared off to turn into SO_2, which is less toxic, and in some chemical processes. It irritates the eyes even in very small concentrations. When inhaled it could cause headaches, dizziness, pulmonary edema, convulsions and unconsciousness.

f) Other Dangerous (Industrial) Air Pollutants

Numerous hazardous air pollutants (both gaseous and particulate), occur in industrial environments, (and in domestic environments to a lesser extent). They have varying effects on health and the environment. Some common gaseous pollutants are—Benzene (C_6H_6), Carbon Disulphide (CS_2), Carbon Tetrachloride ($CCl._4$), Chlorofluorocarbons (CFCs), Phosgene ($COCl._2$), Toluene (C_6H5CH_3), etc.

Benzene, inhaled or absorbed through the skin, gets stored in bone marrow, and could cause anaemia or even leukaemia.

CS_2 is absorbed through inhalation into the lungs or via the skin. It can cause damage to peripheral vision, and affects the heart and the brain, (thus can adversely affect the functioning of many organs in the human body, unlike most hazardous substances that directly act, usually only on the functioning of a single organ).

Carbon Tetrachloride, a suspected carcinogen, is absorbed into the blood through the lungs, also gets in through the skin, and the digestive tract. It could cause damage to kidneys and the liver.

CFCs, commonly used in refrigerators and air conditioners, are due to be phased out due to their adverse affects on the environment understood to cause depletion of the ozone layer in the stratosphere.

Phosgene was used as a poison gas during wars in the early part of the twentieth century. Its affects are similar to those of Nitrous oxide. Toluene, inhaled or ingested, can cause damage to kidneys and the liver.

Particulate, hazardous air pollutants include several substances like *Arsenic* and its compounds, *Asbestos dust, Beryllium* compounds, *Mercury, Silica dust,* etc. (There could be many others such as *Cadmium, Chromium, Manganese, Nickel* and so on). Arsenic cause irritation of the skin and could lead to skin cancer. When exposed to high concentration levels and inhaled, it can lead to lung cancer, and is thus an occupational hazard.

Repeated inhalation of Asbestos particles, (an occupational hazard), causes Asbestosis and malignant tumours (cancer in the lung/abdomen).

Beryllium dust leads to breathlessness, cough, chest pain and even bloody sputum.

Inhalation or ingestion of Mercury could cause acute/chronic effects-that could be reversible or irreversible, in nature. The affects could vary from simple breathlessness, to speech impairment, malfunction of the nervous system, ulceration, loosening of teeth, bloody diarrhoea etc.

No wonder air pollution is so dangerous and injurious to the health of the community, and needs to be tackled on an emergency and permanent basis!

NOISE POLLUTION

Noise Pollution is something that you tend to ignore, suffer in silence, put wads of cotton in your ears or just get away from the source if you can. Seldom do you do something positive about it, except perhaps complain to your immediate neighbour about the nuisance of the high decibel sounds in the neighbourhood! You do not build sound barriers between your house/environs and the traffic noise. When going in for an household appliance, you do not select the least noisy one, but the one that is least expensive that will meet your work requirement. You do not complain to the police about the loudspeaker nuisance in the neighbourhood. Nor do you cause suitable legislation to be made to prevent landing and taking off of airplanes form your neighbouring airport/noisy vehicular traffic at night, or agitate for curbing of noise generation by vehicle exhausts/rickety old vehicles! (Of course, you do have the *Environment (Protection) Act 1986,* that stipulate several things to minimize the adverse effects of noise on the health of human beings-including harmful psychological effects. We shall dwell more on these aspects later on). Are you aware that *Noise Pollution* is not just a nuisance but a real, *dangerous health hazard.*

Apart from the nuisances of annoyance, stress and even fright, (notice how sudden loud noises easily startle babies), loud sounds/ noises can cause hearing losses. Such noise induced damage to hearing could be *temporary or permanent.* A mere two minutes exposure to an ambient noise level of about 90 dBA. Could induce a temporary change of the threshold of hearing called as "*temporary threshold shift*" or TTS. Such a shift may last for a few seconds to as long as several hours! Such shifts are easily detected by *hearing tests/with audiometers.* When noises (or tinnitus) accompanies such TTS, *it is a dangerous indication;* consider it as a sign of possible *irreversible damage to hearing/ deafness* or *permanent threshold shift* (PTS*)!*

Note that dB or decibel is one tenth of a bel. The bel is a notation used to compare power levels, which can be very, very large indeed. For instance, the power level of a sound you may hear could be a very small fraction of a *millionth of a watt* (microwatt), where as the power output of a TV transmitter could be *millions of watt* (Megawatt). And the ratio of the two power levels is over a million million, a difficult number to handle, in calculations etc.! So, you have the notation bel, a logarithmic ratio of two powers P_1 and P_2. Thus one bel = log P1/P2, the logarithm being to the base 10. It is usually more convenient to use one tenth of this value or a decibel, that is the ratio in *dB* becomes *10 log P1/P2.* When you deal with voltage levels, intensity levels, current levels etc. as the power levels are proportionate to square of these quantities, the dB becomes in these cases equal to 20 log V1/V2 etc. That is, the ratio in *dB = 20 log V1/V2, 20 log* I_1/I_2*, etc.* Sound pressure levels are expressed in relation to the Threshold of Hearing, which is taken as 0 dBA. The Threshold of Pain is about 130 dBA!

The onset of permanent deafness/irreversible hearing loss could be gradual or sudden. Loud noisy work environments such as in some industries (noisy machinery in operation, use of pneumatic drills/tools), loud discotheques/unusually loud entertainment surrounding, proximity to high noise traffic centres etc. cause gradual, imperceptible permanent shifts in the hearing thresholds. (How many are aware of the dangers of playing a music system/tv too loud?). Such damage is noticed when it is found difficult to understand speech that is heard-one cannot make out the consonants, in the first instance which makes it difficult to comprehend the speech that is heard. *An indication that partial deafness has occurred!* On the other hand, when you are close to a loud explosive sound, such as due to an explosion or even a powerful cracker burst, there can be an immediate, very perceptible and permanent hearing loss-result a PTs/deafness! This is the situation in the battlefield or proximity to a bomb-burst, etc., if you are not wearing protective muffs over the ears.

The main features of the Environment (Protection) Act 1986 are:

- Normal use of *Public Address Systems* (PAS) and *Loudspeakers* (LS) only in closed premises like Auditoria, Conference Halls, etc. BETWEEN 2200 and 0600 *hrs only*. Permission from competent authority essential for their use in other public places.
- Use of vehicular horns, playing of music, public performances, beating of drums etc. banned in silence areas and within 100 metres of hospitals, courts, educational institutions etc.
- State governments to designate industrial, commercial, residential and silent zones to enable implementation of the standards laid down by the Act. And the standards being 75 dBA, 65 dBA, 55 dBA, and 50 dBA respectively during the day and 70; 55; 45 and 40 dBA respectively at night. Competent Authority to take action against violators, usually on receipt of complaints.

Note that normal conversation levels are about 50 to 60 dB and a shout is at about 70-75 dB, depending on the noise level in the immediate neighbourhood. And the Central Government is looking to ensure use of quieter technologies for use in the domestic appliances etc.

For specific high noise levels which cannot be avoided due to any reason the limiting periods of exposure that are generally accepted are as indicated below:

Noise levels (dBA)	:	87	90	93	96	99	102	105
Exposure Period (hrs.)	:	16	8	4	2	1	0.5	0.25

So, beware of being anywhere near blasting sites, habitual listening to loud music etc. And in high ambient noise environments which you cannot avoid, as (an occupational) safety measure use appropriate protective ear gear without fail.

Earth Surface Pollution

The problem of soil salinity affecting agriculture has been known to exist for thousands of years. Even the fall of the Mesopotamian civilization has been attributed to the failure of agriculture that intensively exploited irrigation, with its fallout of increasing salt content in the soil and consequential ultimate failure of crops. Arguably, this could be considered as an instance of Earth Surface Pollution! Salt dissolved in the water due to various natural processes is carried to the agricultural land by the water used to irrigate the land. The water evaporates, drains away leaving behind the salts to mix with the topsoil and percolate down to the sub-soil levels. Such salts mainly consist of calcium, carbonates, chlorides, magnesium, nitrates, potassium, sodium, etc., and even boron; to varying degrees. Naturally, excessive salinity affects crop growth/yield and could well make agricultural efforts a failure. Where there is good enough natural rainfall, and proper surface drainage the salts (soluble ones ofcourse) dissolve in the water and are carried away (by the water flowing on the surface, the subsurface water-ultimately to the seas/oceans), thus reducing/minimizing the adverse problems of excessive soil salinity. Prawn cultivation in some regions of India has resulted in excessive salinity in the soil, and hence the land in many parts of the region has become unfit for agricultural purposes! These problems get exacerbated when use of pesticides and fertilizers is excessive, improper and is uncontrolled. Further, these artificial additives find their way into the food chain and adversely affect the health of humans and the farm animals to say the least. The problems become terrible when unprocessed/uncontrolled industrial effluents too add to such pollution. (People of Delhi are fortunate that the Supreme Court intervened and ensured that the polluting industries in the capital region be closed down/ moved out of Delhi! Unfortunately, this is not happening elsewhere in the country, to control this bane of pollution all over the country).

Reports suggest that import and dumping of toxic wastes such as lead acid batteries, arsenic compounds and hydrogen sulphide which are disposed of in trenches and pits create hazards by mixing with ground water with resulting increase of arsenic, lead etc., content in water. Ship-breaking is another very environmentally hazardous activity. Reports indicate that soil pollution and mixing of toxic elements from industrial effluents, as well as non-biodegradable plastics and plastic based detergents are root causes for health disorders. To check pollution it is essential to have proper training, adequate public awareness and effective enforcement of environmental protection laws and policies.

Urban conglomerations are major sources of Earth Surface Pollution *too*. (You have already seen how they are major contributors to Atmospheric Pollution). In this, water (municipal waste-water, industrial effluents, storm water, etc.) plays a considerable part to carry and spread pollution over wide areas and down into the soil/earth surface layers through pipes, channels, storm water drains, streams, lakes, sewage disposal systems, percolation and so on. It almost looks as if more the water usage by the population more the pollution! Percolation of the contaminated/polluted water/effluents downward through the surface layers of the soil taints the sub-soil/underground water sources (including even deep borewell streams). Solid waste pollutants are mainly distributed around by the municipal rubbish (including hospital waste etc.) disposal/landfill arrangements.

In the rural areas, it is mainly the agricultural operations, agricultural waste water/effluents that cause water/earth surface pollution. (Apart from intensive irrigation leading to the unwanted problem of high salinity of the soil). Aqua culture, coffee pulping operations, extensive use of fertilizers and pesticides, and so on create their own environmental problems to the extent of maybe even making the land unfit for further cultivation, for years!

Industries that use water extensively to produce immense quantities of waste water/effluents are major causes of pollution that extend down streams to the riparian states, lakes and the seas. Oil industries can be major concern because of the inherent dangers of oil leaks; whether in the production, refining, processing, storage and transportation systems.

Littering is another cause for earth surface degradation. Plastic wastes clog cities' gutters, sewers and storm water drains. Fortunately, the recent legislation banning/curbing the use of thin non-biodegradable carry bags will go a long way to hopefully make this problem a thing of the past, in India.

In almost all cases of pollution, the contaminants/pollutants/chemicals/toxins ultimately gets into the food chain/potable water and water for personal hygiene/washing purposes to adversely affect the health of the population. And thus results in bio-hazards. Pollution changes the characteristics of the water in regard to its colour, smell, pH value, bacteria/virus content, presence of suspended particles/sedimentation, presence of poisonous chemicals/toxins and dangerous heavy metals and so on; to varying extent. No wonder polluted water is unfit for human consumption and maybe even for ablutions, unless and until it is suitably treated/processed, (usually an expensive business), in the first instance, before use.

Table XII.1 The Complete coverage of various types of Pollution

Types of Pollution	Sources	Effects	Preventive Measures
1. Atmospheric pollution a) Air Pollution	* Smoke from factories, power plants, automobiles etc. * Eruption of volcanoes * Major forest fires and disasters emitting harmful gases. * Oxides of nitrogen, hydrocarbons and carbon monoxide * Combustion of fossil fuels.	* Causes cold, cough, irritation in eyes and throat, dizziness etc. * Respiratory diseases like bronchitis, asthma emphysema, reduction in lung capacity, pulmonary edema, cancer etc. * Global warming and depletion of ozone layer in stratosphere. * Responsible for disappearance of chlorophyll, breakdown of plant cells and premature leaf fall.	* Greater usage of electrostatic filters in chimneys of factories. * Proper turning of all motor vehicles * Encouragement of CNG run, pollution free vehicles. * Planting large number of trees and extending forest cover (afforestation).
b) Noise Pollution	* Domestic appliances, loudspeakers etc. * Noise from horns of vehicles, vehicular exhausts, usage of rickety old vehicles. * Noise at traffic signals, airports etc.	* Causes irritability, tension, nervousness and anxiety, infertility etc. * Rest and relaxation are interrupted; efficiency at work decreases. * Increases pulse rate, raises cholesterol and blood pressure. * Produces peptic ulcers and affects digestive system * Severe pain in middle ear; permanent deafness or irreversible hearing loss; loss of equilibrium and nausea.	* Introduction of laws curbing noise pollution and taking strict action against offenders. * Avoid proximity to blasting sites, traffic signals, airports etc. * use appropriate protective ear gear always * Horns to be used only when necessary. * Silencers of vehicles should be in proper condition.

Types of Pollution	Sources	Effects	Preventive Measures
2) Earth Surface Pollution a) Land/Soil Pollution	* Massive amount of solid wastes disposed by consumer society like household refuse, commercial rubbish, garbage etc. * Industrial wastes, construction debris, and agricultural wastes. * Pollutants washed out of atmosphere. * Extensive use of artificial fertilizers, pesticides biocides etc.	* Various health hazards and diseases; stomach ailment. * Excessive salinity of soil which makes land unfit for agriculture. * Artificial additives get into food chain and can even cause irreversible damage to humans and animals.	* Avoid artificial fertilizers and carbides for cultivation; encourage natural fertilizers. * Secure disposal of harmful and toxic waste in large vessels, so that it does not come in contact with soil. * Use of bio-degradable materials for all purposes wherever possible. * Curbing excessive consumerism.
b) Water Pollution	* Fertilizers used for plant growth washed out by rain,, eventually drain into rivers and streams and pollute it. * Various pollutants like DDT, petroleum cadium, nuclear wastes, human wastes, sewage arsenic, lead etc. * Environmentally hazardous activity such as ship-breaking or oil slick etc.	* Organic substances deoxygenate water which is harmful for fish and vegetation. * Responsible for several kinds of bacteria and virus which cause Cholera, typhoid, jaundice, nausea, tuberculosis, gastro-enteritis, paralysis and liver diseases.	* Sewage treatment of polluted water. * Ban on discharge of industrial wastes into rivers. * Enforcement of environmental protection laws and policies. * Imparting proper training and adequate public awareness.

The best way to minimize environmental pollution is ofcourse to tackle the problem at the source of pollution; that is, by avoiding processes and use of products that generates polluting waste products, in their turn. Curbing excessive consumerism naturally goes a long way in this connection. Most of the damage is due to the compelling force that the profit motive of businesses thrives on the concept of quick obsolescence of products/the throwaway concept of usage. This has to be curtailed, contained and replaced with the concept of products with trouble free longlife and easy and sustainable maintenance to further prolong its useful life; and minimize waste production. Any resulting waste products must be bio-degradable/recyclable or harmless to the environment (with simple, economical and effective waste treatment methods if at all required). It helps, ofcourse, when waste can be suitably processed to reduce its bulk/to compact it. This enables its far easier/safer and more secure disposal on long-term basis.

So, the mantra in regard to product usage, product design and any waste generation/disposal should be the five-fold action path—the "*Pancha Tantra*" of environmental protection, as follows:

- "Renounce" (excessive consumerism and trying to "keep up with the Joneses").
- "Reuse" (forget "the throw away concept"; discard "the design theme of rapid obsolescence" and extend life cycle of products).
- "Recycle" (to minimize waste production).
- "Recover" (to conserve natural resources); And
- "Reduce " (by reducing toxicity, by concentrating, compacting etc to simplify/minimize/improve security of waste disposal systems).

Bio-hazards

The quality of life in the modern society has improved tremendously in the recent past with the ease and comforts provided by the technological innovations and consumer oriented products. But not much thought appears to have been given to the consequences of the product design, production and usage-the resulting environmental degradation, and the possible biological hazards that arise with extensive utilization of these modern conveniences. As may be observed from the paragraphs above, pollution is a major culprit in this regard. It is both a cause for environmental degradation and, consequently, also an overwhelming generator of bio-hazards.

The environment we live in is a constant source of bio-hazards. Be it the air we breathe, the water/fluids we drink, the food/the edibles we consume, the medicines we take, the articles/substances we daily handle and so on. The hazards abound in the home environment itself to start with. Clean fresh air, pure water, wholesome food, sufficient exercise, adequate sleep and silent calm atmosphere—the basic necessities for "a healthy mind in a healthy body"—have all degenerated in modern life. This is particularly so in the urban conglomerations. The match box-beehive like apartment complexes structures, piped municipal water supply, vegetation-less "concrete jungle" with its abundance of smoke/dust/noise/waste generation that also encourage multiplication and ease of movements of germs/pests/vermin etc. that all play their part in degradation of the living environment. To these we have to add of course the "modern conveniences", the canned, the wrapped, the packet and bottled kinds-the aerosol cans, the detergents, the house/toilet cleaners (such as phenyls, Vim, Domex, Lysol, Harpic and so on). Add to all these unscrupulous businesses and spurious products; they can make life a hell. The scary headlines we encounter almost daily in the newspapers/TV are practically indicators of the innumerable bio-hazards that perforce we have to surmount in our life-environment. Here are some representative, revealing samples that have appeared recently:

- "Bangalore is gradually turning into a toxic city".
- "Keep that prowling gastric bug at bay".
- "Toxic Tonic" (referring to the poor quality of drinking water in Bangalore).
- "Four women die after drinking borewell water".

- "Contaminated water results in village of deformed children".
- "Bangaloreans go red and gummy in the eyes".
- "Don't be fooled by pollution masks".
- "Bhopal still reeks of toxic gas".
- "Infected salads can damage the brain".
- "Fizz bubbles with Caffeine, Phosphoric acid. Cool loads of calories and side effects are an added attraction".
- "Dangerous sweetener".
- "Spurious saline kills 3 women, two babies".
- "Some beauty products can bespoil your face".
- "Beware that pill may prove life threatening".
- "Any drug that has any effect on your body can cause side effects".
- "Drug firm chiefs jailed for contaminated blood scandal".
- "Multiple medicines can do harm".
- "Beauty is skin deep in the culinary catwalk. Deliciously deceitful, white paint for milk, fried bread for fish".
- "Wheat flour with pesticide recidues".
- "It was meant to be sweet death for policemen".
- "Unsafe toys may lurk on your child's shelf".
- "That paint on your walls could be poisoning you".
- "Workers exposed to nuclear radiation after leaks".
- "Three radioactive waste cans found in Thailand's car park".
- "11 killed in tanker blast".
- "Prctect our Earth save the Ozone layer".
- "Cradling your phone could kill you".
- "Suicide linked to electromagnetic field".
- "Telephone Department crosses wires with KPTC, woman hurt".
- "Data on deaths. 925 electrical accidents claim 259 this year".
- "28 electrocuted as HT line falls on Ramanawmi rallyists".
- "Experts warn against the genomes of greed".

One could go on and on, it could be an endless list of scary situations that we could encounter in our lives; due to degraded environment, poor design and manufacturing practices, greedy businessmen, unscrupulous traders, or because of unexpected and unfortunate accidents, sheer folly, crass negligence/ carelessness, abounding superstition or unremitting ignorance. The price we pay is ofcourse too heavy to bear!

Some elaboration of the causes of the bio-hazards may be more illuminating. To start with the domestic environment is replete with bio-hazards. Many are aware of the common dust-mite and the problems of allergic reaction etc., they create. Some would also know how the mites thrive and the hygienic actions required to minimize the dust-mite problem. But it is a moot point as to how many are actually aware of the dangers of the common household aids like the detergents, the toilet cleaners, the vessel cleaning agents, the cosmetics, the colouring agents, the music system, the TV, the computer and so on. Particularly, as hardly any of them highlight a word of caution/ essential safety actions recommended to circumvent their inherent bio-hazard characteristics.

A recent report of a study of 832 cases of poisoning, by the National Poisoning Information Centre (NPIC), of the All India Institute of Medical Sciences (AIIMS), indicates that over 45 % causes of poisoning occur due to the swallowing of household agents! A high incidence of poisoning in male children was found particularly in the 1 to 5 year age group. The most common substances consumed were found to be Baygon, phenyls, detergents, kerosene, antiseptics, camphor/naphthalene balls, mercury from broken thermometers and cosmetics! Poisoning by drugs were noted amongst some 16 % of the cases. It was also opined that "chronic use of mosquito repellent in a closed room can be toxic". But it would be extremely inconvenient to try to live without those household aids; nay, it is practically impossible to do so! So, resort to the old advice, which still holds good—*keep away, such dangerous stuff beyond the reach of children.* But children being active, ever curious and adventurous to boot will find ways and means to investigate the cupboards "beyond their reach", by pushing a stool/chair/box etc., and standing on that to reach into the prohibited location. Note that kids will play with empty plastic bags, may put it over their heads and choke, or toddlers reach out and pluck bits and pieces form artificial flower arrangements and swallow them with possible serious consequences! Therefore, keep away all such dangerous stuff-do lock up dangerous items safe from those prying eyes and hands!

It is understood that in 1985 the EPA (Environmental Protection Agency-of USA) issued a list of over some 400 toxic chemicals that are "immediately dangerous to life and health" if accidentally spilled and could have "Bhopal like" consequences, if mishandled. It is also reported that "there are over 50,000 pesticide products registered for use but not fully tested for health effects"! (No wonder that with the meagre current testing resources/economic considerations the effective testing of all the above are yet/unlikely to be completed!).

Thousands of food poisoning illnesses and deaths occur every year inspite of improved awareness of the danger by the public, use of advanced technology in processing of food, its storage and consumption. The increasing incidences are mainly attributed to higher consumption of fresh fruits, vegetables without cooking, fresh salads, cold meat, pre-cooked food, seafood and so on. Thus, the chances of infection through bacteria and viruses increases, particularly with unhygienic handling, through source of supply upto actual consumption. It is a real wonder that the food poisoning occurrences are not much more, by many times over.

The presence of allergens and pollutants in the air around us leads to allergic reactions, which could be severe in some cases. Watery eyes, running nose, or the dry eye syndrome are milder effects of possible reactions to the air pollution. The dry eye syndrome can also occur due to Computer Vision Syndrome or CVS (particularly in an air-conditioned environment). The term CVS includes other eye-related problems of working on a computer terminal for long periods-blurred or double vision, visual fatigue redness of eyes or even headaches. The remedy is to blink your eyes more often and take frequent breaks from looking at the monitor (say at least a few minutes off every hour or two).

There are other attendant hazards too if you are a computer buff or computer professional. The dangerous buzzwords such as: Repetitive Strain Injury (RSI), Carpal Tunnel Syndrome (CTS) and the Cumulative Trauma Disorders (CTD) represent computer-related problems that are best avoided. Good ergonomics, proper posture, appropriate lighting, taking frequent breaks away from computer work and doing suitable exercises are the answers to minimizing computer-related injuries.

Aggressive advertisements, endorsements, and ready availability of all varieties of pills and potions at the neighboring drugstore are perhaps even a bane for maintaining good health in these times. Homeopathy practitioners have a saying: "I treat and God heals", a truism since apparently it is the body itself that takes corrective actions and the drugs administered assist/fight infections. It has been said, *"Any drug that has any effect on your body can cause side effects"*. There have been innumerable reports of allergic/other dangerous reactions to medicines taken without competent supervision leading to emergencies and even deaths as a consequence. Recently, (Nov.11, 2001) serious tragedy struck some people of Assam, death took its toll of some children after they were given massive doses of Vitamin A as a part of UNICEF project (the occurrences are under investigation)! So, beware of popping a pill for any ailment/discomfort without consulting your physician. Do tell/remind him also of any other medicine(s) that you have been prescribed/taking and any other long-standing problems/your medical history that is (like heart trouble, diabetics, chronic asthma etc). Even so, take only the specified dose of the prescription drug, in the exact manner prescribed and for the entire duration advised, unless the case has been reviewed in the meantime and fresh directions are given by the doctor. Though common, most times drug reactions may not be reported, or the reactions may themselves look like disease symptoms/even may not be noticed! Simplest reaction could be a rash eruption, whilst there could be dangerous, severe reactions like deep state of shock, serious toxicity, coma or even renal failure/death. Most people may be aware of the possibility of serious allergic reaction to penicillin; but how many are aware that the commonly used effective antibiotics such as tetracycline, cotrimoxazole and ciprafloxacin could become life threatening? Even some drugs taken in combination could have deadly reactions what to talk of dangers of consuming alcohol when on some medication!

During the eighties two major calamitous accidents took place—the Bhopal Gas Tragedy (1984), in India and the Chernobyl Nuclear Power Plant Disaster (1986), in Russia. Both resulted in untold suffering of multitude of people and major environmental pollution effects. The world woke up to the horrendous dangers posed by poor maintenance/operational negligence where hazardous industries are involved. The tragedies are well investigated and documented. We in India are well aware of the extent of the Bhopal Gas Tragedy, but not so well informed about the Chernobyl Nuclear Disaster.

The accidental explosion at the Chernobyl Nuclear Power Plant, which is located about 1,000 kms. Southwest of Moscow, occurred on April 26, 1986. It was estimated that thousands of cancer deaths could be expected due to the cloud of radioactive debris resulting from the explosion and the fire that occurred, in following decades. Over 100,000 people had to be evacuated and hundreds hospitalized with radiation sickness, immediately following the accident. The released radioactive material could be detected in the atmosphere, worldwide! In May 1986 itself the European Community imposed a ban on meat, live animals and produce from an area within 1,000 kms. of Chernobyl to protect the community from nuclear fallout effects. Western Europe witnesses much higher radioactivity due to radioactive debris being swept down from the skies due to heavy rains. Iodine -31 and Cesium-137 were detected not only in the soil but even in fresh milk, as the cows had munched the vegetation that got contaminated as a result of the pollution! (It was reported that on May 4, 1986, the EPA detected the first Chernobyl fallout *in the far, far away USA*! So, the reach of modern bio-hazards is tremendous to say the least!).

The domestic scene (and outside the domestic environment too), is home for the extremely helpful genii, the energy type, which however can turn into deadly monsters in case of ignorance/negligence/carelessness on the part of those taking recourse them. They are the household gadgets and facilities that make life in the modern home comfortable, pleasant and joyful-electricity, gas and other petroleum products! Turn on a switch or a remote control and you have the wonderful inventions of the refriegerator, the microwave oven, the coffee maker, the air-conditioner, the TV/Home entertainment system, the electric blanket and a host of tidy facilities at your fingertip, to do your bidding. The gas facility helps in cooking and central heating, and so on. But carelessness in their usage or negligence in use/maintenance will make one pay a heavy price—from simple shock/burns to serious dangers of electrocution/conflagration/violent explosions—not just bio-hazards but real bio-disasters!

There is yet another genie on the verge of being unbottled, which could open the Pandora's Box of unknown maladies and disasters—the GM or Genetic Manipulation! Fortunately, at the moment only "Hope" has been claimed to be released with synthetic formulations for GM food (still under study for acceptability), vaccines, life saving/assisting drugs such as insulin, interferon etc. But, inspite of cautioning by scientific communities and governments on the possible dangers, already private enterprises seem to be pushing ahead with research on human cell cloning (note that Dolly the sheep was cloned back in 1997), ultimately leading to possibly cloning of humans! The general opinion is that use of GM to combat pests, infirmities and diseases is important and alright, but not at the expense of issues of ethics and hazards posed, particularly cloning of humans and the implications to society/even the human race. At present, the general consensus is on a moratorium on such research, till enough concrete knowledge is gained about the possible risks and gains. (As the saying goes—the Devil is in the details—and in this case, *no one can as yet predict what detail will cause what problems to humanity*).

From all the foregoing material it is quite evident that ensuring Safety and Security of the people and the nation is no mean task. The responsibilities are onerous, the problems become more and more complex and horrendous, facilities and resources remain meagre, legal coverage inadequate and tardy, training at best touches the fringes of needs, and the general public are ever overcritical/seldom appreciative to boot. To add insult to injury, in general, security personnel are treated as only fit to be at the lowest end of the employment chain; their remuneration and perquisites leave much to be desired. (Ofcourse, there are plenty of boodles awaiting those who can organize and supply "Security Guards"—the sentry type; and so also in hiring out/ sale of security gadgets). So, why do '*security-wallahs*' take up the assignments? You wonder! Fortunately, there is this *redeeming feature*-"Technology" that goes on providing newer and newer, helpful gadgets/methods that greatly assist and relieve the "Safety and Security chores". And one thing is for sure, without technology to assist them in their tasks, nowadays, *security guys can do little to discharge their Safety and Security responsibilities, even satisfactorily-let alone well!* The wrong-doers, the criminals, the anti-socials, the ungodly, the terrorists and the hosts of villains of all shades of colours and hues resort to technology to gain their respective aims. So, all you guys who desire to get into Safety and Security business can ill-afford not to *whole-heartedly embrace* "Security Technology". It is best to, at least, get a nodding acquaintance with technology and make friends with the right technology experts!

Appendix "A"

First Aid

First-aid can make all the difference between someone's (victim of an accident etc.), life or his collapse, say into a coma, or death. A Bangalore Daily had a headline screaming "A DOG CHAIN NEARLY COST 6-YEAR-OLD HER LIFE", and adds, that, "Doctors fear she may suffer partial brain damage due to delayed resuscitation". The story was that the child was playing with a metallic dog chain clamped to a window. She got entangled in the chain, stopped breathing and became unconscious. Basic resuscitation measures were not administered to restore blood circulation, which had stopped as the chain had got tightly entangled around her neck. Failure of blood circulation for a few minutes only could lead to irreversible brain damage. Hence, any resuscitation efforts have to be made promptly-that is First Aid must be given within seconds (or as soon as possible), preferably at the site of the accident to save time, and thus possibly save the victim from major problems or even from death. The recounting of the case also listed some helpful tips, steps to be taken in an emergency, as follows:

- Check the victim and see if patient responds.
- Open his airways by tilting patient's head and lifting the chin.
- Look, listen and feel for breathing.
- Open the airway, pinch the nose, open the mouth, but keep the chin lifted.
- Blow steadily into the mouth.
- Maintaining the tilted head and lifted chin, take your mouth away from the patient. Watch for the patient's chest to fall as air comes out.

- Re-check the patient's mouth and remove any obstructions.
- Check the carotid pulse in the throat region.
- Attempt a heart massage when necessary.

This is what first-aid is all about. But, obviously, the steps as detailed above *can be carried out by "any man* in the street", mere mortal, *if he has been properly trained to carry out the procedures.* Effective first-aid, therefore, depends on how well the person administering it is trained and is experienced, apart from the very basic requirement of promptness in the administration of the first-aid.

It is unfortunate and inexplicable that schools and other educational institutions do not give adequate importance to impart education and training on first-aid to its students, which would stand them in good stead later on in their lives as adults. No one is above accidents, nor inured, or have the good fortune of not witnessing any accident at all during his /her lifetime! Hence, a healthy dose of first-aid education will provide some protection to survive accidents, better, and equip one to go through life with more confidence, and to be a good samaritan when he is a witness to an accident, to others.

First-aid means just that, *immediate temporary help, care, or assistance rendered to an accident victim, a person who has been injured or has suddenly taken ill.* This is just, temporarily, to *take care of an emergency situation, say, due to an accident, and help the victim in what is possible, and in a preferred way, till proper medical/other help arrives. It does not mean your assuming the role of a medic, unless you are properly qualified to do so,* that is. But it does mean that any business must have on-site arrangements to ensure good health, safety and welfare of its people. You must have proper emergency procedures, telephones to call up aid, first-aid facilities including personnel trained in imparting necessary first-aid relevant to the on-site operations and environment. This must include competence to render first-aid dressing, immobilizing fractured limbs and injured parts, artificial respiration, control of bleeding, treatment of all types of injuries, burns/scalds etc., and so on, as well as record keeping (for later analysis or even legal protection that maybe needed).

Note that in the description of first-aid activities where a victim is referred to as 'him' it is not gender specific but refers to both genders, 'him' or 'her'. Also, to be effective, the 'First Aider' must have had formal training in first aid as well as periodic retraining as necessary. (In India, in some ways we are indeed very fortunate. For example, in (some) Western countries you would not find a medical doctor's car sporting the familiar Red Cross symbol, since he is unable to render any immediate medical assistance to any accident victim on the road! He can only call up Police/Emergency assistance and it is only those paramedics, in the Ambulance that arrives on the scene, that can/do provide the necessary 'first-aid' to the victim. This situation appears to be from considerations of relevant specific training, availability of necessary "first-aid" facilities for the effective handling of the accident situation, and possible Insurance Claims against "alleged improper handling of the accident victim/situation". Thus, a doctor directly rendering any medical assistance/"first-aid" to the accident victim could well lay himself open to heavy insurance damages! Ofcourse most of the times, in India if an accident victim has to await arrival of paramedics/an ambulance before 'first-aid' is rendered to him, the victim could well lose his life, due to the resultant delay in the help arriving. No wonder the general public witnessing any accident is encouraged to rush the victim to the nearest hospital without delay, and the emergency unit of the hospital is urged to render necessary "first-aid" to the victim, without waiting for the arrival of the police.

Most common accidents that occur are burns, scalds, abrasions, cuts, fractures, foreign object getting into the eyes/ or ears, obstructing breathing, swallowing of an undesirable substance, electric shock, food poisoning, and so on. With the constant advances in modern living conditions, conveniences and the environment, the list can be endless. *It is, therefore, neither feasible nor desirable to try to cover all "first aid" aspects in this ANNEXURE, but only, briefly, indicate some common occurrences, as illustrative cases.*

Each organization has to evolve their own FIRST-AID and EMERGENCY procedures, 'First-Aid Boxes' and 'First-Aid Training' appropriate to its own set up and functioning. Appropriate First Aid Instruction Posters" *should be prominently displayed* at relevant work-spots, (such as, posters on first-aid against Electrocution where electric machinery/apparatus are in use). "First Aid Boxes" should be distinctly marked, usually with the 'Red Cross' Logo *topped with the words* 'FIRST-AID', and they should be placed at appropriate and prominent locations that are easy to access, and make use of. (There is no point in tucking away the "First-Aid Boxes" in some nook or corner seldom seen or visited by any employee). Each location in the plant where people are at work must have at least some persons trained in the application of the appropriate "First-Aid" procedures and facilities. These must include *Techniques of Resuscitation, Control of Bleeding, Treatment of Shock, Treatment of Injuries, Recognition of Illnesses,* and so on. It is also important to ensure requisite simple record keeping.

It is necessary to ensure that atleast someone present knows how to treat unconscious persons, dress and immobilize fractured limbs, recognize effects of poisons (and what to do about it), what is to be done with victims suffering with burns, scalds, wounds and so on. Note that, personal hygiene is all-important when dealing with the injured and the sick. Use the nearest telephone to summon help (it is one of the first actions that may need to be taken). Proper and timely transportation of the accident victim to get adequate medical and prompt attention needs no emphasis. The above call for some delegation of responsibilities-who will call the ambulance, who will notify the doctor, who will inform the authorities/police, who will fetch the "First-Aid Box", the stretcher and so on. *You must, therefore, ensure that there is someone in charge of the* "First Aid"!

Simple First-AID Procedures

Simple "First-Aid Procedures" should be evolved *that could be readily invoked to take care of some common ACCIDENT situations* covering injuries, burns, electric shock, suffocation etc.

What follows should not to be taken as comprehensive, but as illustrative. You would need to refer to a good reference manual on "first-aid", and lay down suitable procedures appropriate to your organizations working. They would also need to be updated from time to time, to keep up with the sophistication of modern living and developments in medicines and good living.

Please note that 'First Aiders' should, as the very first task, cover any cuts and abrasions on their own hands and exposed portions of their bodies with suitable waterproof dressings, before they attend to any injured, bleeding persons. This is to protect themselves and the victim from any possibility of *HIV or HEPATITIS* B infections etc. Victim's wounds should be thoroughly irrigated with pure, clean and cool water before dressing. After attending to the victim, do make sure you wash your hands properly too.

Do consult experts in the field and evolve suitable/appropriate procedures and setup for your organization.

Injuries

Bruises, Cuts, Wounds and Broken Bones are the commonest injuries that occur, any time, and at any place; despite all the care that one may exercise. Naturally, bleeding occurs in most such cases. In serious instances, unconsciousness may also occur. Such injuries could occur at any place. But at home, do lookout when you are in the kitchen; for that is the location where one usually gets burns and scalds, mostly due to carelessness.

On the other hand, you have situations where there may be no actual injuries, unless carelessness follows. Take for example cases of some foreign object getting into your eyes or ears; or a child swallows a button or a coin. These events are not injuries by themselves, nor has damage occurred. But if you leave them unattended, (or what is worse, if one tries to dig out/force out the offending object), serious injury could be the result. Prompt and proper "first-aid" is therefore imperative.

Strains and Sprains

Strains occur when muscles, ligaments and tendons are injured due to, usually, overstress/severe exertion. The muscle fibres etc. are unduly stretched and may be torn. The resulting pain may be felt only hours after the injury! Swelling and pain may be reduced by use of an ice pack on the affected area. You may recuperate faster by using suitable elastic bandages and taking rest.

Whilst *strains* occur with muscles, tendon etc. *sprains* occur at joints. Usual causes for sprains are excessive twisting, wrenching, compressive or pulling movements on the concerned joints, beyond their normal range of actions. The result is difficulty in movements, pain, and swelling of the joint due to the injuries caused to the soft tissues surrounding the joint. It is most common to sprain ones fingers, wrists, ankles or knees. Do note that it is best to treat a suspected sprain as if it was a fracture, and then await a doctor to deal with it.

Foreign Body in the Nose

Leave it alone. Ask the victim to breathe through the mouth. Let the doctor deal with the situation.

Foreign Bodies in the Eyes

A foreign body entering an eye is a very common occurrence. If the object can be easily removed with a clean piece of moist material without affecting the eye, you may do so taking all due care. If the foreign body adheres to the eyeball or is embedded, do not attempt to remove it. Your eye is a sensitive organ and can get injured very easily. If the eyes water, so much the better. With blinking, the tears help remove the object without damage to the eyes, but take care to first see that any movement of the eyelid does not cause any irritation. If not, irrigate the eyes with pure, clean and cool water, preferably, for 10 minutes or more. Irrigate in such a way that water flows out from the inside of the eye to the outside. (Use of clean water is essential, as otherwise the water itself can be a cause for infection of the eyes). Restrain any eye movement, till a doctor has examined the eye. When the foreign object happens to be lodged over the Iris, the coloured part of an eye, or an eyelid it is best to let a doctor deal with it.

When the foreign body cannot be removed with this simple procedure, you must rush the person to the nearest hospital or eye clinic. In the intervening period of transportation, etc., do cover the affected eye with a sterilized eye pad. It is considered that natural tears are the best cleaning agent/lubricant for the eyes, and it may be harmful to use water to bathe the eyeballs due to bacterial infection that may result. Thus, even blowing into the eye to remove foreign object/dust particles are frowned upon, as bacteria in the breath could cause infection of the eyes!

Perhaps in view of the above, medical opinion tend to support the view that any foreign body in the eye-attempt NO first-aid, *but just rush the victim to competent medical assistance.* However, this may not be practicable, always, unless a 'doctor is in the house'.

Chemical Substances Getting into the Eyes

There are instances when some chemical substance gets into the eyes, be it an acid, an alkali, a cleaning fluid, a petroleum product, or what have you. Here prompt attention is absolutely essential to protect and save the eyes. Keep the affected eye open. Flush it with pure and cool water for a period of atleast thirty minutes, till all traces of the chemical are totally washed out/removed. If loose particles of granular chemical compound etc. are present, remove them with a clean moist handkerchief /soft cloth or cotton swab, then cover the eye with clean dressing to reduce eye movements till a doctor examines the eye. And let a doctor follow up with further, necessary treatment.

Foreign Bodies in the Ears

When the foreign body is an inanimate substance, and if it can be carefully removed with a pair of tweezers, without hurting the ear, you may do so. On the other hand, if the substance is animate (alive), like an ant or an insect etc., what you could do is pour warm oil (note, not cool water), into the affected ear, and let the oil drain out, it may bring along/out the troublesome body. (But at first, before you pour in the oil, do make sure that the victim does not have any perforation in that ear. Do seek medical assistance, in any case, to see that there are no possible complications.

Bleeding

Minor oozing of blood/ or a little bleeding is not of much consequence and needs little attention, apart from, ofcourse, a bit of cleaning up; let the blood clot and nature take its normal (healing) course. Remove any visible foreign bodies that can be easily picked out/wiped off with a piece of clean dressing. (*But do not disturb any blood clot already formed!*). If however, the blood streams out, or the bleeding is appreciable you must control it by direct application of pressure. Where possible, apply a pad of sterilized dressing; press the pack over the bleeding area. Continue to apply pressure till the bleeding stops. If the pad of dressing becomes blood-soaked, do not remove it, leave it there and apply another dressing on top of it. Where required, apply direct pressure with fingers or thumb. Note that, raising the bleeding part of the body, or the limb above the level of the heart, and putting pressure on the artery supplying blood to the affected part helps to reduce the flow of blood, (unless the limb is fractured that is). This also lets the blood clot sooner to seal up the cut/wound.

In very serious cases of bleeding, such as arterial bleeding, obviously, application of mere direct pressure, and elevation of the limb concerned will not control the bleeding. You will need to apply a tourniquet to stop the bleeding. To do this, wrap a piece of cloth twice around the affected limb, above the wound, that is closer to the heart, and tie a half-knot. Place a stiff and unbreakable piece of stick, or rod over the knot and tie it up. Twist the stick to tighten (the tourniquet) until the bleeding stops, and secure the stick in place. If proper medical attention is likely to take undue time, do check with the doctor to see whether some release of pressure (due to the tourniquet) would be necessary, now and then. Such periodic release of pressure may be needed to permit some flow of blood to the limb, lest the lack of blood flow affect the limb. Some tissue damage occurs when a tourniquet is applied. Hence, such an action should be carried out only in emergencies, when not doing so could lead to a fatality, because of excessive bleeding.

Note two particularly dangerous cases of bleeding. A chest wound may result in air being directly sucked into the lungs and being blown out, as the victim breathes, a serious condition. In this case what is advised is "apply a dressing and pad to cover the wound and bandage it firmly before rushing him to the hospital". Victim showing distressed efforts at breathing; excessive thirst and restlessness are indications of some hidden, continuous and dangerous bleeding, immediately rush him to the hospital.

Shocks

Shock denotes a condition when the vital functions of the body are severely depressed. (A temporary weakness or a permanent /complete failure of the circulatory system; a common cause of death resulting from serious injuries). The effect of shock, (immediate or delayed), may become evident by features such as the face turning pale, pulse becoming weak and rapid, breathing is laboured or irregular, nausea, giddiness/faintness, vomiting, and cold clammy skin. The cause of shock could be unexpected bleeding, an accident, a bad burn, a sudden unpleasant surprise, and so on. Reassure the victim, in the first instance. Treat the cause and make the victim relax. He may be made to recline, (unless there is a head injury) and put up his feet. Keep him warm, without over-heating, and give some stimulant (sips of water, coffee or tea, *but no alcohol*). But do note that in *serious cases where surgery or blood transfusion could be needed* do not give anything through the mouth, as the victim may need to be anaesthetized! Shocks should not be taken lightly, as unexpected shocks have been known to kill a person!

Broken Bones/Fractures

A fracture is a break or a mere crack in a bone, (and the fracture may be simple/closed or an open one/compound). In a simple/closed fracture there is no wound leading down to the broken bone. In an open/compound fracture a wound extends from the skin to the broken parts of the bone(s) (allowing bacteria/germs access into the body through the site of the fracture). Fractures could be complicated when they have some associated injuries to internal organs/spinal cord, etc., of the body. The first requirement in case of suspected fractures or injured joints is that no attempt be made to move the accident victim, unless he is in a position that exposes him to a far greater danger, such as the possibility of being run over by vehicular traffic/stampede, etc. He should normally be moved only after the affected parts are suitably supported (so that the broken parts do not move/move separately from the body) when the victim is moved. In traffic accidents head injuries are common; but most often the victim may lie injured with bones, joints and muscles crushed due to the impact/crash/fall on the ground, (that may have dangerous stone/projections too). A layman cannot easily make out whether there is a fracture or not. Therefore, it is better and safer to treat the injury as a fracture. As reported, "It is best to use the LAF technique. *L* stands for *LOOK* at the injured part for any abnormality such as swelling/deformity, *A for ASK* the victim to quantify/qualify the pain and *F for FEEL* the injured part for tenderness (feel gently along the bones to detect any fracture)".

Apply clean splints to stabilize the body part, as well as to prevent any penetration of soft tissues by the fractured bone. You may use clean pieces of wood, structurally stiff material, even (folded) newspaper/magazine or cardboard, to bind the affected parts to provide the necessary support. *In case of an open fracture, do not try to push back the protruding bone.* Apply splints without repositioning the broken parts—leave the job of bone setting to qualified medical personnel. The *splints should extend to above and below the joints of the broken bone.* Application of a cold pack to an injury helps to reduce the swelling, and the pain. Clean all fracture wounds with clean water. If more than a couple of hours have elapsed, you must cover the wound with sterile dressing. In brief, *control the bleeding, apply sterile dressing and keep the victim relaxed/ quiet.* DO NOT EVER USE MUD or DIRTY RAGS TO CONTROL BLEEDING. *Treat him for shock.*

In cases of serious accidents, you could suspect a spinal injury. As a check for a spinal injury ask the victim to move his foot against your hand. In case he is unable to do so, he may have injured his spine. *If so, do not move him* until an ambulance with medical personnel arrives and they take charge *unless the victim is in dire danger of being run over by the traffic.* (In that case you have no other alternative to have him moved out of the danger zone to a safer spot). It is advisable to keep in continuous touch with the doctor where feasible, about the condition of the victim until he is able to get adequate medical attention. Note that skull fractures and spinal injuries require very special attention, so that apart from keeping the victim warm /comfortable and ensuring that his breathing is not obstructed it is best to seek/await proper medical attention.

Unconsciousness

Unconsciousness could be one of the two types—Partial (in *Stupor*); Complete (in *Coma*). If in stupor, victim's eyelids twitch or contract when you try to draw back his eyelids. On the other hand, if he is in a coma, there is no voluntary/involuntary response by the victim to the raising of his eyelids. So also, if a bright light is flashed on his eyes his pupils contract when he is in a stupor, but remains unaffected by the light when he is in a coma! In deep coma the pupils are usually highly dilated. Common causes of unconsciousness are—shock, head injury, asphyxia, apoplexy, hysteria, epilepsy, convulsion, diabetes heart attacks, etc.

If the accident victim is/becomes unconscious due to any reason, care must be taken to see that the airways of the victim do not get blocked and are kept open. Ensure abundant fresh air supply. Clean the mouth and see that the tongue does not block the back of the throat. (Remove false teeth if present). Nor should there be a possibility of the victim, unconsciously, bite his (own) tongue! When the face is pale, keep the victim's head and shoulders flat; whereas when the face is flushed you need to raise the head and shoulders slightly, without affecting his breathing. If breathing is noisy turn him into a "three-quarter prone" position, and not on his back. Do not leave the victim alone, until a responsible person is available to be in charge! Also do not attempt to give food/fluids to the victim when he is unconscious. Wait and watch his condition till competent medical attention reaches.

Burns and Scalds

Burn is an injury that is caused when the skin comes in contact with Dry Heat, (hot surface, fire, direct Sun's etc.), or objects that are (alive) with high voltage/lightening. It could also be friction of fast moving rope/wire/rotating wheel that is responsible. Corrosive Burns occur when the skin contacts corrosive chemicals (acids like sulphuric acid, nitric acid, and alkalis such as caustic soda, or quicklime). Scalds are injuries that are caused when the body comes in contact with Moist Heat viz., steam or hot liquid (like boiling water, hot oil or tar). Depending on the exposure there could *be reddening, blistering or destruction of the skin* in cases of both Burns and Scalds. *In Corrosive Burns, however, sub-cutaneous layers of the skin are affected.* In all cases, severe pain is present. Note that the area affected remains temporarily sterile; and you should keep it so.

Burns are categorized into three types and are treated accordingly and differently too. The three types are named as *First Degree Burns, Second Degree Burns* and *Third Degree Burns.* When only *superficial change in appearance of the skin occurs such as reddening* of the skin, it is termed as First Degree Burn. Simply let clean, (as it is easy to get infection which would be deadly dangerous), cool water flow over the area of the burn, or apply a wet compress to it, until the pain subsides. A clean dry dressing may be applied if necessary. Avoid application of any lotions, ointments and creams, unless under doctor's advice.

Second Degree Burn manifests itself with *raised blister formation on the skin.* Give simple first aid and let cool clean water run over it or apply cold compresses. See that your hands are clean and *dry the area* with clean, dry cloth, *without breaking the blisters,* (this is important, see that the blisters do not break), and cover with clean, dry dressing till proper medical assistance is received. *Any dressing or bandage must be light so as not to break the blisters.*

Third Degree Burn occurs when the burn extends into the sub-cutaneous levels of the skin/flesh. The skin gets charred. *Get the victim to a hospital as quickly as possible.* First-aid treatment in this case is as indicated in the following paragraphs.

Before doing anything else, flush the affected area with plenty of clean, cool water. Only then apply suitable balm, as advised by a doctor. Cover with a dressing or a clean towel, if required. Where the *affected area is large, or it is a deep burn sterilized dressing is the answer.* Note that in this case you must not immerse the body part in water, or apply wet compresses, as damage has already been done to the skin and infection can result. Do not attempt to remove clothing that may be sticking to the burn/scald, nor try to burst any blisters that may have formed. This is very important and must be scrupulously observed.

In case of Corrosive burns, contaminated parts of clothes that are definitely not sticking to the skin may be removed, and thoroughly flood all the affected parts with copious, clean water. Do ensure that all chemical/materials are totally diluted, and reduced (use warm solution of baking/washing soda with water for acid, and in the case of alkalis treat with weak acid solution of vinegar or lemon juice, etc. in warm water). General rules for the treatment of burns apply here too. Do remove contaminated clothing immediately taking desirable precautions, ofcourse. A sterilized dressing must be applied to the damaged areas of the skin that is exposed and tie clean towels to those damaged areas of skin where the clothing cannot be removed. Do take care to ensure that such victims are not exposed to infection, (contaminated air, personnel etc.).

Note that the sun can cause serious discomfort and even skin burns with blister formation! So do avoid unprotected exposure to the sun, particularly the mid-day sun. Prevention is always better than the cure! Usual advice should be to see a doctor, unless the case is serious. In which case the same general treatment apply as for burns and scalds.

Suffocation/Gassing

When adequate fresh air does not reach the lungs, vital organs and the nerve centres in the brain are deprived of the all-essential oxygen. This is the cause for the dangerous condition of suffocation/asphyxia. If oxygen supply/fresh air is not quickly restored, the result wold be unconsciousness, cessation of breathing, circulatory failure, and ultimately death! Early symptoms that appear are dizziness/weakness, shortness of breath, rapid pulse, blueness of lips and cheeks, fingertips, etc. Immediate removal of the victim to expose him to fresh air, to a gas free environment is essential. Note that the First aider may need to wear suitable protective breathing aids.

In cases of building collapses, collapse of walls of a pit/trench being dug, landslides, earthquakes, etc. people may get buried in loose material, and the victims may simply suffocate due to lack of air, and lead to results as indicated above. This must have happened to many of the casualties in the recent collapse of the World Trade Center Towers after the terrorist attacks on them. You need to make sure that the debris is immediately and quickly cleared, to promptly expose at least the mouth and the nose, so that the victims manage to get some air to breathe in. In many occasions, it may be necessary to carry out mouth to mouth resuscitation without delay, as soon as the victim is located and uncovered. Once, the victim revives he can be rushed to get a proper checkup/any medical attention that he may specially require.

Suffocation could also occur when the air passages are filled with harmful gases /fumes like vehicle exhausts, smoke, ammonia, methane etc. (or fluids in the air passages as in drowning/foreign bodies in the wind pipe causing choking, etc.). Some gases also affect the respiration system, in addition. Inhalation of gases such as carbon dioxide, carbon monoxide, methane etc. can be deadly and lead to quick fatalities, without the victim becoming aware of the danger. In such situations, the victim should be immediately removed to a fresh air environment. If the victim's breathing is laboured he needs immediate artificial respiration. Giving the victim oxygen may facilitate proper respiration. Keep the victim warm, and give some stimulant. In extremely severe cases, even blood transfusion may be required.

Electric Shock/Electrocution

The very first thing to do when you encounter an accident situation concerning electricity, is to "SWITCH OFF", without delay, the mains/electric current, (if possible), before detaching and removing the victim to safety, away from the spot. When this is not feasible, use a rigid, dry, insulating block such as a piece of dry timber, or heavy duty rubber (insulating) gloves or even a rope or dry part of victims clothing to pull the victim away from the live electric wire/circuit to a safe place. During this process do take care to see that you do not come in direct contact with the victim's naked skin or wet clothing etc. (unless the current in the circuit is positively switched "OFF").

As in the cases of suffocation, gassing, drowning etc., in the case of electric shock too you may need to give artificial respiration (resuscitation) to the victim.

Note that almost any sudden shock could result in death when the shock is totally unexpected.

Drowning

Unfortunately, drowning is quite a common occurrence, whether with children or grown ups; either due to ignorance of the persons getting into the water, or unexpected under water currents etc. In all such cases it is imperative to get the victims onto the shore, as quickly as possible. Unless the victim is conscious, and throws out any water he may have swallowed, and starts to breathe naturally, it is necessary to immediately remove all debris from the nose and mouth, and quickly start artificial respiration. *The first few minutes are valuable/vital in this regard, since any delay could prove to be fatal.* When the rescue is by boat, start the resuscitation in the boat itself. Do not wait to reach the shore. The artificial respiration should be continued without a break, until either the victim starts to breathe naturally, or a doctor pronounces him dead.

Heat/ Cold Exposure

If the air and the immediate environment are hot and humid, particularly, the body cannot get rid of heat by evaporation of the sweat. Also the sweating removes fluid and salt form the body. These conditions lead to heat exhaustion/heat stroke, even when there is no physical exertion! Undue exposure to cold can lead to frostbite. Heat exhaustion leads to profuse sweating, clammy skin, headache, feeling of tiredness or weakness, or even cramps, dizziness, nausea, and vomiting or even unconsciousness. The pulse can be weak, but the temperature may be normal or only slightly higher than normal. Heat stroke is *more dangerous* and may follow a heat exhaustion or occur suddenly. In this case the face is flushed, pulse strong, the skin hot and dry, and the temperature rises rapidly and can reach *as high as even 42 degrees C or more*! The victim may complain of a headache, be irritable, even vomit, which is quickly followed by unconsciousness. *Death is sure to follow if the temperature is not brought down quickly!*

Remove the victim quickly to a cool and shady place. Make him recline with his feet elevated. Cool the victim (by loosening his clothes, may be wetting them without chilling him). If he is conscious, give him plenty of cool water, with some salt (to make up for fluid and salt loss). If the victim complains of feeling cold, cover him up to keep him warm, *but not hot.* Keep a watch on him to see that the condition does not change to the more dangerous heat stroke! It is vital to quickly lower the victim's temperature. So remove him to the coolest possible place close by, remove his clothing and sponge/swab him with cool water/wrap him up in a wet sheet, (without chilling him), fan if necessary till the temperature is lowered to say 39 degrees

C. Then, dry him and wrap him up in a dry sheet, but continue fanning to bring down the temperature to normal. *In case the temperature rises again, repeat the treatment!* Thereafter, you treat him as for heat exhaustion.

When exposed to extreme cold and your extremities (usually the feet, fingers, nose or ears) lose sensation, it is a sign of Frostbite, particularly when the body parts turn waxy and white! The victim is usually totally unaware of the condition, because of the lack of sensation! Move the victim to an environment at/ near room temperature. Cover the concerned extremities and let the affected parts warm up gradually to normal body temperature. *Rapid heating up by exposure to heating appliances could be harmful and should not be done. Do not rub either, to warm up by friction heat.* Rush medical assistance to the victim as quickly as possible.

Dog Bites

Every year tens of thousands of unwary householders, pedestrians, and even two wheeler riders, fall prey to stray dogs. The persons get bitten by such dogs, particularly in cities. (This is apart from the thousands who get bitten by domestic pets). Many of the victims end up with rabies due to lack of necessary, immediate, and correct treatment. And some even after being subjected to the painful anti-rabies (vaccine) injections. All attempts should be made to detain and observe the behaviour of the dog for a period of over ten days. This must be done with caution as the dog may bite others too, and could very well be rabid, (in which case it should be put to sleep). No doubt, in the rural areas people may not have easy accessibility to proper medical facilities and may resort to local methods of treatment involving herbal medicines/procedures, etc. No statistics would be available regarding their effectiveness, or otherwise, in preventing/curing rabies.

In rabies the concerned virus is understood to reach the central nervous system via the nerves, and not through the blood. So using a tight bandage to constrict bleeding will not stop the virus from reaching the brain. Maintain the bitten part of the body at a lower level and bathe the wound with a weak solution of potassium permanganate, if possible. If the dog is known to be rabid and there could be more than a few minutes *delay in getting treatment for a doctor it is best to cauterize the bite wounds* (each one probed and cauterized separately to destroy all the virus that has got in by the bite). You could do the Cauterization by applying to the wounds carbolic acid or nitric acid, (with a pointed matchstick or sharpened piece of wood). Dress the wounds. But note that if there is a *delay of more than half-hour since the mad dog has bitten the victim do* not cauterize!

It is best to rush the victim to the nearest hospital, immediately to be treated, advisably with Anti Rabies Serum, (ARS). Reportedly, the recent, but more expensive, tissue culture vaccine/Anti-Rabies Serum (ARS), are safer. But, for availability and cost considerations hospitals continue to use the painful older nerve tissue/sheep brain based vaccine, (which are not hundred per cent effective), that is also understood to be banned in many countries. (The WHO *recommends that the nerve tissue vaccine* (NTV*), prepared from sheep brain, should not be used any longer.* It is reported to produce serious reactions in some, resulting in paraplegia, bowel and bladder problems, etc). Very recently the safer, tissue culture based vaccine is understood to have become available, and at affordable prices too.

The Do's and Don'ts that the first aid to dog bite victims include:

- DO NOT apply any irritants like turmeric .
- Wash the wound immediately with soap and water (clean of course).
- Dry with clean cloth or cotton and apply tincture of iodine or similar good antiseptic on the wound.
- DO NOT close the wound.
- DO rush, now, the victim to a doctor, for further treatment, which may include administration of anti-rabies injections, where/when needed.

Snake Bites

About 350 of the over 1700 varieties of snakes that exist around the world are known to be poisonous. Fortunately, their habitat is different and usually separate from that of humans. Therefore, Snakebite is a far rarer occurrence, (than dog-bites). Also, most snakebites are not fatal, except that the very fear of snakes induces severe shock in the victim which could be fatal. Ofcourse there will be much pain and swelling at the site of the bite. It may not be possible to identify the kind of snake that has bitten either.

What is required is to stop the snake venom due to the bite from getting into the blood circulation. So, quickly, (well within an hour of the bite, as otherwise it is useless), tie a suitable tourniquet immediately above the puncture wound, towards the heart. (This will prevent the snake venom from entering the blood stream, through the veins of the bitten body part, and travelling up). There is no need to atop arterial circulation! Do make sure that the constrictive bandage or tourniquet is relaxed for say half a minute every half-hour and should be maintained till the anti-venom injection is given. (Note if after three hours the victim does not develop any symptoms he is safe and the bandage can be removed!). Clean the wound with a weak solution of potassium permanganate in clean water. Make cuts on the puncture wounds, lengthwise along the limb, with a sterilized knife or sharp instrument; (this will enable the infected blood alongwith the venom to drain out). Treat the patient for shock, as the shock of snakebite can have a deadlier effect than the snakebite itself. (Keep the victim warm, comfortable and resting). *Now rush him to the nearest hospital for further treatment, including administration of suitable serum.* (If at any time the breathing fails, immediately artificial respiration should be put to effect).

Poisons

Poisons can enter the body by *inhalation* (breathing in the gas or fume), *ingestion* (consumed through the mouth), or *through the skin* (injection or absorption). It can then be injurious to health or cause death, if the quantity of the poison in the body is large enough (varies with the poison concerned). Depending on the nature of the poison, they exert dangerous affects like suffocation, vomiting, pain, blurred vision, diarrhoea, corrosive burns, unconsciousness and death.

Poisons could be broadly classified under seven groups as follows:

1. Corrosive Type (mineral/organic strong acids, alkalis etc.)
2. Irritant Type (metallic and vegetable irritants like arsenic, ammonia, SO_2 etc.)
3. Narcotic or Hypnotic Type (like barbiturates, morphine etc.).
4. Convulsants and Delirants (such as strychnine, cocaine etc.).
5. Paralytic Type (curare, nicotine etc.).
6. Volatile/Gaseous Type (CO, H_2S, HCN etc., deadly gases/ fumes).
7. Others (hormones etc).

Each of the above type has their own particular symptoms and specific reactions of the human body. They also need different type of treatment. Therefore, it could be dangerous to the victim if the first aider were to take on himself to treat the victim. It would be best if he rushes the victim to/get competent medical assistance. He should provide particulars of the occurrence, the symptoms displayed by the victim, any poison left and the original receptacle/bottle/carton of the poison. He should also make sure that any vomited matter etc., is taken along for analysis etc. When the victim is unconscious the first aider should arrange the victim's body in such a way as to make sure that the victim does not have his tongue in the way or any vomit that could choke him, that is keep the airways clear. Artificial respiration may need to be given when the victim's breathing is laboured. If the victim is conscious make him vomit to get rid of the poison, *unless the poison is the corrosive type-* evidenced by yellow/grey stains on the skin, lips and mouth showing acid/alkali burns. So, to reiterate, *do not induce vomiting if, the victim is unconscious, or if his lips and mouth show yellow or grey stains* indicating burns due to corrosive poison. If you know what the poison, *neutralize the poison by giving* appropriate antidote. Give lots of water/soothing drinks, like milk to dilute/delay absorption of the poison, replace lost fluid due to any vomiting, and soothe the irritation of the digestive tract. Relevant reference works should be consulted and suitable first aid procedures/instructions evolved and prominently displayed/put into the S.O.Ps of the organizations that have anything to do with poisons. Specific instructions MUST BE PRESENT *for first aid in case of any accidents in regard to the specific poisons being handled in the organizations*!

In brief, for corrosive poisons (like strong acids, strong alkalis, disinfectants etc.) give the victim plenty of water, but do not make him vomit! Give suitable antidote, if possible-milk of magnesia say for acid poisons; weak acids like vinegar, orange or lemon juice diluted with water, in case of alkali poisoning; and water with Epsom salt in case of disinfectants (like Carbolic Acid, Lysol, etc).

Make the victim vomit if the poison happens to be arsenic, aspirin, sleeping tablets and hypnotic/narcotics, (like, barbiturates, morphia, opium etc.), lead, paraffin, petrol, phosphorous, prussic Acid, and for delirants/convulsants (like strychnine). Also give water, soothing drink, coffee/tea, white of an egg etc. as appropriate. For example, soothing drinks for arsenic poisoning, water/strong tea/strong coffee for aspirin, water with epsom salt/hot coffee for sleeping tablets, and so on.

Some Do's and Don'ts for the First Aider

- Respond immediately when there is a call for help, (drop the other activities).
- Adopt a systematic and calm approach with the victim.
- Do not wait to make a complete diagnosis, (let the doctor do it), but treat quickly the obvious injuries and conditions that endanger the victim's life! That is, Do First Things First quickly, quietly and without panic, reassuring the victim all the time.

- Give artificial respiration without a second delay, if breathing has stopped.
- Stop any bleeding, (without delay, waiting for the arrival of First Aid Box, etc.).
- Watch out for possibility of victim going into shock, treat him suitably for shock.
- Do not try to do too much. What is needed is the minimum that is essentially required to save life/prevent deterioration of the condition of the victim.
- Fresh air is essential to the victim, so keep the crowd/ people away from the victim.
- Do not unnecessarily divest the victim of his clothing.
- Ensure as speedy a removal of the victim to competent medical aid/hospital as possible.

Appendix "B"

Natural Hazards and Disaster Management

Between 1900 and 1987 over two million lives were lost, (yes over 2 million!), as a result of *Natural Disasters/Hazards*, as per the studies carried out a report published by the US National Research Council/National Academy of Sciences/National Academy of Engineering, what to talk of damage to properties! No wonder the United Nations Organization (the UN) declared the 1990-2000 period as the International Decade for Natural Disaster/Hazards Reduction (or IDNDR/IDNHR). The Objective was to reduce, (especially in the Developing Countries), through international co-ordinated actions, the *calamitous outcomes of Natural Disasters*. That is to say, "the loss of life, property damage and social and economic disruption caused by Natural Disasters such as Earthquakes, Windstorms (Cyclones, Hurricanes, Tornadoes, Typhoons), Tsunamis, Floods, Landslides, Volcanic Eruptions and other calamities of Natural Origin, such as grasshopper and locust infestations." Hence, came about the United Nations Disaster Relief Organization, (the UNDRO), and the International Disaster Management Information Network (or the UNDRONET). The intention was to collect and disseminate disaster-related information and enable the vital information flow sans borders/frontiers.

In India the National Informatics Center, (NIC), the interactive information network for use by the Central Government and the State Governments, down to the District level, set up a

Natural Hazards Information System Division at Bhubaneswar, to develop and implement a Distributed Natural Calamities Relief Management System, (NCRMS). Between this and the DISNIC, the District Level Information/Database system one could develop an integrated, macro-level, decision support information system for appropriate Relief Management at the regional, state level and at the national level. The Government of India has also the Information System on Natural Calamity, (the ISNC) to help in providing appropriate Central Assistance to the State seeking its help for relief operations on occurrence of a natural calamity, etc. in the state. These enable proper studies to be carried out, collection of appropriate data and creation of good databases on natural hazards and the destruction that follow, the impact of relief measures and so on. The information support provides for proper policy evolution, planning, administration, monitoring of programmes, coordination, control of budgets and expenditure to effectively help in disaster administrations and management efforts.

In above kind of work the Geographic Information System or the GIS can be of tremendous help as also Satellite Observation Systems. The weather radar network of the Meteorological department helps in formulation of precipitation forecasts, storm warning, cyclone warning, forecast of flash floods and so on. The telecommunications infrastructure assists in the issue of timely warnings to all concerned of impending natural disasters and thus reduce substantially, likely damage, destruction and particularly loss of life. Further, it helps in quickly ascertaining the locations requiring immediate help and the quick rendering of assistance to the affected regions and faster rehabilitation of the displaced populace. Fast communication is imperative in all phases of disaster management, be it the initial expectation phase, the occurrence stage of the disaster, the relief rendering phase, or rehabilitation phase of even the evolution of the disaster management plans and the setting up of the necessary associated infrastructure. More than anything else, it is perhaps the effective communication that helps to greatly reduce the likely loss of life and rendering of timely evacuation and safety work as well as implementation of early disaster warning to the general public likely to be affected.

One aspect has to be mentioned here. In developing countries like India, the main reliance of the community appears to be total dependence on Governmental systems and very little leaning on private agencies/NGOs, except perhaps for the assistance sought from HAM operators (for communication from/to remote/ inaccessible locations). With the greater and greater liberalization and globalization, such as privatization of the communication systems and the media in the country far greater involvement of the private sector and the NGOs can be expected in the future. One can also expect some behavioural changes in the populace that would minimize the effects of hazards and prevent them from turning into disasters! (For example, why should the Governments alone play a major role in rehabilitation programmes, constructing low cost tenements for the deprived? This should be an area of concern for the private sector and NGOs who could quickly build inexpensive shelters for the poor/ displaced persons. Then, the Governments could concentrate on, say, building community shelters to protect the community from natural hazards, etc.).

Now, let us take a closer look at possible Natural Disasters/ Hazards. The Table below is indicative of the major characteristics of natural hazards.

Table of Natural Hazards and some of their Characteristics

Hazard	**Possible Distance Spread (of hazard-coverage/effects)-upto**	**Precursor/Warning Indication (possible lead time for protective actions?)**	**(Disaster?) Communications-Systems Affected?-(Partial/complete)**
Collision Asteroid/Comet/Meteorite	Major Portion of Earth/Large/Small Area of Earth	Years/Long Term/Days	Complete/Partial. Rare/Unlikely-Life *Extinction Level Event (E.L.E).
Global Warming/Ozone Layer Depletion Volcanic Eruption	Thousands of kms. Thousands of kms.	Decades/long term Weeks/Days?	No
Pollution	Thousands of kms.	Years/Hrs/Seconds?	Over a long period?
Cyclone	Over thousand kms.	Days	Yes
Drought	Over thousand kms.	Months/Years?	No
Floods	Over thousand kms.	Weeks/Days?	Possible
Heat/Cold Wave	Over thousand kms.	Weeks/Days?	No
Major Forest Fire	Over thousand kms.	Hours?	Possible
Earthquake	Hundreds of kms.	?	Yes
Avalanche	Tens of kms.	Days/Hours?	Yes
Landslides	Tens of kms.	Days/Hours?	Yes
Flash-flood	Tens of kms.	Minutes?	Yes
Thunderstorm	Tens of kms.	Hours?	Yes
Hail	Tens of kms.	Hours?	Yes

As may be seen from the columns three and four in the above table, the early warning period available and possible effects on communication systems are variable, depending on the occurrences. For example, the effects of automobile emission-pollution could be immediate such as watering of the eyes, choking sensation etc.; also long-term effects as well-such as degeneration of the lungs and the health of the affected persons. Pollution of the atmosphere due to release of poisonous gas, as in the Bhopal Gas Tragedy, affected thousands of people within seconds! And the long-term effects are lingering for the persons affected, even after nearly two decades of the tragic event. Effect of an oil spill in the sea could affect marine life for days and weeks. Corrosive chemical pollution could affect landline communications, whereas cyclones, earthquakes and floods could disrupt not only landlines but also the terrestrial tower based microwave communications. Similar problems could arise in case of avalanches, flashfloods and tropical thunderstorms. A closer look at some of the natural hazards could be interesting. Note that as far as India is concerned any volcanic formations are unlikely to be found, nor are there any known sources of volcanoes in the neighbourhood. Hence, no further mention will be made of volcanoes/their effects. (There are some other natural hazards too like tsunamis or tidal waves, locust swarms, wild bee swarms, termite infestations etc., that are not being covered here).

Asteroid/Comet/Meteorite Collision with Earth

Earth's atmosphere is subjected to micro-meteorite incursions, daily. But these burn up before they reach the Earth surface, except for meteorites with some substance that is appreciable in size. It has been estimated, from observance of evidence of past impacts of meteorites on the surface of the Earth, that a meteorite a few metres across in size could on impact on the surface of the Earth devastate an area thousands of square kilometres. A meteorite about fifty metres in size could well raze a city on impact. Whereas, as per inference drawn from observations, it was a collision with Earth by an extra terrestrial object, a few hundred metres across, that is said to have been responsible for the extinction of the dinosaurs and many other forms of life on Earth, about 65 million years ago! So, one can well imagine the effect of a collision by a large sized asteroid/comet with the Earth; Earth as we know today would not exist and life on this planet may well vanish by such an Extinction Level Event! Fortunately for us, approach of such large object close to Earth is expected to be a very rare/unlikely event. Also, enough early warning of approach by such a large extra-terrestrial body would be available. (And it is hoped that by concerted international co-operation, science and technology would be able to provide suitable implementable solutions to alter the orbits of such objects/ explode them into smaller fragments so that no harm comes to life on the Earth!).

Global Warming

Modern civilization has brought into daily use a host of chemicals, both gaseous and liquid, which has resulted in continuous increase in the levels of trace gases in the atmosphere. This undesirable increase is expected to lead to significantly warmer climates over the earth. That is, unless the increase in the concentration of such gases in the atmosphere, is arrested or reversed.

These gases may already be interfering with the way the earth maintains its balancing act regarding its temperature variations in its space time continuum. This is due to what has been termed as the Greenhouse effect, and the gases that particularly play a part in this effect are called as Greenhouse Gases!

A greenhouse is used in nurseries for seedlings or for raising plants in its peculiar controlled environment. Thin transparent glass (or suitable plastic) covers the Greenhouse all around, above the ground. The transparency permits about 90% of the radiation (mainly from the Sun) impinging on the surface to get through into the space within the greenhouse and thus keep the inside environment hot! This keeps the plants within the greenhouse warm, even in cold regions like Ladakh! The design of the greenhouse includes a suitable cooling mechanism to maintain the temperature at a level suitable for the plants. The plastic/glass covering prevents escape of bulk of radiation from the earth out into the atmosphere leading to accumulation of heat energy within the greenhouse, and thus the increase in the temperature within (as compared to the temperature outside the greenhouse. As more radiation energy gets through into the greenhouse, the temperature within rises more and more; and more of radiation energy from within the greenhouse gets out through the glass, until a new balance is struck, but at a higher temperature (within the greenhouse) by the heat exchange. *This in short is the Greenhouse effect.* The temperature of the earth is controlled by a more complicated but somewhat similar exchange of heat energy-between the incoming radiation energy from the Sun, the atmosphere surrounding the earth, (because of the greenhouse gases acting as the glass enclosure of a greenhouse), and the heat energy/radiation from the earth itself. The greenhouse gases in the atmosphere absorb heat radiation from the earth and thus play a part in maintaining the temperature balance, and unfortunately tilts the balance to a higher temperature level viz. the Global Warming!

The main greenhouse gases are CO_2, methane, nitrous oxide and ozone. Except for ozone the increases in the concentration of the other greenhouse gases mainly arise due to the rapid industrialization and consumerism actively pursued by the developed and developing nations. The overall result is an expected and inevitable increase in global warming temperature of a few degrees centigrade (rise) by the middle of the 21st century! (Unless the comity of nations takes suitable decisive steps to arrest, nay to reverse the concentration of greenhouse gases in the atmosphere).

But why should the global warming phenomenon worry anyone? The reasons are simple but far-reaching. The global warming is expected to greatly effect the climatic conditions allover the world. So much so that it could even change the geography of the world! The temperature rises would be higher towards the Polar Regions than at the equator. The higher temperatures can be expected to result in higher rainfalls in the tropical regions, due to the higher evaporation rates; and drier subtropical areas. The temperature rise is expected to lead to thermal expansion of the oceans, and a resulting rise in the sea levels of 20 centimetres to over a metre. This would result in flooding of low-lying coastal areas in the world, to the extent that even Maldives Islands, major part of Florida (in USA), and so on! Many other unpredictable, but adverse effects on society and human existence are expected. A very scary scenario indeed, particularly since about a third of the world's population lives along coastal regions of the world.

The remedy is seemingly simple—reduce the generation of CO_2 and other greenhouse gases. But this is a highly sensitive aspect for both the developed nations who are great energy guzzlers and the developing nations, which need radical improvement in their living standards, which again require considerable increase in their energy consumption. What has energy consumption got to do with greenhouse gases? Simply put the bulk of greenhouse gases generation is tied up with the methods used for energy generation, viz., use of fossil fuels! The answer therefore is either energy conservation, or resort to use of alternative and renewable sources of energy such as direct solar energy, wind energy, hydro-electric, tidal wave energy generation, nuclear power generation and so on. Yet another immediately implementable method would be to prevent the CO_2 and other greenhouse gases generated from reaching the atmosphere by suitable filtration, conversion, neutralizations techniques. Reforestation would be a good complementing scheme too. (Note that use of CFC gases has already been banned and suitable alternatives are now the in thing).

Ozone Layer Depletion

Ozone is one of the greenhouse gases that help to regulate the earth's temperature. Concentration of this gas, though minute in value, occurs high in the atmosphere above about 20 kms to about 60 kms. So you call it "Ozone Layer"! Even though the concentration is small, this layer plays an important part in reducing the strength of the harmful ultraviolet, (UV), energy radiation form the sun at the earth's surface (to the benefit of the humanity). Molecules of ozone gas absorb UV radiation and breaks down into oxygen (molecules and atoms)-that is breakdown of ozone. Oxygen molecules accept UV radiation to form, alongwith oxygen atoms, ozone molecules (that is ozone formation). This is dynamic balancing process result in the overall reduction of UV radiation reaching the earth's surface. The ozone layer is thus self-maintaining.

But, if you now add to this layer, oxides of nitrogen or CFC, etc. even in trace amounts, these trace gases react with ozone in a catalytic manner to convert the ozone molecules into oxygen molecules. The result is reduction in the ozone concentration, and over a period of time depletion of the Ozone Layer! Thus, an increasing concentration of these catalytic gases is deadly for the ozone layer. Already an expanding "hole" has been detected over Antarctica due to such *Ozone Layer Depletion.*

Why should one worry about this *Ozone Layer Depletion?* There are two main reasons. The immediate reason-the depletion leads to increasing levels of UV radiation reaching the surface of the earth that would cause increasing cases of sunburns, blindness, cataracts, skin cancers and so on. (No wonder people travelling to Australia etc. use sunscreen before venturing out of their residences there!). The second reason is that reduction in the concentration of ozone, along with increase in concentration of the other greenhouse gases is expected to increase the temperature of the earth over a period (upto a few degrees centigrade over the next few decades!). Cause enough to worry now itself! No wonder, there is concentrated efforts, particularly by environment groups to prevent forthwith further ozone layer degradation, and use of CFC gases (which, once released into the atmosphere, may linger on in the atmosphere for over 100 years) has already been banned, internationally.

Recently, the Head of the United Nations Environment Programme (UNEP), Klaus Toepfer is reported to have stated that humans were partly to be blamed for the torrential rains that wreaked havoc from Europe to Asia, (TOINS 14 Aug., 2002). He called on the industrialized nations to assume responsibility for their role in causing the freak weather that claimed so many lives. And said that it was above all, the duty of the industrialized countries to fight (this phenomenon); most of all with cutbacks in energy use and the continuing development of renewable sources of energy. Apparently, Africa represented 14 per cent of the world's population but produced only 3 per cent of its polluting carbon dioxide emissions, "yet it's precisely there that the effects of climate change are so dramatic".

Volcanic Eruptions

Fortunately, for us there are no volcanoes in the Indian region, whether active or extinct. A volcanic eruption can cause deadly destruction in the immediate neighbouring region due to the hot lava/debris that occurs as fallout of the eruption. The smoke dust and debris that spew out as a result of an eruption could reach out high in the atmosphere for even thousands of kms. and float around for days or weeks on end. Thus, affecting atmospheric temperature and climatic conditions. The fallout when it settles on the surface of the earth could affect agricultural production.

Pollution

Most problems of pollution are of manmade origin, whether it is an oil-spill, an acid rain problem, contamination of sub-soil water and above ground waterways, atmospheric pollution and so on. Unfortunately, such pollution problems get aggravated/ extended with nature lending a "helping" hand with the wind movements, water currents, climatic changes etc.! However, there are some forms of pollution purely natural in origin, such as atmospheric/earth surface pollution due to spontaneous forest fires, ditto due to volcanic eruptions, methane gas generation of animal origin (cattle), "locust infestation" and so on. Obviously such events cannot be totally avoided. What can be done is to take preventive measures to mitigate the effects of the fallout.

Cyclones

Cyclones are intense low-pressure buildups that can travel with phenomenal speeds, leaving widespread destruction in its wake-over landmasses that are. Tropical cyclones occur over, practically almost, over all tropical oceans. They are accompanied by wind-speeds of the order of 100's of kms and very heavy rainfall. You can usually expect them during the months preceding/succeeding the monsoon period. Such intense whirlwinds with high latent destructive capacity are known as Typhoons in the China seas, as Hurricanes/Tornadoes in the West (also called as Twisters in North America). Believe it or not, super cyclones could have wind speeds of the order of, as much as, a few hundreds of km/h! (Note that wind speeds in the *Beaufort Scale* is a maximum of 12, for a hurricane, that is a wind speed of over 64 knots, or about 128 km/h only). To add to the woes of the people in the tropical cyclone affected regions; torrential rains, which could reach a daily "routine" of about 25 cms, usually accompany such terrible winds. (10 inches)! The coastal areas have to bear the brunt of the additional threats of surging high tides (commonly 3 to 4 metres high, the highest reported sea level rise due to such storm surges is 40 ft. over 13 metres!) to boot. The only saving feature is that the cyclones dissipate their energies as they enter interior areas of land and hence their maximum destructive forces are spent within about 100 kms of the coast, that the cyclones cross. It has been assessed that every year, on an average, about 5 cyclones traverse the Indian coastal regions.

Fortunately, incipient cyclone formation over the seas can be detected. So advance notice is possible for warning the inhabitants of the concerned coastal regions so that destructive effects of the cyclones could be mitigated and consequential cyclone related loss of life minimized/eliminated. (As regards possible loss of property, the only hope is to minimize such losses with suitable, maybe expensive, design of structures and protection of movable property within such enclosures, during the danger period). With the concerted past efforts of the Government of India, the country possesses quite an effective Cyclone Warning System. Cyclone formation and traverses are subjected to satellite observation, tracked by the weather network/cyclone detection radar (covering the coastal areas) of the Meteorological Department, as well as by collation of reports from commercial aircrafts/ships and so on. The Indian Meteorological Department or the IMD had developed a Disaster Warning System, or DWS, so that the cyclone warning messages could be promptly disseminated to all concerned, to the remotest corners of likely to be affected districts. HAM or Amateur Radio Operations have been quite helpful to ensure reliable/effective communication from/to inaccessible cyclone affected areas, when all other established communication links have snapped during/and post (raging) cyclone periods.

Drought

By and large, the country as a whole is good monsoon, dependent for its water requirements and agriculture. So, poor or inadequate monsoon can spell disaster for many regions due to consequential drought conditions, a condition of prolonged deficiency of rainfall with consequential drying up of water sources, land and vegetation. As a result, the people and cattle etc., in the affected regions acutely run short of food, water to the extent of affecting even their survival during the period. Thus, drought is a very dangerous natural hazard/calamity for the country. It brings acute misery to the people, cattle and domestic pets in the affected region, with lack of food and water even for just staying alive. The parched land makes it impossible for any agricultural produce, and thus appreciably reduces food grain production of the country as a whole. The quantum reduction in the water table (ground water levels fall appreciably) leads to soil erosion and degradation of agricultural land, a deadly long-term effect. Note that in many regions deforestation could be a major cause for occurrence of drought, due to consequent reduction in rainfall, land erosion etc.

Is anything possible at all to eliminate/reduce the horror of drought? The answer is a qualified yes-because it calls for dedicated and meticulous planning, as well as effective implementation of such plans. Both short-term and long-term measures are called for in the fight against drought. As an immediate basis suitable drought relief measures are called for to alleviate the sufferings of the affected populace and cattle etc. Such drought relief measures include supply of essential commodities to the people-drinking water, food, fodder for cattle, proper sanitation measures, medical aid, kerosene and so on. Naturally, provision of alternative suitable, stopgap employment till normal agricultural activities can restart, suitable loans/ex-gratia payments to the affected people to tide over the crisis situation etc. would also be necessary.

Long range weather forecasts help immensely by providing an advance warning of possible occurrence of drought conditions in specific areas that could be affected. Ensuring judicious use of limited water resources available, and increasing the storage capacity of lakes, ponds and tanks alongwith measures to reduce evaporation, help tremendously both as short-term as well as long-term remedial measures. As a result of its intense research and analysis, the IMD is now able to provide fairly useful monsoon forecasts, quite a few months in advance! Long-term measures would ofcourse include construction of suitable canals, construction and recharging of reservoirs/lakes, inter linking of rivers and waterways to deliver excess water from one region to regions with deficiency of water and so on. Afforestation cannot be overemphasized as a long-term measure to fight drought.

Floods

Flood is an antithesis of drought condition, "the opposite side of the coin"; and it could be extremely destructive. The usual causes are excessive rainfall in the catchment area of a river, (excessive snowfall/hail etc. could lead to floods too), a river in spate or a breach in the riverbank embankment, change in the course of a river, inadequate or blocked drainage or, even, a sudden obstruction in the river. (One may add to the above a dam-burst, due to natural or manmade causes, as an unusual cause for a flood). A flood can be an extremely destructive natural hazard, (or a manmade one like-dam-busting operations during WW II, intentional change ofcourse/rerouting of a canal/ river, sudden unplanned/unthinking opening of sluice gates of an overfull dam, etc.)! The almost annual feature of the river Brahmaputra in spate leads to untold suffering for people in Assam and Bangladesh. (China has its meandering river of woe- the Huang Ho, which often changes its course, causes almost annual flooding, bringing in its wake untold suffering to the people living beside the river).

Fortunately, damage and destruction due to floods can be minimized when suitable remedial measures are in place -in advance that is. Of course, you do need immediate flood relief measures such as-ex-gratia payments, rehabilitation, supply of essential commodities, arrangement for adequate supplies of drinking water etc. to the affected people. Affected public properties like damaged roads/rails, destruction caused to railway installations, downed telecommunications links, flooded airport runways etc. has to be restored as quickly as feasible. For example, the Central Water Commission or the CWC set in place, decades ago, set up an early warning system by its flood forecasting, currently using computer models. Rainfall and precipitation data collection even uses radar to get appropriate estimates. Flood damage limitation/control involves short-term measures like evacuation of population from the likely to be flood affected areas on an early warning of incipient flood in the region; and long-term measures such as construction of suitable structures such as dams, embankments, drainage ditches and so on. Obviously, periodic and timely desilting of river beds/tanks etc. is advisable. Reducing soil erosion with suitable Afforestation programmes is advantageous. Ofcourse effective flood management must start with reliable system of hydrological data collection, estimation/prediction, analysis and flood warning system, (should be an element of the Disaster Warning System).

Heat/Cold Waves

Year after year, in India, hundreds of precious human lives are lost, apart from livestock, due to heat waves in summer season and cold waves during winter. Prolonged heat/cold waves adversely affect agricultural production, apart from possible man-hours lost in industries due to sickness and other causes as a result of such adverse weather conditions.

The human body in good health is able to regulate the body temperature and maintain it at a normal average of 36.9 degrees C (98.4 F), at rest, (the temperature as measured in the rectum), with some slight variations between individuals. The body exchanges heat with its surroundings by the three principles of Conduction, Convection and Radiation. This Auto Regulatory system however, fails under extremes of environmental temperatures, be it due to the surroundings, the habiliments worn by the subject body, heat generated within the body as a consequence of food intake/heavy exercise or workload, heat lost due to sweating etc. (Note that food intake for dietary purposes are measured/estimated in calories. And it has been estimated that loss of one litre of sweat by evaporation leads to a heat loss of about 1500 kilo-Joules! Further, under severe desert working conditions the sweat losses could be as much as 10 litres per day!).

Now, of all the organs of the human body the functioning of the brain is highly sensitive to any temperature variation. A change in the normal body temperature by as little as 0.5 degrees C, higher or lower, causes quite serious malfunctioning of the brain and consequently the organs of the body that the brain controls. Greater the change or departure in the temperature from the normal (of 36.9 C, that is 98.4 F), worse the malfunctioning. An increase of 2 degrees C (38.9 C or 102 F) results in clear signs of sickness. And a fall in the temperature by 2 degrees C (TO 34.9 C or 94.8 F) leads to hypothermia-defined by the temperature limit of 35° C/95 F).

The human body is a wonderful mechanism and has the remarkable ability to acclimatize itself to survive in difficult environmental conditions. Gradual exposure and day by day increases in the activity levels help to achieve such acclimatization. The adaptive processes help train the sweat glands to produce more sweat, start to sweat more quickly and continue without fatigue, as well as train the body to retain more salt in the body whilst absorbing larger and larger quantities of water (from stomach/intestines). Depending on how severe the heat environment is and the conditions of the body concerned, the adjustment period could vary from one to three weeks. Such acclimatization is easier for desert (dry-hot during the day/dry-cold at night) conditions than to the moist-heat conditions of tropical jungle environment. This is because of the high humidity that prevents evaporation of sweat to cool the body in the moist or wet-heat conditions. Also one acclimatizes more easily from a jungle to a desert condition than from a desert to jungle condition! Note that there is no such adaptive condition of the body to acclimatize to cold conditions!

But note that the body can acclimatize to quite some extent to high altitude environment!

Earthquakes

Every now and then, somewhere around the world, a major disastrous earthquake occurs, causing massive destruction of property, terrible loss of life, injuries and untold suffering to thousands of people. The reason is not far to seek—Earthquakes are unpredictable—neither science nor art has an answer as yet, to forecast with any certainty, where and when, the next dangerous earthquake will occur.

Not too long ago, on January 26, 2001 on the Republic Day to be precise, a major earthquake occurred in Gujarat, in the Kutch-Ahmedabad region. What began with a booming sound and rocking of the earth surface resulted in unheralded crash of buildings and structures. Thousands lay buried alive in the debris of collapsed buildings and structures, for days together! Most people in the city of Ahmedabad slept outdoors for days and weeks after the event out of fear of re-occurrence of another earthquake, particularly in view of recurring earth tremours.

Fortunately, competent rescue teams equipped with suitable high-tech detectors, Sniffer Dogs etc., got to work immediately to rescue/extricate/save most of them within about 48 hours! It was the prompt contingency measures put into effect that really saved the situation and prevented it from turning into a holocaust. Even so, thousands of lives were lost and the estimated loss of property/business was placed at about Rs.10, 000/= crores, in that brief appearance of a deadly Natural Hazard!

Follow up visits by engineers to the locations of the collapsed buildings/structures revealed that faulty construction practices, poor design of structures that flouted building norms due to greed or ignorance were the main cause for the failure of those structures to withstand the seismic shocks. And that was, primarily, responsible for the terrible loss of life (apart from the loss of property-of course). Identification and re-classification of seismic regions, were necessary and design of structures that are raised should be to appropriate seismic/quake-proof standards.

What is an Earthquake?

The solid portion of the earth's surface or crust, called the Lithosphere, rides over the molten magma. It is not a single block of spherical surface but is composed of irregularly broken up areas called Plates. These plates are in constant relative motion, albeit very slow. They jut into each other, slide over one another, rub against each other and so on. There are large plates like the Eurasian plate, the African plate, the Indo-Australian plate, the North American plate and so on. And there are the minor ones such as the Arabian plate, the Philippine plate etc. The behaviour/study of the plates is called by the name-'Plate Tectonics'. In the region of the broken up areas where large plates abut, and rub, occur zones called Faults. (A well-known fault is the St. Andreas Fault along the Californian coast of the continental North America.). These are zones/fissures between two blocks of rocky earth crust that could extend to hundreds of kilometres. These are active seismic regions prone to tremours and earthquakes. When the plates rub against each other without moving (that is, slide smoothly), pressure is built up and the energy is released radiating from the region. The result is an earthquake when the energy release reaches the surface of the earth, with the attendant rocking and sliding movements of the earth's surface that can be so devastating. (The Himalayan mountain range is understood to have been formed millenniums ago by the jutting in of the Indo-Australian plate with the Eurasian plate over a period of time. The plate's movement continues-some millimetres per year. It is one of the youngest mountain ranges to boot).

The seismic energy, radiates from the region of occurrence of the disturbance, resulting in an earthquake on the surface. The source area is known as the 'Hypocentre' and the point above the same on the surface of the earth is termed the "Epicentre". Apart from the energy content radiated from the subsurface disturbance, the destructive effects of an earthquake depend on the nature of the earth's crust at the Epicentre, the human habitat, the construction and socio-economic factors in the region, etc. The released seismic energy moves in the form of (what are called as) seismic waves-radiating in the crust as "Body waves" (known as Primary/P Waves and Secondary/S Waves) and on the surface of the earth as "Surface Waves" (known as Raleigh Waves and Love Waves). The P wave, is a fast seismic wave that travels through the body of the earth's crust-rocks and fluid-pushing and pulling the matter, it moves through. The S wave, is a slower seismic wave moving through the body of the crust generating an up/down and sideway movements of the substances it moves through. The surface Raleigh wave creates an up/down or sideway movements of the ground (earth surface). Whereas the "Love waves", the fast surface wave, shakes the ground from side to side. The intensity of an earthquake is measured in the Richter's Scale of 0 to a max. value of 10. Intensities of earth tremours could be around 1 or 2 on the richter scale, whereas a major /severe earthquake would have an intensity value of *around 6 or more on the richter scale.*

Mitigation techniques for minimizing the adverse affects of an earthquake include a host of actions, not least of which is the identification and classification of seismic zones/regions. Proper selection of locations for human habitats/conglomerations, appropriate design and construction practices for buildings and structures best suited to the locations concerned, which are scrupulously observed/enforced, cannot be overemphasized. Suitable education of the population, proper contingency plans, rescue and rehabilitation systems, and so on are a must.

The Indian Bureau of Standards, the BIS, has brought out a standard on quake proof structures the IS-1893 (of 1962 revised and updated periodically-1970,1975,1984), "Indian Standard Recommendation for Earthquake Resistant Structures. However, it appears that the construction industry is not much aware of it or its importance, as this standard is rarely followed/referred to, thus contributing to erection of poor structures (that are not quake resistant), that too in seismic zones!

Earthquake Prediction

An earthquake is a natural phenomenon that occurs unheralded, with unparalleled suddenness but with a devastating fury that can cause unbelievable destruction, havoc and loss of life. Unfortunately, it is also not a one-time phenomenon that would spare an area and have subsequent occurrences elsewhere only! It can occur, repeatedly, but at irregular intervals of time and unpredictable intensity too (in seismically active regions). Studies have been carried out in the Indian Sub-continent and it has been classified into five seismic zones. Zone I region is least earthquake prone, like the Deccan Plateau; whereas a Zone V region is seismically very active and most earthquake prone areas like the Northern and North-Eastern regions. The worst known earthquake in India occurred in Assam in 1897 with an intensity of 8.7 on the richter scale. But the death toll was comparatively small, less than two thousand, as compared to the thousands and thousands during the recent January 26, 2001earthquake in Gujarat! Also only a few died during a major earthquake in Assam in 1988, with an intensity of 7.2. So, high earthquake intensity is per se not an indication of possible loss of life that could occur! Naturally, close to seismic gaps bigger earthquakes are to be expected and could lead to bulges, fissures, land sinks and land tilts around the region on the earth-surface.

To study the possibility of an early warning system, geologists monitor water levels in borewells; release of Radon/Hydrogen gases and even water through the earth crust; and others study animal/birds behaviour patterns for possible correlation with occurrences of earthquakes. The basic problem is that, as yet, very little is known about earthquakes and what to look for, in order to be able to make reliable predictions.

There are numerous seismic stations spread around the world designed to detect seismic disturbances/earthquakes, with deep, underground sensitive seismic detector systems and signal analysis centres installed. They are designed to detect P waves, S waves etc. and locate the sources/occurrences of seismic disturbances/earthquakes, occurring even thousands of kilometres from the detection centres. Their detection sensitivities are so high, that it is understood that they can detect the minute local seismic disturbances that would occur due to, say, an underground explosion of a mere kiloton range, and locate the position of such an occurrence! Notwithstanding all this, there are *as yet no instrumentation or methods available to reliably predict in advance the occurrence of an earthquake,* the time, location of the epicentre and its intensity. The current thinking of most geologists is that an earthquake cannot be predicted; it is still an unsolved, most challenging problem to the scientists.

Avalanches

Avalanches occur in mountainous terrain that has heavy snowfall. Because of the steep slopes of the mountainsides, movements of snow-mass, gather volume and momentum, and thus velocity as they rapidly descend the mountain slopes. No wonder that avalanches occur frequently in the Himalayas—estimated to be about 100,000 a year! There are different types of avalanches: loose snow avalanche, airborne (snow) powder avalanche, slat avalanche or a combination of all, known as mixed avalanche. Its speed of descent and the density of the snow-mass determine the destructive power of an avalanche. Anything that stands in the path of an avalanche is destroyed/damaged by the momentum or impact, pressure of the snow-mass, and the velocity thrust. Depending on the type of the avalanche, its velocity and density could range between 10 to 70 m/s and 2-kg/cubic metre to about 400-kg/cubic metre!

The Snow and Avalanche Study Establishment (*SASE*) of the *Defence Research and Development Organization* (*DRDO*) has been carrying out very commendable, useful studies into the nature of avalanches in the Himalayan range of mountains. The studies include prediction of an avalanche occurrence, suitable protective measures and schemes, estimate of snowfalls etc. Obviously, an early warning system helps in possible saving of lives and property.

Forecasting an avalanche involves data on snowfall/met conditions, the terrain data, physical/mechanical characteristics of the snow-mass etc. and the ability to interpret the data to anticipate occurrence of an avalanche in advance. The lead time should be say at least 24 hrs in advance to be able to generate and issue early warnings, (over the radio and TV channels and any other system), that would reach the target people well in time to take protective measures.

The preparations required to mitigate the damage/destruction possibilities of avalanches are covered by what are called as *the six "A's"* indicated below:

- Afforest the areas wherever possible.
- Erect suitable control structures to arrest avalanche/dissipate its destructive energies.
- Artificially trigger an avalanche, at suitable times to prevent an unpredictable occurrence.
- Anticipate an avalanche (with suitable study/analysis) and issue early warnings.
- Educate the population about the hazards.
- Have properly designed shelters/structures in avalanche prone areas where people could be accommodated in an emergency.

Landslides (Mud-slides)

Landslides occur in hilly terrain/mud-slides mainly occur around manmade constructions/trenches, when excessive precipitation occurs or seismic disturbances happen. These cause poor soil stability that result in masses of earth surface/hillsides collapsing and gathering momentum as they hurtle down the slopes. In the process, the masses of earth destroy/cover any obstacle in the way-most damaging being when they happen to be human habitations. Landslides are very common occurrences in the Himalayan region, (the mountain range being geologically young), of the North-Eastern states of India. The general results being the local destruction of property, blockage of roads with resultant affect on transportation and sometimes lives are lost too.

Not much study seems to have been done for having a suitable early warning system in place. Some studies carried out in the; J&K region seems to have indicated fairly good correlation between annual rainfall and extent of landslide activity—not enough to evolve an early warning methodology. It would seem that educating the people living on/near hillsides to be alert during periods of heavy precipitation would be an answer for the present, till deep studies are carried out to enable reliable system of prediction of landslides.

Flash-Floods

Unlike flood control which needs long-term appropriate policy and state/interstate/national efforts, by and large flash floods should be avoidable/controllable phenomena with minimal/local/regional efforts. Note that *flash floods* could be *manmade* problems. Such as unannounced sudden opening of sluice gates when reservoirs are full-say to avoid danger to the dam concerned. Or it could be due to a sudden collapse of a dam structure because of poor design/construction/maintenance, etc. and the structure gets overloaded when the reservoir gets full, (as happened at Pune during the sixties). But, most often it is due to the sudden extreme precipitation that may occur in an area because of a cloudburst or intense thunderstorm, a *Natural*

Hazard. Obviously, lack of proper drainage system in the catchment area for the unexpected precipitation to quickly and properly drain away without damaging human habitations is the main culprit in such cases. Flash floods could cause terrible destruction when they occur in towns and villages, particularly because of the unexpected suddenness of the occurrence, before the people could take suitable protective measures/flee the location, etc. Obviously, provision of proper drainage system, and erection of suitable barriers at the human conglomerations would largely abate the destructive fury of flash floods. Vehicle users should be extremely cautious of crossing causeways, lest they be swept away by raging waters of a flash flood. (Ofcourse people should be educated to watch out for cyclonic weather/ thunderstorm activity in the region, and what to do under those circumstances). Obviously, appropriate disaster management system should be in place to mitigate damage and destruction that could be caused by flash floods too.

Thunderstorms/Hail-Storms

Thunderstorms/Hailstorms are quite common occurrences in the tropical and sub-tropical regions. Luckily, the likelihood of their occurrence in a region could be fairly reliably forecast with availability of suitable weather radar in the region. This greatly helps in the issue of early warning to the populace in the concerned areas so that they do not get caught in dangerous situations out in the open, when the thunderstorm/hailstorm do happen. Hence, the damage and destruction that could otherwise be wrought on unsuspecting population could be mitigated to a very large extent, by the early warning system and education of the populace on precautions to be taken. A severe thunderstorm could well result in a flash flood with its attendant danger, apart from the direct destruction of property that can be caused by the attendant raging wind and heavy downpour/precipitation. Human/livestock lives could be lost when they are caught out in the open during a severe thunderstorm/hailstorm activity.

Appendix "C"

An Introduction to Cryptology

"Cryptology" is a term used to denote the art and science of codemaking as well as codebreaking. That is to say, the term *"cryptology"* includes *"cryptography"*, as well as *"cryptanalysis"*. *"Cryptography,"* ofcourse, is the art and science of ensuring security of messages by use of various techniques of secret writing-such as steganography, ciphers or encryption/decryption processes, etc. And *"cryptanalysis"*, or *codebreaking*, represents the processes/techniques/methods used to unscramble a coded message, (called the *ciphertext*), and obtain the original message that was encoded, (called the *plaintext*), when you do not have the code or key required to decipher/decode the ciphertext, mainly because you are not the intended recipient of the message! It looks like that a whole series of cryptic terms—equally or more confusing has been let loose to indicate what cryptology stands for! So, it is worthwhile in the first instance to start with these terms of usage and find out what exactly each of them mean.

From time immemorial, when man started to exchange messages to communicate with each other from time to time, need arose to make sure that a particular message reached/made sense only to the intended recipient and any interloper would not come to know the actual content of such a message. In the earliest times, sending the message through a trusted messenger who would deliver the message to the required party only-ensured this. It was not enough to have a trusted messenger to carry the message. It was also necessary to make sure that the message contents was neither known to the messenger, nor would it become obvious to any unauthorized person intercepting the message or getting at it by accident/subterfuge etc. The message should make sense only to the intended recipient. So, some secret method of communication, that is, *"Secret Writing"*, (or SW), known only to the sender of the message and the intended recipient became necessary.

This business of *"Secret Writing"* could be achieved in several ways. You could camouflage, or disguise your message in some way to hide it from prying eyes, to hide it in some innocuous text/picture object etc. Such a technique of hiding a message is known as *"Steganography"*, (from the Greek words steganos-meaning covered and graphein-meaning to write). Or you could code the message to apparently look like something else, a meaning less jumble, or meaning something totally different from the original message, by using a suitable process called *"Coding"*. "Coding" involves use of some mutually arranged, preselected method and a "Key". On receiving the coded message, the intended recipient uses the pre-arranged key to get at the plain message contained/camouflaged in the coded message that he has received. Since codes can be broken without too much of effort, by code-breakers, if high security is desired for a message, one has to go in for more complex systems, and resort to "Cryptography" or "Ciphers". Here also you use "Keys" kept secret from all except the actual sender and the intended recipient; but the process of "coding", (hence the decoding too) is more mathematical and complicated.

As mentioned before, in *"Steganography"* you use some method to hide the message. This maybe by making the message "invisible" to all but the intended recipient of the message by suitable camouflage, hiding it in some apparently meaningful communication/image, use of "Invisible Ink", (invisible to the naked eye, and becomes visible on treatment with some chemical or device), and so on. An old historical anecdote mentions how one HISTAIAUS sent a secret message to one ARISTOGORUS through a trusted messenger, in an ingenious manner. He shaved the head of the messenger, wrote the message on the shaven head. He let the hair grow and then sent his messenger to ARISTOGOROUS. The latter, (obviously, as per some earlier mutual agreement), shaved the head of the messenger and read the desired message on the baldpate of the messenger, and acted as desired in the message! (Ofcourse in modern times the unconscionable delay involved in waiting for the hair to grow would be totally unacceptable; but the example indicates the basic simplicity of steganography to keep messages confidential). Modern examples of steganography would be use of invisible inks, images, holograms, microdot, etc.

During World War II, SW became more involved with use of invisible inks to write messages on innocent looking "communications", using all types of chemicals, body fluids etc. Such messages could not be observed/read with the naked eye, without some processing with suitable chemicals/techniques, such as use of ultraviolet light etc. The ultimate technique in this regard was perhaps the use of "microdots", use of photographic techniques to reduce the image of the message/document to the size of a punctuation mark—the full stop. This highly reduced image is then stuck on a regular punctuation mark on an innocent document. (Or, the microdot could be hidden on the envelope, under the stamp and so on). The intended receiver of the document would then scan through the document and look at the microdot with a suitable microscope or a suitably fabricated high magnification device! (It would appear that in ancient India several types of SW were practiced as may be noted for the "Artha Shastra" of Kautilya.).

"Coding" is a means of hiding required information in a message that conveys some other apparently valid/innocuous information. It is simple, and well suited to the modern methods of correspondence/communication. For example, suppose you want to inform someone to meet you at 6 P.M. and you do not want others to get to know this, you could pass on to him an innocuous looking message, such as, say, "come for tea on the 18th". As per your mutual prior understanding he will interpret the 18th as 1800 hrs, or, 6 P.M. You could mutually agree upon a set of code words, (a codebook), that stand for entirely different set of actual words you desire to convey. Or the code could be a system or key, (mutually agreed to beforehand, of course) you use with, say, a popular/common book/magazine, (say the Bible or dictionary etc.), to securely pass on your message. For example

you may convey to your chap a message saying that since Feb. 25, '03, your telephone number has changed to 2568795. This would indicate, as per the codebook/prior agreement, say, start with the word on the 25th page of the book, paragraph 2 line three, word two and then follow up with words in subsequent pages at the 25th, 68th, 79th etc. places! You could of course use codewords in any language, and use those codewords when the message has to be kept confidential from others. Obviously, there are any number of ways to "code" your messages to make them invisible to those who are not authorized to receive them, (by misdirection, loss, interception and so on).

Those who are fans of Sherlock Holmes, may recall use of a coded message, (steganography), in one of the stories in the "*Memoirs of Sherlock Holmes*", viz. '"*The Adventures of "Gloria Scott*"'. A terse, apparently nonsensical message drives the recipient to die of shock. The message stated, "the supply of game for London is going steadily up. Head keeper Hudson, we believe, has been now told to receive all orders for fly-paper, and for preservation of your hen pheasant's life". The Maestro was ofcourse able to find the hidden message by analyzing the situation and a study of the communication. He found that noting down every third word in the message, (the "key" for the message), gave out the secret message; which was-"the game is up. Hudson has told all. Fly for your life"!

But, there is a limitation in this type of coding systems. The number of variations possible are finite. The number of commonly used words in any language is also usually only a few thousands only. A dedicated code breaker who suspects clandestine contents in messages could put in enough efforts to come up with the system used to code/decode such messages, and decode the secret message. And in real time! Hence, for a message to remain confidential long enough, one will have to resort to *"Cryptography"* (or Ciphers or Encryption/Decryption/ Crypto-systems). The message may no longer look like an innocuous sentence and be hence obvious as a secret communication. But it would remain incomprehensible except to a very dedicated code breaker, if he puts in sufficient efforts, and what is more important—length of time too.

Let us first get out of the way many of the cryptic terms used in *cryptography* for easy understanding of this science (and art).

Plaintext—this term refers to the original plain language message (or text) that is encoded by the sender of the message. It also refers to the plain message that the intended recipient gets, on decoding the coded received message he receives, (or a codebreaker gets, when he is successful in his attempts at decoding an intercepted message).

Ciphertext—is the term used to refer to the result of the coding process on a plaintext.

Thus, a *"plaintext"* on coding becomes a *"ciphertext"*; and a *"ciphertext"* on decoding becomes the *"plaintext"* of any coded/ cipher message/communication.

Encryption/(ciphering)—is the process, methodology, technique/ algorithm used to convert a plaintext into a ciphertext.

Decryption/(deciphering) is the (usually, reverse) process used to get the original plaintext out of a ciphertext.

Ciphers/cryptosystems is a generic term used to refer to methods of/equipment for coding/decoding messages.

(The) KEY is the jumble of letters, (may be numerals, or even alpha-numerals), that have to be used with a particular Crypto-system, to code or decode a particular message. (This is analogous to the Key used to lock/unlock locks used to provide physical security-whether a lever lock, magnetic lock, number lock, digital lock, combination lock etc. In the case of digital locks, combination locks, number locks the number/combination required to be used are referred to as the Key to that lock).

The intention of a *"Cipher"* is to ensure that an important message is kept secret and secure from unwanted/prying eyes/ (ears) etc. To code a specific message you use a *"Cipher"* (process) and a particular Cipher "Key". This is called the "Encryption Key", as the particular key has been used to encrypt the message. The recipient of the Ciphertext uses a "Key" to decode the message and get the Plaintext-and that "Key" is called the "Decryption Key".

In most crypto-systems the "encryption key" and the coresponding "decryption key" are identical. And such crypto-systems are designated as "symmetric crypto-systems".

In recent times new cipher systems called "public key crypto-systems" have made inroads into secure communication systems. Such systems have different "keys" for encryption and decryption. Hence, such systems are designated as "asymmetric crypto-systems".

Public key crypto-system—in such systems, the sender has not one but two keys, a public key that is published/made known to all, (like the telephone number in a telephone directory), and a secret key known only to himself. Similarly, the receiver has two keys -one public and the other secret. Thus, the *"encryption key"* and the *"decryption key"* are entirely different. The R.S.A. (Rivest-Shamir-Adleman) public key system is first of such asymmetric key systems. We shall touch upon such systems later on.

Kerckhoffs's principle postulates the fundamental rule for judging the security of a *cipher system*-"the security of a crypto-system must not depend on keeping secret the (crypto) algorithm. The security depends only on keeping the keys secret". That is, you must make the worst case assumption that the system is compromised, (as generally all systems will be sometime or other). That is, the opposition has identical crypto-system with them, (after all the manufacturers/sellers of the systems are few only)/ know fully the encryption/decryption processes/algorithms used. Only the sender and receiver of a secret message know the specific keys used. Hence, the implication is that for good security a system must envisage a set of (potential) keys that is enormous in number/extent. So that the opposition cannot get at the actual key used in a ciphertext, by trying out all possible keys from the set of valid keys (the key field)-in reasonable period (period of interest for the message to remain secret)/indefinitely. With the advent of fast computers and distributed processing, in recent times, many erstwhile, so-called secure crypto-systems have failed in this regard!

The figure below is indicative of the Cipher Process.

Sender's End	Communication Medium	Receiving End
Plaintext -Algorithm -The Key -Ciphertext	(Note, Messenger, post, Telegram, Telex Fax, Telephone, e-mail Sat-link, SMS, cellphone etc.)	-Cipher text -Algorithm -The key -Plaintext

For convenience, and to avoid confusion, the convention is to use the lower-case letters for the letters of a message, that is the Plaintext. And it is referred to as the Plain Alphabet. On the other hand, the letters of the Ciphertext are denoted in upper-case/or capital letters and are termed the Cipher Alphabet. Thus, for the English language:

- Plain Alphabet— a b c d e f g h I j k l m n o p q r s t u v w x y z
- Cipher Alphabet— A B C D E F G H I J K L M N O P Q R S T U V W X Y Z

Thus, the *"plaintext"*, the original plain message/decoded message is in plain alphabet or lower case letters; and the *"ciphertext"* or coded/encrypted message is in the cipher alphabet, that is in upper case/capital letters.

There are two main types of methods used in *"cryptography"*, those that use "transposition" and those that use "substitution". (Hence, they are known as "transposition ciphers" and "substitution ciphers", respectively).

In transposition ciphers the letters of a message are merely re-arranged within the message itself. The result is a sort of a longish "anagram", as long as the message itself. Here each letter/character of the message retains its identity, but is displaced from its position, (that is, you transpose the position of each letter).

In substitution ciphers, you substitute each letter/character of the message by another character (may be a letter, numeral, etc, say a Greek alphabet for Roman alphabet). Hence, in this case, each letter/character of the message changes its identity, but retains its position!

To understand the principle of Transposition Ciphers, let us consider a trivial example. Suppose you desire to code a single word, say RUN, using transposition cipher principle. The letters in this "message" are just three in number viz., R, U and N. These letters can be re-arranged in any of just six (permutation) different ways as—RUN, UNR, NRU, URN, RNU and NUR. But when the number of letters in a message increases the possible transposition combination increase dramatically. (A short message with just, say twenty letters, will have millions of possibilities for getting distinct transposed messages). Note that each of the letters in the message remains same, that is retains their identity, but their location is changed, that is their position is altered. Does this mean that with random transposition of letters in a message we have a simple and secure Crypto-system? For it should be quite impossible to unscramble the coded message by undesirable persons. But, then, how will the intended recipient himself decode the *"ciphertext"*, since the transposition is truly random? (The problems of secure Key transfers!).

Hence, it is impractical to expect foolproof security from transposition ciphers. However, it is a simple practical method for getting some confidentiality. Let us take a short message, say:

THIS IS A SECRET BETWEEN US. Let the transposition be a simple interchange of adjacent letters. Then the result of the transposition is we get a apparently nonsense sentence-

HTSI SI S ACEERB TTEEWNE SU. We can remove the spaces to get a seemingly more difficult message to crack:

HTSISISACEERBTTEEWNESU

Ofcourse the intended recipient of the message has the "key" for this transposition cipher, that is to interchange adjacent letters and thus easily gets the decoded message: *This is a secret between us,* and for it the plaintext-this is a secret between us, by introducing the missing spaces.

The sender could make it more confusing by say splitting the message into two (two-rail system)/three

(Three-rail system) rows etc. thus:

T I I A E R T E W E U

H S S S C E B T E N S to get TIIAERTWEUHSSSCEBTENS, as the coded message. The receiver then just splits the ciphertext into two halves, places one below the other and reads the original message by combining the two rows. (Similarly, a three-rail or four-trail etc., system can be accomplished).

This type of ciphers looks quite complex. Obviously, one can have few practical transposition "Keys". Hence, the feasibility of decrypting such ciphertext by undesirable recipients by just trying out practical alternative transposition methods makes it a very risky proposition for anyone to use it to get even reasonable security of the message. In modern times, therefore, transposition type Crypto-System is hardly ever used.

Substitution Ciphers

As we have seen earlier the name itself is indicative of the method employed in this type of Cipher system viz., substitute each letter of the message by another letter, (or symbol or character), in a practicable way. It is said that Julius Caesar was the first person to have used the substitution method in his message to Cicero during a war-hence that particular method is still called the *"Caesar cipher"*. As mentioned before, in substitution Cipher each letter retains its position but changes its IDENTITY.

Let us take a case where the *"Cipher Alphabet"* is a two-place shift to the left of the *"Plain Alphabet"*. Then we get:

- Plain Alphabet— a b c d e f g h I j k l m n o p q r s t u v w x y z
- Cipher Alphabet— C D E F G H I J K L M N O P Q R S T U V W X Y Z A B

Note that this *"Cipher Alphabet"* is same as the *"Plain Alphabet"*, (but in upper case letters of course), except that each of the letters is shifted two places to the left. Note also that each letter of the *"Cipher Alphabet"* is directly located below each letter of the *"Plain Alphabet"*. Now this can be used as the "Key" to code a message. Take a simple *"Plaintext"* (message)-,"This is our secret". Then the *"Plaintext"* and *"Ciphertext"* become as shown below, (you get the Ciphertext letters by noting down the character in the *"Cipher Alphabet"* that is directly below the letter in the

"Plain Alphabet" corresponding to each of the letters in the Plaintext):

- Plaintext— t h i s i s o u r s e c r e t
- Ciphertext—V J K U K U Q W T U G E T G V

English language has 26 letters in its alphabet. So, since a zero shift means the *"Plaintext"* itself, the shifts possible are from a minimum of one letter to a maximum of 25 letter (shift). That is 25 distinct "Keys" are possible and hence 25 distinct encryption can be done. And in this *encryption process* the algorithm is just the substitution of each *"Plaintext"* alphabet with a ciphertext alphabet; the Key being the distinct cipher alphabet that is used in a particular encryption.

"The decryption process" is the reverse of the *"encryption process"*. The *"ciphertext"* alphabet is placed above the *"Plaintext alphabet"*; and for each letter in the *"ciphertext"* you note down the corresponding plain alphabet to get the *"Plaintext"*.

Thus:

- Cipher Alphabet— C D E F G H I J K L M N O P Q R S T U V W X Y Z A B
- Plain Alphabet— a b c d e f g h I j k l m n o p q r s t u v w x y z

Now for each of the *"ciphertext"* character you read and note down the corresponding *"Plaintext Alphabet"* below it, to get the *"Plaintext"*. Thus, for the first letter "V" in the *"ciphertext"* the corresponding *"plaintext"* letter is "t". The next *"ciphertext"* letter is "J", for which we find the *"plaintext"* letter to be "h". Following this process we finally get the *"plaintext"* characters involves as "thisisoursecret". By inserting relevant spaces in this message we get the original plaintext "this is our secret". Obviously, this is a "Symmetric Key Crypto System" as the "Key" used for both encryption and decryption is the same! Naturally, the Key has to be kept secret by; both the sender and the recipient to prevent the opposition from straightaway decoding intercepted cipher messages. But remember *"Kerckhoffs Principle"*—unless the potential Key-space is immense, the opposition can in course of time get at the *"Plaintext"* by trying out all possible Keys. (So, the Keyspace is so large that it is practically impossible to test out all possible Keys, even with a modern highspeed computer and distributed processing techniques!). With substitution cipher using the (English language) cipher alphabets of maximum possible 25, as noted before, (the zero shift being a trivial cipher alphabet, being the Plaintext itself), the estimated potential Key combinations is an astronomical over 10 raised to the power of 26! Remember that the number of molecules in a mole is under 10 raised to the power 24 only, so the possible Key-space is truly enormous!

From the above, it is obvious that substitution cipher is not only easy to implement, but is also elegant and what is more important, it can be highly secure, (when the available large Keyspace is utilized). Where one is satisfied with some amount of reduced security simpler Crypto equipment are possible by resorting to use of limited Keyspace. You must have noticed that the method of securely exchanging the *"Keys"* between the sender and the recipient becomes a vital and difficult function. When the system caters for use of simplified Key usage it helps immensely in the process of *"Key-exchange"*. So, instead of using all the 25 cipher alphabets one could restrict oneself to use of a few only and that too by use of simple, and easily remembered "Keyword" or "Keyphrase", like say "MUMBAIKER", "GETMESHORTY". Note that you use upper case letters and avoid use of any spaces etc between the letters of the *"Keyword/ Keyphrase"*.

Let us take a look at how a *"Keyword"* is used in substitution cipher. (Method of use of Keyphrase is similar). What you do is quite simple. You arrange the letters in the *"Keyword"* in sequence, eliminating any repetitions. Then you add to the letters the remaining letters of the cipher alphabet as indicated below:

- M U B A I K E R S T V W X Y Z C D F G H J L N O P Q

Thus, you will notice that the second M in the *"Keyword"* is removed, and the other letters—U, B, A, I K E and R in the *"Keyword"*, are also removed from the cipher alphabet, as they are already present/placed in the beginning of this new "Cipher Alphabet". You still have the 26 letters of the English alphabet in this new *"Cipher Alphabet"*, but differently arranged, with the letters in the *"Keyword"* placed in the beginning, and no repetitions of any letter. All you have to do now is carry out the encryption process with this new *"Cipher Alphabet"*.

Of course, you could simply repeat the *"Keyword"* continuously, for a less secure system as:

- M U B A I K E R M U B A I K E R M U B A I K E R M

Even with this limited permutations, the possible keyspace is quite enormous and normally it may well be impractical to unscramble an intercepted message by usual diligent testing of all possible keys, that is the "Brute-Force" method. But then a clever cryptanalyst does not try to test all possible keys but tries out shortcut techniques to arrive at his goal-quickly and more practically. He resorts to use of statistics and linguistics! (That is the "Frequency-Analysis" or "Frequency-Attack" method).

From the linguistic basis, one would expect that in the English language the vowels A, E, I, O and U would appear most frequently in any English sentence/paragraph. But, statistics show otherwise. Studies carried out in the form of frequency analysis of a large number of text show that the vowel "e" *occurs most frequently,* followed by the consonant "t"! Independent trials conducted on English language *"plaintext"* for frequency of occurrence of the alphabets resulted in the following order of frequency of occurrence—highest to lowest:

- 1 2 3 4 5 6 7 8 9 10 11 12 13 14/15 16/17/18 19 20 21 22 23 24 25 26
- e t a o n r l s h d l f c m u g p y w b v k r j q z

The above is termed as a one-gram probability distribution, (highest probability of occurrence to the lowest), as the frequency of occurrence of single English alphabet distribution is tested.

Similar studies have been carried out on English language *"plaintext"* for probability of distribution of combination of letters-twos or 2-grams, threes or 3-grams, fours or 4-grams and so on.

So, by studying the *"ciphertext"* for frequency of occurrences of particular cipher alphabets, 1-grams, 2-grams etc., considerable simplification occurs in the code breaking process. Ofcourse, this presumes that a; large enough body of *"cipher text"* is available, and using he same Key, for applying this technique. Hence, the need in *"cryptography"* is to make EACH '*Ciphertext*' SHORT and each use a DIFFERENT "Key"! Therefore, use of Keywords/ Keyphrases which are used again and again are fraught with chinks in the security armour, in this cipher technique.

So, one obvious way to greatly improve security of the substitution cipher method would be to add other characters/ symbols/numerals etc., that will not substitute *"plaintext Alphabets"*, but represent maybe even null characters such as blanks. For example, one could represent the plain alphabet with any 26 numbers in the range of say 1 to 99. This would leave an excess of 73 numbers (between the 1 and 99 number space, excluding the 26 numbers actually chosen to represent the *"plaintext Alphabet"*). These numbers could be randomly interspersed in the ciphertext in a manner that is known to the recipient. Anybody who intercepts such a *"cipher text"* would be at a loss to decode it using frequency analysis etc.

A simple stratagem of using a (codebook and) codewords in the *"plaintext"* would further enhance the security of the system. (Like, using the codewords "lion" to refer to the head of the family/organization, "offshoot" to refer to a child/department in an organization and so on).

The above types of substitution ciphers (also termed the CAESAR CIPHER, after Julius Caesar who is supposed to have used it first), are known as "Monoalphabetic Ciphers". The reason being that the cipher alphabet uses characters, (letters, numbers, symbols or a combination of these), to substitute the letters in the Plaintext alphabet in a one-to-one manner, that is in a repeated fashion-without a change from occurrence to occurrence of the plain alphabet. Is it possible to improve further the security of the substitution cipher? VIGNERE found a simple enough method to do this, hence the system is known as the "Vignere Cipher", using what is known as the "Vignere Square"! What you do is use a different *"cipher alphabet"* for each *"plaintext alphabet"* from the 25 different cipher alphabets available, and also, preferably in a random way. (Recall that a cipher alphabet is obtained by displacing the plain alphabet by from a minimum of one to a maximum of 25 places). With this system, you now have an additional *"cipher alphabet"—"the plain alphabet"* itself, as it could be interspersed between the other 25 *"cipher alphabets"*. This results in the availability of total 26 *"cipher alphabets"* for use in this cipher system. When you place these *"cipher alphabets"* one below the other what results is the Vignere Square!

The Vignere Square

"Plain Alphabet"

a b c d e f g h i j k l m n o p q r s t u v w x y z

"Cipher Alphabet"

B C D E F G H I J K L M N O P Q R S T U V W X Y Z A

C D E F G H I J K L M N O P Q R S T U V W X Y Z A B

D E F G H I J K L M N O P Q R S T U V W X Y Z A B C

E F G H I J K L M N O P Q R S T U V W X Y Z A B C D

F G H I J K L M N O P Q R S T U V W X Y Z A B C D E

G H I J K L M N O P Q R S T U V W X Y Z A B C D E F

H I J K L M N O P Q R S T U V W X Y Z A B C D E F G

I J K L M N O P Q R S T U V W X Y Z A B C D E F G H

J K L M N O P Q R S T U V W X Y Z A B C D E F G H I

K L M N O P Q R S T U V W X Y Z A B C D E F G H I J

L M N O P Q R S T U V W X Y Z A B C D E F G H I J K

M N O P Q R S T U V W X Y Z A B C D E F G H I J K L

N O P Q R S T U V W X Y Z A B C D E F G H I J K L M

O P Q R S T U V W X Y Z A B C D E F G H I J K L M N

P Q R S T U V W X Y Z A B C D E F G H I J K L M N O

Q R S T U V W X Y Z A B C D E F G H I J K L M N O P

R S T U V W X Y Z A B C D E F G H I J K L M N O P Q

S T U V W X Y Z A B C D E F G H I J K L M N O P Q R

T U V W X Y Z A B C D E F G H I J K L M N O P Q R S

U V W X Y Z A B C D E F G H I J K L M N O P Q R S T

V W X Y Z A B C D E F G H I J K L M N O P Q R S T U

W X Y Z A B C D E F G H I J K L M N O P Q R S T U V

X Y Z A B C D E F G H I J K L M N O P Q R S T U V W

Y Z A B C D E F G H I J K L M N O P Q R S T U V W X

Z A B C D E F G H I J K L M N O P Q R S T U V W X Y

A B C D E F G H I J K L M N O P Q R S T U V W X Y Z

(Note that the last column and the last row are similar to the *plain alphabet,* but in capitals as *cipher alphabet,* and the 26 *cipher alphabets* form a 26 by 26 square—the Vignere Square!).

This simple additional technique results in a radically enhanced security for the substitution *cipher system.* It is called as a *Polyalphabetic system,* as a number of come into play. Here, too, you could simplify the encryption/decryption processes by going in for use of simple *Keywords,* instead of using randomly the *cipher alphabets.* But you still retain very high cipher security. You associate each letter of the *plaintext* with a letter of the *Keyword.* For example, let us use the Keyword "PLAIN" with the *plaintext welcome to India* as an illustration.

- The Plaintext—w e l c o m e t o I n d i a
- The Keyword—P L A I N P L A I N P L A I
- Ciphertext— L P L K B B P T W V C O I I

You get the *"ciphertext"* by taking each *"plaintext letter"* and checking the "ROW" of the Vignere Square (that is the cipher alphabet in the Vignere Square starts with the cipher alphabet letter associated with the Plaintext letter. Thus, the letter "w" at the start of the *"plaintext"* is associated with the *"cipher alphabet"* letter "P", below it. So, look down the *Vignere Square* for the row which starts with the letter "P", and look along this row for the cipher text letter that is below the plain alphabet letter "w". In this case it happens to be the letter "L". And, this is the *"ciphertext letter",* (for "w"). By following this process, you identify the remaining *"ciphertext letters"* to get the full cipher text as "LPLKBBPTWVCOII" for the plaintext "*welcome to India*". If you like you could then group these letters into groups of five letters for ease of transmission through letter, telephone etc.

Now, you would have noticed that in the Vignere Square the first row and the first column are identical in the sequence of letters. So, it is not really necessary to have a big chart of the square to carry out the above task. You can simplify the process. Have just the first row for reference and work with that only.

Also since you have 26 cipher alphabets in the Square you can start the first row with "A" itself! Thus, use the sequence:

• A B C D E F G H I J K L M N O P Q R S T U V W X Y Z

for carrying out the task. So, if the *cipher alphabet* starts with the letter "P", then consider the *plain alphabet* a to start there and count along the row the *plain alphabet* letters till you reach the required *Plaintext letter* to arrive at the required *Ciphertext* letter for the cipher. Thus, for the "w" of the Plaintext with "P" of the *Keyword* as the *Cipher Alphabet,* you get "L" as the *cipher text letter.* And for the *plaintext letter* "e", with "L" as the *cipher alphabet letter* you arrive at "P" as the *cipher text letter,* and so on. Definitely, a far simpler process than the use of he entire Vignere Square for the task. Ofcourse, with use of personal computers it does not matter what way you do the job! Then, naturally it would be convenient too to use the Vignere Square and to highlight (or different colour) on the computer screen the relevant rows of cipher alphabet, in this particular case those starting with "P", "L", "A", "I" and "N". This enables easy identification of the character at the intersection of the column containing the concerned *plaintext letter* and the concerned *cipher alphabet* row, (starting with the relevant cipher alphabet letter).

To decrypt the message you employ the reverse process. You first note down in sequence a row of the *"Keywords"*, in capital letters of course. Below each of the letters of this row of letters you note down in sequence each of the letters of the cipher text, (also in capitals). You then look at the *"cipher alphabet"* rows starting with the concerned letters of the Keywords, and find the intersections with the relevant columns containing the *"ciphertext"* letters to find the letters of the *"Plaintext"*.

Thus, for the example given above the steps are as indicated below:

Step 1. Note the Keyword/Key — P L A I N P L A I N P L A I N

Step 2. Note the ciphertext letters — L P L K B B P T W V C O I I

Step 3. Note intersection letters — w e l c o m e t o I n d i a

It is obvious for the above that the longer the Keyword more complex and secure the resulting cipher! The design of the Vignere cipher system makes it immune to frequency analysis/ attack. Further, it provides an immensely high Keyspace, or number of distinct and valid Keys possible. It is also very easy for the sender of a message and its recipient to securely exchange the concerned Keywords/Keys. These qualities make Vignere cipher an excellent Cryptosystem.

You would have noticed from the above that the *Vignere Cipher* utilizes multiple *cipher alphabets,* one for each of the (non-repeated) letters in the Keyword (cipher Key). It continuously alternates between a number of distinctly different *"cipher alphabets"*-as per the Keyword/cipher Key. Therefore, this is a *"Polyalphabetic cipher system"*, (whilst the Caesar cipher system described earlier uses only a single cipher alphabet and is hence a typical *"Monoalphabetic cipher system"*). This does not mean that this cipher is impregnable. Since the *"Keyword"* is repeated to the extent of the Plaintext/(ciphertext), the system is amenable to attack by linguistics and statistics. Repeated 1-grams, 2-grams, 3-grams etc. such as a, an, the etc. give a structure to the ciphertext that helps in *"cryptanalysis"*. Techniques are available to estimate the number of letters in the Keyword used.

As far back as 1854, Charles Babbage, the mathematical genius who proposed the design for the first electronic computer is attributed to have suggested a cryptanalytic technique to decipher the *"Vignere cipher"* using *"Keywords"*. The ultimate result was that mathematicians got the upper hand in *"cryptanalysis"* as against cryptographers who had the upper hand till then in designing secure ciphers! Not too much later any cipher designed could be broken up pretty fast, by *"cryptanalysis"*. But the World War II saw lot of activities in generation of variety of cryptosystem and in the post war period cryptographers were able to come up with unbreakable ciphers! Initially they were mostly based on the *"Vignere cipher"*! So, now you can design an Inherently non-breakable secure cipher, which cannot be cryptanalysed on the basis of the *"ciphertext"* alone. Ofcourse, one could attempt to get the Key by subversion, subterfuge, surveillance, interception and so on, and break the "unbreakable" cipher, with the help of the Key! (No system can be 100 % safe against such attacks).

Cipher Security

You need to use a Key, which is as long as the message itself to guarantee the security of the cipher system. Further, the Key should have random occurrence of letters and should not be used again! This is the principle used in what are termed as "One Time Pad", (OTP), "One Time Tape", (OTT), etc. They use a *"Key"* once only and do not repeat the *"Key"* again, apart from using randomly, (in practice Pseudo-randomly), generated letters for each key. These are truly secure cipher techniques. But there is a flaw-the problem of securely exchanging the *"Keys"*! (Apart from the problems of securely maintaining, using, and disposing of used *"Keys"* which accumulate fast as they are not reused again. The difficulty in regard to getting high speed of operation of the cipher system does not hold good now in view of the fast advancements in the computer speeds and technology). Naturally the security of the system depends on the true randomness of the Key generation; and any compromise in this regard compromises the cipher system security. The assertion is that, a it is mathematically proved that it is "IMPOSSIBLE" for a cryptanalyst to unscramble a message that has used an OTP/(OTT) to encrypt it. Apparently, this type of system is the only one that is (inherently), totally secure and immune to cryptanaytical attacks and yet practical to use, (apart from the drawbacks of secure generation, exchange, maintenance use and destruction of truly random Keys). The reasons are not far to seek. The total randomness of such a cipher eliminates any patterns, structures-in fact anything that a cryptanalyst can latch on to and use as a wedge to break to the *"ciphertext"*. No wonder such ciphers are absolutely secure.

Block Ciphers

The rapid growth in economies and commerce in the post World War II period after the initial recession, necessitated exchange of highly confidential commercial and financial information between and within commerce houses, customers and so on. Need for rapid and secure exchange of financial transactions over fast expanding telecommunication system became an absolute necessity. Any compromise in the confidentiality of such information could entail heavy, unacceptable economic losses to the concerned organizations/units. Thus, it became essential for them to go; in for extensive use of ciphers. Till then it was only the government organizations and the military that used ciphers, it was quite their very own domain! And the business houses had far little stake in that area.

So, came the field days for commercial cipher systems. The giant computer company, the IBM, got into the act and developed a computer based technique for rapid encryption/decryption of blocks of characters at a time for bulk ciphering purposes—the Block Cipher. The US government desired to ensure that the business houses could have a fairly secure ciphers system-that is the cipher for commerce-but which could also be capable of being cryptanalysed by the US government for their security concerns, (the National Security Agency or the NSA). So, based on the IBM techniques the *National Bureau of Standards of the USA* developed a *"Standard Cipher System"* for commercial use that was called as the *"Data Encryption Standard"* or the DES. This has come into use in a very big and extensive way, all over the world, till very recently. The cryptosystem is quite secure, but not so secure that the cipher cannot be crypto-analyzed by competent agencies!

The DES was the harbinger of field days for secure commercial transactions. I could also be used for encryption/decryption of bulk data on almost "real-time" basis. Later on, came crypto-systems based on suitable mathematical formulae like some Polynomials, which permitted running texts/large volumes of data or bulk information to be encrypted/decrypted on on-line transaction basis. Such systems are known as "Stream Ciphers". Since most of the cipher systems are based on the use of "micro-processing," operating on "Binary Logic", it is worth the while to take a look at "Boolean Algebra" that encompasses the binary logic.

Boolean Algebra

The Algebra based on binary logic, that is number system with a base of two, (as against the usual decimal number system based on the base of ten), is named after George Boole, who explored the possibilities, as the Boolean Algebra. It was found that for efficient computer operations the best logic/number system is Ternary or Binary logic-that is a number system based on either a base of three or a base of two, and not the usual system of base of ten! When it came to using switches, Electro-mechanical or Electronic, the normal "ON"/"OFF" conditions represented a two state condition—a binary and hence the binary logic was found to be most convenient and efficient for computer design; manufacture and operations.

What is binary logic? In the *"decimal system"* the individual digits of a number has a value dependent on its position in the number. Thus, the right-most digit has a value of units (the digit value multiplied by 10 raised to the power zero). The digit next to it on its left a value of tens (the digit value multiplied by 10 raised to the power 1). The one next to it has a value of hundreds (the digit value multiplied by 10 raised to the power 2), and so on to the n-th position where the digit represents a value equal to the value of the digit multiplied by 10 raised to the power (n -1). Thus, a number say 573 stands for 5.10 squared +7.10 + 3.1; since 10 raised to 1 is 10 and 10 raised to the power 0 is 1. That is the number is 5 hundreds + 7 tens + three units or 573. In the binary system each position has a value of two raised to the power of 0, 1, 2, ---- n; instead of 10 raised to those powers for the relevant position/place. And each position can have only 0 or 1, called as Binary Digits or "bits" for short, as against the decimal 0, 1, 2, ---- 9, called as "digits". Thus, a binary number say 11010 stands for 1.2 raised to power 4 + 1. 2 raised to power 3 + 0. 2 raised to power of 2 +1. 2 raised to the power off 1 + 0. 2 raised to the power 0. Thus the value of the number in decimal system works out to 16 + 8 + 0 + 2 + 0 or 26. Note that in digital systems and computers a stream of eight, (8), (binary) bits is referred to as a "Byte".

This two-bit, (0 or 1), binary system works out into some strange logical combinations/operations. Thus, when you add two numbers, each 0, you will of course get the result as 0 too, but when you add 1 and 1 the result is 1 with a carry of 1 to the next higher position in the binary number system. Basic Boolean (Algebra) Relationships, symbols associated with some basic binary logical operations in the Boolean Algebra which one should be familiar with are indicated below:

Boolean Relationships/	**Symbols**	**Associated Binary Operations**	**Thus**
A.B = B.A	.	"AND"	1.1 = 1; 0.0 = 0
			1.0=0.1=0
A + B = B + A	+	OR	1 + 1 = 1; 0 + 0 = 0
			1 + 0 = 0 + 1 = 1
$A.\overline{A} = 0$	-	"NOT"/"NEGATION"/	
$A + \overline{A} = 1$			
A + 0 = A; A + 1 = 1; A + A = A			
A.0 = 0; A.1 = A; A.A = A			
(A.B).C = A.(B.C) = A.B.C		Associative	
(A + B) + C = A + (B + C) = A + B + C		Law	
A.B + A.C = A.(B + C)			
A + B.C = (A + B).(A + C)			
$\overline{A.B.C} = \overline{A} + \overline{B} + \overline{C}$		De Morgan's	
$\overline{A + B + C} = \overline{A.B.C}$		Theorem	
	+	"EXCLUSIVE OR "NOT EQUIVALENT"	1 + 0 = 1; 0 + 1 = 1 0 + 0 = 0 & 1 + 1 = 0

A Negation operation on "AND" is called "NOT AND" or "NAND". And a Negation operation on "OR" is known as "NOR". These are popular operations along with "EXCLUSIVE OR"/ "XOR".

The wonderful thing is that all the Boolean expressions can be easily designed into compact integrated circuits and cheaply manufactured into millions in very short time. So, design and manufacture of computers becomes a "no big deal". The result is for all to see inexpensive digital diaries, compact *"Personal*

Digital Assistants" or PDA's use by all and sundry, and the PC or the Personal Computer used all over the world in quite hundred's of millions! One may ask what has all the above Boolean Algebra, binary system of numbers etc., got to do with Cryptology or the DES?

Much before the idea of computers and the binary system came into vogue, a sort of digital communication had already got established with the invention of the "Morse Code" for telegraph transmission. In this method each alphabet and number (alphanumeric character), is represented by a group of combination of short transmission duration referred to as a "Dot", and a longer duration, (about at least three times longer), of transmission called a "Dash". The dots and dashes forming a character are interspersed with pauses when there is no transmission, with duration of about three dots. There is a pause with no transmission between characters, of about five times the duration of a dot. There is no precise time interval laid for these dots, dashes and pauses. This *"Morse Code"* was extensively used till recently when it went into oblivion (though may still be used in experimental/amateur transmissions). Then came the truly binary, more efficient digital communication code called the "Baudot Code" in which each character was represented by a suitable combination of five (5) bits-that is pulses, or "ON" and "OFF" transmission conditions. Then came the Teleprinter communication, using the *"Baudot Code"* and later the formation of the *"Teletype Code"* for Teletype transmissions. Somewhat later arose digital/computer & communication techniques using 7 or 8 bit codes like the ASCII or the *"American Standard Code"* for Information Interchange. In this code each character (letters of an alphabet, numbers, punctuation marks etc.). is represented by a 7-bit or an 8-bit, (or Byte), binary "Character". So any piece of writing, passages, messages or communication could be converted into these digital binary representations for efficient coding and transmission. So, cryptology too came to depend on these digital techniques using ASCII or similar codes and Boolean Algebra to do its stuff! Thus, the DES also depends on conversion of the alphabets/characters of a message into binary bits on which relevant transformations of substitution etc. are carried out. Thus, any information is first converted to a stream of binary bits/(bytes). Suitable cipher operations are carried out on this stream of bits, with a specific key that modifies the stream of bits into a totally different stream of bits, which is, then transmitted to the recipient. The recipient, knowing the cipher system and the key used carries out a reverse operation process on the received stream of bits to get the original stream of message bits that he then reconverts into the plaintext.

The DES uses a 56-bits long Key. But with use of a parity bit with every 7 bits of the Key, the actual length of the key becomes 64 bits or 8 Bytes. Therefore, the plaintext is first divided into blocks of 64 bits in length. Each of these blocks is encrypted separately. Hence, the designation of block encryption to this system. The system of transformation using the Key is quite complex, with splitting of each block into two halves the right and the left-each treated in a different way, use of permutations, "XOR"-ing, a number of cycles of switching around and so on to get the ciphertext. Space does not permit going into the full details of the DES process. Those interested in understanding how the DES works should refer to the large number of books/ articles in journals available that detail the process.

The *"decryption process"* is the reverse with the same Key as is used for the *"encryption"*, as it is a symmetric cipher system. The *encryption* and *decryption* rates can be very high with the DES-say around 200 Megabits/sec with a PC having a clock speed of about 200 MHz! Perhaps a possible drawback of he system is that transmission errors in noisy communication channels could result in completely corrupted output-that is you will not be able to get the *"plaintext"* for the *"ciphertext"*, unless suitable error correction codes are used in the transmission system. This is because the method used is intentionally designed for good error propagation! Thus, one bit of received error in the ciphertext results in the following bits of the block getting adversely affected during the decryption process.

About a decade ago, when computer speeds were low and sizes were considerable one could not dream of breaking a ciphertext encrypted with the DES, by the simple means of trying out all the possible keys—that is the *"Brute Force Method"*. Recent reports suggest that with the high-speed efficient hardware available now, and use of distributed processing etc. The DES is no longer secure and can be cryptanalysed in fairly short period of say days. However, there are some more efficient methods of attacking the DES, which are expected to permit breaking of a DES encrypted ciphertext in a much faster time. But, ofcourse, this would be quite an expensive task and may not be worth the while for normal commercial communications using the DES. But it could be risky to consider the system for highly sensitive communications like Top Secret ones. If, however, one goes in for a much larger Key-length of say 128 bits or more, and some modifications in the process, then the system would remain quite secure for considerable time to come-not forever ofcourse, like the OTP.

As in any other cryptosystem, in the DES too the same Key should NOT be used for encryption of more than a single message. Otherwise, it would be possible for a cryptanalyst to break the cipher using what is known as a known *"plaintext attack"*.

Public Key-Cryptosystem

So far what we have seen about ciphers is that the Key used for decryption has to be same as that used for encryption, i.e., they belong to what are known as "Symmetric Ciphers". Now, as we have noted, the same Key cannot be used to cipher even just two messages. Single key means a single message only has to be encrypted, for security. So, the problems arise of secure exchange of a large number of Keys between the sender and recipient of cipher messages. (Note that this is apart from the need for a cipher system to have enormous "Key-space" to prevent "Brute Force" attack by a cryptanalyst to break the cipher). Obviously, if one could have a cipher system where you do not have to exchange Keys at all, the sender uses his own Key and the recipient uses his own, to solve the Key-exchange problems it would be wonderful. Since different Keys would then be required for encryption and decryption, such systems are known as "Asymmetric Ciphers". Rivest, Shamir and Adleman together invented for the first time exactly such a system which became popular and has come to be known as the *"RSA Public Key Cryptosystem"*. The system used what are known as one way mathematical functions or Trap-door functions. (Earlier to the RSA some mathematical functions called as Knapsack types were tried out for Public Key type of ciphers. But they were found wanting in regard to security of the systems against attacks).

The idea of a *"Public-Key Cryptosystem"* is for one to have their own separate encryption and decryption Keys. The encryption Key will be in the public domain, like the telephone number of a person being openly available to one and all, in the telephone directory. The Keys should be easy to generate. But, the reverse should be unfeasible. That is, it should NOT be feasible to arrive at the decryption Key from the encryption Key. However, it would be advantages to get easily the encryption Key form the decryption Key, to be able to generate new pairs of Keys easily/conveniently. Since the encryption Key is made public, it is called the Public-Key; and as the decryption Key is kept secret to oneself, it is known as the Private-Key. Note that Diffie, Hellman and Merkle publicized this concept in 1976. Suppose "A" desires to send a secret message to "B", "A" looks up the Public-Key of "B" in a sort off directory similar to the telephone directory, say. None can decrypt this message, (not even "A")—except "B" himself, using his Private-Key. Similarly, others too can send secret messages to "B" by using his Public-Key. If now "B" wants to reply to "A" he will encrypt his message using the Public-Key of "A"! This system, thus, avoids the need for secure exchange of the all-important secret cipher Keys. All that is required is for one to generate his own pair of Keys, (separate, but mutually related, encryption and decryption Keys), and publicize his encryption Key to all concerned, openly without hesitation or any secrecy! Hence, the entire herculean problem of secure Key-exchange is totally avoided/eliminated.

The RSA system is based on the function that it is easy to multiply two large numbers, but it is extremely hard to find the two factors of a product of two very large prime numbers. You take two large prime numbers say "p" and "q". Let "n" be equal to p*q, the product of p and q. Get the product (p -1)*(q -1). Now find a number "e" that is relatively prime to the number (p -1)*(q -1). Then the encryption Key is the pair of numbers n & e. Obviously, everyone must have a different number "n"; but "e" could be a common part of his or her encryption Key, that is to say, that "e" could be a part of everyone's Public Key. Also, each one must keep his or her pair of numbers p and q a SECRET.

So, what do you do to encrypt a message with this RSA system? Here, the binary system, and the ASCII character system, we talked about comes into play. First of all, you have to break down the message into smaller blocks of size "b", which must be kept smaller than, (say by one bit), the bit-length of the number "n" that you have chosen. Obviously, you have to convert the ASCII characters of the message into the binary equivalent binary digits (bits/bytes), to get the message (block) as, say the decimal number "m". Now, to get the ciphertext "C" of this message you carry out what is called a modulo operation.

$C^e = m \pmod{n}$, where n and e are the encryption Key-pair, and m is the message (number)

Now what is this mod business? It is nothing very complicated, as an example will show. Let as for simplicity assume p and q to be the small prime numbers 11 and 13. Then n = 143. Let us take 7 as "e" relatively prime to (p -1)*(q -1), that is 120. Assume that the message converted to decimal number is say 67, that is m = 67.

Thus, the ciphertext C becomes:

$C = 67^7 \pmod{143}$. In this case, (mod 143) means you divide the number 67^7 raised to the power 7, by 143 and find out what is the remainder. That remainder is the result of the operation, in this case the ciphertext C!

You can find out the 7th exponential of 67 more easily by first breaking down the 7 into its constituents 4 + 3+ 1, or even 2 + 2 + 3 + 1 and find the square and cube of the number 67 and multiply these to get the products. Thus, we get 67 squared as 4489; and 67 cubed as 300763 and 67*1 is 67 itself. Thus

C = (67 squared (mod 143)) * (67 squared (mod 143)) * (67 cubed (mod 143)) * (67 (mod 143)).

= 4489 (mod 143) * 4489 (mod 143) *300763 (mod 143) * 67 (mod 143), in this case becomes,

C = 56 (mod 143) * 56 (mod 143) * 34 (mod 143) * 67 (mod 143), that is

C = 56*56*34*67 (mod 143) = 100 (mod 143).

So, in this case the *ciphertext* "C" is 100. So, the sender sends the number 100 as his ciphertext. Obviously, unless you have the decryption Key you cannot unscramble this to get the original message "m"! Knowing "n", in this case the number 143 does not help in finding "m", in this case 67, from the ciphertext (number) 100.

Now, the question is how to get the decryption Key "d"? You know "e", "p" and "q", having started with them to get the encryption Key-pair of numbers n and e. You compute "d" from the equation:

d*e = 1 (mod (p-1)*(q-1)) = 1 (mod (11 -1)*(13 -1)) = 1 (mod (10*12) = 1 (mod 120)

Thus, 7 * d = 1 (mod 120). One has to take resort to a technique called *"Euclid's algorithm"* to calculate "d".

To get the original message "m" from the ciphertext C you use the relation ship:

m = C^d (mod 143), as n = 143 in this case. Note that even when "n" is known unless "p" and "q" are known to compute (p -1)*(q -1), one cannot find the decryption Key-"d".

(Note that you get the encryption Key easily from the decryption Key as the "n" and "e" pair has been chosen by you. But you cannot get the decryption Key "d" from the publicized encryption Key, unless you know the factors "p" & "q").

From the above, it is obvious that RSA is also a block encryption system, with block size close to the bit length of "n".

The system can be implemented by software so it is easy to put into practice with the ordinary personal computer or PC. Note that the size of the Key is not fixed but is dependent on the number "n" that you chose. For convenience and for "n" to be large enough, one may fix the size of "n" to be say 512 / 1024 etc. bits, that is a large enough power of 2, in the binary system.

Has this marvellous cipher system any drawbacks? Unfortunately, the answer is yes. What is of immediate concern is that a reasonably good software encryption process has quite a slow encryption rate of only few kilobits/sec., (kbps). Same thing is true of decryption rate too. So, the encryption and decryption processes are time consuming. Hence, the RSA is totally unsuitable for bulk data transfers (using this cipher). But it is advantageous to combine the high security and simplicity of the RSA and the fast encryption decryption rates possible with other systems like the DES. The RSA is used for Key exchange purposes only (of the DES), and then that particular DES Key is used for the actual transmission of lengthy messages. (Obviously for short messages the time taken for the cipher processes for the messages may well be shorter than the time required to exchange the DES Keys, so it may be simpler to directly use the RSA ciphering of such short messages!).

More serious drawback is what is expected in the future. Suitable shortcuts may be found to factorize the "n" to get the factors "p" and "q" very quickly. Or super speed computers like "Quantum Computers" may be built that are fast enough to factorize "n" in "real-time". Then the RSA system would become totally insecure!

Due to lack of space, we will not go into the areas of "Digital Signatures", "Authentication" etc. that the Public Key Cryptosystems are eminently suitable for deployment.

Pretty Good Privacy, (PGP)

The extensive worldwide spread of the Internet communications and the e-mail exchange etc., in the recent times has highlighted the pressing need for ensuring privacy of such personal/

commercial communications. Naturally, such privacy systems must be easy to implement with a PC that one normally uses, and provide sufficient security too. Phil Zimmermann believed that everybody deserved to have the privacy offered by the RSA type of cipher for his or her private communications. Working from his home he formulated in the 1980's a combination of the asymmetric RSA, working in tandem with the older symmetric system of ciphering, the PGP. He introduced unique feature in the PGP that helped easy generation of pair of private and public Key that is required and in a random way with a wiggle of his/her PC so that each user has his/her individual pair of the required encryption /decryption Keys. This also had the advantage of verification of the authorship of the mails received.

In 1991, Zimmermann published for free, on the Internet, this PGP to be public property with no patent problems, Intellectual Property Rights or IPR! This invited the official wrath on him for so called *"security breach"*, as the PGP enabled anyone to communicate securely perhaps, without the NSA being able to decode it! (It is understood that the MIT press published a bulky volume on the PGP!).

Cryptanalysis

Cryptanalysis involves intensive use of Intelligence gathering activities (to obtain information on the cryptosystem system used by the opposition and the Keys used in the cipher messages to be cryptanalysed), mathematics, linguistics, statistics etc., apart form a healthy dose of intuition and hunches. Without doubt, cryptanalysis is a combination of Science and Arts! The techniques and methods of cryptanalytic attacks are so varied and complex that it is difficult to even give an introduction to it here. If would also require a highly dedicated study to even cross the fringes of this field. But interesting books are available that give an idea of the efforts involved in cryptanalysis, such as the "Ultra", "The Enigma" and so on, covering cryptanaytical efforts by the Allies during the World War II, in Codebreaking.

"Cryptanalysis" is a highly specialized task. The basic tools available to a cryptanalyst are linguistics, statistics, probability

theory, linear algebra, group theory, information theory, intelligence activities to get at-systems/Keys used, side information etc. Anyone interested in *"cryptanalysis"* will hence need to carry out an extensive and deep study of available literature on the subject and see whether he or she has the penchant for it. Some ground rules have been indicated by Kerckhoffs in his book on military cryptography, as far back as the 19th century! Aptly they are known as Kerckhoffs' rules/criteria, for good Crypto-systems.

1. The system should be unbreakable, (theoretically as well as practically).
2. Method of choosing a particular Key of the cryptographic system should be easy to remember.
3. Cipher text should be transmittable by Telegraph.
4. Any compromise of the system should not inconvenience the correspondents.
5. The equipment must be portable.
6. The system should not require a long list of rules or mental strain.

Kerckhoffs criteria (for Cryptanalysis) state:

- Cryptographic systems that have a finite Key-space may always be cryptanalysed by Key trials-testing of all Keys until a Plaintext occurs. (Ofcourse such a system could still be practically, unbreakable if the time required with available computational capabilities for an exhaustive Key trials is impractical. Obviously, this is a technology driven cryptanaytical limitation).
- Any cipher system has two-information components—one that is public and the other that has to remain private or secret. The public aspects are the cipher rules/algorithms, hardware specifications, service manuals and so on. Even the software information cannot indefinitely remain secret. In the private domain are the Key-space and parameters, which select one/several of many transformations possible.

In this connection, compromise of system means knowledge of the public information. Hence, security achieved in the substitution systems is the lack of knowledge as to which specific transformation has been used-the private information!

- The need for a short memorizable Key remains an important design consideration—the human factor—hence a chink in the armour!
- In the 19th century, the text may be represented in a form suitable for transmission and recording. This criterion is no longer relevant, as with suitable *"steganographic"* methods you should be able to hide the very presence of a message.
- Since the user has to bear the cost of the equipment, it is very important to see that the selected cryptographic system does meet the cipher objectives.
- The opposition may usefully exploit side information/ Auxiliary information provided in the ciphertext. Hence, the need for ciphertext to look as random a series of characters as possible.
- Effectiveness of cryptographic systems does depend on whether:

1. Only ciphertext is available to the opposition.
2. Both ciphertext and the corresponding plaintext become accessible to the opposition.
3. The opposition is able to get at the ciphertext of a chosen plaintext!

So, watch out for carelessly discarded plaintext, the context of the information being transmitted (as ciphertext ofcourse), as side information, etc. (Obviously, when one has adequate supply of ciphertext and the corresponding plaintext, Key recovery becomes easy). *"Cryptanalysis"* is not for the weak. It needs knowledge, dedication, meticulousness, grit and the "sixth sense", a combination that very few persons can be expected to possess.

Appendix D

Some useful Reference Information

1. World Times

Country/city		Time Difference (hrs)	Time when 1200 Hrs. Ist (India)
India, New Delhi		0000	1200 (Noon)
	Mumbai		
	Chennai		
	Kolkata		
	Bangalore		
	Hyderabad		
Nepal, Kathmandu			
Sri Lanka, Colombo			
U.K. London; (GMT)		-5.5	06–30
Algeria, Algiers			
Gambia, Banjul			
Ireland, Dublin			
Morocco, Rabat			
Portugal, Lisbon			
Senegal, Dakar			
Austria, Vienna		-4.5	07–30
Angola, Luanda			
Belgium, Brussels			
Cameroon, Yaounde			
Congo, Brazzaville			
Czech Republic, Prague			
Denmark, Copenhagen			
France, Paris			
Gabon, Libreville			

Country/city	Time Difference (hrs)	Time when 1200 Hrs. Ist (India)
Germany, Berlin		
Bonn		
Frankfurt		
Holland, Amsterdam		
Hungry, Budapest		
Italy, Rome		
Milan		
Nigeria, Lagos, Abuja		
Norway, Oslo		
Poland, Warsaw		
Romania, Burcharest		
Spain, Madrid		
Sweden, Stockholm		
Switzerland, Geneva		
Zurich		
Bulgaria, Sofia	-3.5	08–30
Cyprus, Nicosia		
Egypt, Cairo		
Finland, Helsinki		
Greece, Athens		
Israel, Jerusalem, Tel Aviv		
Jordan, Amman		
Lebanon, Beirut		
Libya, Tripoli		
Malawi, Blantyre		
South Africa, Johnnesesburg		
Pretoria, Cape Town		
Sudan, Khartown		
Syria, Damascus		
Turkey, Ankara		
Zambia, Lusaka		
Zimbabwe, Harare		
Ethiopia, Addis Ababa	-2.5	930
Iraq, Baghdad		0
Kenya, Nairobi		
Kuwait		
Russia, Moscow		
Saudi Arabia, Riyadh, Jeddah		
Tanzania, Dar-Es-Salaam		
Qatar, Doha		
Uganda, Entebbe		

Country/City	Time Difference (hrs)	Time when 1200 Hrs. 1st (India)
Iran, Teheran	-2.0	1000
U.A.E., Abu Dhabi, Dubai	-1.5	1030
Bahrain		
Mauritius		
Oman, Muscat		
Seychelles		
Afganistan, Kabul	-1.0	1100
Pakistan, Islamabad	-0.5	1130
Karachi		
Bangladesh, Dhaka	+0.5	1230
Myanmar (Burma), Yangon	+1.0	1300
Thailand, Bangkok	**+1.5**	**1330**
Indonesia, Jakarta	+2.0	1400
Malaysia, Kuala Lumpur		
Singapore		
Brunei, Bandar Seri Begawan	+2.5	1430
China, Beijing		
Shanghai,		
Guangzhou,		
Hong Kong		
Australia, Perth		
Philippines, Manila		
Taiwan		
South korea, Seoul	+3.0	1500
Japan, Tokyo	+3.5	1530
Australia, Canberra	+4.5	1700
Brisbane		
Melbourne		
Sydney		
Papua New Guinea		
Fiji, Suva	+6.5	1830
New Zealand, Auckland		
Wellington		

Country/City	Time Difference (hrs)	Time when 1200 Hrs. 1st (India)
Honolulu	+8.5	2030
Canada, Vancouver	+1030 (-1330)	2230
U.S.A. Los Angeles	(Pacific Time)	
San Francisco,		
Seattle		
U.S.A. Chicago	+12.5 (-11.5)	0030 (Previous Day)
Houston		
Winnipeg		
Mexico, Mexico City		
Canada, Montreal	-10.5	0130 AM.
Ottawa		
Toronto		
Panama, Panama City		
The Bahamas— (U.S.A) Nassau		
Freeport		
Colombia, Bagota		
Peru, Lima		
U.S.A., Washington, Boston,	**(Eastern Time)**	
New York, Philadelphia		
Cuba, Havana		
Argentina, Buenos Aires	-8.5	0330
(Caracas	-10.0	0200)
Brazil, Rio-de-Janeiro		
Urugury, Montevideo		
Chile, Santiago	-9.5	0230

(Note that the U.S.A. has four time zones, viz., Eastern, Central Midwestern and Pacific Times; and the clock is advanced by one hour during summer—Summer Time.)

Thus, the coastal California time is three hours behind New York time. So the Los Angeles and San Francisco cities will have local time of 1030 PM (the previous evening), when it is noon in India, (and the summer time will be 1130 PM local time, there).

2. Countries of the World (some general information)

Country	Capital	Continent	Population (millions)	ISD Country (code)	Language	Religion (primary)
Afghanistan	Kabul	**Asia**	22+	+93	Pushtu	Islam
Albania	Tirana	**Europe**	3+	+355	Albanian	Islam
Algeria	Algiers	**Africa**	30+	+213	Arabic	Islam
Andorra	Andorra-la-Vella	**Europe**	<1	+376	Catalan	Christianity
Angola	Luanda	**Africa**	13+	+244	Portuguese	
Antigua & Barbuda	St. John's	**C. America**	<1	+1-268	English	Christianity
Argentina	Buenos Aires	**S. America**	37+	+54	Spanish	Christianity
Armenia	Yerevan	**Europe**	8+	+374	German	Christianity
Australia	Canberra	**Australia**	19+	+61	English	Christianity
Austria	Vienna	**Europe**	8+	+43	German	Christianity
Azerbaijan	Baku	**Europe**	8+	+994	Azeri	Islam
The Bahamas	Nassau	**C. America**	<1	+1242	English	Christianity
Bahrain	Manama	**Asia**	<1	+973	Arabic	Islam
Bangladesh	Dhaka	**Asia**	140+	+880	Bangla	Islam
Barbados	Bridgetown	**C. America**	<1	+1246	English	Christianity
Belarus	Minsk	**Europe**	10+	+375	Belarussian	Christianity
Belguim	Brussels	**Europe**	30+	+32	Flemish	Christianity
Belize	Belmopan	**C. America**	<1	+501	English	Christianity
Benin	Porto Nova	**Africa**	6+	+229	French	
Bhutan	Thimphu	**Asia**	2+	+975	Dzongkha	Buddhism
Bolivia	La Paz	**S. America**	8+	+591	Spanish	Christianity
Bosnia Herzegovina	Sarajevo	**Europe**	4+	+387	Serbo-Croat	Islam, Christianity

Country	Capital	Continent	Population (millions)	ISD Country (code)	Language	Religion (primary)
Botswana	Gaborone	**Africa**	1+	+267	English	Christianity
Brazil	Brasilia	**S. America**	170+	+55	Portuguese	Christianity
Brunei	Bandar Seri Begawan	**Asia**	<1	+673	Malay	Islam
Bulgaria	Sofia	**Europe**	7+	+359	Bulgarian	Christianity, Islam
Burkina Faso	Ouagad ougou	**Africa**	11+	+226	French	
Burundi	Bujumbura	**Africa**	6+	+257	Kirundi, French	Christianity
Cambodia	Phnom Penh	**Asia**	13+	+855	Khmer	Buddhism
Cameroon	Younde	**Africa**	15+	+237	French, English	
Canada	Ottawa	**N. America**	30+	001	French, English	Christianity
Central African Republic	Bangui	**Africa**	3+	+236	French	Christianity
Chad	N'djamena	**Africa**	8+	+235	Arabic, French	Islam
Chile	Santiago	**S. America**	15+	+56	Spanish	Christianity
China	Beijing	**Asia**	1.200+	+86	Chinese	
Colombia	Bogota	**S. America**	35+	+57	Spanish	Christianity
Republic of Congo	Brazzaville	**Africa**	3+	+242	French	Christianity
Costa Rica	San Jose	**C. America**	4+	+506	Spanish	Christianity
Cote D'Ivore (Ivory Coast)	Yamoussoukro	**Africa**	16+	+225	French	
Croatia	Zagreb	**Europe**	4+	+385	Serbo-Croat	Christianity
Cuba	Havana	**C. America**	11+	+53	Spanish	
Cyprus	Nicosia	**Europe**	<1	+357	Greek, Turkish	Christianity
Czech Republic	Prague	**Europe**	10+	+420	Czech	Christianity
Denmark	Copenhagen	**Europe**	5+	+45	Danish	Christianity
Dominican Republic	Santa Domingo	**C. America**	8+	+809	Spanish	Christianity

Country	Capital	Continent	Population (millions)	ISD Country (code)	Language	Religion (primary)
Ecuador	Quito	**S. America**	12+	+593	Spanish	Christianity
Egypt	Cairo	**Africa**	70	+20	Arabic	Islam
El Salvador	San Salvador	**C. America**	6+	+503	Spanish	Christianity
Eritrea	Asmara	**Africa**	3+	+291	Tigrinya	Christianity
Estonia	Tallinn	**Europe**	1+	+372	Estonian	Christianity
Ethiopia	Addis Ababa	**Africa**	64+	+251	Amharic	Islam
Fiji	Suva	**Australia-Oceania**	<1	+679	English, Fijian	Christianity, Hinduism
Finland	Helsinki	**Europe**	5+	+358	Finnish, Swedish	Christianity
France	Paris	**Europe**	60	+33	French	Christianity
Gabon	Libreville	**Africa**	1+	+241	French	Christianity
Gambia	Banjul	**Africa**	1+	+220	English	Islam
Georgia	Tbilisi	**Europe**	5+	+995	Georgian	Christianity
Germany	Berlin	**Europe**	80+	+49	German	Christianity
Ghana	Accra	**Africa**	19+	+233	English	
Greece	Athens	**Europe**	10+	+30	Greek	Christianity
Guatemala	Guatemala	**C. America**	11+	+502	Spanish	Christianity
Guinea	Conakry	**Africa**	8+	+224	French	Islam
Guinea-Bissau	Bissau	**Africa**	1+	+245	Portuguese	
Guyana	Georgetown	**S. America**	<1	+592	English	Christianity, Hinduism
Haiti	Port-au-Prince	**C. America**	8+	+509	Haitian. Creole, French	Christianity
Honduras	Tegucigalpa	**C. America**	6+	+504	Spanish	Christianity
Hungary	Budapest	**Europe**	10	+36	Magyar	Christianity
Iceland	Reykjavik	**Europe**	<1	+354	Icelandic	Christianity

Country	Capital	Continent	Population (millions)	ISD Country (code)	Language	Religion (primary)
India	New Delhi	**Asia**	1,000+	+91	Hindi, many regional Languages, English, Hundreds of dialects	Hinduism, Islam, Sikhism, Christianity Buddhism, Jainism, Zoroastrian & Tribal Beliefs.
Indonesia	Jakarta	**Asia**	200+	+62	Bahasa Indonesia	Islam
Iran	Tehran	**Asia**	70+	+98	Farsi, Kurdish	Islam
Iraq	Baghdad	**Asia**	24	+964	Arabic	Islam
Ireland	Dublin	**Europe**	4	+353	Irish, English	Christianity
Isreal	Tel Aviv	**Asia**	6+	+972	Hebrew	Jewish
Italy	Rome	**Europe**	60	+39	Italian	Christianity
Jamaica	Kingston	**C. America**	3	+1876	English	Christianity
Japan	Tokyo	**Asia**	125+	+81	Japanese	Shintoism, Buddhism
Jordan	Amman	**Asia**	5+	+962	Arabic	Islam
Kazakhstan	Alma-Alta	**Asia**	16+	007	Kazakh	Islam
Kenya	Nairobi	**Africa**	30+	+254	Swahili, Eng.	Christianity
Korea (North)	Pyongyang	**Asia**	22+	+850	Korean	
Korea (South)	Seoul	**Asia**	47+	+82	Korean	
Kuwait	Kuwait City	**Asia**	2	+965	Arabic	Islam
Kyrgyzstan	Bishkek	**Asia**	5	+996	Kirghizian	Islam
Laos	Vientiane	**Asia**	5+	+856	Lao	Buddhism
Latvia	Riga	**Europe**	2+	+371	Latvian	Christianity
Lebanon	Beirut	**Asia**	3+	+961	Arabic	Islam
Lesotho	Maseru	**Africa**	2+	+266	Seotho, Eng.	Christianity
Liberia	Monrovia	**Africa**	3	+231	English	
Libya	Tripoli	**Africa**	5+	+218	Arabic	Islam

Country	Capital	Continent	Population	ISD Country (millions)	Language (code)	Religion (primary)
Liechtenstein	Vaduz	**Europe**	<<1	+41	German	Christianity
Lithuania	Vilnius	**Europe**	3+	+370	Lithuanian	Christianity
Luxembourg	Luxembourg	**Europe**	<1	+352	French, German	Christianity
Macedonia	Skopje	**Europe**	2	+389	The Denar	Christianity
Madagascar	Antananarivo	**Africa**	16+	+261	Malagasy, French	Christianity
Malawi	Lilongwe	**Africa**	11+	+265	English	Christianity
Malaysia	Kuala Lumpur	**Asia**	22	+60	Malay	islam
Maldives	Male	**Asia**	<1	+960	Divehi	Islam
Mali	Bamako	**Africa**	11+	+223	French	Islam
Malta	Valletta	**Europe**	<1	+356	Maltese Eng.	Islam
Mauritania	Nauakchott	**Africa**	2+	+222	Arabic	Islam
Mauritius	Port Louis	**Africa**	1+	+230	English	Hinduism
Mexico	Mexico	**N.America**	100+	+52	Mexican/Span	Christianity
Moldova	Kishinev	**Europe**	4+	+373	Romanian	Christianity
Monaco	Monaco	**Europe**	<<1	+377	French	Christianity
Mongolia	Ulan Bator	**Asia**	2+	+976	Mongolian	
Morocco	Rabat	**Africa**	30+	+212	Arabic	Islam
Mozambique	Maputo	**Africa**	18+	+258	Portuguese	
Myanmar	Yangon	**Asia**	50	+95	Burmese	Buddhism
Namibia	Windhoek	**Africa**	2	+264	Eng. Afrikaans	Christianity
Nepal	Kathmandu	**Asia**	24	+977	Nepali	Hinduisim
Netherlands	Amsterdam	**Europe**	16	+31	Dutch	Christianity
New Zealand	New Zealand	**Australia**	4	+64	English	Christianity
Nicaragua	Managua	**C. America**	5+	+505	Spanish	Christianity
Niger	Niamey	**Africa**	11+	+227	French	Islam
Nigeria	Abuja	**Africa**	115+	+234	English	Islam

Country	Capital	Continent	Population (millions)	ISD Country (code)	Language	Religion (primary)
Norway	Oslo	**Europe**	5	+47	Norwegian	Christianity
Oman	Muscat	**Asia**	2+	+968	Arabic, Eng.	Islam
Pakistan	Islamabad	**Asia**	140+	+92	Urdu, Eng.	Islam
Panama	Panama City	**C. America**	2+	+507	Spanish	Christianity
Papua New Guinea	Port Moresby	**Oceania**	5	+675	English	Christianity
Paraguay	Asuncion	**S. America**	5+	+595	Spanish	Christianity
Peru	Lima	**S. America**	25+	+51	Spanish	Christianity
Philippines	Manila	**Asia**	75+	+63	Filipino	Christianity
Poland	Warsaw	**Europe**	40	+48	Polish	Christianity
Portugal	Lisbon	**Europe**	10+	+351	Portuguese	Christianity
Qatar	Doha	**Asia**	<1	+974	Arabic, Eng.	Islam
Romania	Bucharest	**Europe**	22+	+40	Romanian	Christianity
Russia	Moscow	**Europe**	140+	+7	Russian	Christianity
Rwanda	Kigali	**Africa**	8	+250	Kinyarwanda	Christianity
San Marino	San Marino	**Europe**	<<1	+378	Italian	Christianity
Saudi Arabia	Riyadh	**Asia**	20+	+966	Arabic	Islam
Senegal	Dakar	**Africa**	9+	+221	French	Islam
Seychelles	Victoria	**Africa**	<<1	+248	Eng. Fr. Creole	Christianity
Sierra Leone	Freetown	**Africa**	4+	+232	English	Islam
Singapore	Singapore	**Asia**	4+	+65	Malay, Chinese	Buddhisim
Slovak Republic	Bratislava	**Europe**	5+	+42	Solvak, Magyar	Christianity
Sloveina	Ljubljana	**Europe**	2	+386	Solvenian	Christianity
Somalia	Mogadishu	**Africa**	9+	+252	Somali	Islam
South Africa	Pretoria	**Africa**	44	+27	Afrikaans	Christianity

Country	Capital	Continent	Population (millions)	ISD Country (code)	Language	Religion (primary)
Spain	Madrid	**Europe**	40	+34	Spanish	Christianity
Sri Lanka	Colombo	**Asia**	19+	+94	Sinhalese, Tamil	Buddhism, Hinduism, Islam
Sudan	Khartoum	**Africa**	30+	+249	Arabic	Islam
Suriname	Paramaribo	**S. America**	<1	+597	Dutch	Hinduism, Christianity
Swaziland	Mbabane	**Africa**	<1	+268	Swazi, English	Christianity
Sweden	Stockholm	**Europe**	8+	+46	Swedish	Christianity
Switzerland	Berne	**Europe**	7+	+41	French, German, Italian	Christianity
Syria	Damascus	**Asia**	16+	+963	Arabic	Islam
Taiwan	Taipei	**Asia**	22+	+886	Chinese	
Tajikistan	Dushanbe	**Asia**	6+	+7	Tazhik	Islam
Tanzania	Dodoma	**Africa**	36	+255	Swahili, Eng.	Christianity;
Thailand	Bangkok	**Asia**	64+	+66	Thai	Buddhisim
Togo	Lome	**Africa**	4+	+228	Arabic	Islam
Tonga	Naku'alofa	**Oceania**	<1	+676	English	Christianity
Trinidad and Tobago	Port of Spain	**C.America**	1+	+866	English	Christianity
Tunisia	Tunis	**Africa**	9+	+216	Arabic	Islam
Turkey	Ankara	**Asia**	65+	+90	Turkish	Islam
Turkmenistan	Ashkhabad	**Asia**	4+	+993	Turkmenian	Islam
Uganda	Kampala	**Africa**	24	+256	Swahili, Eng.	Christianity
Ukarine	Kiev	**Europe**	49+	+380	Ukrainian	Christianity
U.A.E.	Abu Dhabi	**Asia**	2+	+971	Arabic	Islam

Country	Capital	Continent	Population	ISD Country (millions)	Language (code)	Religion (primary)
United Kingdom	London	**Europe**	60	+44	English	Christianity
U.S.A.	Washington DC	**N. America**	280+	+1	English	Christianity
Uruguacy	Montevideo	**S. America**	3+	+598	Spanish	Christianity
Uzbekistan	Tashkent	**Asia**	25+	+7	Uzbek	Islam
Vatican City	Vatican City	**Europe**	<<1	+39	Latin, Italian	Christianity
Venezuela	Caracas	**S. America**	25	+58	Spanish	Christianity
Vietnam	Hanoi	**Asia**	80	+84	Vietnamese	Buddhism
Yemen	Sana	**Asia**	19+	+967	Arabic	Islam
Yogoslavia	Belgrade	**Europe**	11	+381	Serbo-Croat	Christianity
Zaire	Kinshasa	**Africa**	50+	+243	French	Christianity
Zambia	Lusaka	**Africa**	9+	+260	English	Christianity
Zimbabwe	Harare	**Africa**	13	+263	English	

Note:

1. Population figures are approximate and are in millions.
2. The + sign before the ISD code indicates that two zeros, the international access code precede the code digits, (Country Code, Area code, and the distinct subscriber number (upto 8 digits)).
3. There are several (other small) countries that are also members of the United Nations (UN). The UN now has nearly 200 countries principalities as its members.
4. Other languages/local dialects may also be in use.
5. Where no religion is mentioned mostly the inhabitants observe traditional beliefs. This may also be in addition to others who observe some formal religion.

3. Major International Organizations and Other Agencies

A) The United Nations and Organizations operating under its aegis, (and their Headquarters location)

The United Nations, (UN)	New York (U.S.A.)
The Food & Agricultural Organization, (FAO)	Rome (Italy)
The World Health Organization, (WHO)	Geneva (Switzerland)
The World Meteorological Organization, (WMO)	Geneva (Switzerland)
The World Trade Organization, (WTO)	Geneva (Switzerland)
The World Intellectual Property Organization, (WIPO)	Geneva (Switzerland)
The World Food Council, (WFC)	Rome (Italy)
The International Court of Justice, (World Court)	Hague (Netherlands)
The International Bank for Reconstruction & Development , (IBRD or World Bank)	Washington (U.S.A.)
The International Atomic Energy Agency, (IAEA)	Vienna (Austria)
The International Civil Aviation Organization, (ICAO)	Montreal (Canada)
The International Development Association, (IDA)	Washington (U.S.A.)
The International Finance Corporation, (IFC)	Washington (U.S.A.)
The International Fund for Agricultural Development, (IFDA)	Rome (Italy)
The International Labour Organization, (ILO)	Geneva (Switzerland)
The International Telecommunications Union, (ITU)	Geneva (Switzerland)
UN Disaster Relief Coordinator, (UNDRO)	New York (U.S.A.)
UN Environment Programme, (UNEP)	Nairobi (Kenya)
UN Educational, Scientific and Cultural Organization, (UNESCO)	Paris (France)
UN Children's Education Find, (UNICEF)	New York (U.S.A.)
UN Industrial Development Organization (UNIDIO)	Vienna (Austria)

B) Some well-known International Organizations/Associations

ASEAN, (Association of South East Asian Nations)	Jakarta (Indonesia)
IATA, (International Air Transport Association)	Montreal (Canada)
International Bureau of Weights & Measures	Sevres (France)
ICPO, (International Criminal Police Organization)	Paris (France)
ISO, (International Standardization Organization)	Geneva (Switzerland)
NAM, (Non-Aligned Movement)	
NATO, (North Atlantic Treaty Organization)	Brussels (Belgium)
OAU, (Organization for African Unity)	Addis Ababa (Ethiopia)
OPEC, (Organization of Petroleum Exporting Countries)	Vienna (Austria)
Red Cross (International)	Geneva (Switzerland)
SAARC, (South Asian Association for Regional Co-operation)	Kathmandu (Nepal)

C) Well-known/Famous Intelligence/Security Agencies

ATF	Agency for control of illegal/dangerous activities—Alcohol, Tobacco & Firearms	(U.S.A.)
BND	German Intelligence & Security Agency	(Germany)
BSF	Border Security Force, (Peacetime protection of the Nation's Border)	(India)
CBI	The Central Bureau of Invesigations, (Fedreal Investigations)	(India)
CIA	The Central Intelligence Agency, (External Intelligence/Actions)	(U.S.A.)
CISF	Central Industrial Security Force, (Protection of PSU'S, Airport Sy. Etc.)	(India)
CRPF	Central Reserve Police Force, (Deployment for (mainly) Internal Security)	(India)
DMA	Disaster Management Agency, (Federal Agency-Organize/coord. Activities)	(India)
DHD	Department of Homeland Defence, (Federal Agency-Anti Terrorist Activities)	(U.S.A.)
FBI.	The Federal Bereau of Investigations, (Federal Investigation/Internal Sy.)	(U.S.A.)
GSG-9	Premier German Anti-Terrorist Unit	(Germany)
IB	The Intelligence Bureau, (Federal Agency for Internal Intelligence/Security)	(India)
ISI	The Inter Services Intelligence (Agency), (Intelligence/Security/Actions)	(Pakistan)
KGB	Russian Intelligence & Security Agency, (Internal & External Security Actions)	(Russia)
MOSSAD	Intelligence & Security Agency, (Internal Intelligence/Security)	(Israel)
MI-5	The Military Intelligence- SECTION 5, (Internal Intelligence/Security)	(U.K.)
MI-6	The Military Intelligence- SECTION 6, (External Intelligence/Security)	(U.K.)
NCB	Narcotics Control Bureau	(India)
NCRB	National Crime Records Bureau	(India)
NSC	National Security Council	(India)
NKVD	Military Intelligence Agency, erstwhile USSR	
NSA	The National Security Agency, (Federal Agency-Intel. Gathering &Co-ord.)	(U.S.A.)

NSG	National Security Guards, (Commandos for anti-hijacking, VIP Sy. etc.)	(India)
RAW	Research & Analysis Wing, (External Intelligence/ Secuerity Advice)	(India)
RCMP	Royal Canadian Mounted Police, (Federal Agency for Intelligence/Security)	(Canada)
SDECE	French Intelligence & Security Organization	(France)
Scotland Yard	Premier British Agency for Investigations/ Anti-Terrorist Activities etc.	(U.K.)
SPG	Special Protection Group, (Security of selected VIP's like the President & PM)	(India)
SS, (US/UK)	Secret Services, (Security of the President, President designate, PM etc.)	(U.S.A./U.K)
US Marshals	(Witness Protection Programmes, etc.)	(U.S.A.)

4. Flight Distances (Approximate) between some Major cities

Flight between Cities		Distance (in Kms.)	Flight between Cities		Distance (in Kms.)
Amritsar	Moscow	4,600			
Chennai	Abu Dhabi,	3,050	Singapore	Jakarta	900
	Kuala Lumpur,	2,600		Kuala Lumpur,	350
	Singapore	3,000		Perth	3,950
				Sydney	6,300
			Jakarta	Sydney	5,500
			Perth	Sydney	3,300
Delhi	Abu Dhabi	2,500			
	Bangkok	3,000			
	Dubai	2,400			
	Frankfurt	7,100			
	Kuwait	2,900			
	London	7,550			
	Moscow	5,000			
	Mumbai	1,200			
	Muscat	2,100			
	Rome	7,050			
	Sharjah	2,400			
Kolkata	Bangkok	1,650	Bangkok	Hong Kong	1,800
			Hong Kong	Tokyo	3,100
			Tokyo	Moscow	7,500
				Osaka	400

Flight between Cities		Distance (in Kms.)	Flight between Cities		Distance (in Kms.)
Mumbai	Abu Dhabi	2,000	Abu Dhabi	Dubai	130
	Aden	3,050		Kuwait	850
	Baghdad	3,700		Sharjah	130
	Bahrain	2400			
	Chennai	1,050	Dubai	Doha	400
	Doha	2,300		London	5,950
	Dacca	1900		Kuwait	950
	Dar-Es-Salaam	4,700		Muscat	350
	Delhi	1,200			
	Dubai	2,000	Kuwait	Baghdad	1,000
	Frankfurt	6,600		Geneva	4,500
	Kolkata	1,700		Frankfurt	4,000
	Kuwait	2,800		Jeddah	1,250
	London	7,700		Muscat	1,250
	Mauritius	4,700			
	Muscat	1,600	Sanaa	Sharjah	2,850
	Nairobi	4,600			
	Rome	6,650			
	Sanaa	3,700			
	Seychelles	3,300			
	Sharjah	1,900			
	Singapore	4,000			
Tiruvanatha-puram	Abu Dhabi	3,000	Amsterdam	London	400
	Dhahran	3,500		Los Angeles	8,950
	Dubai	3,000		Paris	500
	Sharjah	3,000			
Frankfurt	Algiers	1,550	Casablanca	Rio de Janeiro	7,300
	Amsterdam	500			
	Barcelano	1,100	Copenhagen	Oslo	500
	Berlin	450			
	Boston	5,900	Geneva	Amsterdam	900
	Brussels	300		Paris	440
	Budapest	850		Rome	750
	Cairo	2,900			
	Caracas	8,100	Lagos	Accra	400
	Casablanca	2,300		Nairobi	3,900
	Chicago	7,000			
	Copenhagen	700	Lima	Santiago	2,450
	Geneva	450			
	Helsinki	1,550	London	New York	5,750
	Istanbul	1,850			

Flight between Cities		Distance (in Kms.)	Flight between Cities		Distance (in Kms.)
	Lagos	4,850	Nairobi	Johannesburg	2,900
	London	650			
	Madrid	1,400	Rome	London	1,550
	Montreal	5,850		Paris	1,150
	Moscow	2,000			
	Nairobi	6,300	Toronto	Montreal	500
	New York	6,200			
	Paris	500	Frankfurt	Stockholm	1,200
	Rome	1,000		Tel Aviv	2,950
	Toronto	6,350			

5. Phonetic Alphabets

Alphabet/Numbers	ICAO Phonetic Alphabet	Morse Code (Now mostly Obsolete)		
		Code	in words	pronounced as
A	Alpha	·–	dot dash	did dah
B	Bravo	–···	dash dot dot dot	dah did did did
C	Charlie	–·–·	dash dot dash dot	dah did dah did
D	Delta	–··	dash dot dot	dah did did
E	Echo	·	dot	did
F	Foxtrot	··–·	dot dot dash dot	did did dah did
G	Golf	––·	dash dash dot	dah dah did
H	Hotel	····	dot dot dot dot	did did did did
I	India	··	dot dot	did did
J	Juliet	·–––	dot dash dash dash	did dah dah dah
K	Kilo	–·–	dash dot dash	dah did dah
L	Lima	·–··	dot dash dot dot	did dah did did
M	Mike	––	dash dash	dah dah
N	November	–·	dash dot	dah did
O	Oscar	–––	dash dash dash	dah dah dah
P	Papa	·––·	dot dash dash dot	did dah dah did
Q	Quebec	––·–	dash dash dot dash	dah dah did dah
R	Romeo	·–·	dot dash dot	did dah did
S	Sierra	···	dot dot dot	did did did
T	Tango	–	dash	dah
U	Uniform	··–	dot dot dash	did did dah
V	Victor	···–	dot dot dot dash	did did did dah
W	Whiskey	·––	dot dash dash	did dah dah
X	X-ray	–··–	dash dot dot dash	dah did did dah

Alphabet/Numbers	ICAO Phonetic Alphabet	Morse Code (Now mostly Obsolete) Code	in words	pronounced as
Y	Yankee	–·––	dash dot dash dash	dah did dah dah
Z	Zulu	––··	dash dash dot dot	dah dah did did
1	Wun	·––––	dot & four dashes	did dah dah dah dah
2	Too	··–––	2 dots & 3 dashes	did did dah dah dah
3	Tree	···––	3dots & 2 dashes	did did did dah dah
4	Fo-wer	····–	4 dots & a dash	did did did did dah
5	Fife	·····	5 dots	did did did did did
6	Six	–····	dash & 4 dots	dah did did did did
7	Sev-en	––···	2 dashes & 3 dots	dah dah did did did
8	Ait	–––··	3 dashes & 2 dots	dah dah dah did did
9	Nin-er	––––·	4 dashes & a dot	dah dah dah dah did
0	Zero	–––––	5 dashes	dah dah dah dah dah
Punctuation marks in Morse code:				
	Full Stop	·–·–·–		did dah did dah did dah
	Comma	·––––·		did dah dah dah dah did
	Colon	–––···		dah dah dah did did did
	Dash	–····–		dah did did did did dah
	Slash	–··–·		dah did did dah did
	Semi Colon	–·–·–·		dah did dah did dah did
	Question Mark	··––··		did did dah dah did did
	Exclamation	––··––		dah dah did did dah dah

There are a few other Morse Codes foe SOS, Wait, end of session, error etc.

6. Conversion Tables (and Abbreviation of Units)

1 Angstrom (A) Unit = 100 millionth of a Centimetre (cm). (1 cm = 100 million A)

1 micron (u) = 1 millionth of a metre, or 1 metre = 1 million microns.

1 cm = 1/3.94 inches (in), or 1 inch = 2.54 cms. (1 cm = 1/100th of a metre (m); or 1 m = 100 cms).

1 foot (ft) =12 Inches. 1 Yard (yd) = 3ft. = 0.9144 m. 1Furlong = 220yds. 1 Mile (M) = 8furlongs = 1,760 yds =5280ft)

1 Kilometre (Km) = 1,000 metres or = 0.6214 miles. 1 miles = 1.609 Kms. = 1,609 ms.

1 Knot (kn) = 1 nautical miles per hour. = 1.152 Miles per hour (MPH). And 1 MPH = 0.868 knots. 1 nautical mile = 6,080ft, (approx. 2,000 yds) = 1.853 Kms. And 0.539 nautical miles. = 1 kms).

1 calorie = 0.239 Joules (J). 1 J = 4.186 calories.

1 radian = 57.3 degrees. = 1,000 mils. 1 degree = 0.01745 radians.

60grains = 1 drachm. 2.888grams = 1 drachm. 0.1371ounce (avoirdupois)= 1 drachm. 0.9115ounce (troy) = 1 ounce (avoirdupois). 0.125ounce (troy) = 1 drachms. = 0.4558 drachms = 1 dram. 1.772gram. = 1 dram. 13.166 ounces (avoirdupois) = 1 pound (1b. Troy). 14.583 ounces (troy) = 1 pound (1b. Avoirdupois).

(1.829ms = 1 fathom. 608ft = 1 cablelength = 219.5ms = 120 fathoms).

4,546litres (l) = 1 gallon. 1l = 1,000 cubic centimetres (cc).0.2199 gallons= 1l. 35.196 ounces (fluid)=1l.

27.77 cm/sec. = 1kilometre/hour, (km/hr. km.p.h). 44.70 cm/sec = 1 miles/hour, (MPH).

0.355 Kilometres/litres (Kmpl) = 1 mile/gallon (Mpg). 2.82 Mpg = 1 Kmpl.

28.35 points (printing) = 1 cm. 72 points (printing) = 1 inch. 1/12 picas = 1 point (printing).

(929 square cms = 1 square ft. 0.155 sq. in. = 1 sq. cm. 247 acres = 1 sq. km. 2.471 acres = 1 hectare.)

1000 kgs. 1 tonne (metric). 1016 kgs. = 1 ton = 2,240 lbs.

746 watts (W) = 1 horsepower (H.P.) = 42.41 Btu/minute = 10.69 kg-calories/minute. 1,000 W = 1KW. 1,054.8 J = 1 Btu. 1 kg-calories = 4.186 kilo-joules = 426.9 kg-metres; 1 kg-calories/minute = 69.77 W.

3600 Coulombs = 1 kg Ampere-hour. 10.764 Lux = 1 Foot-candles.

1 Standard Atmosphere = 1,013.2 millibars. = 760 mm. of Hg at 0 degree C at sea level. =29.92 mm. of Hg. = 14.70 lbs. per sq. in. = 1,033 gm. wt. per sq.cm.

Freezepoint of water = 0-degree centigrade (C). = 32 degrees Fahrenheit (F) = 0 degree Renmar (R).

Boiling point of water = 100 degrees C. = 212 degrees F. = 80 degrees R.

Hence to convert degrees F. to degrees C., temperature in (F-32) *5/9 = in C. and in (C* 9/5 + 32) = in F.

Absolute temperature is in degrees Kelvin (K). 0 degree K = 273 degree C.

Hence Boiling point of liquid helium which is 4.2 degrees K. = -168.8 degrees C.

Melting point of solid hydrogen is 14 degrees K = -259 degrees C.

Boiling point of liquid hydrogen is 20.3 degrees K = -252.7 degrees C.

Boiling point of liquid air is 83 degrees K= -190 degrees C.

Boiling point of oxygen is 90 degrees K = -183 degrees C.

Boiling point of water is 373 degrees K = 100 degrees C.

Some common conversion factors:

0.3937 ins. = 1 cm.	**2.54 cms = 1 in.**	**3.28084 ft. = 1 metre.**	**0.3048 m = 1 ft.**
1.0936 yds. = 1 m.	**0.9133 m. =1 yd.**	**0.62137 miles = 1 km.**	
1.60934 km = 1 mile.	**0.155 sq. in =1 sq. cm.**	**6.4516 sq. cm. = 1 sq. in.**	
10.7839 sq. ft. = 1 sq. m.	**0.0829 sq. m. = 1 sq. ft.**	**1.196 sq. yd. = 1 sq. m.**	
0.83613 sq. m. = 1 sq. yd.	**2.471 Acres = 1 Hectare.**	**0.40469 Hectare = 1 Acre**	
0.3861 sq. miles = 1 sq. km.	**2.5899 sq.km. = 1 sq. mile**		
1.75976 Pints = 1 Litre	**0.5683 l = 1 Pint**	**0.8799 Quart = 1 l.**	
1.1365 l = 1 Quart.	**0.21997 Gallons = 1 l**	**4.546 l = 1 Gallon.**	
0.03527 oz. = 1 gm.	**28.3495 gms. = 1 oz.**	**2.2046lbs. = 1 kg.**	**0.4536 kg = 1 lb**

Decadic Values-Conversion Factors

S.No.	Symbol Name	Symbol	Read as	Value
1.	atto	a	10 to the power minus 18	millionth of a billionth part of-
2.	femto	f	10 to the power minus 16	thousand of a billionth part of-
3.	pico	p	10 to the power minus 12	millionth of a millionth part of-
4.	nano	n	10 to the power minus 9	thousand millionth part of-
5.	micro	Greek letter mu	10 to the power minus 6	one millionth part of-
6.	milli	m	10 to the power minus 3	one thousandth part of-
7.	centi	c	10 to the power minus 2	one hundreth part of-
8.	deci	d	10 to the power minus 1	one tenth part of-
9.	deca		10s of	ten times
10.	hecto	H,h	hundreds of, or 10 to the power 2	hundred times
11.	kilo	K, k	thousands of, or 10 to the power 3	thousand times
12.	Mega	M	10 to the power 6	one million times
13.	Giga	G	10 to the power 9	thousand million times
14.	Tera	T	10 to the power 12	million-million times
15.	Peta	P	10 to the power 15	thousand billion times
16.	Exa	E	10 to the power 18	million billion times

Some Examples:

picofarads means a value that is —10 to the power minus 23 farads.
nanoseconds means—one thousand millionth of a second.
micrometre means—a length or distance that is one millionth of a metre.
milligram means—one thousandth of a gram.
decibel means—one tenth of a bel.
hectolitres means—one hundred litres.
GigaHertz or GHz means—thousand million Hz.
Terabits means—million million bits. (or billion bits).

Note: U.S. billion is only one thousand million.

Physical Constants

Avogadro's Number (N) 6.0238*10 raised to the power 23 molecules/mole
(Number of gas molecules per c.c. at 760 mm of Hg. at 0 degree C. = 2.69* 10 to power 19.).

Boltzmann's Constant (k) 1.3803*10 to the power minus 23 watts/Hz/degree K.

Exponential (e) 2.7183

Electronic Charge (e) 1.6019*10 to the power minus 19 coulombs.

Electron Mass (m) 9.1083*10 to the power to the minus 31 kgs.
Electron Radius (r) 2.8179*10 to the power to the minus 15 m.
Mass of proton = 1.673*10 to the power to the minus 27 kgs.
(Ratio of mass of hydrogen to mass of electron = 1, 838.)
Faraday's Constant (F) 96,493 coulombs/gm.-equivalent.

Acceleration due to gravity (g) 981 cm./sec.Squared. (Varies slightly from location to location, from about 978 at the equator to about 983 at the North Pole).

Planck's Constant	6.6238*10 to the power to the minus 34 Joule.sec.
Latent Heat of Water (fusion)	79.63 calories/gm. at 15 degrees C.
Latent Heat of Steam	539.55 calories/gm. at 15 degrees C.
Pi	3.1416
1/Pi	0.3183
Pi squared	9.8696
Log of e to the base 10	0.4343
Log of 10 to the base e	2.3026
Log of Pi to the base 10	0.4971

Velocity of light (c) = 299,800 kms. Per sec. = 186,300 miles per sec.
1 Light year is 9.460 million million kms.

Melting point of—	platinum..	1,773 degrees C.
	Copper..	1,083 degrees C.
	Gold.....	1,063 degrees C.
	Silver...	960.5 degrees C.

Temperatures at/of—	low red heat...	500 to 600 degrees C.
	White heat...	1,500 - 1,800 degrees C.
	Oxy-hydrogen flame...	2,200 degrees C.
	Electric arc...	3,300 - 3,500 degrees C.

(Estimated) at sun's surface.... 6,000 degrees C. (approx.).
(Estimated) of hottest stars... 35,000 degrees C. (approx.).

Solar System data

Distance from the earth to the sun-: 149.7 million kms. = 93 million miles.
Distance of moon from the earth-: 384,000 kms. = 239,000 miles.
Mean radius of the earth -: 6,638 kms. = 3,957 miles.
Mean radius of the moon-: 1,738 kms. 1,080 miles.
Mean radius of the sun-: 0.69 million kms. = 0.43 million miles.

1 Year = 365.242 mean solar days.
1 solar day = 86,164 mean solar seconds.

1 lunar month = 29.53 mean solar days.

Velocity of sound in air-: 331.3 m. per sec. = 1,087 ft. per sec.
(Note that the velocity of sound in other materials is far higher. For example it is 1,410 m. in water and 5,000 m. in steel!).

Composition of air -: about 78% nitrogen (N), 21 % oxygen (O), 0.95 % Argon (Ar) and trace gases of carbon dioxide (CO_2), Helium (He), Krypton (Kr), Neon (Ne) and Xenon (Xe).

Solar constant is the amount of Solar Energy incident on the surface of the earth, at Earth's mean distance from the sun. And it is equal to 0.137 w/sq.cm. Or 1.37 K.w. per sq.m.
(Note that the sun loses mass of about 4 million tons per sec. by its radiation of energy to its surroundings (vacuum)).

8. Units (Fundamental and Derived)

The International System of Units, the SI system, was adopted in 1960. Till then the basic units of length, mass and time were in the CGS system, (Centimetre, Gram and the Second), and the Electromagnetic Units (EMU) were based on the CGS system. The SI system is based on the MKS units of Metre, Kilogram and the Second.

The Fundamental or base units are those of Length, Mass, Time, Electric Current, Temperature and Luminous Intensity. From these the other units are derived such as Force, Energy, (Power), Electric Potential Difference, (EMF), Resistance, Capacitance, Inductance, Pressure and so on.

The main units of general interest alongwith the symbols used for them are indicated below:

Quantity	Unit	Symbol	(Old CGS units)	Comments
Length	Metre (m).	l	Centimetre (cm).	Metre is taken as specific multiple wavelength of a specified radiation
Mass	Kilogram (kg)	m	Gram (gm).	Mass of specified alloy cylinder maintained at Bureau of weights & Measures, Paris.
Time	Second (s).	t	Second (s)	Specified period of specified radiation (Cs-133)
Electric Current	Ampere (Amps./A).	I	Ampere	Current in two parallel conductors 1m apart that generates specified force between them.

Quantity	Unit	Symbol	(Old CGS units)	Comments
Temperature	Kelvin (K).	T		Fixing Triple point temperature of water at 273.16K.
Illumination	Lux or Lumens/sq.		Ft. candle	1 ft. candle = 10.76 Lux
Luminous Intensity	Candela (cd)/ Lumen	I		1 Candela = 12.57 Lumens
Force	Newton(N)	F	Dyne	Force that accelerates a 1 kg Mass by 1m/s. sq.
Energy	Joule (J)	E., W.	Erg.	Work done when 1 N Force applied moves 1 m onward
Power	Watts (W)	P	Erg/s.	Rate of energy of 1 J/s.
Electric charge	Coulomb (C)	Q	Coulomb	Amount of electric charge flow in 1 s. for current of 1 A.
Electric potential difference	EMF. Volt (V)	V	Volt	Potential difference between 2 conductors carrying 1 A current, when power dissipated is 1 W.
Electric resistance	Ohm ( )	R	Ohm	R that has 1 A current flow when 1 V is applied across it.
Capaçitance	Farad (F)	C	Farad	C that has 1 V across it when gets a charge of 1 Q.
Inductance	Henry (H)	L	Henry	L that has 1 V across it when tha current in the circuit changes uniformly at 1 A/s.
Magnetic flux	Weber (Wb)	Phi. (cp)	Maxwell	The magnetic flux linking a 1-turn circuit, when reduced at uniform rate to zero in 1 sec. Produces 1 V in the circuit.
Conductance	Mho ( )	G	mho	Inverse of resistance.

Quantity	Unit	Symbol	(Old CGS units)	Comments
Magnetic induction	Tesla (T)	B	Gauss (G)	Weber/m-squared
Magnetic field	Ampere-turn/metre	H	Oersted (Oe)	1 Ampere-turn/metre.
Frequncy	Hertz (Hz)	*f, v*	hertz	(Up and down) variation in magnitude of one cycle/s. (voltage, current, pressure, flux, etc.)
Pressure	Newton/m. squared (N/m. squared)	P		
Reluctance	Ampere-turns/Weber	R		
Angular velocity	Radians/ second	w (2.pi.f)		
Reactance	*wl; 1/wC*	X		Inductive or capacitive.
Impedance	(R+X)	Z		Combined effect of resistance & reactance.
Admittance	1/Z	Y		Inverse of impedance.
High ratios (Of power; voltage current etc.	Decibel (tenth of a Bel)	dB		10 log to base 10 of the power ratio; and 20 log to base 10 for voltage. ratio, current ratios etc.

9. Approximate Equivalent Sizes-Paper Clothing, Shoes

a). Paper Sizes:		
	Metric	**Imperial**
A0= 841 mm. by 1189 mm.	B0=1000 mm. By 1414 mm.	Antiquarian---53 by 31 in.
		(1346 by 787 mm)
A1 = 594 mm. by 841 mm.		Double Elephant-40 by 26-1/2 in.
		(1016 by 679 mm)
A2 = 420 mm. By 594 mm.		Imperial----30-1/2 by 22-1/2in.
		(775 by 572 mm.)
A3 = 297 mm. By 420 mm.	B4=250 mm. By 353 mm.	Double Crown-30 by 20 in.
		(762 by 508 mm.)
A4 = 210 mm. By 297 mm.		Royal--------24 by 19 in.
		(610 by 483 mm.)
A5 = 148 mm. By 210 mm.	B5 = 176 mm. By 250 mm.	Medium------22 by 17-1/2 in.
		(559 by 444 mm.)
Paper-weights are normally metric-- in grams/sq. m. or ---gsm:		
	Light --100gsm, (or 72 pounds--light); heavy--64 gsm, (or 300 pounds-heavy	

b). Men's Suits: **Sizes**

Indian:	36	38	40	42	44		
European:	42	44	46	48	50	52	54
U.K./U.S.	32	34	36	38	40	42	44

c). Lady's Dresses: **Sizes**

Indian:	32	36	38	40			
European:	38	40	42	44	47	50	52
U.K.	10	12	14	16	18	20	22
U.S.	8	10	12	14	16	18	20

d). Men's Shirt (Collar Sizes):

Indian (cm):	36	38	40	42	44		
Metric (cm):	37	38	39-½	41	42	43	44
U.K./U.S. (in):	14-½	15	15-½	16	16-½	17	17-½

e). Shoe Sizes: **Sizes**

American	English	European	(Approximate) Cms
5	-	38	25
-	5	38	25½
6	-	-	$25\frac{2}{3}$
-	6	39	26
7	-	40	$26\frac{2}{3}$
-	7	-	27
8	-	41	$27\frac{1}{3}$
8	42	28	
9	-	-	28¼
-	-	43	28½
-	9	-	28¾
10	-	44	29½
-	10	-	$29\frac{2}{3}$
11	-	45	30
-	11	46	30½
12	-	-	30 ¾
-	-	47	31
-	12	-	31¼
13	-	48	$31\frac{2}{3}$

American womens shoe size								
5	6	7	8	9	10	11	12	13
(APPROXIMATE) cms								
24	25	25¾	26½	27 1/3	28¼	29	29¾	30 2/3

10. (Perpetual) Calender (Upto Next Generation)

a) Grouping of the Years. (Note down the Group number for the year of interest)

Group. I Year >	1990 to 1999	2000 to 2009	2010 to 2019	2020 to 2030
1	1990	2001; 2007	2018	2029
2	1991	2002	2013; 2019	2030
3	1997	2003	2014	2025
4	1998	2009	2015	2026
5	1993; 1999	—	2010; 2011	2021; 2027
6	1994	2005	—	2022
7	1995	2006	2017	2023
8	1996	—	—	2024
9	—	2008	—	—
10	1992	—	—	2020
11	—	2004	—	—
12	—	—	2016	—
13	—	2000	—	2028
14	—	—	2012	—

b) Code for the Group and the Month. (Note the Code alphabet for the month of interest)

Month-Year-Group	Jan.	Feb.	Mar. & Nov.	April & July.	May.	June.	Aug.	Sept & Dec.	Oct.
1	A	D	D	G	B	E	C	F	A
2	B	E	E	A	C	F	D	G	B
3	C	F	F	B	D	G	E	A	C
4	D	G	G	C	E	A	F	B	D
5	E	A	A	D	F	B	G	C	E
6	F	B	B	E	G	C	A	D	F
7	G	C	C	F	A	D	B	E	G
8	A	D	E	A	B	F	D	G	B
9	B	E	F	B	D	G	E	A	C
10	C	F	G	C	E	A	F	B	D
11	D	G	A	D	F	B	G	C	E
12	E	A	B	E	G	C	A	D	F
13	F	B	C	F	A	D	B	E	G
14	G	C	D	G	B	E	C	F	A

See the next page for the calendar (for the month of the chosen year): the column for the Code

c) Monthly calendar: read the column under the concerned Code for the month involved; (as found at (b) above.

Simply put, the steps involved are:

1. For the year of interest, note down the Group number from the table at (a).
2. For that Group number (year of interest) look up the Code alphabet from the table at (b), for the month of interest.
3. The column in table (c), given below, for that Code alphabet (noted at step 2. Above), gives the calendar for the concerned month, for the year of interest.
4. Note: for uniformity and ease of checking 31 days are shown in each column, though, there are only 28 days in Feb. except in leap years when it is 29 days, and only 30 days in April, June, Sept, and Nov.

Code>> Day	A	B	C	D	E	F	G
Monday	1						
Tuesday	2	1					
Wednes.	3	2	1				
Thursday	4	3	2	1			
Friday	5	4	3	2	1		
Saturday	6	5	4	3	2	1	
SUNDAY	7	6	5	4	3	2	1
Monday	8	7	6	5	4	3	2
Tuesday	9	8	7	6	5	4	3
Wednes.	10	9	8	7	6	5	4
Thursday	11	10	9	8	7	6	5
Friday	12	11	10	9	8	7	6
Saturday	13	12	11	10	9	8	7
SUNDAY	14	13	12	11	10	9	8
Monday	15	14	13	12	11	10	9
Tuesday	16	15	14	13	12	11	10
Wednes.	17	16	15	14	13	12	11
Thursday	18	17	16	15	14	13	12
Friday	19	18	17	16	15	14	13
Saturday	20	19	18	17	16	15	14
SUNDAY	21	20	19	18	17	16	15
Monday	22	21	20	19	18	17	16
Tuesday	23	22	21	20	19	18	17
Wednes.	24	23	22	21	20	19	18
Thursday	25	24	23	22	21	20	19
Friday	26	25	24	23	22	21	20

Saturday	27	26	25	24	23	22	21
SUNDAY	28	27	26	25	24	23	22
Monday	29	28	27	26	25	24	23
Tuesday	30	29	28	27	26	25	24
Wednes.	31	30	29	28	27	26	25
Thursday		31	30	29	28	27	26
Friday			31	30	29	28	27
Saturday				31	30	29	28
SUNDAY					31	30	29
Monday						31	30
Tuesday							31

11. Caution/Safety Guidelines for use of Electrical/Electronic/Computer Equipment/Systems.

Extensive use of electricity and equipment/systems using electricity, such as illumination devices, the electric iron, electric oven, Refrigerator etc. have become almost all pervasive in modern life. In recent times electronic equipment and devices such as the Radio, Tape Recorder, Music System, TV, VCR, Video Camera, Computer System etc., are becoming more and more popular even in the remotest corner of the country. But the general public, the user of these various gadgets is, most of the time, not fully aware of the safety precautions that are necessary when using such devices. It is usual for each equipment/System to have it own specific safety instructions that are to be scrupulously observed by all that use, install, service and maintain the devices, including their safe storage. What are given below are general guidelines that apply to all such equipment.

General Do's & Don'ts:

1. Before connecting the equipment to the mains do make sure that:
   a) The power switch is OFF.
   b) The main supply voltage is appropriate, as specified for the equipment by its manufacturer.
   c) The power switch on the equipment, if any, is kept in the "OFF" position.
   d) The equipment power plug matches the mains socket, and the power cord is long enough and is not damaged.
   e) Also make sure that the proper fuse if any is in position in the equipment.
   f) Ensure that nothing rests on the power cord and there is no spilt water, beverage etc. to wet the equipment nor the cord; nor anyone is likely to trip over the cord at any time.
2. Connect and disconnect the equipment to the mains holding the plug attached to the cord and not the cord itself.
3. Do NOT disconnect the equipment without first switching "OFF" the power, both on the equipment itself and on the switchboard.

4. Use only the controls on the device, and Do not touch the equipment itself lest an electric shock results.
5. Do not insert any metallic item like a pin/screw driver etc., into any sockets or openings in the equipment. This may result in an electric shock. Such provisions are meant for specific plug connections/proper cooling of the equipment.
6. Do not let any liquid (like water, beverage etc.), solid (like screws, powder, dust etc.), nor gaseous substances (like smoke, polluting gases, incense etc.) get into the openings/vents-lest harm results in the functioning of the equipment system. Nor should you use aerosol sprays, cleaning agents, solvents, abrasives etc., for sprucing up any electronic device. Protect the equipment when not in use by properly covering it with suitable 'Dust Cover'.
7. Placement of the device during use must be such that all its vents are clear of any blockage or obstructions and there is free flow of air all round for effective cooling of the inside of the instrument.
8. Do place your electronic devices in clean, well-ventilated and cool location, well away from direct sunlight and sources of heat.
9. Do make sure that the device is well grounded, (connected to a properly grounded 3-pin power outlet), to avoid possibility of shocks if you accidentally touch the body of the device.
10. Do make sure that you have switched "OFF" the device after use. Unplug the equipment if it is not going to be used in the near future, and cover it with its dust cover. If the period of non-usage is likely to be months, it may be preferable to properly store it away in its packing carton.
11. For any maintenance, servicing or repair it is advisable to call in the authorized service personnel to open and do the needful, with the appropriate tools and necessary knowledge that they possess, on sophisticated electronic devices and systems. (Amateurish efforts may result in (additional) damage to the sophisticated/costly systems).
12. DO NOT:
    (a) Touch or tamper with any electrical conductor or apparatus, (nor electronic one for that matter), till you have made sure that the system is not active/line, and has a proper earth.
    (b) Close any switch unless you are knowledgeable about the circuit it is connected to/operates, and also you are aware of the reason for the switch being in the "OFF" state; and you have the need to energize the circuit.
    (c) Replace a fuse that has blown, until the cause for its fusing has been found out and properly rectified.
    (d) Modify or alter circuits/equipment without proper authorization and supervision.
    (e) Try to use water to quench an electrical fire; or use a fire extinguisher on an electrical fire that is not appropriate.

(f) Work on live electrical circuits/electrical or electronic equipment without having necessary knowledge/without taking required precautions, (such as rubber gloves, insulated tools etc.).

(g) Use wires/cables/fuses/components etc. that is not appropriate, for making connections etc. in circuits/devices/systems.

13. For many working on a computer, or playing video games has become a daily ritual, whereas the computer professional can hardly spare a few hours away from the computer! However, everyone will need to observe certain elementary precautions when working on a computer, the DO's and the DON'Ts, some that are meant to protect the health of the user and many that are devised for safety of the computer system itself. Some of them are given below for ready reference:

(a) Even before you start your work on the computer, see to the correct ergonomics.

aa. See that proper, even illumination of the work area is present and you can see the monitor screen clearly and without any glare. (Do keep the monitor screen clean for good readability).

bb. Do ensure that the chair you use and the computer table is of proper design. Your knee must clear the underside of the table by a few centimeters (say 5 to 6 cms at least). When you sit down your knees and your hips should be at the same level, (knees could be a little higher). And see that the work area surface is level with your elbows. Use a footrest if needed to rest your feet comfortably.

cc. Do sit erect and support you back suitably. And see that the top of the monitor screen is at eye level.

dd. When seated the chair should not be so far as to make you lean forward or backward to look at the monitor properly.

b) Do NOT keep staring at the monitor continuously, for hours, without taking a break at least every hour or so, without fail, and look away from the monitor every few minutes, lest the deadly RSI (Repetitive Strain Injury) or defects in vision occur! More frequent the breaks, the better it is for you.

c) Type gently as the computer keyboard is quite sensitive and does not require the hard pressure that normal typewriters need. Excessive use of typing force increases the possibility of RSI. Note that excessive use of the mouse also can lead to RSI.

d) When working for long periods oftime on a computer it is better to fidget and keep adjusting/moving the body now and then to stay continuously fixed in a static position!

e) Have a good and effective virus protection software installed in your computer, and do update it frequently, that is as and when add-ons are released by the company. Be wary of opening attachments to e-mails until you are positive that it is from your reliable correspondent. So also being circumspect in downloading free software/computer games is advisable.

f) Save frequently whilst working on the computer and make regular backups of your important data, without fail and store them separately. Take care to see that they are write protected!

g) Use only authentic, certified software from reliable dealers.

h) It makes sense to ensure only duly authorized use of your computer by others; even then, preferably under proper supervision!

i) In case of problems with your computer have it attended to in-situ whenever possible and only by known reliable computer expert/technician.

j) As far as possible use your computer as a stand alone mode only, connecting it to the line (with telephone etc. modem) only when essential, like for sending/receiving e-mails. Even so it is better to prepare the letters documents etc. "Offline" and connect to the line for transmitting the pre-prepared work.

Index